The Cosmology of Freedom

Robert C. Neville

New Haven and London, Yale University Press

1974

Designed by John O. C. McCrillis
and set in Baskerville type.
Printed in the United States of America by
The Vail-Ballou Press, Inc., Binghamton, N. Y.

Published in Great Britain, Europe, and Africa by
Yale University Press, Ltd., London.
Distributed in Latin America by Kaiman & Polon,
Inc., New York City; in Australasia and Southeast
Asia by John Wiley & Sons Australasia Pty. Ltd.,
Sydney; in India by UBS Publishers' Distributors Pvt.,
Ltd., Delhi; in Japan by John Weatherhill, Inc., Tokyo.

For
Gwendolyn Elizabeth Neville
(June 4–October 10, 1966)

Contents

Preface

This is an essay in systematic philosophy. Two particular advantages of the genre should be pointed out as encouragements to readers accustomed to impatience with such philosophy. First, systematic philosophy is the only philosophic discipline attempting to provide a critical vision of the whole of things. Although philosophers may have eschewed this goal in recent years, the public justly continues to regard it as philosophy's task. Second, systematic philosophy has the advantage of a special kind of self-criticism unavailable to other philosophic genres. Instead of examining its presuppositions only in their ad hoc appearance, systematic philosophy formulates its presuppositions with the additional principles of formal system; examining the system of presuppositions, it elicits even higher systematic presuppositions, and so on. Systematic philosophy with a dialectical orientation toward itself is the only internal check on dogmatism available to philosophy. My hope is that this essay, in conjunction with my other work, enjoys these advantages.

The disadvantages of systematic philosophy should also be acknowledged, even though this essay attempts to mitigate them. First, the formal principles of systematic interconnection tempt one to discuss matters that simply are not important to discuss except for formal reasons. I suspect there is a touch of pedantry in those inclined to systematic philosophy. My colleagues, friends, and editor have worked hard to minimize the system-overkill in this essay. The second disadvantage of systematic philosophy is that, whereas its expressions are finite, its aspirations are not. The contours of this essay on freedom, for instance, reflect systematic concerns with topics not treated here. Its original motive, in fact, was to prove that views expressed in an earlier book of mine, *God the Creator*, do not entail a rejection of freedom. Although many other motives underlay the writing of this book, and although the explicit discussion of the relation between freedom and God is not to be found here at all, those systematic considerations still shape the present argument. I have nevertheless attempted to make this essay as self-contained as possible, not presupposing any acquaintance with or acceptance of its theological connections.

The third disadvantage is that systematic philosophy is hard to read. I have tried to simplify the formal arguments, to forestall the need for previous acquaintance with the philosophers I criticize, and to use examples that are not themselves controversial. But I fear it would still be of help to readers to have a paideia much like my own for the sake of understanding the argument. The difficulty in reading systematic philosophy is that one must have a sense of the whole before one can see what any particular argument is about. Without such a sense it must seem as if the argument is now a matter of historical commentary, now a matter of practical policy, now a matter of spinning out speculative concepts, with no continuity of mutual relevance. I have attempted, however, to provide as many road signs and instant replays as possible.

Systematic philosophy not only has horizontal problems of coverage, it has vertical problems of moving from one level of abstraction to another. Systematic philosophy is often associated with its speculative component, its most abstract categoreal scheme; on this level its arguments are those constructing a formal system. But the system only has philosophic meaning as an interpretation of experience. Therefore interpretations of the most concrete affairs are just as much part of systematic philosophy as of speculation. The basic form of systematic argument is dialectic, moving up and down the ladder of abstractions, correcting categories in light of experience and refining experience in light of categories. Such a dialectical argument is difficult to follow, however. Surely it must seem that formal speculation just does not fit with discussions of art and responsibility. Furthermore, because most educated people today are not accustomed to systematic philosophy, they identify only one of its components as "the real thing." And they are impatient for it to come around. With regard to this book, patience pays off; if the reader does not like the kind of argument he is reading, another kind will appear in the next section. Meanwhile, he will have to accept on faith the view of my wife and other similarly trenchant critics that the arguments do add up to a systematic whole.

My intellectual debts are many and diffuse. Besides my teachers and colleagues at Yale University who were acknowledged in an earlier book, Robert Brumbaugh, Charles Hendel, John E. Smith, Carl Vaught, and Paul Weiss, I have profited immeasurably from colleagues at Fordham, especially Norris Clarke, Bernard Gendron, Quentin Lauer, Elizabeth Salmon, and particularly Alexander von Schoenborn. My views on freedom have been carefully criticized by graduate and undergraduate students, especially by three who are now colleagues, Elizabeth Kraus, John Chethimattam, and Aldo Tassi. Robert Mulvaney is my greatest intellectual creditor at Fordham; he has repeatedly renewed my confidence in the importance of speculative philosophy and has continually been an example of precision in moral thinking.

The experience reflected in this book has been equally enriched by my association with the Institute of Society, Ethics and the Life Sciences. The problems of freedom, both personal and social, are dealt with there on a daily practical basis. I have profited especially from conversations with Daniel Callahan, Willard Gaylin, Marc Lappé, Peter Steinfels, and Robert Veatch. Robert Veatch's views on individual responsibility and consent form the background for much of the discussion in chapter 11.

Public discussions of my published work, although sometimes painful, have been great educational experiences. I wish to thank especially Anselm Atkins, David Burrell, and Lewis Ford.

Thanks are also due Jonas Narbutas, Philip Pecorino, and William Briel for mimeographing portions of the manuscript for use in classes during the last eight years. My parents, Rose and Richard Neville, undertook the final preparation of the typescript, one of the least benefits for which I owe them thanks. I am especially indebted to Jane Isay and Judy Metro of Yale University Press for their support and assistance in transforming the manuscript into a book.

My wife joins in dedicating the volume to our daughter, Gwendolyn Elizabeth, whose life taught us to measure freedom against the fateful limits of fixity and chance.

PART 1

Freedom and Cosmology

1

Freedom as an Intellectual Problem

The Task

The Bible records the career of the tribes of Israel as they forged a society based on the worship of a divine moral lawgiver, a God who identified both himself and Israel through a covenant of obedience. So successful was this career that the Kingdom was established, the Temple built, and the people settled in a homeland. This, as we know, was the undoing of the moral covenant, the adulteration of the religion, and the beginning of the end of the national state. But in the time of crisis the Deuteronomic editor set down the foundations of the moral law and religion in a classic way. He preserved the ideals that made Israel's unsurpassed contribution to civilization. Pity Babylon and Nineveh, who had no Deuteronomy!

The moment inevitably comes, it seems, when the ideals guiding the career of a given culture succeed so well in taking root that they undermine the social organization that developed them. The changes taking place as new cultural forms replace old ones constitute a crisis, Will the values inherent in the old ideals come to fruit in the new forms? Or will the changes destroy any possibility of incorporating the old values?

One of the most decisive factors in the time of transitional crisis is the role of intellectuals like the Deuternomists. Those who discipline their love for the breadth and depth of wisdom can articulate abstractly and succinctly what is worthwhile in the passing culture and what may be done to reincarnate it in the coming one. This is the intellectuals' conservative function. Beyond this, they can imagine and articulate, again abstractly and succinctly, the new possibilities opened by the social changes. The values of the old culture should be carried along in some form

3

to enrich the new values; a crisis that fails and comes to chaos has fewer, not more, possibilities for cultural life.

In both its conservative and imaginative function intellect must work *abstractly* and *succinctly*. Abstractly, because it must hit upon the important, leaving aside the trivial that can be changed harmlessly. Succinctly, because its insights must be communicable to all stations in social change where intelligence might be employed. There are many kinds of intellectual abstraction and succinctness—poetic, philosophic, religious, scientific. Where the intellectual community succeeds in this task the crisis stands a better chance of enriching rather than impoverishing human experience.

Our own time is a crisis, marked by revolution and violence, by a strange inappropriateness of all ideologies, by sudden shifts in power from centers of Western civilization to places untouched by the West a few years ago. These signs only mark the crisis. But this point is unexceptional—and it constitutes the problem for this study—that the promise of full freedom to participate in society and in the world's wealth has been heard by nearly everyone. And everyone is demanding the freedom. More pointedly, the freedom to participate is being demanded by peoples whose cultures have not been part of the civilization that developed the ideal of freedom. Some participated in other cultures; others were *in* Western societies but were deprived of the power to *participate* in them. In either case they are not able to take up freedom according to the organized social forms of participation. It seems they can take it up only by revolution of one sort or another.

The freedom of participation demanded throughout the world is the fruit of Western civilization. It derives from Israel and Greece, from the Christian middle ages, from the development of European and American democracy and sense of social responsibility, and most of all from the consummate and peculiarly Western combination of hope and technique. Our crisis is whether the social forms of the various societies of the world, both within and without the civilization of the West, can be changed to fulfill the promise the West has put forth, or whether the violence of revolution will lead to such chaos that freedom anywhere is only a pipedream.

Understanding freedom is at the center of the present crisis.

As an intellectual topic it is profitably approached through many disciplines, especially through the physical and social sciences, through art, literature, law, politics, religion, and philosophy. There is a special advantage to the approach through philosophy, however. Since the crisis forces the question of freedom to be asked radically, the disciplines asking it are forced back to their own roots, to their philosophical foundations. No approach to freedom can escape at least a quasi-philosophical form, and in this sense a philosophical questioning of freedom is the most direct approach. Only religion and art equal philosophy's direct and concrete touch.

Freedom has a history as a philosophical problem. When bondage was associated with the dominance of imitation on decision-making, as it seemed to Plato, freedom was associated with educated and intelligent judgment. When bondage was associated with personal will, as it was in the eleventh and twelfth centuries, freedom was law.[1] For quite different experiential motives, having to do with fear of political anarchy, Hobbes also appealed to law as the guarantor of freedom.[2] To Rousseau, on the other hand, the very network of legalized convention that had provided the experiential ground of freedom in the middle ages seemed the source of bondage, and he took freedom to be freedom from the artificial.[3] In times of pressure freedom has seemed to be the assertion of a strong will against obstacles. When science has made men feel subject to blind but knowable forces, freedom has seemed to be a disenagagement from the natural order. When disengagement from nature and society has seemed to bind men into meaningless isolation, freedom has been construed as commitment. Of course, the development of philosophical theories has exercised a causal role in the construction of these larger experiential situations. But the philosophical concept of freedom has been directly responsive to the changes in experience.

This means two things for the philosophical study of freedom. First, it means that freedom must be studied with an eye to con-

1. See R. W. Southern, *The Making of the Middle Ages* (New Haven, Conn.: Yale University Press, 1953), pp. 107–08.

2. See Hobbes's *Leviathan* (New York: E. P. Dutton & Co., 1950), pt. 2, chap. 21, p. 179.

3. See, e.g., Rousseau's *Emile*, trans. Barbara Foxley (New York: E. P. Dutton & Co., 1911), bk. 1.

crete experiential conditions. The study must be sensitive to literature, the arts, history, social studies, and other areas of reflection dealing with concrete experience. It will have its dialectical aspects as well, to be sure. But there is a necessary inelegance to the study of freedom resulting from the need to appeal to deliverances of experience that have not previously been formed by philosophical discipline.

Second, an adequate study of the concept of freedom must pull together seemingly unconnected strands of the concept's history. What relation is there, for instance, between freedom from jail and freedom from necessitation by antecedent causes? One way of unifying the most diverse historical strands is to do so historically, that is, to tell the story that includes them all. Philosophy's task, however, is to provide a normative concept; it aims to say how freedom *ought* to be conceived if we are to grasp reality well. It must show how the various strands of freedom *ought* to fit together, which is a different kind of fit from a historical one. History enters for the understanding of the various strands of freedom, but it does not dictate the way to unite them in an adequate concept that can articulate and guide culture.

THE HYPOTHESIS

There are *personal* and *social* as well as *religious* dimensions of freedom. At a level of subdivision, there are many dimensions of personal freedom, many of social freedom, and at least two of religious freedom. A "dimension of freedom" is any aspect of human life that can in its own right be called a matter of freedom, or a definition of it.

The dimensions of personal, social, and religious freedom cannot be reduced to one another. No one completely includes the others as proper parts of itself, and none is superior to the others except in ways defined from its own purview. Nor is there a formula integrating all the dimensions together into one unified sense of freedom. What unity there is comes from the concrete unity of the human life or social history.

Personal freedom has to do with the structures or capacities or ways of life that can be considered in relative abstraction from the person's social and religious context. Social freedom has to do with the dimensions of freedom individuals have particularly because they participate in social groups. Religious freedom has to do with the experience of transcending the ordinary world of experience and returning to it without being bound by it; this experience is religious insofar as it is possible because of some particular connection with God.[4]

Of course, the person is not in fact abstracted from society, and all the dimensions of personal freedom themselves have social dimensions. For instance, freedom of choice is a personal dimension insofar as it is a matter of the determination of the individual will; but the choices open are usually socially structured, and a person learns to choose well, perceptively, and steadfastly through his social interactions. Likewise, a social dimension of freedom, for instance the freedom to appropriate a heritage, involves personal dimensions, in this case the choice involved in appropriation.

The dimensions of personal freedom articulate what it is to be autonomous. The philosophical traditions influenced by epistemological and moral problems usually identify freedom as such with self-determination or autonomy. The dimensions of social freedom emphasize participation in or access to the institutions and organizations of social interaction particularly important for human life. Some political philosophers, most social scientists, and nearly all liberal social leaders, especially activists, interpret freedom in terms of participation.

Autonomy and *participation* are concepts each of which indicates an approach to characterizing the heart of human life. Autonomy defines people in terms of their individuality. Participation defines them in terms of their interrelations and achievement of humanity through society. *Personal freedom* will be interpreted in Part 2 in terms of four basic dimensions of freedom: external liberty, freedom of intentional action, freedom of choice, and creativity. The main problems involved with each dimension can be spelled out in introductory fashion here.

External liberty, roughly speaking, is the freedom from restraints of all sorts and, according to Thomas Hobbes, is the paradigm of freedom:

4. The dimensions of religious freedom will not be treated in this book. For treatments systematically connected with the approach here, see Robert C. Neville, *God the Creator* (Chicago: University of Chicago Press, 1968) and *Spiritual Liberation* (New York: Seabury Press, 1975).

By liberty, is understood, according to the proper significa-
tion of the word, the absence of externall Impediments:
which Impediments, may oft take away part of a mans power
to do what hee would; but cannot hinder him from using the
power left him, according as his judgment, and reason shall
dictate to him.[5]

Although external liberties can be considered apart from the
character of the people possessing them, considered apart they are
not ultimately interesting. The liberties must be prized in some
way. Furthermore, the distinction between the external and the
internal is more subtle than Hobbes thought necessary to take into
account. There is a sense in which the external environment
through which a person uses his power freely is not as external as
the environment that restrains him. This calls for a consideration
of more internal factors and raises the general question of how
what is internal to individuals and what is external ought to be
distinguished.

The second dimension, more internal than external liberty, is
a person's freedom of intentional action, his freedom to do that
toward which he most inclines, "a mans power to do what hee
would," in Hobbes's words.[6] Concerning freedom of intentional
action, an account must be given both of action beyond the person and of the initiation of the action.

Someone is sometimes said to be unfree if he cannot act in the
world because the world is so controlled by causal laws that his
intentions cannot interrupt, modify, or get expressed in deeds.
The difficulty would be that freedom makes no sense because the
course of nature is determined without regard for the influences
of people's intentions. Assuming the difficulty, if a person thinks
he can do something involving the causal processes of nature, he is
deceived. This kind of restraint differs from the restraint of external liberty in that it involves the very connection of the intentions, inclinations, and powers of the will with the external world.
The problem here is not that the external world impedes certain

5. Hobbes, *Leviathan*, pt. 1, chap. 14, p. 106; see also pt. 2, chap. 21, p. 177,
"Liberty, or Freedome, signifieth (properly) the absence of Opposition" and "A
Free-Man, is he, that in those things, which by his strength and wit he is able to
do, is not hinderd to doe what he has a will to."
6. Ibid., p. 106; but see Hobbes's own definition of power, pt. 1, chap. 10, pp. 69ff.

actions, nor is it that a person is restrained from willing or choosing; rather it is that he is restrained from translating his intentions into actions. If a person is to be free in this sense, then an account must be given and justified of genuine human agency in the natural and social world.

Many thinkers maintain that freedom of intentional action is all that can ever be intended intelligibly when speaking of the will's freedom.[7] But the further question can be raised whether a person has the further freedom of choosing what to intend, want, or incline toward. Now if there is the further freedom of choosing, it would seem we are involved in an infinite regress, as Jonathan Edwards pointed out.[8] The only reason a person would incline toward one alternative rather than another is some prior inclination toward it; and that prior inclination, if freely chosen, would be so chosen only by yet a prior inclination, and so on. To avoid this regress it would seem that if there is this further freedom of determining intentions, it must be freedom in a different sense from the freedom of intentional action.

The third dimension to be distinguished, then, is the freedom to choose between alternatives, a dimension clearly different from the freedom to do *in concreto* what one intends. The third dimension is considerably harder to defend than the second, however, and just because of what is involved in the justification of that second kind. To show that a willing agent can be able to do what he wills, it is necessary for him to be a natural agent of some sort. But if he is a natural agent, is he not determined in his intentions by the causal laws that govern the natural world? Jonathan Edwards claimed that a person's free will consists solely in his ability to do what he is inclined toward and, asserting that every happening must have a sufficient cause, denied that the person has any further freedom of choosing the inclination.[9] Kant, on the other hand, insisted on a person's freedom in determining what is to be

7. Jonathan Edwards said, in *Freedom of the Will,* ed. Paul Ramsey (New Haven, Conn.: Yale University Press, 1957), p. 164, "But one thing more I would observe concerning what is vulgarly called liberty; namely, that power for one to do and conduct as he will, or according to his choice, is all that is meant by it. . . . Let the person come by his volition or choice how he will, yet, if he is able, and there is nothing in the way to hinder his pursuing and executing his will, then man is fully and perfectly free, according to the primary and common notion of freedom."

8. Ibid., pp. 171–74.

9. Ibid., pp. 180–89.

willed and, agreeing that every event in the natural world has a sufficient cause, excepted the will from that world; he gave up the freedom Edwards insisted on and limited intention to the ideal realm of types.[10] Is there a way of having both sides?

Libertarians often have thought that by denying the doctrine common to Edwards and Kant, namely that the natural world is wholly conditioned by causes, it would be possible to hold both dimensions of freedom.[11] One of the reasons it seems imperative to hold to both, however, is that both are essential to account for a person's responsibility for his actions. Without the freedom of intentional action a person would have no actions for which he could be held responsible, and to hold him responsible only for motives seems prima facie to be a reduction unreasonable to our moral experience. On the other hand, without the freedom to choose the alternatives willed, a person could be held no more responsible for what he did than the series of causes that gave his will its inclination, causes as far reaching as the whole society.

Yet to deny the complete conditioning of the natural world by causes, to say that the process of events is indeterminate to a degree, seems on its own account to run afoul of responsibility. A person must be the cause of his actions if he is to be held responsible, and he is not responsible for what happens adventitiously. Yet if the causal chain is so indeterminate that the person escapes the conditions prior to him, it seems to be so indeterminate that he is no longer the condition of his actions. If he *is* conditioned, on the other hand, the conditions are responsible and the person is not. So it would seem that simply to deny the determinateness of the process of events is not sufficient to save both intentional action and freedom of choice.

To have both kinds of freedom together involves a more extensive reinterpretation of the causal process of nature than the relatively simple assertion of indeterminateness. A person can employ natural laws to accomplish his ends, but he must have the power of determining which laws of nature will be given occasion to operate in a situation where alternatives are presented. If this

10. See Immauel Kant, *Critique of Practical Reason*, trans. Lewis White Beck (New York: Liberal Arts Press, 1956), pp. 70–74.

11. See, e.g., the views of Austin Farrer in his *Freedom of the Will*, Gifford Lectures, 1957 (New York: Charles Scribner's Sons, 1958).

distinction between the causal processes of nature and the causal power natural to the self to interrupt and modify the external process is allowed, then the indeterminateness of the natural process must also be acknowledged. But the indeterminateness is required here, not to cut a person off from prior conditioning, but rather to allow an opening in the environment into which he can insert the causal sequences that fulfill his intentions.

The distinction between the causation of nature and that of the will makes room for the two kinds of freedom in question. But it does not of itself give an account of how a person goes about deciding between alternatives. It shows only how, if he can choose between alternatives, he can make that choice bear upon what he does in the world. How does a person determine his will or intentions with respect to alternatives? If there is indeterminateness within the deciding process, then the determination may be adventitious. Or the determination may be made by prior inclination, as Edwards maintained. In the former case, a person could be said to be free in his determination of choices, but he would be irresponsible. In the latter case, even if the distinction between the two kinds of causation were to be allowed, the person could not be said to be free in his choice of what to work out in the natural course of events. A third alternative is that a person chooses by adopting a *potential* intention as his own actual one. Making a choice is not just a matter of being a cause that determines an effect to happen but is the adoption of a reason for acting this way rather than that way as one's own reason. In this sense it is a free constitution by the agent of his own moral or intentional nature. Arbitrarily to establish a usage of words, we can say that a free *choice* between alternatives stems from a free *decision* as to what moral reasons one identifies with, a free decision regarding what one's own intentions are to be.

A free agent is one making free choices and acting with intentional freedom in the ways chosen. Over and above being a free agent, however, is the matter of acting well, being a good agent. A good agent is skilled and disciplined to make choices for good reasons. To be able to determine what are good reasons for acting, a person must be sufficiently free from his past and from convention so as to be sensitive to what may uniquely be appropriate. He must, in other words, have a capacity to be creative in determining what the best alternative is in each new situation. Without creativity, moral process can be only reiteration of standards that gradually lose their value as the conditions they originally measured well erode away. Moral process is either progress or retrogression, and only creativity can generally bring about the former.

Creativity is the fourth dimension of freedom. Not only is it a freedom from the bondage of the past, it is freedom from the alien character of the world. The more a generally creative person works with his environment, the less alien it is to him in each instance. The longer he works, the less likely will he be to find something he has not already influenced before. There are limits to this. A person cannot fully domesticate another person's subjectivity, especially the person's creativity: that is private. Furthermore, even the most creative person will influence things mainly in the proximate environment, and the vast reaches of the universe are beyond his significant power. The alien forces of the universe will get him in the end. But the degree to which a person can be autonomous in the universe depends on his creativity.

Social freedom will be interpreted in Part 3 in terms of four dimensions roughly parallel to those of personal freedom. The first is that of *freedom of opportunity*. Opportunities are viewed here, not as cosmological possibilities for individuals, but as possibilities both valued by the individual and sustained by the structure of society. How is it that certain opportunities come to be valued as matters of social freedom? In one way or another, it must be because the society itself conveys their value to individuals in culture. Understanding freedom of opportunity, therefore, requires a discussion of social values and their relation to other values a person might have.

For an opportunity to be viewed as a matter of social freedom, it must be one that somebody believes important enough to be sustained by the resources of the society as such. If this belief is generally shared through the society, the opportunity can be called a *right* the society should guarantee its citizens. The importance of the social guarantee is that the control of social resources becomes itself an issue, appearing in the other dimensions of social freedom.

What are the basic kinds of opportunities prized as social freedoms? The cosmological model developed in earlier parts of the book will suggest that a person's fundamental relations to the environment is one of receiving and giving. In terms of social rights, this means a right to profit from the environment, and a right to express one's intentions in it. The opportunities therefore can be divided into those of culture and those of participation in organized society.

The opportunities of culture have to do with opportunities for taking up cultural resources as components of one's own experience. This means both that the resources must be available and that the person must be able to appropriate them, an ability arising from experience. The three most important opportunities of culture appear to be (1) the freedom to have an historical heritage, identifying with a civilization-building group; (2) the freedom to enjoy a high culture, bringing the values of civilization and cultured life into personal experience; and (3) the freedom to use one's cultural experience in the concrete interactions of a society. These three add up to the freedom to have a culturally rich identity informing one's social participation.

The freedom to participate in organized society involves opportunities for acting. The most important opportunities appear to be again of three sorts: the freedom to participate in social media, including economic and educational media (without these a person has no power); the freedom to organize for cooperative pursuit of common goals; and the freedom to participate in organized society with a life style unique to oneself, expressing one's heritage, culture, particular stations, and personal choices.

The freedoms of opportunity find their integrating expression in the ideal of a free historical agent, one who is sufficiently in control of historical forces so as to make his personal choices historically efficacious. The possibility of a free historical agent, however, supposes that society does indeed offer live options of how to live—in other words, alternative social forms.

This points to the second dimension of social freedom, *social pluralism*. Without a pluralism of social forms, the freedom of opportunities could be limited to a consistent, totalitarian few, and people could be conditioned to prize them; this is something of the ideal of B. F. Skinner. Without genuine options between social forms, there is no such thing as freedom of choice on the social level. The problem here, however, has to do not with the mechanism of choice but with distinguishing private choosing from public limitations. The main concept to be analyzed in this respect is the distinction between the public and the private. The hypothesis is that the public has to do with concerns for sustaining an environment for prized kinds of creativity, and the private has to do with concerns for the creativity itself. Social pluralism entails a public guarantee of a plurality of social forms. It also entails a right to privacy and integrity.

How can a person live in a society with many options for social forms without losing his integrity? Does not the unity of life come from consistency of the social patterns in which one lives? The discussion of personal freedom of course suggests that the integrity of life comes from styles of choosing, and indeed this is the third dimension of social freedom, *freedom of integral social life.* The question to be asked here is what kind of experiential style is appropriate for living in a pluralistic situation, so that one is not in bondage to social fragmentation. This raises the prior question, on the cosmological level, of how a person's choosing can be related to his social environment. The experiential style hypothesized has to do with characteristic ways of relating perceptions, thoughts, and actions.

If the environment provides opportunities and options, and the person has an integral social style, how is the social order itself structured? How does change take place in society that reflects the other dimensions of freedom? The answer defended in the hypothesis is *participatory democracy,* the fourth dimension of freedom. A participatory democracy is a social order in which persons influence the conditions under which decisions are made to the extent they are potentially affected by the decisions. Understanding this requires an interpretation of relevance to decision-making, power, authority, and publicity. The concept of participatory democracy is an ideal making demands on all the other dimensions of freedom, but fulfilling them all. So runs our hypothesis.

As philosophers have long known, what one says directly about personal and social freedom is not half as controversial as the categories one selects to set up the problem in the first place. The hypothesis formulated and developed in this book is perhaps idiosyncratic in its use of cosmology. But it gives a fairly typical American account of social values, in the tradition of Edwards, Emerson, and Dewey; its methodology of social analysis reflects this tradition too. The greatest impact on social thinking in recent years, however, has been that of John Rawls's *Theory of Justice*. Rawls's strategy, stated briefly, is to attempt to formulate social values from a position that brackets out special perceptions and interests. He believes that justice should be defined in its root sense from a nonhistorical perspective, the "original position." The prima facie sense of "equality," so important for the concept of "justice," requires a nonhistorical perspective. The hypothesis regarding freedom put forward in the present book, however, takes just the opposite view. Social values, including justice and freedom, can be appreciated only from concrete historical perspectives. The practical problem is not to abstract from special interests to a position of minimal equality but rather to broaden one's special perspective to include the breadth of the human tradition. The problem is parochial bias, not historically conditioned bias. Although there are many advantages of logical clarity to Professor Rawls's approach, it neglects the very important contribution of the American tradition of social thought and as a result separates social ideals like justice from the push of concrete affairs, perpetuating the unfortunate dichotomy of norms from facts.

A final point must be made about the neglect of religious freedom in the formulation of the hypothesis. For many people, of course, it is the most important kind of freedom, and it certainly has a cosmological character to be investigated. Essential to religious freedom, however, is the fact that it stems from a person's connections with the foundations of existence, the divine, God. Those ultimate foundations are not part of the cosmology to be discussed in this book. Nevertheless, all the other kinds of personal and social freedom also have connections with the foundations of existence. And because this book prescinds from those connections there will undoubtedly be a feeling of flatness about the discussions of personal and social freedom. For instance, the discussion of intentional action will treat intention as a kind of causality but will ignore the deep existential problem of making an act of will, of pulling oneself together to "will one thing" in

Kierkegaard's phrase, or to act "possessed of the self" and "without regard for the fruits," as the *Bhagavadgita* puts it. Yet again, the character of creative invention and judgment is discussed, but without treatment of the sense in which one's creativity is at root the action of the elemental powers of the universe. In these and many other ways, the problem of existential freedom in its most poignant depths is a religious or spiritual problem, resting on the connection of cosmological entities with their ground. In other words, the cosmology of freedom is somewhat superficial compared with the ontology of freedom. But the cosmology must come first if the ontology is not to be empty; and it is deep enough for most practical interests.

Freedom is better than bondage, in all the respective dimensions. This fact can be noted in the relentless demands of people for freedom in all guises. But it can be *understood* only in terms of a theory of value. There are several reasons why a theory of value must be developed to defend the hypothesis about freedom, but the most concrete is to show why freedom is good. The answer will be that freedom introduces an intensity of contrast lacking in the bondage appropriate in every dimension.

ABSTRACTIONS

It might be argued that the hypothesis as briefly stated already reveals a fundamental confusion. Some of the elements of freedom and the topics to be discussed in their regard are concrete and practical: the problems of external liberty and social participation are clear examples. Others are abstract and theoretical, problems of philosophers, not of men, as Dewey would say: an example is the choice between alternatives, involving the determinism controversy. This confusion is an instance of the attempt to give philosophy a positive subject matter by intertwining abstract (and empty) problems with concrete, experiential, and positive ones better handled by practical persons, not philosophers. A true philosopher's job, according to this objection, is to show that the abstract problems rest on category mistakes so that people's creative attention is focused on the real practical ones; this is especially true of the problems of freedom.

The answer to this problem is that the really practical problems include the abstract ones. Granted there is a distinction between problems of adequate conceptualization and those of concrete experience, where the latter involve direct action and brute forces, it is not obvious that only the latter are of practical import. Quite the contrary. In the first place, the way people understand things is important for how they deal with them. This is more true for freedom, close as it is to a person's own identity, than it might be for clearly concrete but impersonal things like rocks and trees.

In the second place, the distinction between the abstract and the concrete is not clear, and it is dubious that freedom is all on the concrete side. Suppose it be said that the concrete is particular and the abstract universal—the view of many nominalists. Then freedom is mainly abstract: even "particular" external liberties are not really particulars; they are general opportunities to do particular acts. Suppose that the concrete is said to be the direct content of consciousness and that the abstract is the classification of the contents—the view of William James.[12] Surely the deliberation about alternatives is abstract then. No matter how the distinction is drawn, the original point still holds; that is, a most practical part of freedom is a person's understanding of himself as free.

"Experience" is not a contrast term to "abstraction." Rather it includes both the abstract and the concrete. But supposing experience does include both the concrete and the abstract, it may still be objected that the hypothesis just mixes the two in a hodgepodge. If there is any distinction between the abstract and the concrete it is incumbent on an adequate account of freedom to make out the distinction and sort the issues accordingly. This criticism is well taken. But the actual sorting of the issues of freedom is so complex it can be done only in the detailed development and defense of the hypothesis, not in an introduction. As to the more general problem of distinguishing the abstract from the concrete, a brief word is in order.

An abstraction is best conceived as a simplification. It is abstract because it leaves out elements of what it simplifies. As there

12. See James's *Some Problems of Philosophy: A Beginning of an Introduction to Philosophy* (New York: Longmans, Green & Co., 1911), chaps. 4–6.

are different ways of simplifying a subject, there are different abstractions of it; as there are degrees of simplification, there are degrees of abstraction.

One might object that this characterization misses the essential point, namely that an abstraction is a mental entity and that at least some things simplified by abstractions are real and non-mental.

On the contrary, to conceive an abstraction as a simplification does render that distinction. Suppose, as will be argued below, that mental activity is the process of simplifying the given. In contrast with this a physical activity is the process of rearranging the given elements in different, perhaps novel patterns. More is involved in the process of simplification than mere simplification; in people at least that process is intentionally directed and self-critical. Human activity, if this suggestion is true, must be conceived in terms of both processes, mental and physical. While the physical activity of a person may be analyzed merely in terms of rearrangement and his thought merely in terms of sign-making, to understand the activity as human it must be shown how the physical rearrangement of elements is directed by the process of simplifying sign-making. As to the distinction between the mental and the real, both physical objects and simplifications are real, each in its own way, and both can be simplified when involved in a mental process.

Abstractions are better or worse simplifications. In more practical terms, things may be conceived in a variety of ways, but some ways are better than others. This means there are norms applicable to the process of abstraction. An abstraction is better if it leaves out the trivial and highlights the important. This seems an unexceptional thing to say, but several crucial things follow from it.

First, if an abstraction (for our purposes an abstract conception) is good or bad according to how it distinguishes the trivial from the important in what it simplifies, then the distinction is intrinsic to whatever can be conceived as well as to the conceptions themselves. It is often said that a conception is good if it represents what its object is, and bad to the degree that it represents the object as being other than it is; this view focuses on the mental repetition of structure. But if abstractions are simplifications, then the structural repetition view is misleading. A simplification *always* is less than what it simplifies, since it leaves elements out. But it is *good* to simplify if what is left out is trivial and what is highlighted is important, a distinction confused in the unsimplified subject.

The second consequence of the claim that abstractions are good if they sort the important from the trivial is that we must ask, Important for what? The only recent school of philosophy to recognize the primacy of normative elements in conception is pragmatism, and at least some pragmatists have answered, Purpose. Things may be conceived in different ways for different purposes. An element is important enough to be retained in an abstract conception if it must be acknowledged in order for the purpose to be fulfilled, and an element is trivial if it can be ignored. According to some kinds of pragmatism, an element that can be ignored for all purposes whatsoever is unreal, merely imagined to exist.

The pragmatic answer is limited, however. In the long run, what is important in the world determines what people's purpose *should* be. Moral questions have the form, Given such and such important conditions, what should be done? Some pragmatists have a tendency to think that the setting of purposes is an arbitrary matter. In small and partial elements of life, it is indeed often arbitrary. But in the large matters people insist that their purposes be good ones. Given a life with friends to enjoy, fulfilling work to do, and an environment to enhance, how should people live? One answers that question according to the apparent real importance of the various conditions.

This suggests that in the long run importance is determined, not by a purpose external to the thing with important and trivial elements, but by some character of the relations of those elements themselves. Here is another way of saying that values are intrinsic to things. Suppose the ranking of importance and triviality in a complex of elements is a function of the relations of elements. Then, to conceive a thing well abstractly is to simplify it by highlighting the particular function of the relation of the elements. This allows for abstract knowledge of objects apart from the knower's specific purposes. *In the long run the best theory is the way things ought to be conceived in order to be dealt with accord-*

ing to their real importance, and the best purposes are those reflecting the theories most adequately simplifying what is important.

Since this interpretation of abstraction depends on unusual metaphysical views, it can be attacked through its metaphysics in many ways; and in those ways it can be defended only through its metaphysics. Those important objections will be dealt with in the defense of the metaphysical position in the next few chapters. But there are two direct attacks that can be dealt with briefly here.

Everyone knows, the objection goes, that there is a crucial distinction between facts and values, and therefore we must be able to conceive the one without the other in some sense. In fact, we can prescind from all questions of value and deal only with the cognitive problems of facts, as the scientists do. Since scientists employ abstractions, abstractions cannot intrinsically be involved with value notions like importance.

The difficulty with this attack is that it is contrary to experience. In experience people rarely deal with things only as facts, but rather as objects of various sorts of interests. A thing is an object of interest because of its apparent importance. Even when there is nothing in an experiential environment to hold a person's attention, and his attentive activity selects first one focal point then another, there is an imputation of possible or real importance to each attentive object. Facts are never brutely experienced as prescinded from values; a person may make the separation, but this itself is to simplify. Even in the case where the simplification aims to state fact prescinded from value, the abstract simplification is determined *normatively* to do just that. It is a good abstraction precisely because it leaves out the value elements as trivial. The norms for a good scientific theory—universality, coherence, elegance, etc.—determine the form of scientific abstractions and what it is good for them to treat as important.

The second attack on the above view of abstractions is that all abstractions distort. Real values are to be found in the concrete content of experience but are distorted when experience is classified by inevitably one-sided abstractions. So, contrary to the claim that abstraction singles out what is important, abstraction distorts the distinction between the important and the trivial by leaving out details in the richness of experience.

This attack amounts to a denial that there are degrees of importance exhibited by things in experience; if there are degrees, then abstractions can distinguish them. Of course there are good abstractions and bad ones; the bad ones are those that do distort. Still there is no reason to say all abstractions distort; they would only distort if there were no differences of degrees of importance so that the relatively trivial could be left aside. This objection serves as a warning, however, against the confusion of abstractions with concrete reality that Whitehead called the "fallacy of misplaced concreteness."

FREEDOM AND THEORY

The various elements of the problem of freedom have been simplified in abstract discussion in various ways throughout the history of philosophy. Even the most concrete issues have been given theoretical treatment. The difficulty in understanding freedom, however, is that the kinds of abstractions used to simplify the various elements of the overall problem have not been unified. External liberties are often discussed in terms of political theory. Intentional action is usually discussed in the language of philosophical psychology. Choice between alternatives sometimes is a matter of physical theory, as in the problem of determinism, sometimes linguistic theory, as in the problem of counter-factual conditionals, and sometimes social theory, as in Dewey's usual approach to the matter. Deliberation has been analyzed in terms of moral example and ethical theory. Discussions of the issues of social participation have been disconnected even more.

For a unified account of freedom, therefore, it is necessary to have an abstract theory of the whole that can capture the insights of history and put them in their places. This means the development of a *very* abstract theory, since the ways in which disparate elements can be brought together are likely to be extraordinarily simplified versions of the original discussions. Until such an abstract theory can be presented, the hypothesis about freedom cannot be stated in proper form. The statement in this chapter has only listed the various elements; it has not presented them as unified in a theoretically proper hypothesis. Consequently, the hypothesis can only be grasped properly at the end of the discussion, after the abstract theory has been presented and made plausible.

Philosophy necessarily lives with abstract theory. But philosophy ought not lose touch with concrete experience. Concrete experience is always more ambiguous than theoretical abstractions can articulate. Not only does it include the trivial with the important, experience is uniquely located in temporal and spatial existence. The meaning of an experience is rarely exhausted in itself but depends on other existential connections. An action can be free in one sense, unfree in another. It can appear to have freedom in a certain dimension but be in fact the opposite of what it seems. And there is an irony in concrete experience that theory cannot articulate.

The fulcrum of a philosophical account of freedom is a theoretical model comprehensive enough to exhibit all the dimensions of freedom in articulated relations. Since the development of this model will involve discussions of topics seemingly unrelated to freedom, the necessity for it should be explained.

Two contemporary schools of philosophy tend to disparage the very task of speculative theoretical models in philosophy. One, linguistic analysis, often claims that "metaphysics is impossible." Of course, it is not impossible as an activity since there are actual examples of it. Rather, the analytical claim is that metaphysics cannot be what it claims to be, a meaningful explanation of experience. Of course few philosophers take seriously today the attempt to develop a reductionistic criterion of meaning; a system or concept is meaningful if people can make progress in understanding it, even if it is silly. Whether a speculative philosophy *explains* is a more serious question. A system that alleges to explain by deducing the world may in fact be impossible; or again it may not. At any rate the system presented here explains as a general hypothesis explains; how well it explains should be determined by a direct examination of it, not by a discussion of its a priori possibility.

Some analytic philosophers, following Peter Strawson, have attempted to distinguish descriptive metaphysics from revisionary metaphysics, cleaving to the former. Descriptive metaphysics articulates the general concepts involved in how we think and talk about the world; revisionary metaphysics tells us how we ought to think and talk. The former seems like safe analysis, though broadened and systematized. The latter seems inventive and to demand from philosophy a special kind of knowledge it lacks. The distinction, however, is safe only at its extremes. Descriptive conceptual analysis is a kind of simplification; to ignore the examination of the values directing simplification one way rather than another is to accept uncritically the categories of analysis. Yet to examine the appropriateness of the categories as alternate simplifications is to engage in revisionary metaphysics, even if the only novelty introduced is an explicit approval of what before was implicitly approved. Abstraction or simplification is invariably valuational if there are alternative abstractions; and if there are no alternative abstractions it is difficult to see what progress is made.

Other analytic philosophers, following Sellars, emphasize the transcendental or "linguistic" turn in philosophy. This move requires accepting some domain of experience as authoritative on its own—a priori judgments in mathematics and science for Kant, language as spoken by common people or empirical scientists for our contemporaries—and then asking how this authority is to be understood. Philosophy on this view explains how the authoritative domain is possible and why it is authoritative. But philosophy cannot (ought not) impune the authority itself, or supplant the authoritative domain with some philosophically constructed system. The difficulty with this view is that philosophy's business is to take no authority for granted. To be sure, experience in some sense is the last court of appeals. But just what elements of experience are authoritative should be the conclusion of a philosophic effort, not its starting point. Of course it can be shown why science or ordinary language are authoritative if it is assumed that they are; anything presumed true can be justified as having its own authority. But in the world of practical affairs, for which philosophy should provide wisdom, the important questions are precisely those of what elements are authoritative.

Phenomenology, the other philosophic school disparaging speculation, believes the form of philosophical understanding is a series of acknowledgments of what experience presents, arranged in some kind of order, systematic or otherwise. The arguments for this belief are usually of two sorts. First are "philosophy as experience" arguments: the source of philosophical knowledge ought to be experience; and the acknowledgment of what experience delivers, precisely as deliverance of experience, is how philosophy ought to appropriate its subject. Second, in this way philosophy will deal with realities, not with philosophical constructs; an entity or category hypothesized to solve a philosophical problem is only an intellectual pawn in a conceptual game; these can be called "experience as philosophical reality" arguments.

The "philosophy as experience" argument is correct that the source of philosophical knowledge ought to be experience. But there are two reasons why philosophical understanding should be refined beyond the experiential acknowledgment stage.

The first has to do with what is intended by understanding. We appeal to experience to discover the elements regularly involved in freedom, and these must be acknowledged on the authority of experience in some sense. But we want to understand why the particular occasions when freedom is relevant exhibit these general elements, and for this a theory is needed. Experience may show that a free person must be able to criticize his standards; but a theory is needed to show what structure a particular creature must have to engage in criticism.

The second reason is that we want to understand things so that we know what is important about them *when we act*. Only a theory that simplifies well can distinguish the important from the trivial; yet on the level of experiential acknowledgment philosophy must record the important and the trivial with unprejudiced equality. The "acknowledgment of experience" view of the final form of philosophical understanding cannot distinguish the important from the trivial, and when it tries to do so usually takes some character like regularity or universality as the mark of importance; but there is no reason prima facie why the regular is more important than the individual or irregular, and the contemporary rebellion against "essentialism" in favor of "existentialism" shows a growing appreciation of this.

In sum, the "philosophy as experience" argument for the "acknowledgment of experience" theory fails for two reasons. First, it is better to know both what experience is and why it is that way than just to know the former; as Plato would put it, the man of theory who understands causes knows more than the man who knows only what experience teaches. Second, the "acknowledgment of experience" theory does not have the moral value of distinguishing the important from the trivial in its form of knowledge.

"The "experience as philosophical reality" argument is that theoretical constructs are nothing but pawns in a conceptual game. It analyzes the situation as follows. A certain subject matter is interpreted with a hypothesis. The hypothesis, to make the subject matter intelligible, asserts something about the subject matter that was not apparent in its initial experiential presentation, but since the warrant for the assertion is only hypothetical, what was asserted is only a hypothesis, a concept. This is a logical mistake, however. There is a difference between the asserting, which is conceptual and grounded in the hypothesis, and what is asserted, which might be anything assertable. If a person interprets a knock on the door with the hypothesis that someone on the other side wants in, this does not entail that the person on the other side is a concept instead of an existing individual. The "conceptual pawn" complaint is usually used to object to proofs for God, claiming that the God inferred must be only a philosopher's construction. It is difficult, of course, to find a valid argument for God; but no one ever meant to say that God is a hypothesis. It is a mistake to say that the entities, categories, and so forth, that might be hypothesized to explain something must themselves have the kind of reality hypotheses do.

What are the formal criteria for a philosophical theory that would account for the elements of freedom mentioned above? Attention should be called to four features. First, the theory must be *inclusive*. Unlike a scientific theory specifying its subject matter as a certain kind of physical reality, a theory adequate for freedom must take into account at least all the diverse things specified above. Practically speaking, there is hardly any kind of theory not included somehow among the things a comprehensive theory of freedom must integrate.

Second, the theory must be *systematic*. If it were not systematic then its inclusive character would make it a grab bag of miscellaneous observations. Its systematic character is what gives unity to the model exhibiting how the observed elements of freedom hang together. To defend the systematic elements in the theory requires discussing things not obviously related to freedom, but those things *are* systematically related if the elements of freedom are to be interpreted with an intelligible theory.

Third, the theory must be *abstract*. If it were not abstract, that is, if it did not conceive the elements of freedom in a very simplified form, then it would be unable to articulate what they have in common and how they are connected. This means the various elements and problem areas must be abstracted into categories that fit together systematically. Since the elements of freedom are so various, the system of abstract categories must be very abstract indeed to attain the requisite universality.

Fourth, the system of categories must be capable of being *specified*. That is, the categories must be of such a form that it is apparent how they are exhibited in the various specific problems of freedom. We may speak abstractly of a being in general acting according to norms, which helps us understand a person acting according to ideals, which then sheds light on John's telling the truth in an uncomfortable situation. Specification is by no means a deductive matter since it moves from the simplification to what is simplified, re-relating the simplification to the matter left out as trivial at each stage in the simplification process. The processes of specification and simplification should make the concrete reality more intelligible.

It is convenient to distinguish the various levels of philosophical abstraction with the traditional names: metaphysics, ontology, cosmology, and so forth. In fact, now that the philosophic community has got over its wholesale rejection of classical philosophy, the question asked is how the traditional classifications apply to present enterprises. The classic terms may be used to demarcate levels of abstraction in the following way.

No matter what sorts of things might exist, each of them has some kind of identity, distinguishing it from the others. To this extent the things are determinate; some things may be partially indeterminate, but nothing with an identity is completely indeterminate. Therefore, one philosophical study that is perfectly universal and systematic is that of determinateness as such, of what it is to be determinate. In accordance with tradition, the study of the transcendental properties of determinateness can be called *metaphysics*. It is systematic and perfectly universal in the sense that it studies what is transcendental.

Traditionally, the study of the transcendentals has been distinguished from the study of being as being. In contrast to asking about the characteristics of determinateness as such, we may ask about the conditions for there being anything determinate at all, and for the intelligibility of determinateness. This can be called *ontology*. It is especially complex since the condition for any determinateness is not itself determinate in an ordinary way, and yet the theory about it must be determinate to be intelligible.[13] In the following chapters it will be clear that the ultimate condition of determinateness is better conceived in some contexts as the Good rather than as Being.[14]

In practice there can be no clear separation of metaphyiscs from ontology in the sense defined here. The arguments about the condition for determinateness turn on the characteristics ascribed to determinateness. And what is important in the characteristics of determinateness is what is best simplified in ontology.

A more specific study than either ontology or metaphysics is the examination of the system of categories distinguishing, integrating, and interpreting all the various kinds of determinations there are. This study works with conceptualizations of all the different things there might be on a sufficiently absbtract level that they can be related systematically. It is the kind of speculative philosophy Whitehead and Peirce did, and it can be called *cosmology*.[15] It must be inclusive, systematic, abstract, and capable of specification into the particulars of experience. This is the kind of theory needed to understand the elements of freedom.

This characterization of cosmology must be qualified, however. Metaphysics and ontology, as described here, are independent of experience in the sense that anything determinate is their subject matter; mere ideas would do. They are not a priori studies in all senses, since they must be checked against experience to make sure nothing important about determinateness has been left out; in this sense they are dialectically related to cosmology. But no facts deliverable by experience would make a difference to the strict character of determinateness as such. Cosmology, in contrast, is directly dependent on the various areas of experience it must systematically interpret and integrate. It is not empirical like the sciences or arts, because it does not set the conditions for the em-

13. For a systematic defense of this thesis see my *God the Creator*, chaps. 1–4.

14. *God the Creator* presents the case for Being. Chap. 3 of the present book argues the case for the Good.

15. Whitehead's *Process and Reality*, Gifford Lectures, 1927–28 (London: Macmillan & Co., 1929) is subtitled *An Essay in Cosmology*.

pirical testing of the aspects of experience it tries to integrate, except perhaps with regard to humanistic areas whose experimental
studies have not separated clearly from philosophy. But it is empirical in the sense that it must systematize in simplified form
what experience delivers.

In the present intellectual situation there is no single context
in which a comprehensive view of the subject matter of cosmology
can gather its raw material. Rather there are three competing contexts, none of which is genuinely universal or inclusive. They can
be called *microcosmology, macrocosmology* and *mesocosmology*.[16]
The first two are the provinces chiefly of the speculative physicists,
microcosmology covering the composition of everything in terms
of elementary particles, macrocosmology in terms of the cosmic
origin of matter and energy. But neither gives much prima facie
value to constructing categories as simplifications of the world of
human experience; in no obvious way can they be specified elegantly to deal with things of human scale, the scale in which freedom is a problem. Whitehead was perhaps the last philosopher to
attempt a genuinely comprehensive cosmological system; but
even he can be accused of skimping on attention to the cosmological dimension of human affairs. Mesocosmology is cosmology arising from attention focused on things of a human scale. It must,
of course, be comprehensive, systematic, and abstract; but it is
more easily specifiable with respect to affairs of human life than
with respect to micro- and macro-affairs.

Philosophers have tended in recent years to specialize in subjects requiring expertise outside philosophy proper, subjects usually called "philosophy of . . ." In light of the empirical ground-
ing of cosmology, this is a good thing. It seems, however, that the
natural sciences require such an extreme degree of expertise that
philosophers have tended to divide into those devoted to science
who study that exclusively and those who devote themselves to
the subjects other than science. These latter are the experts in
the things of human scale, the philosophers of art, religion, history, and man; the ethicists; social philosophers; and students of
the history of philosophical thought. As long as this division with
regard to science holds as characteristic of the community, there

16. This distinction, and the terminology, are due to Professor Robert H. Kane
of the University of Texas.

can be no genuinely comprehensive, systematic, abstract, and specifiable cosmology. Even geniuses like Whitehead who seem to be at home on both sides of the division have not found the community able to criticize them in full perspective.[17]

Fortunately for the purposes of the present study the problems of freedom are all those of a human scale (with certain qualifications regarding the problem of determinism) and can be handled by a mesocosmological theory. Of course, it would increase the plausibility of the hypothesis to be developed if it could be shown to have an absolutely general cosmological form. But given the intellectual situation, this is impossible.

Although explicitly the claims of this book must be fairly limited, restricted to how well a theory works for handling a limited experiential problem, of course the implicit claim is much larger. The problems of freedom are not *that* limited in experience, and a theory handling them well is likely to do well with others.

17. Hartshorne, for instance, has concentrated almost exclusively on the problem of God and his relation to actual entities; he deals also with the experiential problem of the worshipfulness of this God. Weiss is much more extensive in his interests but works from the standpoint of mesocosmology, neglecting the more strictly scientific problems. Grünbaum deals mainly with the scientific side. Perhaps Whitehead's most catholic interpreter is F. S. C. Northrop.

2

The Cosmological Scheme

There is no way to be light-handed in presenting a system of philosophical categories. Although such a system is always a hypothesis, its parts cannot be put forward as tentative suggestions. Speculative philosophy has no spirit unless the categories are genuinely intended to mean what they say. Philosophical categories, complex and very hard to state exactly, are nevertheless tissues of concepts gaining meaning from their interconnections. Their logical relations must be followed out rigorously. Of course, whether the scheme is valid, or even worthwhile, depends on its relation to experience. The main emphasis of the later chapters of this book will be to relate the scheme to various experiential dimensions of freedom. The purpose of this chapter is to introduce the categoreal scheme.

According to the distinctions made in chapter 1, the first section of our discussion will deal with metaphysical categories, the second with cosmological ones. The third will develop the doctrine of individuals to the point that allows subsequent chapters to discuss the *freedom* of individuals in cosmological terms.

METAPHYSICAL CATEGORIES

The general metaphysical hypothesis is that, to be determinate, a thing must be some kind of harmony of essential and conditional features.[1] The terms "harmony," "essential," and "conditional" have technical meanings expressing the principles of the metaphysical hypothesis.

For a thing to be determinate it must be itself, different from other things. Therefore it must be determinate with respect to something else. It is inconceivable that a thing be determinate

1. This metaphysical theory has been defended at length in my book *God the Creator* and will be put forward here as a suggested premise.

in absolute isolation. It might of course be in physical and causal isolation. But if it is different from something else, anything else, it is in the metaphysical relation of being determinate with respect to those other things. Only on the more specific cosmological level is it necessary to ask what kind of relation is involved in being determinate with respect to something else, for instance a temporal or causal relation, a relation with reciprocity, a relation of factual to counterfactual, or possible to impossible, of concept to concept.

Because it must be determinate with respect to something, a determinate thing needs *conditional* features constituting it as conditioned by that with respect to which it is determinate. For instance, a thing determinate with respect to its cause has conditional features stemming from its conditioning antecedents; or if it is determinate with respect to its effects, it has conditional features anticipating them. These of course are cosmological examples of conditional relations; the metaphysical principle is quite vague with respect to what kinds of conditions there might be. But the metaphysical principle itself is that a thing is what it is partly and necessarily in virtue of its being conditioned by other things with respect to which it is determinate. The consequence of denying the necessity of conditional features is that the relational character of determinateness is ignored.

A determinate thing must also have *essential* features making it unique, exclusive of those other things to which it is related, since relations require some inner reality in the terms related. This may be shown from the character of conditional features. A conditional feature of a thing appropriates that with respect to which the thing is determinate in a way characteristic of the thing whose feature it is; it conditions the thing with respect to the other by appropriating the other in a conditioning way. But the conditioning way must be characteristic of the thing as defined in some way other than the appropriating conditioning feature, since that feature is characteristic and there must be something of which it is characteristic. Therefore, there must be something essential that the conditional features express when appropriating external things in ways characteristic of the thing of which they are parts.

Essential features are the reasons why the harmony of a thing, including both conditional and essential features, has the pattern it does. In the cosmological theory of freedom, persons will be represented as complexes of essential and conditional features interacting in society. Furthermore, most of the dimensions of freedom will have to do particularly with essential features, since the essential features constitute the inner heart of a thing in terms of which it appropriates the things that condition it. A model must be developed showing what essential and conditional features mean for living individuals. It will turn out that the essential features are those by which people constitute their own being, to the extent that they do. And when the essential value a man has is something he in part determines himself, in an important sense he gives himself his own reason or value for being what he is, his moral justification.

The harmony of the essential and conditional features can be analyzed both as a structure and as a value. As a structure, its parts are immediately together. That is, there is no "third thing," a feature or principle, mediating between the features of the thing. Rather, a thing's nature is the togetherness of its features related to each other according to their own natures. Not to acknowledge the immediate togetherness of things in harmony is to require a higher mediator, in effect only adding to the complexity instead of reducing it, since the relation between the mediator and the mediated features would need a mediator, and so on. Rather, a harmony is a togetherness of things unified just by virtue of the natures of its parts. This is the structural side of harmony.

There is another aspect of harmony—the normative or value. With at least some kinds of things, the features making them determinate can be arranged in a variety of ways; the important features of human beings, for instance body, emotions, and intellect, can be related in many ways. Of course, the different modes of relating or harmonizing the features make a difference to the features themselves, but these differences may not be as important as the differences in the modes of harmony. There are better and worse modes of harmony. Roughly speaking, a mode of harmony is better if the difference it makes to the harmonized features enhances the features. Again, human life is a good example. There are neurotic ways of harmonizing body, emotions, and intellect,

and ways that fulfill the features and enhance them by their connections; the latter are better. Since it is difficult to enhance different and often conflicting things in the same harmonious pattern, the greater the differences between the things enhanced, the
greater the intensity of contrast in the pattern, and the greater the
value.

Every essential feature, being determinate, is itself a harmony,
and every harmony, even if not itself an essential feature in a
larger harmony, has a value by virtue of the degree of contrast
in its pattern. The reason any harmony, be it an essential feature
or not, has its value or contrast pattern is that it itself has essential features with values to be realized in its pattern. The
essential features of a thing determine the thing's overall pattern
to have the contrast or value it does in order to realize the values
of the essential features in the integration of the thing's conditional features.

Although it is not to the point of the theory of freedom to defend its metaphysical underpinnings at length, certain large-scale
alternatives can be discussed.

Beginning with a notion as abstract as determinateness sets this
approach off from the Aristotelian, Thomistic, and existential
philosophies that start with existing things. According to existence
philosophies, only concrete existing things are real and all other
things are abstractions from the existent. On the metaphysical
orientation expressed in this book, however, anything having an
identity is real. Further questions must be raised as to the *kinds*
of reality involved—existential, possible, past, fictional, conceptual, and so forth.

The existence position makes an unwarranted limitation on
what sorts of things there are. It might be said the principle of
parsimony requires beginning with the most obvious kind of
being and making the attempt to reduce other apparent alternatives to it. But this is too simpleminded an employment of the
principle, too quantitative an interpretation of economy; it is
conceptually more economical to speak only of determinateness
and to leave it to further investigation to discover what sorts of
things are determinate.

Another alternative to this metaphysical hypothesis is determinate monism, which would object that the characterization of

things as requiring both essential and conditional features is a
commitment to irrational metaphysical pluralism. Because of the
conditional features in the hypothesis, all definition is relational;
because of the essential features, there is an element in every
determination that is not shared by any other, at least not in the
same respect. Determinate monism takes this to be an admission
of absurdity, since the theory must admit that there is no one
determinate thing that unifies the whole.

Metaphysical pluralism does not imply pluralism in all senses,
however. The solution of the problem of the one and the many,
the functional heart of *ontology,* may well provide a monistic
category as the condition for there being any determinateness at
all, and this would answer the objection of the determinate monist. The determinate monist makes the mistake of believing that
the unity of the determinate things must itself be a determinate
thing; but the unity may well be the ground of determinateness
as such and not determinate itself in any obvious sense. Thus it
is possible to maintain a metaphysical pluralism and an ontological monism together. This would avoid both the "block universe"
objection to monism, since the unity would not be a determinate
block, and the unintelligibility objection to pluralism, since a
unity is still acknowledged.

Cosmological Categories

Moving from the abstract level of metaphysics to the relatively
more specific matters of cosmology, the cosmology introduced in
this book to handle freedom is both pluralistic and axiological.
As a pluralism it acknowledges a plurality of genuinely distinct
concrete individuals that are not related to each other in a cosmological sense by anything as concrete as themselves. They are related by a variety of cosmological elements more abstract than
themselves, for instance common possibilities, common obligations, and so forth. With Whitehead and Weiss, the position says
that all such unifications are dependent on the perspectives of the
individuals, the unifications being abstract relative to the individuals in whose perspectives they are. This cosmological pluralism
is compatible with metaphysical pluralism and ontological monism. God, discerned in ontological reflection, need not be considered among the cosmological categories.

The categoreal scheme here is axiological in the sense that it is dominated by a theory of value. As a cosmology, the scheme must give accounts of individuals, change, causation, developments, groupings, and so forth. And as a mesocosmology it focuses on the cosmological element that can be controlled to some degree in human life and society, especially judgments for intentional action, standards, criticism, and so forth. But all these accounts are dominated by, and in some sense derived from, a theory of value.

The theory of value runs through cosmology, metaphysics, and ontology, but it functions in a particular way in cosmology relative to the cosmological model to be developed. A model derived, in the appropriate sense, from a theory of value is different in ways that will become apparent from all other models—models derived from an underlying sense of the primacy of structure rather than value.

Although it is premature to formulate the sense of value in the axiological theory, the thesis that distinguishes this cosmology from other pluralisms is the following. The reason why the *"real internal constitution" of a thing is such and so, is that such and so is a good way its given or potentially given constituents can be ordered.* The reference to "a good way" is the dependence on the theory of value. In this theory, a good answer to a question about why a thing is as it is, considering its constituents, is that that is a good way for it to be (with the commitment to go on to show how, why, and in what senses that way is better or worse than others). In contrast to most cosmologies, this axiological one justifies turning very quickly to a discussion of assessments to be given the worth of things. Understanding the nature of particular things is primarily understanding their worth or value.

If the metaphysics sketched above is a good simplification of this cosmology, then the emphasis on the theory of value is well placed. What should be expected as most important in the cosmology is the way it illustrates the distinction between essential and conditional features. Although important qualifications to this statement are to be noted in what follows, the constituents of an individual are its conditional features, and its essential features are the values it attains by ordering them one way rather than another (its "reasons" for being this way rather than that). The cosmological theory of value, therefore, is at the heart of what is cosmologically essential.

The importance of value notwithstanding, the central notions of any cosmology have to do with causation and existence. In this regard, Whitehead surely made the greatest advance since the age of Greek philosophy with his concept of "prehension." [2] A prehension is a grasping of an object and an incorporation of it into one's own being. At first this sounds simple, a straightforward analogy with "knowing." But it is a revolutionary concept. To be a thing, in Whitehead's vision, is to be an act of prehending all the objects of one's world as conditions for one's being. From the standpoint of the thing coming into being, at the beginning are the many objects to be prehended. At the end is the complex prehension having them all together. When the act of prehending is finished, it is a fact, over and done with, available for prehension by other beings—"actual entities" or "occasions," as Whitehead called them. Before the act of prehending has done anything to the objects to be prehended, the "initial data," to use Whitehead's term, are potentials for entering into the prehending entity. Between the beginning, with many separate initial data, and the end, with one complex unified new individual, is the process of "concrescence," of making a new concrete entity. Concrescence unifies the many initial data—the given past facts—into a coherent harmony; and it brings them from the status of being mere potentials to that of actual constituents of a new concrete entity.

The "stuff" of a new entity is those components of its initial

2. The second chapter of Whitehead's *Process and Reality,* entitled "The Categoreal Scheme," is the distillation of the greatest speculative thinking of the twentieth century to date. Yet its fate has not been particularly felicitous. To begin with, a zealous page-proof reader of the first edition, noting that "categoreal" was not in his dictionary, changed the running heads to "The Categorical Scheme," which means something entirely different. And then in terms of content, Whitehead's chapter is virtually unintelligible without a thorough understanding of all the rest of *Process and Reality,* an enormously difficult undertaking. Most philosophers of Whitehead's era prized immediate clarity above importance of topic, and learning to think in Whitehead's categories was just not worth the effort for them. The "saving remnant" who persevered have done brilliant service in analyzing and interpreting Whitehead, drawing out the implications of different emphases in his work, applying his principles to concrete problems. And they have carried speculative philosophy to new heights of rigorous discipline in a time when the temptations were to affirm some previous metaphysical system or to retreat to doing history of philosophy. But too many of the interpreters, exhausted by the effort of interpretation, could not bring themselves to ask whether, after all, Whitehead might be mistaken on some fundamental points. Like Kant scholars, they have tended toward acquiescence by exhaustion.

data, of the old entities, that it takes into its own being. Most components of the old beings are incompatible for synthesis in the new entity and are eliminated in the process of concrescence. Whereas the Aristotelian substance philosophy would suggest that the actuality of the old entities would be consumed when taken into the new entities, that is not so for a philosophy of prehension. Although a concrescent process of prehension actualizes a potential new entity, that new actual entity is merely a potential for subsequent entities. Its actuality can be prehended by an indefinite number of later entities as a potential in the concrescence of each. To be an actual entity is to be a process of actualizing one's own unique nature out of the potentials presented by past actualizations.

This notion of prehensive actualization marks two modes of causation. The first is the transference of reality from one occasion of prehension to the next: what is actualized in the former becomes a potential for actualization in the latter. The second is the process internal to the concrescence of integrating the many diverse initial given potentials into a coherent new entity; this is the reduction of many potentialities to one new actuality. In the first mode of causation, the earlier determines the later. In the second, it is truer to say the entity makes itself by adopting the past as its conditioning constituents. The past of course sets limits on how it can be treated by the concrescing occasion, but the past becomes actual in the present only through the creativity of the present occasion.

From the standpoint of an occasion, its conditional features are its initial data, the past world given to it. Its essential features are those it uses to order and harmonize its conditional features into its own concrete unity. Some of its essential features are derived from conditional ones; others are unique to its own present process; yet others derive in a sense from the future. From wherever they derive, the essential features are those characterizing the subjective heart of occasions. They determine how each occasion stands related to each thing conditioning it. They set the limits by which the conditional features are appropriated into the new objective fact of the occasion's unique individual nature.

Where does the organizing principle for a concrescent process derive from? If the initial data in the first phase of an occasion's conscrescence are separate past facts, what gives direction to the process of integration? Whitehead suggested that among the initial data is a special prehension of God's thought for how that particular occasion might unify itself. This divine proposition is prehended as a lure for the process of concrescence, which then is filled concretely by the decisions of the concrescent occasion. This doctrine will not do, however. First of all, Whitehead's concept of God is unsatisfactory for reasons not particularly germane to this study.[3] Second the claim that each occasion prehends a unifying lure from God is too much like a *deus ex machina*. There are many items among the initial data making claims to being ordering values. The very heart of the subjective process of concrescence is the process of deciding how these competing values are to be ordered for the ordering of the other conditional features.

In an occasion, therefore, there is a double-decker process going on. On the bottom is the process of integrating the conditional features into a new objective fact. On the top is the process of developing a consistent order or hierarchy of essential features that would determine the bottom process. The process on the top deck is of "essential" interest (pun intended) to the problem of freedom and will be analyzed in great detail throughout Part 2.

Whitehead pointed out that it is crucial to an "event" cosmology such as this to distinguish two important kinds of "division," or analysis of events: *genetic* division and *coordinate* division. Genetic division is an analysis of the stages or phases in the happening of an event, and coordinate division is an analysis of the outcome or finished fact of the event. "Genetic division is division of the concrescence [the becoming concrete]; coordinate division is division of the concrete."[4]

In coordinate division, the essential features involved in the event appear merely as structures alongside the structures of the conditional features. Whether it is relevant to distinguish essential from conditional features in coordinate division depends entirely on the pragmatic purposes of the analysis. In moral delib-

3. Besides *God the Creator*, see "The Impossibility of Whitehead's God for Theology," *Proceedings of the American Catholic Philosophical Association* (1970); "Whitehead On the *One and the Many*," *Southern Journal of Philosophy* 7 (winter 1969–70) : 387–93; and "Response to Ford's 'Neville on the One and the Many,'" *Southern Journal of Philosophy* 10 (spring 1972).
4. Whitehead, *Process and Reality*, p. 433.

eration, for instance, it is usually important to distinguish the elements in a person's deed that reflect his own contribution from the forces that impinge upon him; moral culpability depends on this distinction.

In genetic division the essential features must be dealt with as such. Genetic division is an analysis of how the essential features govern the process of synthesizing the conditional features into a concrete unity. And as such, the essential features function not primarily in their structural character but in their normative character. Strictly speaking, in an even that is happening but has not finished happening, there is no concrete structure, only the energy or drive to attain concrete structure. In complex individuals like human beings some essential features are brought to consciousness in deliberation, in the form of imagined alternatives for realization. In this sense, their structural side is consciously taken account of. But their real governance of the process of actualization is a matter of their normative side.

As a consequence it is necessary, going beyond Whitehead, to acknowledge three ways in which an essential feature can be in an even: actually, potentially, and normatively. Its primordial status is the normative. That is, in order for an essential feature to be actualized in an event, or even for it to be a potential for actualization, it must be relevant as a norm.

In considering whether an action is morally justified, the relevant essential features of the action must be examined in their normative roles. It is not enough to determine what the structure of a person's "reason" is; one must discover its worth. Its worth is what must be examined to discover his relation to the "reason," whether he could have done otherwise, and so forth.

One more important difference from Whitehead's philosophy should be stated at this point. Whitehead attacked the doctrine of "vacuous actuality," the thesis that something can be real without having a subjective immediacy of its own.[5] The subjectivist bias of modern philosophy, of which Whitehead approved, is the belief that to be real a thing must have a kind of subjective experience of its own, a belief going a long way toward justifying Whitehead's attempt to build a microcosmology out of analogues to ordinary human experience.

5. Ibid., p. 43.

Only a modified version of this thesis should be accepted, however. Fully concrete things of course must have subjective immediacy; in fact, in one sense that defines them as concrete. But abstract things cannot have subjective immediacy. Moreover, contrary to Whitehead, abstract things can have a kind of independent reality, namely that of being norms for relating patterns, even if the patterns are not embodied. Whitehead could admit that abstract things need not have subjective immediacy; but to exist they must be parts of actual entities that do have it. Axiological cosmology is therefore more "realistic" than the philosophy of organism.

The reason for acknowledging the reality of abstractions independently from concrete things is that to be a norm is a kind of reality structures can enjoy irrespective of relations to concrete things. A structure is normative always with respect to some set of structures that need ordering. But the set of structures to be ordered need not be concrete. In fact, the very meaning of normativeness when applied to moral obligation is that some way of doing things is obligatory in a particular concrete occasion precisely because it is obligatory in any situation like that. Its normative character stems from a relation to the structure of the situation, not to the concreteness of the situation.

In summary, the cosmology to be developed here is pluralistic and axiological. The former implies a rejection of organic models for interpreting the world's unity. The latter implies the centrality of concepts of value to the concerns of cosmology. The cosmological approach to causation follows Whitehead's revolutionary notion of prehension. Each occasion or event is an act of prehending a past world into its own new, concrete nature. The data prehended are its conditional features; the ordering principles are its essential ones. These points provide an introductory orientation to the cosmology to be developed here. Now a closer analysis of individuals must be undertaken.

INDIVIDUALS

How is a cosmological scheme best exposited? The most efficient way for the purpose of understanding freedom is to build a model, a verbal picture of the relevant natural structures and processes, in which the scheme is illustrated. Among the relevant things to be modeled according to the scheme are persons as enduring objects, events in which actions and decisions take place, personal interactions, social groups, the causal ramifications traceable to moral agents, norms, critical activities, and the like. Most of these ultimately turn on the account given of enduring personal individuals.

Because of the centrality of the concept of prehension, the simplest account of enduring individuals says they are made up of separate occasions or concrescences. This was Whitehead's own view. The ultimate realities, the *rēs verae,* of the world are individual events; an enduring individual is a series or nexus of these events exhibiting a certain continuity of pattern from one occasion to the next. The continuity of identity, on this view, is attained through form rather than through an underlying matter.[6] Forms or "eternal objects," as Whitehead called them, remain self-identical through many instantiations; only the relations between instances of forms change. Actual entities—the occasions—are what they are immediately, are unrepeatable, and perish with change.

Contemporary philosophers holding to a more Aristotelian substance doctrine, such as Paul Weiss, criticize the doctrine of actual occasions as being inadequate to account for self-identity through time.[7] It is necessary to see just how far this criticism is valid. The crucial point, in the chapters of Part 2, will be whether the cosmology of actual occasions can account for moral continuity, the continuity involved in responsibility.

Suppose we say that an enduring individual is a nexus of occasion in serial order having much the same form. If the individual is living, as opposed to inanimate, then there will be considerable alteration in the common pattern from moment to moment; still, the continuity of identity consists in nothing but elements of form reiterated in each occasion. In a complex individual such as a person, the reiteration of the "identifying characteristic" depends on many factors of continuity in the environment. When this

6. Ibid., p. 44.
7. See, e.g., Weiss's *Reality* (New York: Peter Smith, 1949), p. 207–08; or *Modes of Being* (Carbondale, Ill.: Southern Illinois University Press, 1958), pp. 30–34, 242.

environmental dependence obtains, Whitehead would call it a "society," each train of enduring individuals depending on the other trains for their own continuity of identity.[8]

For human beings the reiterated pattern would include most dominantly a spatial and temporal perspective on the world, a geometrical way of ordering the elements in the world with respect to one's own place.[9] The reiterated pattern would also include a bodily sense that is qualitative as well as quantitative. Part of the reason a person believes in his own identity through time is that he feels much the same way from moment to moment. The times when his sense of identity is upset are those when his bodily feelings are disturbed. A person directly prehends all past events (positively or negatively); but he prehends the bodily feelings of certain events as being *his*.[10]

It is important for freedom to notice that the reiterated pattern can include moral factors like promises. The pattern actualized last week of making a promise stays with the pattern of a person's body, place, and habits of character, so that the intervening events of the week do not negate the fact he made the promise. This is not to say he should keep the promise—ethics courses are filled with discussions of promises that should not be kept—but the reiteration of the promise-making pattern does mean that now he is the one who last week promised.

The question to be raised is whether there is any reason for the reiteration of the identifying characteristics. Presumably, the reason for the reiteration would be at the heart of enduring individuality; it would be the essential identity of the person through time. Then it must be asked whether the reason is sufficient for free human life.

The reason for the reiteration of the pattern depends on the kind of analysis or division made: genetic or coordinate. The genetic reason, the one interior to the process as it were, is that the pattern's reiteration would bring about the *greatest possible contrast* in the completion or "satisfaction" of the moment, and that the greatest possible contrast is always effected. What might this mean? In the raw material out of which an entity or "occa-

8. Whitehead, *Process and Reality*, pp. 50–52, 168–72.
9. Whitehead would call this a "strain-locus" (ibid., pp. 472ff).
10. Ibid., pp. 474ff.

sion" arises, all the past actual entities are given; they are present as objective data to be "prehended" or grasped by the emergent occasion. But they are not all compatible as constituting the physical satisfaction of the moment in its "end," its concrete realization. Some of the initial data must be excluded, "eliminated" or "negatively prehended," depending on the cleverness of the occasion in finding possibilities of coexistence or contrast.

The stupidest occasion gains greatest contrast by reiterating its past exactly, if the environment so tolerates, because there is always greater contrast in its own previous moment's perspective on the whole than in any segment of that world without that perspective. If something drastic has happened to the actual world between the time it was previously prehended and the present, then that relative novelty, which must be taken into account, may prevent exact reiteration. Under ordinary circumstances, the molecules of a rock, for instance, just repeat themselves in their macroscopically solid movement; when the rock is struck by a hammer, the molecules cannot orient themselves in space and time without moving uncharacteristically fast and in aggregately new directions.

Entities with greater complexity in initial data, and therefore with greater capacity for invention of new modes of contrasting their prehensions, can find ways of attaining greater contrast by combining their own past states with neighboring past states; they may, if they are "smart," find ways of giving up some elements of their past identity and reintegrating with the environment in radically changing ways, attaining still greater contrast.

The discussion of contrast in the preceding paragraphs made no mention of consciousness. Human beings have some experience that is conscious in ways allowing for extraordinary depth of contrast. Still, the (genetic) reason one remains the same person is that reiteration of one's past gives experience the greatest contrast. Of course, a human being is living, and this means that the greatest contrast involves some reiteration and some novelty. The continuity in self-identity does not require absolute sameness.

It is to be noted that the reason for continuity, genetically analized, is a matter of the *essential* features in each occasion. The greatest contrast in an occasion is always relative to the initial data that must be integrated in a contrast pattern. And the greatest contrast *possible* is always limited to the forms of contrast prehended in the initial data from the other temporal actual occasions. An occasion with much complex data has greater possibilities of contrast. Although it is the structure of the contrast that allows the real togetherness in contrast of the different data, it is the *value* of the contrast that makes it *normative* for the process of harmonizing the data. The reason for continuity in a particular case is that it is better than discontinuity. And if the data are such that the best contrast involves *dis*continuity, depending on the relative circumstances, then the continuity of the previously enduring individual is broken off. The notion of degree or depth of contrast is an aesthetic one, to be analyzed according to an axiology presented in the next chapter.

According to a *coordinate division* of actual entities, the reason a pattern repeats itself, following Whitehead, is just a matter of laws of nature. A law of nature, roughly characterized, expresses the regularities and relations between natural events. The coordinate division looks at an event not in its process of happening but as a concrete finished fact, and a law of nature expresses a relation between its finished character and the finished characters of other events. A series of events with much the same pattern is an enduring individual, and laws of nature tell us when to expect such continuity, and when not to expect it. Laws of nature are arbitrary.[11]

Whether a genetic or a coordinate division is relevant depends on the problem of freedom involved. When considering how to accomplish a goal, to determine whether it is possible, the events contemplated for the world are examined coordinately. So with any consideration of possibilities, or with most considerations of group activities. On the other hand, in making assessments of moral justification for oneself or for others the deliberation must include genetic division; it must ask the question, Was the contrast adopted really the best available?

The reasons cited here for continuity of personal identity are Whiteheadian ones, but not ones he himself emphasized. He did emphasize, however, that continuity is just a characteristic of our

11. Since we are speaking only roughly here, ignoring many of the subtleties introduced into this topic by Whitehead, Charles Peirce, and others, we can include in the notion of laws of nature the habits of character we observe in other people, societies, and the like.

own epoch and has no metaphysical necessity; there could well be a world of discontinuous events, in the sense of lacking reiteration of strain-loci; but given the kinds of things in our present epoch, there is continuity where we find it.[12]

Are the reasons given in this theory as exposited so far adequate to account for the kind of personal individuality characteristic of free human beings? Or must we adopt a stronger substance doctrine? This question refers only to the reason cited in genetic division, since that is the division relevant to moral continuity. No one doubts coordinate continuity.

The first answer to the question is that the citation of the greatest possible contrast explains why an actualized occasion is or is not continuous with some antecedent occasion, once the occasion is given. But it does not explain why the continuous or discontinuous occasion exists in the first place. According to Whitehead's categoreal scheme, any multiplicity of actualized occasions is necessarily united in the experiences of some subsequent occasion. But then *any* subsequent occasion unites the world of completed occasions, and there is no reason why the perspectives of different previously enduring individuals should be repeated. That is to say, there is no reason why there should be a plurality of occasions uniting in their own experiences, according to their own perspectives that are constituted continuous with previous perspectives, the past world initially common to them all. The successor to the present moment might be only one occasion. This is an important and general deficiency of the categoreal scheme of the philosophy of organism. For individuals the deficiency means that there is no reason to expect that an individual will continue from one moment to the next. This is a serious limitation, since the presumption of ordinary experience is that individuals will continue unless their inner society or external environment prevents it. The best our scheme can say so far is that, if there is an occasion uniting the past from its perspective or with some of its identifying characteristics, then the degree of contrast determines how much continuity there is.

The second answer to the question of adequacy deals with the sense in which a personal individual in a present moment identifies occasions in the past and anticipates ones in the future as be-

12. Whitehead, *Process and Reality*, p. 492.

ing himself, in contrast to other past and future occasions that are not himself. According to the foregoing account of enduring individuals as serially ordered nexuses reiterating an identifying characteristic, the occasions of one's past are those (a) with the identifying characteristic and (b) from which the present has inherited the characteristic. But one's past and future are not prehended only by oneself. Other people can prehend a person's past in significant ways. Furthermore, one does not prehend only one's own past, but also past occasions in the careers of other people. The present experience of each person includes occasions from his own past and that of others. How does each person keep straight which occasions belong to his own identity? In some sense, those which are from his own past experience are dominant in the present, "feeling warm," as William James would say. But dominance is an insufficient criterion for individual continuity. As Hegel pointed out so graphically, experiences of others may be more important than some experiences of oneself; yet this should not entail that those others experienced cease to be separate individuals and have their identities essentially in oneself; it entails only that they are important influences. A person's past, present, and future are his in a sense distinguishing them from the experiences of others, however mutually influential.

An account of human individuality must be able to render our ordinary sense that an individual owns his experiential moments in past, present, and future all from the perspective of any temporal mode. A person's present being includes his having-been-something-particular in the past and his going-to-be-something resulting from his decisions in the future. Likewise, his being in the past consisted in identifying in some way with his present and future being, and his future being in its own way must identify with his past and present being. Many factors of moral responsibility, intentional action, and so forth, depend on making out these connections, and the objective notion of duty points out that the connections are not merely memory and conscious anticipation.

These limitations of the view as developed so far require inventing a notion of a *discursive individual,* that is, one whose life is played out in parts, moment by moment, but whose individuality extends beyond the moment so that at no time is its whole individual nature either actualized or in the process of actualization. Furthermore, a discursive individual must satisfy the demands we have just found the simpler doctrine unable to satisfy, namely, that a reason be given why an individual can be expected to continue, and that criteria be given for distinguishing one's own from other individuals' instantiation of one's identifying characteristics. A discursive individual must be recognized as an irreducibly basic concrete entity, on a cosmological par with actual entities or actual occasions.

The mark of concreteness is that a thing have subjectivity (norms by themselves are not concrete). Therefore, in contrast to the idea of an enduring individual made up of subjective moments, a discursive individual must have a subjectivity or subjective immediacy that extends through its whole temporal length. The kind of subjectivity must be differentiated according to what is appropriate for each mode of time; but it must still be subjectivity in some important recognizable sense. The test for whether the account is sufficient for a genuinely discursive subjectivity is whether it makes sense to give a genetic division of the whole nexus of a person's life—past, present, and future. Or, since our focus will be primarily on the moments in which men make decisions, the question will be whether the subjectivity of a present moment requires taking account of the subjectivity of past and future moments of that person, where the past and future subjectivity is treated as subjectivity per se, not as subjectivity objectified.

For the simpler view (Whitehead's), only present moments have subjectivity and can be given a genetic account. A nexus of moments can be compared only from the standpoint of their satisfactions (excepting the present moment in the nexus), and so the nexus can be treated only in terms of coordinate divisions. This means there is no subjectivity of the personal life as a whole; it really is reducible to a collection of substantially different cosmological entities. A discursive individual, however, is a single and irreducible cosmological entity.

The difficulty with saying subjectivity applies to the whole of a life is that men do live moment by moment. The past presented to an occasion is determinate, and the future partially indeterminate. How can it be said, then, that the whole of a life has a subjective immediacy to it? It would seem that at any one time, only the present is subjective and the past and future are presented objectively, the former having perished in its subjectivity and the latter not having attained it yet. Even Whitehead could admit that, in one sense, the whole of a life has subjectivity, namely, that each moment in the life is subjective when it is present. The difficulty with that view, however, is that the concreteness marked by subjectivity applies only to the moments individually, and not to their unity in a concrete human (of any discursive) life. What can the alternative be?

It cannot be that the unity of a whole life is a determinate pattern ingressing subjectively in a developmental way moment by moment. The very fact that a present moment divides a determinate past from a partially indeterminate future means that the pattern of one's life is not completely determinate in any moment when it is subjectively immediate. If the only two candidates for the continuity of an individual were an underlying substratum of change and an unchanging form, and if the latter were opted for, then the form must be subjectively immediate in each moment separately, not in the series of moments as a whole.

The thesis resolving the dilemma is that in any present moment of a discursive individual there must be essential features, determining the constitution of that moment, that derive some from the past and some from future life of that individual. The subjectivity of the past and future moments, as embodied in their essential features, must function essentially in each present moment. This is over and above the essential features unique to the present moment. Whitehead could admit that the subjectivity of a past moment can enter a present moment objectively; he could even admit that the object of a present occasion's feeling is the subjective form of a past occasions' feeling; but he could not admit that the past occasion contributes essentially to the subjective form of the present moment. The senses in which essential features in a present moment "derive" from the past and from the future are subtle and depend on many issues besides the ones raised here; they will be treated in chapters 4 through 7.

The advantage of the doctrine of the threefold ground of essential features in the present is that the subjectivity operative in any present is a subjectivity of the whole life. Although all change and action of an individual takes place in a present moment, the determinants of the subjective form of any present occasion include not only the present's essential features but also those of past and future.[13] Consequently, the axiological cosmology is committed not only to find an alternative to the doctrine of subjective aim, but also to provide doctrines accounting for the entrance into the present of essential features from the past and from the future.

An ambiguity in the notion of subjectivity ought to be cleared up. For Whitehead, subjectivity is the process of bringing a set of initial data to unity, infecting them with the occasion's own subjective form so that they harmonize in a unique satisfaction. On the one hand, subjectivity can be associated with an emphasis on the process of actualization as such; in this case, a moment's subjectivity is perfectly isolated and cannot be repeated. On the other hand it can be associated with the elements of subjective form appropriating the prehensions to the unique identity of the occasion. The axiological cosmology emphasizes the sense of subjectivity referring to what is unique to the identity of individuals in contrast to what is externally derivative. In this sense, subjectivity would have to do with the essential continuity of an individual as he prehends his world and himself through a stretch of time.

If the doctrines necessary for a discursive individual can be made out—and only the subsequent discussion can see whether that is possible—then we will be able to give a reason for expecting an individual's nexus of present moments to extend into the future. The reason is that the future has already contributed essentially constitutive features in present moments. The kind of reality the future has, of course, is very strange to minds used to thinking of all reality on the model of the past ("the world is made of facts") or at best on that of the present (to be is to exist with power). One of the peculiarities of future reality is its con-

13. This is now another motive for denying Whitehead's doctrine that subjective aim, or the lure for concrescence, is derived solely from a prehension of God in the initial data of an occasion. That doctrine would account only for the origin of subjectivity from the past, essential features arising from that initial hybrid physical prehension of God. If the subjectivity is derivative only from a subjective aim or lure prehended from God in that moment, then the unique present and future do not function essentially so as to contribute subjective form. Whitehead does maintain, for instance in *Process and Reality*, p. 75, that there is an arranging of emphases to be given various prehended data that is utterly unique to the moment. But there are no norms or features determining this arranging.

tingency: a future possibility might never become actual. Consequently, the future contributing an essential feature to a present moment might never be actualized in its own right. But this does not mean its *future* reality is deficient. Although it is premature to introduce this point, the contribution of the future to present essential features has to do with relevant obligations; even if a person chooses to act contrary to his obligations, his present is still constituted by having the obligatory act as his obligation. The difference between having an obligation and performing it is closely tied to the difference between present reality and future reality.[14]

The notion of a discursive individual, if made out, would also provide criteria for identifying which past and which future occasions are members of the same temporally extended life as a given present moment. The criteria would have to do with marking those past and future occasions contributing essential features to the present. The set of all occasions contributing essential features to each other is the set that is united in the subjectivity of a single life. This point must be qualified in many ways, to be sure. Since lives grow temporally, the set of occasions belonging to a life must be specified with respect to some time; a person's life as a child has many fewer moments than his life as an adult just because the future that determined him essentially in childhood has been actualized in adulthood, and his future perspective is much longer. Also, strictly speaking, the future occasions embodying obligations mark the range of the person's possible action, not of his person in the more restricted sense. It is important to be able to say of a distant happening that it is an effect of the agent's acting and a matter of his obligation, but not his very self.

In summary, it should be pointed out that the continuity of individual life is not to be accounted for as a matter of a substratum entertaining changes, or of a structural form. The latter is to be rejected because structures do not change. The former suggestion, although it has not been discussed, has grave difficulties in accounting for "substantial change." The alternative proposed here is that the continuity, the irreducible unity of a life, the subjectiv-

14. Because Whitehead did not acknowledge future reality beyond projections of present reality in what he called the "superject," he could acknowledge intentions for the future, and goods to be embodied in the future, but not obligations where the future has nonactual but yet real normative power.

ity of the whole, is a matter of the normative side of forms, of essential features. The essential features govern the changing relations of structural forms. This is another illustration of the justice in calling our theory an *axiological* pluralism. The doctrine of individuals depends on a theory of value.

3

A General Theory of Value

A theory of value, an axiology, is the strangest of philosophical inventions. Most ordinary theories are "views" (from the Greek sense of *theoria*) of logical structures of facts. The facts might be particulars or they might be general empirical laws. The logical structures might be necessary or hypothetical with reference to what the theory explains. In any case, ordinary theories are understood as having their parts related in a coherent, logical form. A theory of value, however, does not easily fit the ordinary case.

Of course an axiology includes or (presupposes) all sorts of ordinary theories. It should include an account of how people in fact employ values, a matter for empirical theory. It may also deal with how values bind people in obligation, apart from their intentional recognition of obligation; this calls for a transcendental theory that, though strange in its way, has been familiar as a theoretical type since Kant. Also, the relation between values can perhaps be exhibited in a kind of logical structure, of the sort attempted by Robert S. Hartman. But none of these kinds of theories addresses the central question of value theory.

What is value? What is it to be a value? What makes something valuable? These are all formulations of the central problem of axiology. The problem is very hard to pose. The nature of value is not something to be explained by something else in a logically coherent structure. Value, rather, is the presupposition of logical form; among other things, value is the difference between coherent and incoherent theory, between formally good and formally bad form. So although a good theory about value must exhibit value, value is always its presupposed norm. And since a theory is always only an hypothesis, that norm must be transcendent enough to apply to its possible alternatives, even if those alternatives are not as good as itself. So the most an ordinary theory can explain about the nature of value is an instantiation of value, not that which makes the instantiation an illustration of itself. A proper axiological theory must be dialectical, therefore, in the sense that it backs up on itself, asking about its own presuppositions and drawing its conclusions from the process of backing up. The nature of the dialectical form of the value question will be elaborated in the next section.

An axiological cosmology is a philosophical view that not only includes a cosmology and a theory of value but claims that the latter determines the former. Or put aphoristically, structures are as they are because that is a good way for them to be, and therefore to understand structures is to understand what their value consists in.

Explaining a value theory this closely related to a cosmology means employing the cosmology as the theory exhibiting the values. Value will be explained below in terms of harmonies, essential and conditional features, and so forth. In this sense, the plausibility of the value theory is dependent in large part on the plausibility of the cosomology, as so far explicated. But then the most problematic aspects of the cosmology have been those requiring a further axiology to justify them. That axiology is here supplied, or at least sketched.

The general theory of value defended here can be described as *formal, objective,* and *realistic.* A brief discussion of these three characteristics will serve as an introduction to the theory.

To say that the theory is *formal* is to buy into a host of connotations. In the first place, what is meant by "formal" is an association with Plato's theory of forms. Forms, for Plato, not only are structtures things have in common but also ideals. Value will be interpreted in terms of Plato's doctrine of "normative measure." Although the scholarly controversies concerning Plato's own meaning will be avoided, the affinity of the present theory of value with his theory of forms (in at least one interpretation) should be pointed up.[1] The present theory will also employ the notion of the form of the good.

---

1. The scholarly interpretation of Plato's theory of forms followed here derives from the work of Robert S. Brumbaugh. See, for instance, his *Plato for the Modern Age* (New York: Collier Books, 1964), or *Plato on the One* (New Haven, Conn.: Yale University Press, 1961).

In the second place, "formal" means that the general theory of value is presented in structural terms. Instead of a concrete contextualistic analysis (such as Dewey's is supposed to be in principle), and instead of an ethical or meta-ethical analysis drawn from observations about life (such as Aristotle's or Toulmin's), the present argument will be a structural metaphysical analysis of what it is, categoreally, to be a value. This again is closer to the Platonic–Leibnizian–Whiteheadian tradition than to the sons of Aristotle. Of course on due occasion the formal structure must be related to life and experience. Form unrelated to experience is philosophically unimportant. But only a high degree of abstraction allows a clear and honest categoreal scheme avoiding compromise or surreptitious distortion of concrete experience. Furthermore, if the function of a value theory is as important as it was alleged in the last chapter, and as it shall prove below, then it is imperative that it be abstract enough to permit extrapolation into the languages of a great many areas of thought.

In many respects, for instance, the function of the theory of value with regard to free agency according to the axiological cosmology is similar to the views of Dewey. But Dewey's theory of value is so closely tied to the sphere of human action as often to be fruitless when applied to mathematics or even logic; his *Logic: The Theory of Inquiry* shows the limitations of his conceptions by its very brilliance. It is ironic that Dewey, who understood technology so long before anyone else, failed to appreciate the degree of abstraction in technology's mathematics and the consequent need for a quantifiable value theory. If value theory is the basic interpretation of structure, as it is for Dewey, then it ought to be at home with mathematics, the most simplified of structures. Just as the value theory ought to be formal enough to be fruitful in mathematics, so it ought to be capable of extrapolation into art, religion, morals, philosophy of history, and a variety of other fields.

That the theory is *objective* means values are not defined essentially in terms of evaluation, as are many contemporary value theories, even relatively formal ones like Ralph Barton Perry's. To call the present account "objective" is perhaps misleading, since in the Kantian tradition objectivity is defined in terms of subjectivity. There is a truth in this, of course, as indicated in the hypothesis that anything prehended is an object. But the present point is to deny that the form making a thing valuable is something contributed by a valuing subject. To be sure, it must be possible to show how objective values are evaluated, since unappreciable values are philosophically unimportant; this will be attempted in chapter 7. Furthermore, the situation is vastly complicated by the fact that evaluation in many cases changes or reforms objective values; this particular complication is an instance of the general complication stemming from the fact that people are self-referential natural agents.

To say that the theory is *realistic* is a further elaboration of the above point, namely, that the values are what they are, regardless of what people may think of them. Thus it will be possible to say according to this theory that unappreciated or even practically unappreciable values are still values; the unnoticed sunset and desert flower are beautiful in themselves. A seeming exception is that many of the relevant values for people depend precisely on being created by people, even on being thought by them. The values involved in theories pre se, for instance, depend on a person's thinking them. The values involved in thinking theories, over and above those in the theories thought, are even more complicated. But it will be shown that the categoreal nature of the values involved is always one step ahead of the self-referential thought about them; they are appreciated because of their character, not valuable because they are appreciated in the first instance.

These peculiarities of the general value theory defended here set it apart from most competitors. These peculiarities, however, are not meant to be taken as virtues, although in the end it is hoped that they will appear to be such. Rather, the peculiarities are pointed out to forestall criticism of the general theory for not being something that it indeed never intended to be.

THE DIALECTICAL QUESTION OF VALUE

It was pointed out in chapter 2 that a harmony is both structural and normative. The only evidence given was the common sense connotations of harmony people have given to the language, and it is necessary in this chapter to give a more detailed analysis of the relation between structure and value. The importance of this task is shown in the fact that accounts of structure in ignoring the normative side are burdened with a nonexperiential distinction between facts (structures) and values. The Aristotelian tradition in general has emphasized structure to the subordination of value. The Platonic tradition has done better, and the dialectical approach to axiology taken here is explicitly Platonic.

The beginning, then, is a consideration of the categoreal framework for interpreting harmony; the framework should have the status of a metaphysical hypothesis. The notion of harmony supposes a plurality of things to be harmonized. The plurality in a harmony's components is unified immediately, as noted in the previous chapter. The determinate nature of the harmony is not reducible to the determinate natures of its components apart. It *is* reducible to the components harmonized together; this is tautologically true. But because not all things harmonize, harmony is a differential notion indicating something over and above what is in the parts considered by themselves. The problem now takes the form, What is harmony, such that some things fit together in certain ways and others do not? And what kind of question is this?

As Plato pointed out in *Philebus* (23 c–e), finite things are a mixture of limit and the indefinite or purely indeterminate. A harmony has both a plurality harmonized and a form or limit according to which it harmonizes. Since harmonies seem to be a mixture of two very different kinds of being, that which is to be formed and the limit or order that forms, it seems appropriate to consider the extremes in themselves.

But recall the asymmetry in Plato's view. The purely manifold and indefinite is not quite real. The limit on the other hand, is more real than the mixture or harmony. Furthermore, in awarding prizes to things in order of worth, the prizes get higher in the direction of limit, and lowest place goes to the indefinite or pleasure (*Philebus* 64c–67b). This is an unlikely arrangement for allegedly coequal ontological contributors to the finite mixtures of the world.

The difficulty comes from a common confusion about what kind of question is being asked and answered. Consider the following arguments drawing out implications of the conceptual framework:

(a) In any given harmony, the components fit together because of the specific forms of each. Working "down" there is no such thing as pure plurality or something completely in need of form, since everything has the form it does by virtue of the forms of its own components.

(b) Likewise, moving up from a harmony, we never reach a form so pure it is not forming some components. All forms form pluralities, since they are all modes of harmonies, and harmonies unify pluralities. There is no pure limit or undetermined form. (Since some things are partially indeterminate, there are some other things with respect to which they are not harmonized; therefore there is no infinite series of higher forms in this structural sense nor need to fear a block universe.)

These arguments are valid, given the construction put on forms and harmonies above, but it is important to note they are addressed to questions about the *structure* of things. They interpret forms in a structural sense. As Wittgenstein might put it, they show forth the form of harmonic facts. There is another kind of question, however, that Wittgenstein acknowledged but thought could not be asked, the question about why the form of facts is as it is.[2] He called this the Mystical, and it was the very question Plato raised.

We must distinguish two kinds of questions. The kind to which the two arguments were addressed is structural; it asks about the structure of harmonies. Let that kind of question be called *theoretical* or, as Plato says, *dianoetic*. It is to be answered by a theory that has the status of an hypothesis.

The other kind of question aims to know why form or structure is what it is. It cannot be answered by citing facts or showing forth more form; since Wittgenstein at one time thought these the only two proper species of knowledge, he concluded that there was no proper answer to this kind of question, and that consequently it was not a proper question. But Plato would call it a *dialectical* question, to be answered by dialectical considerations. He characterized dialectic in the *Republic* as the art of reasoning that uses theories or hypotheses as steps in a ladder that might be climbed to reach the Good (*Republic* 511b). Put more plainly, dialectic is the art of criticizing claims (theoretical or otherwise) in terms of the norms they presuppose. Only dialectic can deal with questions about why a harmony is harmonious.

If we question the presuppositions of a harmony *theoretically* we ask what is below it and above it in terms of the components it contains and the more inclusive harmonies containing it; this

---

2. See his *Tractatus Logico-Philosophicus*, trans. C. K. Ogden (London: Routledge & Kegan Paul, 1922), props. 2.172, 4.121, 4.1211, 6.13, 6.4321–6, 6.522–6.53.

is a structural question whose answer contains forms functioning structurally. But if we question its presuppositions *dialectically,* the situation is different. There are two dialectical questions here.

First, what does harmony per se presuppose there is to be harmonized? The dialectical answer is, plurality per se. If we cited determinateness in the plurality we would be begging the question, since to be determinate is to be a harmony and the presupposition of harmony per se is not more harmony. Yet pure plurality has no identity and is in fact indistinguishable from nothing. The upshot, dialectically speaking, is that there is *nothing* real presupposed absolutely as contents of harmony, looking down, as it were. The only answer to be given for a question about the contents of a harmony is a theoretical one. In other words the content of the world is brutely given and must be known through theoretical interpretation of experience; empirical science is necessary for the analysis of any content; only form has higher presuppositions accessible to dialectic.

The second dialectical question is the more important. What is it that makes a harmony harmonious? Why is structural form the way it is? What makes some things fit together in certain ways and others not? The answer cannot involve the citation of a higher form or mode of harmony. Those higher harmonies themselves need the same dialectical question asked of them. Harmony per se cannot be explained by citing another harmony. But how is the dialectical question to be answered? Can we say what Wittgenstein thought could not be said?

Plato's suggestion was that the dialectical ground of structure is value; that, more than being a mere structure, a form is also a norm. The question why formal structure is the way it is, on his account, is answered by showing that it is good to be that way. The task here is not only to elaborate this but also to defend it as the appropriate kind of answer.

Consider ourselves in a situation in which finding out why form is the way it is becomes more a matter of urgency than a matter of curiosity. Suppose we were creators about to make a world, wondering whether we should make a world with structural form in it. This is a little fantastic, and when Plato considered the question he hedged and made his chief characters in the *Timaeas* merely theoretical thinkers, not given to dialectic. Although Timaeas attempts to show *what* the structure of creation is, he begs the dialectical questions about *why* form is as it is. An analogue to creating a world is governing a state, however, and in the *Statesman* Plato addressed himself to the dialectical question in analogical guise. A statesman is a man skilled in the art of normative measure. Plato distinguished two kinds of measure, relative and normative (*Statesman* 283e–287b). Relative measure is when components are mixed according to some fixed rule, using conventional or arbitrary units of standard measure. Statecraft has no hard and fast rules, however, since the components to be mixed in the state are always changing, playing new roles, altering in importance. The statesman has the art of knowing just how much of this and how much of that is enough, in what order, and with what timing. Knowing "how much is enough" is the art of normative measure, and we can call the formal proportion arrived at *a* normative measure.

The statesman must look to the form that normatively measures his situation (cf. *Statesman* 286d). Notice what it is. First, it is the ideal that guides his activity. Second, as an ideal it is the best way of harmonizing the components he must mix. And third, its structure is that of the proportion and order in which the components are to be measured.

The notion of normative measure can be broadened to cover all cases of forms, not just those taken as ideals by practical persons.[3] Every form is a normative measure and has a structure that harmonizes the things it measures relative to their own component structures. This structure in the measure is what theoretical concerns pay attention to. But forms as normative measures are also normative; they are ideal ways of harmonizing the components, and the structures they have are the way they are because those are good ways of putting the components together.

What makes a measured proportion or structure normative? This question is not the same as asking what the structure of a normative measure is, since an elucidation of the structure would only show *how* the structure hangs together.

Whatever we say of a normative measure, however, must be

3. Consider the following: "[W]hen one day we come to give a full exposition of the true accuracy in dialectical method, we shall find the need of this postulate concerning due measure which we have just enunciated" (*Statesman* 284d, Skemp trans.).

structural to be intelligible. Any answer that might be given must be in the form of a theoretical hypothesis recommending itself to our critical judgment. An hypothesis is required from which we can move in two directions. We should be able to treat the hypothesis as an explanation of selected harmonies and move down from it to show how the harmonies embody the principles in the hypothesis. On the other hand we should be able to move up from the hypothesis to see why it is the presupposition of any structure whatsoever, including its own structure.

Plato had the clue about the nature of normative measure. The ostensible topic of the *Philebus* is the good life, and the foil from the beginning is the proposal that the life of pleasure is the best. It is quickly apparent to all, however, that the good life is a mixture of components, including more than pleasure; the abstract discussion of limit, the indefinite, the mixture, and the cause of mixture takes place in the context of elucidating those components. The dialogue ends with an awarding of prizes to various components of life, and perhaps of reality, in the order of greater value. It is not that one component would have value by itself or could be left out; rather, the order ranks the values in terms of dependence—the value of one thing depends on the value of another, whose value depends on that of yet a higher one, and so on. Fifth prize goes to pure pleasures, those that are not harmful. These contribute to the good life only if we also have the experiential technique, the knowledge of nature and people, and the art of enjoyment that allow us to attain and maintain the pleasures; therefore technique, science, and the arts get fourth prize. But technique, science, and the arts contribute to the good life only as they are marshaled with genuine intelligence and reason; these get third prize. Intelligence marshals the components of the good life into a whole that requires a sense of "what is proportioned and beautiful, and what is perfect and satisfying and so forth—whatever terms denote that kind of quality" (*Philebus* 66b, trans. R. Hackforth); that kind of quality gets second prize. The first prize goes to the region of "what is measured or appropriate" (66a). The qualities receiving second prize are the norms translating pure measure or appropriateness—normative measure—into relevant terms for the good life. To say that the first thing of worth in the good life is pure measure is to say that goodness in life is an expression of good in the most general sense of goodness. More specifically, it is good in that it is beautiful, perfect, satisfying, and so forth, because intelligence organizes it that way, making use of the various kinds of knowledge available for securing and enjoying things. None of these can be left out, and the order cannot be tampered with. Since the whole conversation aims at discovering the good in human life, we can take the qualities awarded first prize as the first reflection of the form of the Good in things that have to be measured.[4]

The articulation of normative measure must involve something like aesthetic categories. But the proper categories must be even higher or more abstract; they determine why aesthetic categories are the way they are. As Plato pointed out, the aesthetic categories —the proportioned, the beautiful, the perfect, and the satisfying— are normative because they embody a measure for things with beauty and make their parts appropriate for each other. The dialectical question is now, How can the measured and appropriate per se be articulated?

The suggestion to pursue is that the form or normative measure in a harmony, its measuredness or appropriateness, makes the harmony *elegant*. Although the term "elegance" has bad connotations of supersophistication and artificiality, it conveys the sense that what is harmonized elegantly is the way it is because that is a good way to be.

This interpretation of normative measure is the right kind to answer the question at hand: working down we might see that the structure of things makes them elegant, and working up we can see that elegance is presupposed in any formal or harmonizing criteria. It is necessary now to elaborate the metaphysical hypotheses about harmony and normative measure with the conceptual apparatus of a theory of elegance.

Elegance can be defined by hypothesis as a combination of *complexity* and *simplicity*. These are interrelated concepts, each of which is involved in the definition of the other. Every mode of

4. Some excellent Plato scholars, e.g. Edward G. Ballard in *Socratic Ignorance* (The Hague: Martinus Nijhoff, 1965), argue that Plato abandoned the doctrine of the form of the Good in later dialogues. I am convinced, on the contrary, for reasons that appear here and in my review of Ballard's book, "Socratic Ignorance," *International Philosophical Quarterly* 7 (June 1967): 340–56, that the explication of the Good in terms of the world is the chief theme of the later dialogues.

harmony requires some degree of complexity and some degree of simplicity. A high degree of complexity together with a high degree of simplicity gives a high degree of elegance; but a high degree of one without a corresponding high degree of the other gives a relatively low degree of elegance.

A harmony's complexity refers to the number of different forms or modes of harmony entailed as constituents of its overall form. A form is more complex if the harmony it measures has more different constituent forms. Since any harmony's hierarchy has an infinite number of constituents, every constituent having constituents and so on, complexity does not refer to the number of constituents but to the number of different kinds of constituents. A harmony is more complex if it harmonizes more different kinds of things. Minimal complexity of form is to contain only one kind of essential and one kind of conditional feature.

Simplicity means the economy with which the included different forms are harmonized. A harmony includes its constituents in a hierarchy; at each level its constituents are harmonized together immediately, and they themselves have constituents on lower levels, and so forth. A harmony is simpler to the degree that fewer constituents at the higher levels are able to contain more different forms at lower levels. Ideal simplicity would have the fewest components on each level and the greatest depth to the hierarchy that is possible for a given number of *different* constituents. Least simplicity would mean all the different kinds of constituents are homogeneous internally and are immediately harmonized all on the same level; their harmony would be a bare conjunction and no different kind would be a constituent of any other.

The simplicity of a harmony must have some complexity, since it needs constituents to harmonize. The complexity of a harmony needs some simplicity, since it must get its different kinds of constituents together. These are contrast qualities, but also conjoint ones; you cannot have one without the other. Having both together is what makes a harmony (and its form) elegant. Although there is no harmony that is not elegant, since each must have some simplicity and some complexity, they differ crucially in degrees of elegance. A harmony is more elegant if there are high degrees of both simplicity and complexity. A very elegant thing seems easy to grasp because there are few components on each level, but the more we look the more we see contained in depth.

A high degree of complexity coupled with a low degree of simplicity gives an elegance degenerate in depth *importance:* the components of the harmony are not arranged so that they vary greatly in importance. In a hierarchy determined by a form of the lowest possible simplicity, with all the different kinds of components on the same level related by bare consistency or conjunction, no one component would be more important than any other. In aesthetics, depth consists in diversity of importance, not uniformity.

A high degree of simplicity with a low degree of complexity results in an elegance degenerate in *relevance*. That is, not many different kinds of things are relevant to the harmony. A thing is relevant to a harmony if its form is measured or taken account of by the forms of things on higher levels in the harmony's hierarchy. If a constituent could be left out of the harmony without changing anything, it is not relevant. In art we call a work simplistic if it has much simplicity but not much complexity.

In the discussion of complexity and simplicity we have assumed that harmonies could be interpreted merely as a hierarchy of included components. This is an oversimplification, since elements are components of harmonies only in certain respects. Therefore, the characterization of a harmony's elegance should specify the respects in which it is simple and complex. Elaboration is unnecessary here, however, since what has been said is sufficient to make our point: to be structured is to have a normative measure.

PARTICIPATION

Our dialectic has argued that structures are intrinsically normative for the constituents they structure. What is the relation between the structural and normative elements? This is what the Platonic doctrine of participation is about. The thesis is that to have a structure is to participate in a value by being a norm for what is structured.

Although every normative form is a structure, Plato thought that the problems of participation could not be solved if forms were considered only structurally. In the *Parmenides* he made this point two ways, informally and formally. The first part of the dialogue discusses young Socrates's immature conception of form in a direct but informal way, and the conclusion is that no matter what model Socrates suggests (and he suggests only structural ones), participation does not make sense. So devastating is Parmenides's attack that at the end Socrates's only certainty is that there are forms for certain valuable things but probably not for such a thing as mud (because mud is worth too little). Participation, this suggests, cannot be understood without taking into account the normative side of forms.

The second part of the dialogue is a formal analysis of structural unity showing, in Robert Brumbaugh's words, "hypothetical deductive formal systems of any purely descriptive kind to be limited because they are incomplete, and that for their completion we need something that is non-hypothetical." [5] Noting this, Brumbaugh argues that the non-hypothetical ground must be something like value forms. Our axiological cosmology says a normative or value element is needed in all forms.

The fundamental question to which the citation of a form is the answer, is the question of identity—identity for a thing, a process, a program, a state of affairs, and so forth. And a thing's identity is usually thought to be a structure. What the axiological cosmology argues is that a thing's identity is most fundamentally how it relates to its *ideal,* and that its structure depends on the ideal it has. The argument will be that structural participation can be exhibited as an abstract part of ideal participation. This is the key to the connection between structure and value.

Forms and universals are different and should be distinguished. A form was defined before as a normative measure, the structure of a harmony that is normative for what is harmonized. This, however, is a form *in a harmony.* A form *in itself* is the value measuring the harmonic constituents normatively, the reason why the measured structure is normative. This is a dispositional characterization of forms, as it were. A normative measure is a schematization of the constituents of a harmony with the pure value that would measure them when schematized. These pure values in themselves could not be determinate, since everything determinate is a harmony, and the values are the normative ground of harmoniousness. The dialectical investigation of forms in themselves depends on value theory, and it can be undertaken only by characterizing the relation of forms in themselves to harmonies.

5. Brumbaugh, *Plato on the One,* p. 199.

In the early Platonic dialogues, in which Socrates is searching for the form of some *ideal,* the form itself rarely can be defined or explained. Since this happens so often Plato probably meant to show that ideal forms are not determinate things that can be defined or explained. On the other hand, what happens positively is that the various factors the ideal is supposed to govern are exhibited in alternate arrangements with a critical assessment of the alternatives. Furthermore, in the dramatic context the personal characters of the participants are usually given new critical integration by the discussion, so that the ideal in question comes more and more to be exhibited in their lives. What the dialogues exhibit is the ideal form normatively measuring in various ways.

Since forms are identified by what they are to measure, the identifying handle comes loose if they are considered only in themselves. Forms in themselves must be considered under the aegis of pure normativeness, or the form of formness. This is why it often seems in Plato that there is only one really real form, that of the Good, and why the less forms have to do with plausibly ideal categories, the less they are real forms.

Forms are structured only *relative to what they measure,* and as the dialectic examination of a particular form moves from the suggested structure to the norm for the structure, the sense of "form" involved seems to shift. We should recognize this shift by underscoring the dialectical move from structures to forms in themselves. In asking about the identity of a thing we ask for its normative measure, the thing's form; the answer is a description of the form's structure. But if we ask why the form is as it is and mean by this a more fundamental question than one answered by citing what determinate relations it has to harmonize, then we ask about what is normative in the measure. This pushes the dialectic to a new definition of form as that which measures the constituents to be harmonized. Plato said that the first meaning of form is a theoretical or dianoetic one, whereas the second meaning is dialectical. The first concerns structure, the second value.

The discussion so far has justified a certain usage of terms. A form in itself, conceived in disconnection from things it might harmonize, is a pure value. A form in relation to things it might harmonize is a norm, or normative principle. The structure a harmony has in virtue of the norm is a normative measure. A normative measure is the way a harmony embodies or has the value mediated to it by the norm.

Considering a form in itself as that which measures the constituents of the harmony—and not as the structure into which the constituents have been properly measured—the form is a value made determinate only relative to possible instantiations. A thing participates in such a value by having some organization or structural harmony, the normative principle for which is that value. Here the paradigm for participation is the moral situation. In analyzing a moral problem we interpret the alternative connections of factors according to how well they exhibit some appropriate values. The values are made determinate in the various alternate imaginary arrangements of factors. And we say that the situation is or has its appropriate value-identity to the degree that its organization reflects the appropriate principle of measure.

It will help to treat three questions pertinent to participation:

First, how does a set of things to be harmonized have an *appropriate* value or norm? In the moral sphere this is the problem of determining the appropriate norm to be applied in a given situation. On a more general level it is the question of the relevance of possible constituents to given norms. The answer is that where things are determinate with respect to each other they are already harmonized together in some mode or other, and that what normatively determines the elegance they actually have also determines what higher forms of elegance are possible. The value in itself is what determines the elegance, and the higher determinate modes of elegance are its specifications. For different sets of constituents there are different appropriate norms. For a given set of constituents there is always at least one ideal norm that is appropriate if they are harmonious at all; bare consistency is at least a minimum ideal. And for any selection of constituents that are not harmonious together, some others can be added, within the limits of possibility, to make them harmonious and therefore relevant to an ideal. The ideal of normative measure defines possibility itself.

The second question about participation is how it can have degrees. This is the problem of how well a thing attains its ideal. We say, "Jones is a butcher, but not a *real* butcher." How can degrees of participation in an ideal form be rendered in our technical vocabulary?

A given set of constituents can be harmonized more or less elegantly, although any of its harmonies is elegant to a degree. The degree of participation a thing has in an ideal form is the degree to which its structural form is an elegant harmony of its components. The perfect embodiment of an ideal would be the most elegant of commensurable alternatives in which that set of constituents could be organized. The ideal norm itself is that according to which the relatively elegant normative measures are ranked.

As Plato showed, the procedure of ranking alternative structures involves comparison and intuition.[6] The alternatives are compared and ranked according to how elegant they are, and the marks of elegance are complexity and simplicity. Many of the attempted definitions of ideals in Platonic dialogues lack complexity, not taking into account all the factors seen on other grounds to be relevant. The early definitions of justice in the *Republic* are cases in point. Other characterizations of ideals fail in simplicity, being filled with too many ad hoc and unintegrated elements, as is the difficulty with Euthyphro's approach to piety. The ways of being a less-than-perfect butcher are various. Imperfect butchers suffer from two kinds of faults; either they fail to perform some relevant things, like cleaning off the pinfeathers, or they encumber their job with irrelevant tasks that prohibit them from putting first things first, tasks like selling eggs and butter on the side. Plato said butchers should cut at the natural joints, but we have a generation of not-*real* butchers, who hack their chickens into quarters.

The third question arises from the first two. How is a value determinate? It cannot be determinate in itself if there are degrees of participation. If it were determinate in itself, then the actual structure of the participating harmony simply would agree or disagree with it. Two structures can only be different; they cannot be related by the degrees in which one participates in another. The determinateness of an ideal comes only in relation to the determinate character of the constitutents it measures. It can be seen and recognized only in specific embodiments, either actual or imagined. To direct our moral activities we imagine alternate arrangements of situational factors, see that some are more elegant

6. For a detailed defense of the theory of intuition, see my "Intuition," *International Philosophical Quarterly* 7 (December 1967) : 556–90.

than others, and take the most elegant as a norm. But that determinate norm is not the value in itself; it is only the most elegant structural harmony imagined, and the reason it is the most elegant is because the value as norm determines what the formal nature of elegance is with reference to the relevant constituents. The degree of elegance a thing has is the degree to which it participates in its norm.

This is another way of saying that what gives a normative measure its structure cannot itself be a determinate structure, since it could not then account for structure itself. The consequence drawn before was that it is hard to say there is a plurality of ideal forms or values, since they can hardly be said to differ if they are in themselves indeterminate. Suppose, then, we say that there is only one really ideal form, the form of the Good, whose disposition relative to plural things is to give them structurally determinate, harmonious, normatively measured, elegant natures. But *relative* to a given set of things to be harmonized, the form of the Good is the normative ground making elegance for that set what it is, and this is different from the elegance appropriate to some other set of components. Therefore it makes perfect sense to say the form of the Good for a state is Justice, for human life is the Measured or Appropriate, for religion Piety, for enjoyable things Beauty, for claims Truth, and so forth.

The way has been indicated to interpret participation of individuals in ideal norms. The theory of participation has traditionally been construed, however, as the participation of individuals in universals or structural forms, not in norms. If our value theory is true the traditional move has been a misconstruction. This is precisely the point where the tradition has lost sight of Plato's insight into the normative element underlying structure. The thesis of the axiological cosmology from the beginning has been that somehow structures derive from values; now we must come to terms with the "somehow."

According to the general theory, all structure, including universal structure, is the schema of a determinate plurality to be measured with a measuring norm or ideal. A thing has the structure it does because that is a good way of harmonizing its components. It is important, therefore, to become clear about the language of participation on this theory. Instead of saying that several things participate in a common structure, it is better to say several things participate in the same norm, and *the way they participate is by having the same structure.* To participate in a norm is to be structured by it. Things do not participate in the same pattern; they are patterned the same because they have the same patterns in their constituents and they participate in the same norm. This is a departure from traditional participation language and must be explained.

The usual motive for adopting a doctrine of forms in the first place is to handle problems of description, not of morality. The reason people who believe in universal structures do so is because we seem to cite them in applying universal descriptive terms to things. If forms are really norms, what are we to make of the traditional claims for universals? These have to do chiefly with universality, abstraction, independence, eternality, irreducibility, and purity.

Concerning universality, the features of things selected from harmonies in description are structures that might be embodied in any number of other things precisely in the sense that the other things might have constituents measured by the same norm. *The universality is in the capacity of the norm to measure any number of concrete individuals presenting the same structure of constituents to be measured.* Of course, the constituents themselves are structured by norms appropriate to them, and things can have identically structured constituents by the same reason that they can have identical structures as a whole.

Concerning abstraction, since the structure of individuals is individual and not universal, the only elements that could exhibit universals are harmonies abstracted from the individual whole; these in fact are the things we describe. Two individuals could not have exactly the same structure or they would be the same individual; by structure is meant any determination, including existential determination relative to place and proper time. Certain parts of individuals could be structured in a way repeatable in other individuals, however, and the universals we think of in theoretical thought are abstract structures or simplifications.

Concerning independence, there is no such thing as a universal independent of structural constituents to be harmonized and the norm according to which they are harmonized. It is impossible, therefore, to speak strictly about universals as subsistent entities; their reality is entirely that of schemata relating the appropriate norms to structural pluralities to be harmonized. This is not an inconsequential reality, however, so long as it is remembered not to make too much of it.

Concerning eternality, universals have their determinate character quite independently of whether there are any individuals exhibiting them. For their character consists entirely in the *way* constituents are harmonized according to the appropriate norms. Since what is functional here in the nature of the constituents is their determinate structure, and that determinate structure may itself be universal, it is *possible* that there be a world consisting entirely and exclusively of universal forms. Each universal would be a normative measure schematizing other component universals and the appropriate norms.

The reality of universals is not reducible to instances. An instance of a universal is nothing but something structured in that universal way; it is really an instance of a set of constituents being measured and given determinate structure by a norm. The universality consists in the fact that the norm would structure any similar set of constituents that way. The normative quality of the value is not reducible to its applicability in any instance or set of instances.

Acknowledging the eternality of universals we can do justice to the formal theoretical disciplines like mathematics that explore only pure structures. They are articulating modes of harmony. Of course, they do not pay direct attention to the norms that give the harmonies their structure, only to the structural results; this is the nature of theoretical reasoning. It takes dialectic to limn out the normative functions. That formal disciplines admit the functioning of norms is shown in their appeal to consistency, definiteness, coherence, formal economy, and so forth.

The argument of this section may now be summed up. Value is primarily a matter of harmony, and the theoretical interpretation of harmony given by the axiological cosmology was discussed in terms of its contents and its ranking of harmonies in hierarchies. The metaphysical presuppositions of harmony are plurality and a measure for the plurality, and it was found that these can be understood only by asking two kinds of questions, theoretical ones that lay out the structure of the harmony, and dialectical ones that expose the norm for it or the value in it. Since value theory is interested primarily in the latter, it was pursued with the development of Plato's doctrine of normative measure. A normative measure is a mode of harmonizing constituents that has elegance, and elegance was discussed in terms of simplicity and complexity. Having distinguished the normative side of harmony from the structural side, and having analyzed it, the problem then was to interpret the connection between the two, and the interpretation took the form of defending a Platonic doctrine of participation in forms. It was argued that the identity of a thing is not the structure it actually has, but the relation it has to its appropriate ideal or norm. In part that relation consists in having the structure it has so as to embody the norm in a normative measure; but there are degrees in which a thing can harmonize its constituents elegantly, and the more elegant its harmony, the more its norm is embodied. Although the discussion was on the simplified level of metaphysics, it is obvious how important the degrees of possible elegance might be for a free individual who can control himself to some extent.

In conclusion, the value theory can be said to hold the following theses:

1. *For any plurality of things there may be various ways in which they can be together, and the more elegant ways are the better ways.* The "can be" is intended here in a nontemporal, noncosmological, and purely abstract sense; it may in this sense be said that five and seven "can be twelve, "can be" separated by an integer larger than the former and smaller than the latter, and so forth.

2. *A mode of harmony or structure in which things are together is a normative measure—that is, a good way for the things to be together.* Some normative measures are better than others, depending on which have more elegance. Since every determinate thing has a mode of harmony, every thing has a degree of elegance, a normative measure.

3. *A normative measure is the structure of a harmony according to which the particular constituents of the harmony can be elegantly joined.* It schematizes the constituents with

elegance. The principles of elegance must be transcendent of the particular normative measure since the same constituents might be elegantly harmonizable in a variety of different ways. The ranking of the various normative measures according to degree of elegance is itself transcendent of any particular measures. It must be recognized, therefore, that the norm for any given set of constituents transcends the various ways of measuring the constituents.

4. *The transcendent norm cannot be conceived, however, except as it is embodied in some structured measure.* This is because only structures can be conceived. The conceptual employment of norms, therefore, takes the form of comparing alternative normative measures and ranking them. As long as the degree of elegance can be grasped in the alternatives there is no practical purpose served by conceiving the norm directly.

5. *The function of norms relative to things they might measure can be observed, however, and therefore it is possible to have a theory about norms that is not just a commentary on how various specific alternatives are better than others.* This is a point about which Dewey was not clear. It is apparent that norms are indeterminate if they are considered in disconnection with what they might measure; as such, we can speak of norms per se simply in terms of the single form of the Good, or the form of Elegance. But norms are considered primarily in relation to specific sets of constituents, and we can therefore talk about them as relatively distinct ideals; the ideal of Justice for groups, of Beauty for art, and so forth.

The notion of value taken by itself is utterly indeterminate, for the reasons given. Taken with reference to harmonies the notion of value is that of norm for togetherness. The language of value is equivocal, depending on whether one is talking about the principle of elegance as such (the norm), a value a thing might have (a normative measure in which its constituents might be structured), the value it does have (the normative measure it actually has in contrast to others it might have—a cosmological case), the value it ought to have (the most elegant normative measure), and so forth. The relations between these have now been spelled out enough for the equivocation to be determined satisfactorily by the context of discussion.

ARISTOTELIAN CRITICISM AND THE PARADOXES OF PARTICIPATION

In many senses, Artistotelianism is the most radical opponent of Platonistic axiology because it deals with the same issues and comes from the same experience. For present purposes, however, it would be inappropriate to focus on the historical opposition between Plato and Aristotle; it is only necessary to generalize the opposition so as to include the basic tendencies uniting the Platonic and Aristotelian traditions in mutual opposition. The fundamental opposition turns on the primacy of structure versus value. For the Platonic tradition, value is primary and structure is derivative. For the Aristotelian, the primacy goes to structure, and in a variety of ways value is derivative from it. The basic Aristotelian premise is that value is self-sufficiency in structure. Motion aims at eternity, and fulfills this best by circularity; circularity in life and death is perpetuation of the species, and biological final causes are therefore reproduction and the attainment of the species-acme. Value in human life is its own kind of self-sufficiency requiring a balance of friends, fame, and fortune; the stablest person is the one whose virtues are habits, living in a stable society where virtue can be habitual; and the greatest excellence of humans is the intellectual virtue wherein the transient person becomes spiritually identical with the mind of God.[7]

Where structure is primary, there is neither need nor possibility of transcending structure to account for it. Self-sufficiency is a structural notion akin to completeness, and it therefore becomes a question of fact whether something is self-sufficient or what its self-sufficiency would consist in. The habits of mind based on the fundamental hypothesis that structure is primary are so pervasive that most Aristotelians cannot conceive the Platonic theory of participation as even initially plausible. Why should we appeal to transcendent values when all the questions can be answered with reference to only immanent factors?

But that is just the point. Not all the questions can be answered that way, and here is the strength of Platonism. Why is self-sufficiency the paradigm or heart of value? Why is circular motion

7. See, e.g., Aristotle's *Nichomachaean Ethics*, X, vii.

better just because it is nearer eternity than linear motion? Why
is intellectual identity with eternal truths better than a once-and-
forever decisive action? These are all values in their own ways,
but their ways are not the only ones. What about the candle that
shall not last the night, burning at both ends, but with a wondrous
light? What about the great man, the conditions for whose glory
contain the causes of his own destruction? Experience shows that
the price of self-sufficiency is too often dullness and isolation. So
the first reply to the Aristotelian is that he is mistaken in labeling
the valuable things in experience. Who said the greatest need of
the Great Souled Man is a swift kick in the buttocks? Praise God
for dappled things!

The second reply is that, regarding value questions, the theory
that structure is primary must commit the naturalistic fallacy in
an inexcusable way. That is, when Aristotelianism says, "Goodness
is self-sufficiency," or something of the sort, it must be able to give
a further reason why. The fact that self-sufficiency does not characterize many things taken as good testifies to this. Axiology can
handle this problem by saying that goodness is elegance, but that
only structural things show it; the question "Is this really good?"
can be answered by a comparison with alternatives; the claim that
elegance is the criterion is an empirical claim to be tested by ascertaining whether the resultant rankings of alternatives are ordered according to relative maximizations of simplicity and complexity. Elegance is functional as a transcendent principle of normativeness; it is not characterizable itself, as self-sufficiency would
be, but it functions through its structural expressions.

The Aristotelian might retort that questions about why self-
sufficiency is the paradigm of goodness are meaningless. Goodness
is just defined that way. Anyway, a theory such as axiology that
must make reference to factors that cannot be defined in terms of
a categoreal system must be talking nonsense, since in some way or
other meaningfulness depends on systematic connection. But this
is the very question at issue. Structural Aristotelianism believes
the highest form of philosophy is theory, dianoia; nothing can be
self-referential beyond this. Axiological Platonism believes the
highest form of philosophy is dialectical, with the dialectic based
on a doctrine of participation. The Aristotelian cannot accept as
meaningful the very heart of the Platonic orientation. But then

neither can he answer questions the Platonist can. Since no *theory*, for instance that of structural primacy, should limit the *questions* to be asked, the axiological approach is better.

Aristotle and his followers have a more direct critique of Platonic axiology, however. The doctrine of participation is internally paradoxical, they claim. If the theory is plausible that things have structure in virtue of participating in norms rather than in other structures, then it should be able to avoid the traditional paradoxes of participation. Our best source book for the paradoxes is Plato's own *Parmenides*.

The first paradox is the following: if, when a thing participates in a form, it participates in the form as a whole and not just in part of the form, is it the case that several things participating in the same form make that form itself different things? If so, then several things cannot really participate in the same form. It would seem that if the whole form is in one instance, there is nothing left over for any other instances. This is the question, How can a form be universal? Socrates's answer was to say that the form is in many places at the same time and still is not separate from itself (*Parmenides* 131b). Parmenides likened this to a sail covering several men and pointed out that in this analogy each instance participated in only part of the form.

The first-level difficulty lies in conceiving the form as if it were a substance with its own existence of an individual or existential sort. If all existing things have their natures by participation in transcendent forms, then by hypothesis no relation between individuals can be the paradigm for the relation between thing and form. Rather the form is universal, which is just to recognize its capacity to be participated in by many things. The second-level difficulty therefore is in making sense of universality.

There are two levels of answers to the difficulty of universality. On the *theoretical* level, when we ask about the common structures of things we want to know two things: which structures are in the individuals, and what the exact nature of the structures is. The former involves empirical testing; the latter formal or "conceptual" analysis, for which something like mathematics is the paradigm form of reasoning. In theoretical reasoning, the problem is to determine whether the formal structures of two or more things are the same, not how the universal can be common. Formal or theoretical analysis supposes the possibility of universality and concentrates on the problems of just what structure the universal has. The *dialectical* question about how a universal can be real and universal pushes to a new level. If the universal is taken to be nothing more than a self-subsistent structure, then the participation of many things in it is a mystery because its reality can be imagined only as a dessicated abstraction from a concrete being. This is the wrong kind of reality, however, since the reality of a universal consists in the formal relations between the forms of the things it harmonizes; these formal relations are far more stable and untouched by change than any concrete things they may be embodied in and abstracted from. The reality of universals consists precisely in the kinds of formal connections known by theoretical reasoning, and this is nothing self-subsistent.

On the other hand, the reality of universals cannot be dependent upon concrete things that instance them or upon thinkers who know them, for by definition they are not exhausted in any instances, and they are what they are whether anyone knows them (something we must say to account for the possibility of formal error). The hypothesis that forms are norms makes sense of all this. The ideal form, indeterminate in itself, is neither universal nor particular. Yet it functions relative to what is to be measured as the principle of normative structuring, and it does this whenever there is something relevant to measure. It functions universally, therefore, although it is nonsense to say it is universal in itself. Furthermore, the structure the ideal form gives to the plurality it measures has purely universal abstract elements, true wherever embodied and conceivable as determinate even without being embodied. Universal forms should not be conceived as real except insofar as they are construed as the structures possibly to be given things by the principles of normative measure.

The second traditional paradox Parmenides raises is the "third man" argument, the stock in trade of the Aristotelian tradition. If a form is a pattern or determinate structure, then a thing participates in it by being like it, and the form in its way is like the participating thing. But if form and thing are alike, their likeness is in virtue of some third thing, a higher form. Parmenides points out that this leads to an infinite series of forms before getting to one that explains similar things. The answer to this argument, of course, is that real forms are not patterns but rather the principles that give normative structure to patterns. If a form in itself really is an indeterminate *value* then no third-man regress is possible.

There is a truth in the argument that forms are patterns, however, since it is in virtue of having the same pattern that we say things are alike. Socrates's insight was that identity of pattern was precisely the likeness of things. To say things are alike is to say that they have the same pattern. Things do not participate in the same pattern: they participate in the same ideal form, and this gives them the same pattern. The normative way of harmonizing two different sets of components, if the harmonies participate in the same ideal form in the same respect, is the same. So it is false to say that things are like their pattern; their determinate structure is their pattern, and those elements that are universal can be repeated in other things.

The third paradoxical element in the traditional theory of forms is harder to state briefly. Forms are defined in terms of one another. The structure of a universal or structural form is a harmony of things fitted together in virtue of their own structures, and the determinateness of the universal stems from mutual determination with other universals. The harmony depends upon the fit of other harmonies, and whether there are any concrete things so harmonized makes no difference to the structural connections of the harmonies. On the other hand, when we know concrete things in the world, we know them not in terms of their forms in themselves but in terms of other concrete things concretely related to them. Plato's example is that of slave and master; the slave is the slave not of masterness itself but of some concrete master. So it would seem that if we know concrete things to begin with we would not ever have to get to forms in themselves, only forms embodied; and if we know forms in themselves we would have no connection with the concrete world.

This crucial misunderstanding comes from conceiving the forms as if they could exsist by themselves as mere universals. The universals may be contemplated and formally analyzed by themselves, but they cannot be conceived to exist by themselves. They exist only as the schematization of ideal forms to determinate pluralities. The pluralities, of course, may be other forms, not concrete things; so it is possible for there to be a world of only forms. But it is not possible that the forms can be conceived as anything determinate without conceiving them as universal possibilities for the infinitely complex world. Furthermore, as argued above, it is hard to conceive of concrete things without conceiving of them as formed by universal structures. Structural forms, including universals, ought to be taken as the mean between concrete things and the kind of forms that can exist on their own without reference to change.

The interesting part of this alleged paradox, however, is the question it raises about how we can speak of forms "apart" at all. When speaking we always consider universals as structures that might be in concrete things; this fact has led many thinkers to say universals are only abstractions from concrete things—a mistake, considering the universality of universals and the particularity of the concrete, but one that is understandable. To consider forms in themselves it is necessary to appreciate them as ideals. The ideal forms in themselves, however, are indeterminate, which poses no amount of embarrassment for a position like young Socrates's, which claimed there are different forms for every distinct kind of thing (except perhaps the least valuable kinds). What shall we say?

It should be remembered that the only difference between ideal forms comes in their measuring different pluralities. Pure formness is the principle that harmonizes any set of components by structuring them with some degree of elegance. In itself this can be called the form of the Good; with reference to specifiable sets of components it has different names. Since the dialectic of forms usually starts with a given structured thing we are not at a loss for some differential name for the ideal appropriate to the thing. It is true to say with Socrates that every kind of thing has its own form, since for every specifiable set of components there is a specification of the form of the Good, a normative measure for the set that functions as an ideal. What is genuinely and purely ideal in the normative measure, however, is that which makes that particular structure elegant and structurally coherent as a norm for those components—the form of the Good as relative to the things measured.

The three paradoxes considered so far are the basic arguments lodged against an axiology based on participation. The reinterpretation of the doctrine given here shows that they do not hold against this particular form of the doctrine. Of course, the advocate of a theory is not likely to give the most cogent presentations of the arguments against his own view, and it is open to opponents to rephrase the arguments. The keynote in the defense against the objections is that the doctrine of participation is different from a structural account and that most objections do not take the difference seriously enough; consequently they usually beg the question.

EXPERIENTIAL EVIDENCE

Having dealt with at least some of the traditional charges of internal difficulties in the axiological theory, we may now turn to positive evidence, not from theory but from experience. Where in experience, if anywhere, do we find normative measure used as the interpretation of the meaning of something's value? Note that the issue here is not whether there is such a thing as value. Rather the issue is to determine whether the given account of what value means finds exemplification in experience. Of course, most experiences are partial in the sense that they do not exemplify all the logical ramifications of the structures forming them. But there are certain domains of experience that collect experiences together into a pattern with some integrity, and these do exemplify the logical structures. Several self-critical disciplines will be examined here, namely physics, mathematics, history, and aesthetics. The area of morals will be examined in connection with deliberation in chapter 7.

In the history of the development of modern physical science we are accustomed to thinking of radical changes in fundamental theory as revolutions of sorts, as, for instance, was involved in the acceptance of Copernicus's theory, and Einstein's. In both cases fundamental models of physical reality were overthrown and replaced. The point of interest here is why the changes were made, since they should illustrate the kinds of principles and judgments appealed to in science to justify one theory as being better than another.

The purpose of a theory is to explain something in experience. Therefore, when there is something in experience that a theory ought to explain but does not, that is a good reason for changing the theory. The change in theory may be minor, or it may involve the adoption of a whole new model. The changed or new theory should account for as much as the old one and also handle the unexplained anomoly. But neither in the case of the Copernican revolution nor in that of Einstein's were there clear cases of anomolies that could not be accounted for under the old systems. Nor was it the case with either revolution that the scientific community's acceptance of the new model waited until after some newly predicted evidence turned up. The accounts of both revolutions are well enough known that they can be retold briefly.

As E. A. Burtt has pointed out, known celestial phenomena could be accounted for with the Ptolemaic astronomy at the time of Copernicus. Furthermore, there were grave difficulties with Copernicus's suggestion. Without a theory of gravity, it seemed that things would slide off the earth if it were moving itself at great speed. Without a modern theory of dynamics, it seemed that objects thrown straight up in the air ought to come down west of the place from which they were thrown if the Earth were spinning. In fact, according to Burtt, other objections to Copernican theory, "such as the objection that according to Copernicus the fixed stars ought to reveal an annual parallax, due to the 186,000,000-mile difference in the position of the earth every six months, were not answered till Bessel's discovery of such a parallax in 1838." [8] In the face of these difficulties and others, what was the attraction of Copernicus' theory? Copernicus could

> plead only that *his conception threw the facts of astronomy into a simpler and more harmonious mathematical order.* It was simpler, since in place of some eighty epicycles of the Ptolemaic system, Copernicus was able to "save the phenomena" with only thirty-four, all those which had been required by the assumption that the earth remained at rest being now eliminated. It was more harmonious, in that the major part of the planetary phenomena could now fairly well be represented by a series of concentric circles around the sun, our moon being the only irregular intruder.[9]

In other words, the formal construction of the theory was more elegant, and even though strictly speaking it may have been more

8. Burtt, *The Metaphysical Foundations of Modern Science* (Garden City, N.Y.: Doubleday, Anchor Books, 1954), pp. 37–38.

9. Ibid., p. 38.

paradoxical in that day than the Ptolemaic theory, Copernicus's idea was enough more elegant that it carried the field. The Copernican revolution played a part in the larger revolution of the times that involved a rearrangement of what was taken to be important and relevant. Modern science was fully formed when, by the time of Newton, and largely due to his work, the model for understanding physical reality was given a mathematical formulation. But as Burtt notes, even this was but a development of the claim Ptolemy himself had made, that the reason to adopt *his* theory was that, in his time, it offered the simplest geometric interpretation of things.[10]

In much more complex but analogous fashion, the conclusive proof for the relativity theories of Einstein did not come until the predicted observation of the perihelion of Mercury. As noted by A. d'Abro, "When this precise angle predicted by Einstein was observed during the subsequent solar eclipse of 1919, interest in relativity became widespread; for it was recognized at last that the theory was not a mere mathematical dream." [11] Before this time, however, the elegance of Einstein's special and general theories of relativity had persuaded people to reject or at least to consider rejecting the other theory and its correlative elements. The mathematical elegance of relativity theory, in comparison with the cumbersome transformations required by the older view to account for observed phenomena, recommended it simply as a better theory, a more "theoretical theory," if that phrase can be understood.

Concerning mathematics, allusion has already been made to the frequent appeal of mathematicians to elegance in the construction of theoretical connections and inference patterns. This in fact is the origin of the desirable connotations of the term "elegance." The point to be made here concerns the new conception of the notion of form arising with and following the discovery of non-Euclidian geometries. It became apparent that formal relations were not something read off externally given elements, and that rather they depended on initial principles of the formal system having themselves a peculiar status. That they govern what is al-

10. Ibid., pp. 46–47, 51.

11. *The Evolution of Scientific Thought from Newton to Einstein*, 2nd ed. (New York: Dover, 1950), p. 278.

lowable within the system depends on their being accorded the authority to do that by the thinker. In this sense, the structure of the system depends upon the mathematician's will, which in turn is usually guided by *expedience,* a practical category, or *interest,* an aesthetic one. But the authority the first principles have is objective and realistic in the sense that it governs what is allowed in the system quite apart from the wishes of the mathematician. The structure of the system that follows from the accepted first principles has no dependence on the thinker. The domain known through mathematical systems, therefore, must be a pure set of structures whose features are made known through the construction of different systems according to various sets of first principles.

But since the various authoritative first principles—the patterns of inference, the specific theorems—differ from system to system, and the differences depend on the will of the mathematician, what precisely would be that objective and real structure mathematics knows per se? It could not be simply the articulated mathematical structures, since these in some cases are contradictory. Nor could it be simply a tremendous variety of different complex structural relations set forward in 'if–then" fashion side by side, for this would not make apparent the obvious unity of mathematical thought. But what all their systems have in common is their internal hang-togetherness. Furthermore they are connected in such a way that if they were arranged in hierarchies, some could be seen to be alternative variations on parts of others. The suggestion is that, just as Newtonian mechanics can be represented as a limited domain within the revolutionary model, so mathematical systems, depending on their first principles, can be hierarchically ordered. The fundamental content of the domain known by mathematics is thus not so much the alternate systems but the systems as ordered in a hierarchy.

Of course, the implication of this is that the important things in the domain known by mathematics are those governing the harmonious ranking and structuring of the diverse systems. If there is a single hierarchy within which all possible mathematical systems can be interpreted, then the important things in it will be those determining it to have the structure combining them all, in a word, its essential features. And the relevant things in mathematics will be those determined to be in need of harmony with each other due to the chosen first principles, namely, all the things true in any mathematical system. This accords with the way relevance was described before: all components are relevant to the degree that their structure needs to be taken account of by the whole harmony to have the elegance it does.

The final suggestion is that, just as elegance functions to order each system of formal relations, so it functions to order them together. The true mathematical reality known by mathematicians is the purely formal structure of normative measure. What is conditional in mathematics is the particulars of systems coming from the choice of first principles according to the interest and expedience of particular mathematicians. What is essential is the set of normative elements giving the interrelations of formal systems the elegance they have. Even if there is not one ideal mathematical system that would include all others as proper parts, the normative elements still would have, but in a limited way, the essential and regulative importance claimed. This general interpretation, if true, gives substantial confirmation to the claim that the value in mathematical systems is elegance.

The writing of history also exhibits the decisive function of elegance as the criterion for valuable historical form. Like natural science, history has a subject matter to which it must do justice. But it does not "do justice" in the same way natural science does, that is, with an abstract model. The development of the writing of history is not that of modifying or replacing theoretical models as science discovers new domains and sharpens its experimental instruments. Rather, even in writing history about the long past, the changes are more like telling the story a different way. Whereas the form of understanding in the natural sciences is that of an abstract model, the form of understanding in history is that of a story.

When an historian asks what is important to say or study, he answers his question by determining what story there is to be told. The formal structure of the story gives both relevance and importance to the possible details. It also suggests what to look for, by analogy with other stories. And in a way that is difficult to formulate, the historian knows he has explained what he set out to explain when he can tell how things happened in a satisfactory story. The novelist and storyteller are to the historian what the mathematician is to the natural scientist.

The story is itself a formal harmony whose outcome is the inclusive mode containing the elements that lead up to it. In fact, the story form well illustrates the complexities noted in the previous section stemming from the fact that a thing is in a harmony in some respects and not in others. Many things enter a story tangentially but are very important. They play their role in the story but are not only or wholly in that story. It is crucial for the historian to determine what is relevant to a story, articulating the features of its ending. And the way he tells the story must reflect what is important, for that is the guiding essential element that makes the relevant things fall together the way they do.

An historian's story must be true to the facts. Yet there are good stories and bad stories, all of which may reflect something of what happens. A good story puts the facts together in an elegant way—a way showing maximum inclusiveness with simplicity. Of course the data required to make a good story must be checked with the facts, and it is entirely possible that what really happened does not make a good story. To the extent that what happened does not make a good story, to that extent it is somewhat unintelligible or absurd. The form of valuable historical understanding is elegant.[12]

Developments in modern art also illustrate the thesis about elegance. The significance of various forms of abstraction—abstraction from accurate representational drawing, from realistic color representation, from common-sense definitions of space and perspective, from representation per se, from any meaning beyond the physical art object—is that interpretation is thrown back more and more on formal elements within the work itself. As the New Critics dealt with poetry, so critics in general recognize that value judgments about a work of art depend on making out the formal

12. A different account of the proper form of historical understanding is given by Geoffrey Barraclough in *An Introduction to Contemporary History* (Baltimore: Penguin Books, 1967), chap. 1. His thesis is that at least his kind of history writing centers on the discernment of contemporary patterns rather than on the tracing of causal developments with a story line. It should be apparent, however, that the judgment between competing pattern structures is an aesthetic one and that the better pattern is the one that includes the most with the greatest economy. The view defended here follows that of Jack Hexter in *A History Primer* (New York: Basic Books, 1971).

interrelationships of elements. The limitation of the New Critics is that they did not recognize the roles that external context, authorship, and participant interest play in the real formal integrity of a work of art.

Furthermore, differences of style can be interpreted in terms of differences in kinds of elegance in the hierarchies of works of art. The overall elegance of the work depends on what is essential in the work, and in different styles different things are essential. To use gross examples, line and color may be essential in one style whereas texture and sense of space may be essential in another. These examples are gross because the real differences come in *kinds* of line, *kinds* of texture, and so forth. If elegance is interpreted in terms of complexity and simplicity, not in terms of decorativeness, it can be applied to the kind of harmony peculiar to art.

Having exhibited that the interpretation of value given is in various ways what we mean in critical experience by value, it is now fair to restate the conclusions.

A harmony has a value and it contains many values. It has a value because its mode is a normative measure. To be a normative measure is to proportion and arrange constituents so that their hierarchy is elegant. Elegance is the formal property of a harmony's hierarchy containing its complexity of constituents in a simple way. There are degrees of complexity and simplicity, and their integration in the form of a thing gives rise to degrees of elegance. Although these notions can be characterized, they cannot be formally defined, since they themselves define formal definition. They can, however, be exhibited.

That a harmony contains many values means its mode of harmony contains many other modes as constituents, and that each of these other modes is itself a value. This allows for a new definition of elegance and normative measure.

A mode of harmony is elegant to the degree that it compounds constituent values. The greater the constituent value integrated together, the greater the elegance of the containing mode. If complexity alone were the character of elegance, then the more elegant harmony would be the one that contains more different values. But although they may be infinitely different they may not add up to much. On the other hand, if simplicity alone were the character of elegance, then the more elegant harmony would be the one that contains least value. Put together the most elegant harmony is the one that compounds the most constituent values.

Accordingly, a normative measure is a mode of harmony whose structure enhances the value of its components. That is, the structure of a normative measure gives the components their compossible structures with their own elegance. Deliberation is based on the interpretation of normative measure that seeks ideals as compossible structures to enhance the values of things already having a value of their own.

This brief presentation of a general theory of value surely raises more questions than it answers. This itself is something of an achievement, considering how hard it is to raise these questions today. The presentation here is sufficient for the purposes of examining freedom in light of the cosmological scheme. The general concepts of value can be made specific to the cosmological categories in the appropriate contexts. After so much metaphysics, cosmology, and axiology in Part 1, the discussion would lose all sense of orientation to the problems of freedom if these are not now directly addressed.

PART 2

Personal Freedom

Preliminary Remarks

The four chapters of the discussion of personal freedom derive their order from two concerns. The first has to do with the contents of the dimensions of freedom. External liberty is the simplest approach to autonomy and creativity is the most complex; the first and fourth chapters are the ends of the bridge developing the theme of autonomy. The reason true autonomy must be creativity and not merely external liberty is that human agency constructs a world of its own choice. The two chapters on free agency—the discussion of intentional action and the discussion of free choice —lie between external liberty and creativity.

The second reason for the order of the discussion is that it allows the cosmological categories to be elaborated in a fairly straightforward fashion. The chapter on external liberty develops the basic categories defining individuality and the relation between a person and his environment. The chapter on intentional action develops the concept of voluntary action, or the causation peculiar to responsible agents; this emphasizes the *dynamic* categories relating an individual with his environment. The chapter on free choice develops the categories interpreting the process of the experience of autonomy within the individual. The chapter on creativity not only introduces the moral categories involved in deliberation, interpreting them in terms of the value theory, but also sums up the categories interpreting the autonomy of the individual in the environment.

4

External Liberties

On the simplest level, a person thinks he is free if nothing prevents him from doing what he wants. Of course this is a naïve view of freedom. He may be enslaved to a narrow ideology or inhibited by deadening pyschological pressures. He may have a weak image of himself as an agent. He may be ignorant of real opportunities, undeveloped in his taste, alienated from social identifications, or prevented from integrating his separate choices into a coherent personal style. Although not impeded from doing what he wants, he still can be in bondage in all these senses.

Naïve though it is, this simple view of freedom makes a powerful claim. After all the fancy psychological and sociological contributions are in, a man simply is not free when he is prevented from doing what he wants. The practical force of this point is in the tradeoffs in external liberty we have become willing to make for the sake of the more internal kinds of freedom. Compulsory education is an established example. New techniques of behavior control force the issue even more. Our folk wisdom is coming to counsel caution in purchasing inner powers with the loss of external opportunity.

In the passage quoted in chapter 1 from *Leviathan,* Pt. I, chap. 14, Hobbes gave the classical definition of this simple kind of freedom, part of which reads:

> the absence of external Impediments: which Impediments, may oft take away part of a mans power to do what he would; but cannot hinder him from using the power left him according as his judgment and reason shall dictate to him.

Two elements of this definition are especially significant for the general discussion of freedom.

The first element is the decisive distinction between what is internal and what is external. Freedom has to do with external impediments, but Hobbes is careful to say the Yea or Nay of external opportunity is distinct from the person's internal powers and affects only their external expression. A person still has his identity defined in terms of his powers, as directed by his reason and judgment. We would be inclined to say today that the actual free exercise of powers determines their growth and contours more than Hobbes's statement would suggest. Nevertheless, Hobbes is likely right that we carry our identities around with us somewhat independently of external impediments or opportunities. What we carry with us from one situation to the next is who we are. Even if our identities are bad or unfree in any of the internal senses mentioned above, enjoying a personal identity is thought to be a right, or at least a valuable thing. And one aspect of freedom is being able to act on the basis of inner identity, a freedom consisting in external opportunity. Putting the point the other way, no matter how virtuous, sophisticated, or free one's internal choices are, freedom is drastically incomplete if those choices are impeded from external realization.

How are external liberties attained? Which ones should be prized? What are the social and personal conditions for their maintenance? Whose responsibility is the protection of liberties? Which liberties are for all, which only some? Which liberties should be traded off for other values, and under what conditions? These are all questions pertaining to the social dimensions of freedom, to be treated in Part 3.

What is the difference between a person with his individual identity and the external environments in which he acts? What are the relations between his choices at one moment and those at another? What is the difference between one's powers and his exercize of those powers? These are fundamental cosmological questions at the base of personal freedom.

One's cosmological image of the relation between an individual and his environment is by no means irrelevant to one's conception of freedom, especially of external liberty. Hobbes's atomistic cosmology, for instance, is expressed rather plainly in his simple distinction between a person with his powers and the environment that might contain impediments. His distinction seems simplistic to us because we know of the complex relation between the structure of internal identity and the influence of the environment. What alternative conception will do justice to our critical, psychological, and sociological knowledge? It is essential to answer this question. The present chapter and the next will develop hypotheses to answer it.

The second significant element in Hobbes's definition of freedom is his remark that a person's powers are directed by reason and judgment. Hobbes himself was a determinist regarding reason and judgment and therefore saw no point to considering whether they might be free in some senses. That is an open question to be discussed in the next two chapters. The import of Hobbes's remark, however, is that external action is not free unless humanly directed in some way. The problematic of (free?) human intention, (free?) choice, and (free?) rational deliberation is intrinsic to the very conception of an individual freely acting in an environment. An unimpeded rock would be called free only in a trival sense.

Therefore, the cosmological hypotheses required for making sense of external liberty must be comprehensive enough to render a model of intention, choice, and deliberation. The care that must be taken in the presentation of categories for use in later chapters is justified because those later topics are in fact crucial for understanding external liberty.

INTERNAL AND EXTERNAL

The clue to the distinction between internality and externality is in the distinction between essential and conditional features. The two distinctions are not identical, because the essential and conditional features are *both* parts of the thing, internal to it. The relevance of essential and conditional features stems the role conditional features play in how a determinate thing appropriates and makes internal reference to what is outside it. Whatever is external and yet *relevant* enough to a thing to be an impediment or opportunity, must be something grasped by a conditional feature of it.

Furthermore, the distinction between what is internal to a thing and what is external is not a neutral distinction made from some third standpoint. By its very logical structure it supposes the standpoint of the thing that has internal elements. Therefore, the distinction must be made from the standpoint of the thing itself, expressed as a union of essential and conditional features.

The theoretical solution to the problem of distinguishing between what is external to a person and what is internal is that his essential and conditional features are internal and what conditions his conditional features is external. But this is very abstract and applies to all determinate things whatsoever. Talk about "external impediments" is important with reference only to persons. Although the effort of this chapter is to become more specific in the application of the distinction between externality and internality to persons, the discussion cannot aim at completeness until later chapters where intentionality, choice, and social interaction are discussed.

Persons are existing individuals with discursive, that is, temporally developing, harmonies, Persons exist because they act and change within themselves, occupy places and interact with other individuals singly and in groups. They are discursive because their total identity includes changes in development. Furthermore, the discursive harmonies of persons are such that they include within themselves other discursive harmonies as well as nondiscursive harmonies. Most of the categories necessary for the distinction between what is external to a person and what is internal may be introduced with a discussion of *non*discursive existing individuals.

Nondiscursive individuals are important for freedom because they have momentary existence, and decisions are made in the moment. Without an account of the kind of thing that can exist at a moment wherein change can take place "freely," the theory would be incomplete. Such a momentary existent would not be a person, only part of a person. A nondiscursive individual is one that has its complete reality at a moment. This nondiscursiveness of such individuals consists in the fact that their parts are not related as earlier and later. A discursive individual does have its parts related as earlier and later.

An existing individual occupies a moment of time. This is a timeless use of the present tense of "occupy." In this timeless sense it is proper to say Napoleon occupies a past duration of time, the reader occupies a present moment, and the events of the year 2500 occupy a future duration. To occupy a time in this timeless sense, it must be true that there has been, is, or will be some time in which the individual occupies a present moment. It is misleading to limit existence to the present moment any more than this. To say Napoleon existed once but does so no longer is only to say that he does not at this present time occupy a present time; it should not be taken, as Thomists are prone to do, to mean that Napoleon lacks present reality. Rather, so long as he is determinate, he has reality—in this case, the present reality of occupying a past time. To deny this is to fall into the paradoxical position of saying that Napoleon now has no reality except as thought of by someone, and then his reality is only that of an idea. But it is essential to Napoleon that by now he would be entirely past, and it is not essential that anyone think of him; whether anyone thinks of him is not connected with the order of his lifetime such that all his presents becomes pasts. To say that the events of the year 2500 do not exist should only be taken to mean that they do not have present existence now. They do have future existence now, although it is very hard to give them identity in the face of the future's vagueness. To deny future existence is to fall into the analogous paradoxical position of saying that a future event has no reality except as thought of. But how a future event can get from present existence as a mere idea in someone's mind, into the kind of brute future existence that forces hard decisions, and back into present but nonmental existence, is more cumbersome to understand than existence with three modes, past, present, and future. When momentary existence is discussed in the pages following, a present moment is meant unless otherwise specified.

The momentary existence of an individual existing nondiscursive harmony is such that its existence articulates space and time and that it grasps or "prehends" other harmonies into its own momentary harmony. This is the hypothesis to be elaborated in what follows. The existential aspect will be taken up in this section, and the notion of prehension in the next.

Its mode of existence reflects how a thing is together with other things. To have past existence means to be related to other past things in a system of realized and compatible facts. To have future existence means for a possibility to be compatible with at least some other possibilities in a way that would not be compatible in present or past existence; to have a sea battle at time T and not to have a sea battle then, are compatible as future possibilities but not as present or past facts. To have present existence means to be causally isolated from contemporaries and to be constituting or making a change, bringing about a new fact in oneself; present existence separates contemporaries, allowing each one to be self-creative.

As there are kinds of togetherness appropriate to past, present, and future modes of existence, so there are different relations between the modes, and the difference is made by causal relations. A causal happening takes place within a present existent. But this happening takes its rise from what happened before; hence the past happenings can be said to cause, in the sense of determining the conditions for, the present happening. The present does the same for the future. Two things are in the same present if they are caused by the same things and yet do not cause each other. This is Whitehead's definition of a temporal duration.[1] To be sure, each thing has its own present existence, so it would be better to say that each has its present existence in the same duration. As Whitehead pointed out, it is possible for a thing to be presently existent in the same duration with several other things that are not in the same duration with each other; that is, one of those other things causes the other. In this case we can speak of the present existence of a thing having several durations. The meaning of this doctrine of existence will be made clear with respect to each of several dimensions of personal freedom. Only its general propriety will be considered here.

The position amounts to the claim that "existence" is a real predicate. Is there any direct proof of this? It makes perfect sense to ask whether something exists or not, and although perception may be the criterion we use for answering the question, the meaning of the answer is that of the thing has its own place, time, and causal connections relative to where we have our places, times, and causal connections. Although it is true that "I perceive a tree" entails "There exists a tree," this is not because perception means existence. Rather, it is because we suppose that the perception of a thing depends upon causal connections with the thing that place it in the existential field. Contrary to Kant, it is impossible to think something with all its inner determinations without thinking that the thing exists or not, since the inner determinations depend upon existential connections. Only the most abstract thought can think of ordinarily existing objects without applying

1. *Process and Reality*, p. 487.

or denying the characteristics of existence to them; the only way this can be done is by prescinding from all conditional features that relate to existence.

To claim "existence" is a predicate is not yet to specify what kind of predicate it is. Most modern nontranscendental philosophers have thought of existing as being in an existential field of some sort. The field is spatial and temporal, and in one way or another it is a medium of action and causation. For the present axiological cosmology, this conception characterizes *only past existence*. Such field is a locus of systematically related past facts. The action depicted in an existential field is a *course* of action, where a route of entities does something significant, the following of which in retrospect leads from the beginning to the end of action. No action really takes place in an existential field; the field is the systematic gathering together of many actual entities, each of which has already acted in a present-existence sense, so that there is an actualized pattern of a whole large-scale action.

An existential field is analyzed by what Whitehead called coordinate division. That is, the analysis prescinds from the genetic development of concrete unity in each actual entity and studies the objective patterns or "eternal objects of the objective species" as they pass from one part to another of the existential field.[2] "Pass" is used metaphorically; more strictly, a *route* of passage exists in the existential field. The character of the existential field is determined by the actual entities in it analyzed coordinately.

For Whitehead, the formal reality of the existential field is a mode of the experience of a prehending entity; it is a potential for division in that entity's experience, but it is neither actually divided nor real in itself independent of that entity's experience so that it could be divided. This position presents a great many difficulties unrelated to freedom, and the axiological cosmology is not committed to Whitehead's view of the ontological status of the existential field.[3]

2. Whitehead, *Process and Reality,* pp. 445ff.

3. It is conceivable that the field has independent reality really distinct from presently existing entities, conditionally related to them by way of the objective realities of its components. Axiological pluralism's treatment of discursive individuals requires that past existence render essential features to presently existing entities. Also, certain aspects of responsibility argue for the plausibility of independent past existence. At this point the issue may be kept open.

Spatial relations in the existential field are spacey. Temporal relations are timey. Temporal and spatial relations are unique kinds of concrete harmonies and must be recognized as such. No intellectual analysis of relations can substitute for the experience of them. The experience may be very sophisticated, having to do with calculations on the basis of light trajectories and so forth. But the experiencing body of the calculator and the physical character of the trajectories must enter into the summary calculation of the nature of space and time. It is sometimes thought that Whitehead, following Leibniz, wanted to reduce the spatial and temporal character of the coordinate field to logically definable relations. It is not clear, however, that his attempt to define points, lines, and flat loci antecedent to measurement amounts to that; they are intended to allow the possibility of measurement, and anything measurable, that is, the character of points, lines, and flat loci, is conditional upon the cosmic epoch we happen to be in. He even said that the continuity in the coordinate division of our own epoch is a contingent affair not necessarily descriptive of other epochs.[4]

Future existence has been rather neglected as a philosophical problem in its own right, and most thinkers have assumed it is like past existence; this is probably because remote future existence is known only by inference, whereas past existence is known by memory, a more familiar kind of knowledge.[5] To be a future existent is to be a possibility in a field of possibilities. That the future is a field means that it puts possibilities together, and there are two senes in which this is true.

In the first sense the possibilities are together with each other as past facts are together with each other. But the character of the togetherness of possibilities differs from that of facts. Whereas facts must be consistently actualized to be systematically together, future possibilities can be contraries and still be together. The possibility of tomorrow's witnessing a sea battle, and the possibility

4. See Whitehead, *Process and Reality*, pt. 4. For the discussion of continuity, see pp. 467–70.

5. Some of the most interesting studies of future time, and those that most influenced the development of the present theory, have been done by Robert S. Brumbaugh. See his "Kinds of Time: An Excursion in First Philosophy," in *Experience, Existence and The Good*, ed. Irwin C. Lieb (Carbondale, Ill.: Southern Illinois University Press, 1961); "Logic and Time," *Review of Metaphysics* 18 (June 1965); and "Applied Metaphysics: Truth and Passing Time," *Review of Metaphysics* 19 (June 1966).

of tomorrow's peace, exist together in the future without conflict.

In the second sense, the future possibilities for everything presently actual exist together. The field of future possibilities is common to all present entities. Entities in the present are united by the fact that they must carve their own futures from a common integrated future. The possibility of interaction depends on the interrelation of possibilities for different present entities.[6]

The integrated character of possibilities in the future and their characters as compatible contraries are no more to be reduced to logical relations than the spatial and temporal characters of the existential field of past existence.

The specific characters of future possibilities come largely from their connection with present existence. Future possibilities are related to present existences as ways for realizing value. Many philosophers would say that common sense interprets possibilities in relation to how they would be as past facts. They say most ordinary people think of possibilities as alternative imaginary *actualized* states of affairs. However, common sense is more complex. In wondering about the future, or in moral deliberation, common people make a coordinate analysis of what it would be like if such and so possibility were realized. More important, however, ordinary people grasp individual future possibilities according to their aesthetic appeal in present experience. Present experience of the future is mediated by knowledge of the past, but it is appreciative before it is structurally analytical, and the analysis generally serves the purposes of appreciating goals more accurately and of calculating how to attain them.

Present existence is not to be in a field but rather to be involved in a process of self-constitution. As such, a presently existent thing is unrelated to other presently existent things and is related only to past and future existences; as Whitehead pointed out, the relation to past and future shared with all other presently existent things allows a kind of mediate relation between contemporaries that he described in terms of presentational immediacy.[7] But there is no existential field of contemporaries.

To exist in the present is to take up the results of the past in

6. Of contemporary philosophers, Paul Weiss has best emphasized the unity of the future and the role this plays in integrating present existence. See his *Modes of Being* (Carbondale, Ill.: Southern Illinois University Press, 1958), pp. 105–20.

7. See Whitehead, *Process and Reality*, pt. 2, chaps. 2 and 4; pt. 4, chap. 4.

prehensions, to sort and grade these according to certain criteria for harmony and to actualize oneself as a concrete unity or prehensions of the past. Depending on how innovative the entity is, novel possibilities of harmony enter its process so that *its* way of uniting the past is unlike anything that happened before and unlike any of its contemporaries. Most of the problems of freedom concern the process of harmonization of the initial data given in prehension so that an actual satisfaction is reached at the end of the present moment. The axiological cosmology follows Whitehead closely here.

The process of actualization is the locus of change, and it gives an order of past and future. All actual entities prehended in a given moment must be past with respect to that moment, and all actual entities that prehend that moment must be future to it; all that neither prehend it nor are prehended by it must be contemporaries of it. That two actual entities are contemporaries of a third does not mean they are contemporaries of each other; one can prehend the other. Therefore, as Whitehead pointed out, we should define a present duration as the set of all actual entities in which each is contemporary with any other; a given present existent may therefore have many present durations in its one moment of self-constitution.[8] The relation of prehension, or causation, which amounts to the same, defines temporal seriality.

Most elements of personal freedom have to do primarily with present existence, where decisions are made. Most elements of social freedom have to do either with the appropriation of past existence or the development of possibilities in future existence. Present existence is involved in taking advantage of the past and future.

The cosmological continuity between the modes of existence lies in present existence. The present existent begins with what is past, incorporates future possibilities, and creates a new finished fact. This process is the reality of present existence. Because the burden of argument at this point is to define the integrity of a personal individual through an extent of time, so that it can be determined what is internal to him and what external, the next task is to examine the doctrine of prehension in the present existent.

8. Ibid., p. 487.

PREHENSION

The problem of the presence of one thing to another cannot be solved, either by a super relation that swallows up the things into a larger whole, or by representations different in existential being from the thing represented. The continental tradition of transcendental philosophy has exhibited the shortcomings of the former approach and the British empirical tradition has boxed its way around in the other. It was Whitehead's great genius to conceive the notion of prehension as an alternative to both impasses.[9] An actual entity is a concrete patterning of prehensions, each one of which is a grasping in a subjective way of the actual and full being of another actual occasion. A prehension is the way one thing grasps another thing—not a representation of that other thing but its very being.

There are two factors that must be discussed in an analysis of prehension: (1) the objectivity of what prehensions prehend and (2) the subjective form of the prehensions.

Each prehension has an object it prehends. The object has a being of its own. In scholastic terminology this is its "subjective reality." If the prehended thing is another momentary existing individual, its subjective reality is what it is as an existential non-discursive individual, realizing harmoniously its own pattern or unity of prehensions. The subjective reality of the thing *as available for prehension by another thing* is its "objective reality."

The objective reality of existing individuals is in a sense *less* than their subjective reality. Subjectively, an existing individual works changes with its initial data. This changing is not prehended or carried into objective reality, but the change made is. The objective reality includes both what the prehended object had given to it and what it added to what was given. The full reality of the prehended object consists both in its existing change as made and in the subjective "working up" of its objective data. The changing, as contrasted with the change, implies the distinction between before and after; it does not denote a passage from earlier to later. Consequently, the changing in itself cannot be said to exist in serial time; present time is not serial. Therefore the changing

9. Whitehead himself gave credit to Francis Bacon. See *Science and the Modern World*, Lowell Lectures, 1925 (New York: Macmillan Co., 1927), pp. 6off.

is the *incomplete* existence of the thing. Since the changing does not itself fully exist, it cannot be prehended as part of the existing object.[10]

Present existence is momentary. It comes in drops. Each moment is an occasion in which objective realities are taken up as initial data, sorted, and worked into a unity satisfying the process of that present moment. The final form the objective realities take in the momentary satisfaction is called their objectification. Having attained satisfaction, the entity in the present moment is itself an object to be prehended by a subsequent present existent, and its objective nature consists in the totality of objectifications of what it initially prehended itself. Even in a discursive individual, a moment of present existence prehends a past moment of the same individual as an objective reality, and its own presence consists in rendering itself an objective reality for the next present moment. In this way, a discursive individual lives moment by moment.

The subjective side of prehension stems from the fact that the objective data prehended must be harmonized together in the individuality of the prehender. Whereas things prehended may have formal realities relatively independent of one another, as objective data in the prehending individual they are internally related elements of that individual's nature. And elements closely connected in the things prehended might be widely separated in their subjective locations in the prehender. The uniqueness of the prehending individual stems both from the uniqueness of the universal character of the pattern or harmony it imposes on the various things that are given it as conditions and from the haecceity of the pattern in the individualizing harmony.

10. Whitehead argued that a present actual entity prehends in its initial data all the actual entities in its world. Most of these are negatively prehended in the subsequent process so as not to achieve final objectification or are given very insignificant positions; even the most complex of final satisfactions is a radical simplification of the infinite complexity of the past. An alternative to this doctrine would be to say that there is selection in the initial data of prehensions. There are two reasons for preferring Whitehead's doctrine, even though it seems contrary to common sense to believe that the totality of the past is prehended. The first is that adequate reasons can be given for eliminating most of the significant past and for the simplification that takes place in a present process; Whitehead did this in Part 3 of *Process and Reality*. Second, Whitehead's is formally the simpler hypothesis; it is simpler to say "all" or "none" rather than "some," since "some" needs a further account in terms of selective principles.

The subjective side of a prehension is its features deriving from its place in the harmony of the prehending individual. A prehension is what it is subjectively according to the modes and ranks of harmonies in which it is involved in the individual's harmony. The harmonies in which a prehension subjectively participates are not necessarily themselves prehended as objective data but may be the prehender's own contribution, deriving from its own principles of selection and organization.

The subjective harmony of prehensions in an individual is important for most topics discussed in subsequent chapters. How the harmony is brought about is important for the concept of decision. The connection of the subjective harmony with harmonies outside the individual is important for the concept of action. The principles determining the form of the harmony are important for the concept of responsibility. And the internal structure of the harmony is important for the theory of value.

This discussion of existing individuals was entered into in order to find a way of distinguishing what is external to man from what is internal. The suggestion was made that the clue lies in the metaphysical distinction of essential and conditional features. At this point it is necessary to say how momentary nondiscursive individuals specify this distinction.

The conditional features of presently existing individuals are the prehensions considered as wholes, with both their objective and subjective sides. This is because the conditional features of a thing must grasp other things in a way characteristic of the appropriating thing, according to the metaphysical hypothesis. The things grasped are the objective realities prehended. The characteristic way they are grasped is the subjective form of the prehensions that prehend them. This is a way of rendering in cosmological terms the metaphysical notion of a conditional feature. The essential features of such individuals, on the other hand, are those factors that determine what the subjective form of the whole harmony of prehensions is. The subjective form is characteristic of the individual because it is determined in part by the selective principles that are the individual's essential features.

Most of the problems of personal freedom have to do with essential features. Before these can be dealt with, however, and before the distinction between the internal and external can be made, the discussion must be broadened from nondiscursive to discursive individuals, such as people.

DISCURSIVE INDIVIDUALS

Merely to be a discursive individual is not to be a person. A person is a unique kind of discursive individual exhibiting organic relations between bodily parts and interrelations with a human physical and social environment. This section will consider the notion of discursive individuals as such, and the next will take up organic ones.

A discursive individual is a temporal nexus of existing entities that has an individual unified developmental harmony exhibiting how any component entity receives essential features from past and future entities in the nexus. To elaborate this characterization, first the notion of "temporal nexus" will be discussed and then the rest of the definition.

"Nexus" is Whitehead's term, and it can be characterized within the present scheme in the following way. A temporal nexus is a set of momentary or nondiscursive individuals so ordered that each prehends one and only one other as its immediate past and is prehended by one and only one other as immediately past for that other. The momentary individuals are arranged contiguously in a linear temporal order. An exception must be made for the first and last members in the series. If a momentary individual prehends two other momentary individuals as immediately past and contemporary to each other, there are two temporal nexuses involved as well as a spatial nexus relating the contemporaries.

If a particular pattern is ingredient in all the individuals in a temporal nexus, and the reason it is in each one is that it has been prehended from the contiguous antecedent in the nexus, then the nexus can be called a "patterned nexus." A temporal nexus can have one pattern characteristic of one of its segments of individuals and other patterns characteristic of other segments. There is no reason why one pattern must continue through the whole nexus, although the whole cannot be called a single patterned nexus unless such a pattern is continuous. The general notion of a nexus is important for a variety of problems to be taken up in the discussion of freedom. A patterned nexus, for instance, is important for understanding a causal chain in which the imprint of the agent is carried to the effect. This is a necessary concept for causal responsibility. Moral responsibility, moreover, requires the ability to plot out alternate nexuses of causation in the process of deliberation, and therefore the *knowledge* of nexuses is important. Furthermore, the complex structure of an organism sufficiently diverse in its functions and integrated in its personality to be a free agent makes the *interrelation* of nexuses an important topic. The prime nexus of a discursive individual, however, is an individual harmony, an haecceity not to be reduced to simpler parts except by being broken up.[11] The problem for the axiological cosmology is to show what is peculiar to the individual harmony of a discursive individual, making it a unique kind of individual harmony.

A unified developmental harmony is a career. It has a fixed past history at any given point. Its future is partially determined and partially undetermined at that point, and the career is in the process of being made somewhat more determinate in that present moment. The career is not a pattern abstracted from the person living it but is the whole personal development itself; there is a distinction between the pattern of the career and the career itself. What makes an individual career possible, in distinction from a chain of slightly altered patterns replacing one another in separate events, is that any presently existing moment contains essentional features derivative from the past and from the future of that individual.

How do essential features derive from the past? An essential feature is a factor determining the way in which the prehensions in an actual entity are to be organized to bring about the satisfaction of the moment. In the moment itself, they function as values to be realized. Those coming from the past are patterns with their own values prehended as objective realities in past actual entities. *All* objective realities prehended are harmonies with their own values, and the labor of the process of unifying prehensions is to find a way of putting all those values together so as to maximize them in some sense. Whereas most objective realities only present values to be integrated, some present values that contribute to the

11. Whitehead could admit that nexuses are particular, but not that they are individuals themselves; for him, the component entities in the nexus are the individuals.

integrating itself. That is, some prehensions entering as conditional features also function as essential features.[12]

How can an objective reality be an essential feature? One might be tempted to say that any objective reality whose value qualifies the whole of the satisfaction of the prehending entity is an essential feature. There are two reasons why this is inadequate. The first is that merely to qualify the whole of a satisfaction is not necessarily to be a matter of subjective form or an essential feature; it is only to be very important for that satisfaction. The second is that many things experienced are important enough to qualify the whole of experience without being part of one's own past self. A profound musical experience is a case in point. According to the considerations in the previous chapter, however, the essential features that derive from the past are supposed to derive from the past states of the discursive individual in question, and in fact to be the mark of whatever past states belong to it.

This last consideration gives a clue to the answer. The essential features from the past are objective realities that make up the discursive individual's past. In fact, they are the essential features, not the conditional features (except insofar as conditional features are also essential), of the past occasions of the individual's experience. As determinants of subjective form in past occasions, they must be objectified to be prehended into the present occasion; but once objectified they function again subjectively, being some of the values directing the present.

Now the *reason* these essential features objectively prehended from the past function essentially in the present moment is that the present moment is part of that discursive individual. There is *no* reason given within the present occasion itself why some objective realities function essentially. It is precisely because a discursive individual is a basic and irreducible reality that its past moments contribute essential features to the present; the present moment of a discursive individual must have such to exist, and no reason for it can be found within the moment prescinding from

12. This is analogous to Whitehead's claim that a peculiar prehension, that of God's conceptual valuation of possibilities appropriate for the occasion, contributes the subjective aim subjectively forming the way in which that and all other initial prehensions are to be integrated.

its place in the discursive individual, the very thing we want to explain.[13]

There are two important kinds of illustrations of essential features coming from the past. The first (which holds only for an organic discursive individual, something not discussed yet) is the inheritance of character, either in a "spiritual" sense or in a physical one. The factors determining a person's behavior—his personal character—are inherited as essential features; so are those that determine his basic bodily constitution. The relative importance of these factors in a given moment depends on circumstance and the other essential features—people sometimes act out of character. This illustration may be misleading, since, for the physical characteristics at least, there is a whole society of discursive individuals in the organic hierarchy of the person, each inheriting essential features from the past and each inheriting a place in the pattern of the society.

The second illustration is on the moral level. The essential factors that commit one to a promise or a contract, to love or hate, or to any decision with a moral dimension, are inherited in a moral way. That is, in whatever sense turns out to be appropriate under further analysis, a person has essential features obliging him to recognize responsibility for what he has done in the past.

The essential features deriving from the future, like those from the past, are basic and irreducible elements of discursive individuals, not to be explained on the basis of a present moment considered in abstraction from the rest of the individual life. There

13. In Whitehead's language, although contrary to his theory, there must be a categoreal obligation that the subjective form of a moment in the life of a discursive individual reflect the determinants of the subjective form of past moments in that life. There would also be an explanatory category to the effect that the members of the temporal nexus of a discursive individual, and only those members, convey in serial order the inheritance of essential determination. Whitehead himself, denying the categoreal primacy of discursive individuals, does have a reason why one of the objective realities, that is, God's conceptual valuation, functions essentially to determine subjective form; the value in it is greater and is felt as a greater lure than the values of anything else physically prehended. The axiological cosmology has no reason to say that the objective realities of the past life of a discursive individual are more valuable than other values that might enter in. The problem of adjudicating the essential features coming from the three sources is one yet to be conjured with in chapter 5. On the complex level of human life it is the problem of decision itself.

are two senses in which essential features enter from the future. The primary sense is that they enter through obligations relative to a present decision. The essential features from the future are elements that will figure essentially in determining future acts of harmonization, or decisions. So in the first sense, relative to *this* present decision rather than *that, this* future possibility will be obligatory rather than *that*. Part of the worth of choosing this alternative rather than that depends on what future obligations it entails.

The secondary sense in which essential features enter from the future is that, relative to past objective realities given certain objectification in a present moment, certain future possibilities are goods rather than evils. Put in human terms, if a person takes up *this* stance toward some past condition rather than *that,* then *these* possibilities will be good and *those* bad, relatively speaking. Considered separately, the essential features that enter in the primary sense involve categorical imperatives, those in the secondary sense hypothetical. In the process of integrating prehensions, these two senses are brought to unity so that once the decisive elements in the process are reached for the stance toward the past and the orientation toward the future, there are only categorical obligations.

Essential features deriving within the present moment itself are spontaneous values that affect the process of harmonization. They are not objectified in prehension until a subsequent moment prehends their effects. Within the process of events from one moment to another, such essential features might be only adventitious and therefore of little interest to most senses of personal and social freedom. Yet in moments of important human decision, these precisely are the decisive features.

It was said in chapter 2 that the axiological cosmology ought to be able to give a genetic as well as a coordinate analysis of a discursive individual. The specification of that sense now will bring the discussion up to date regarding the distinction between what is inside and what is outside a discursive individual.

A genetic division is an analysis of a moment that begins with initial data; sorts, arranges, and evaluates the data; and finishes with a concrete harmony or satisfaction, the depth of which being a measure of the contrasting data harmonized. This is an analysis of the work of the essential features operative in the moment reducing the initial data to the satisfaction with the unique subjective form of that particular occasion. By extension, the genetic division of a discursive individual is the analysis of the development of essential features *through* the series of moments. The essential features of a relatively early moment in life function essentially in a middling moment; that middling moment has other essential features deriving from the future and from the moment itself. All those essential features may function in a relatively later moment, and so on. A genetic analysis of a discursive individual, containing past, present, and future moments of experience, is an analysis of the development of the essential features through the whole life; that analysis would have as its units the individual moments (or at least the important ones), but its form would be to treat the moments as phases in the development of the lifelong complex career of the individual. A genetic analysis would amount to a description of the individual's norms or values and how they are decisive through its life.

A coordinate analysis of a discursive individual would depict its development through the series of satisfactions the nondiscursive components would have. In the satisfactions all the rest of the world, relative to the moment of each satisfaction, would be objectified. Therefore, a coordinate division would show only how the whole world is evaluated in each moment, and how that evaluation develops through the whole life. The only way by which it would mark the essential features of the individual in contrast to the world would be by noting empirical regularities of structure. There need be no irreducible discursive individuals for natural science.

The genetic analysis of a discursive individual must note both essential and conditional features. Neither is determinate without the other. The essential features are determinate only in ordering the conditional prehensions in each moment, and those developing through the history of the individual and the world with which it interacts. The conditional features—the prehensions—cannot exist in a momentary individual or in an occasion of experience except as together, and their togetherness or order is a matter of essential features.

It is now possible to specify what is internal to a discursive individual and what is external. Internal are the conditional and essential features of actual entities that contribute essential features *as essential* to past or future entities in the temporal nexus of the individual. External are all the actual entities, and nexuses of actual entities, that condition members of the discursive individual's temporal nexus but that do not contribute essential features functioning essentially in its moments of present existence.

It should be noted that this distinction between internality and externality is not yet appropriate to be applied to human beings. Human beings are organisms containing societies of discursive individuals, and some sense must be given for internality to the society.

Organisms and Persons

A human being is a live, intentionally directed, bodily organism, and his organism contains many suborganisms with quasi-independence from the intentional direction of the whole. His limits are obviously flexible and do change. A human being is a society of occasions set in a larger society of the human environment.[14] In the human society are organic and inorganic societies, and many nexuses, living and nonliving, that are not themselves societies. A society is a set of actual occasions with a defining characteristic of the set exhibited by each of the occasions, such that the reason the defining characteristic is in each occasion is that the relationships of the society promote its being there. A society is, therefore, its own reason for being and provides its own stability. A human being is a society of subordinate societies.

In many societies some nexuses are more important than others for determining the defining characteristic of the whole, and they are more important by reason of the greater intensity of experience they afford. A complex society such as a human being is organized so that the lines of inheritance of intense experience tend to converge to a controlling point, probably the brain; as a result brain events seem to be the most intense of any in the body. Intensity of experience is also a matter of life, that is, of an occasion's capacity to originate novelty to attain intensity greater than that inherited. The greatest kind of intensity in a human being seems to be a nexus of brain events, such that each (a) prehends

14. See Whitehead, *Process and Reality*, pt. 2, chap. 3.

from its predecessor in the nexus its *conceptual* activity, (b) prehends the intensities of other bodily organs as conveyed through the nerves, and (c) has a great capacity for novelty. The personal life of a human being is this nexus of events jumping from one part of the brain to another and connected by the prehension of the *conceptual prehensions* of their antecedents.[15]

Along with William James, Whitehead knew to emphasize that the kind of human experience of which we can be conscious is characterized by the "withness of the body." Objects experienced always bear the stamp of the bodily route by which their characters were transferred from their own subjectivity to the brain of the experiencer.[16] Although every occasion prehends every past occasion directly, when the brain prehends the chair entity and also the retina-imaging-the-chair-entity, the latter is more complex and is given more importance in the brain occasion. It may be that in our epoch, although there is direct prehension of every past event among the initial data, only prehensions of contiguous or nearly contiguous events reach objectification in the final satisfaction.

What is the reason for saying that a person's foot is more a part of him than his hat? It is much farther from his brain. The only argument is that his foot has tighter social connection with the brain. Both hats and feet can be removed without destroying the brain. To resolve this, the axiological cosmology must say the following.

The proper model—perhaps "metaphor" is the better term at this stage—is that of a discursive individual, each of whose present existences is at the top of a hierarchy of other present existences. The contained existences may themselves be members of discursive individuals that maintain a constant relation to the hierarchy dominated by the personal discursive individual. Some of the contents of the hierarchy (called a personal hierarchy) are merely ter-

15. In Whitehead's terminology, the initial data in an occasion are physically prehended, and conceptual prehensions have as objects not physical things, but eternal objects that have been abstracted from physical things or gained through conceptual reversion. The conceptual prehensions determine the novelty that can be introduced over and above the initial data of physical prehensions. A hybrid physical prehension is the physical prehension among initial data of the conceptual prehensions of a prehended object.

16. Whitehead, *Process and Reality*, pp. 474–83.

mini of causal nexuses originating outside any hierarchy determined by a member of the personal discursive individual; an example would be food being digested.

A human being, on this model, would be a changing, temporally developing hierarchy of actual entities, including discursive individuals arranged in various ways. The personal discursive harmony at the top depends on the maintenance and development of various elements within the hierarchy, on various rhythms of activities. Were the hierarchy to break down, or not develop in the right way, the personal discursive harmony would cease to exist.

Any existent member of the personal discursive individual prehends three kinds of antecedents: those of its own past, those of the various components of its hierarchy other than itself, and those outside the body altogether. From this it follows that at any given present moment, the contained hierarchy is not then presently existent, but past. The elements in the hierarchy contemporary with the given present existent of the personal discursive individual are components of the immediately future member of the personal discursive individual. In this sense, the members of the developing hierarchy of the person do not have to be exactly in phase—a person can at once feel appreciation for a whole dinner, not just for the last bite. The physical ingestion of dinner, a component in his present personal experience, is not a matter of even a contiguous flow of bites and secretions but rather is punctuated by conversation and other interruptions. Insofar as a person's physical and social environment is constant, the enduring elements in his developing hierarchy are important. Insofar as the environment changes, the flexibility of the hierarchy to support its personal discursive individuality in a variety of different ways is important.

An organic individual can be said to include its hierarchy as proper parts of itself, whereas it cannot be said to include, except in unusual senses, things outside its hierarchy. The distinction is this. The hierarchy and only the hierarchy includes all those conditions necessary for the mutual contribution of essential features that characterize the continuity of the personal discursive individual. The experience of the personal discursive harmony can be defined as those actual entities prehended in any present moment of the personal individual. Entities prehended that are not necessary to the continuity of the discursive individual, however important they might be for its experiences (such as the musical experience cited above), are not proper parts of the organism. They might be inside the skin, but they are external to the person.

This model can be illustrated to distinguish what is internal from what is external. The inheritance of those essential features from the past within the personal discursive individual having to do with *physical* characteristics require sustenance of physical elements in the hierarchy. The brain needs food, so the stomach must digest, the blood must carry the oxygen, and so forth. The continuity of intention of physical purpose in the personal discursive harmony requires that the body act. A foot may be cut off, interrupting the continuity of intentional action; the personal discursive individual in a person, however, is very adaptive and is likely to find some other way of getting around; the loss of a foot is not likely to affect the physical inheritance within the personal discursive individual. The loss of a heart, unless it is replaced, does eliminate the possibility of inheritance of essential features from the past; so would loss of certain nerves and other vital organs. The loss in these cases is not so much the organs themselves but their structural contribution to the personal discursive individual at the top of the hierarchy.[17] Man-made substitute organs can be used if they make the same contribution, and they become part of the organic individual precisely to the extent that they contribute to the continuity of the personal discursive individual at the top of its hierarchy by way of making its derivation of essential features from past and future possible. Death occurs when the physical character of certain elements in the hierarchy is such as not to provide vital contributions to the personal discursive individual. The death of an organism is progressive in the sense that the noncontribution of one element in the hierarchy, although not directly affecting the personal discursive individual, causes another to become noncontributive, and so forth; death can be arrested anywhere along the way to the personal discursive hierarchy.

A physical analysis of the whole hierarchy of a person, i.e., his

17. Whitehead correctly noted that the "variety sought" for intensity of experience "is the variety of structures, and never the variety of individuals" (ibid., p. 485).

body, is a matter of coordinate division; as such it is difficult to locate those entities that constitute the personal discursive individual, since their mark consists in essential features not available to coordinate division. The best we can do is to find those organs that make moral decisions, since the essential features are most distinctively operative there. Physical analysis does tell us, however, that the personal discursive individual is associated with the brain and central nervous system; a person can be revived with the resuscitation of most bodily systems except the nervous, and even parts of the nervous system, when no longer functioning, can be restored and the person can be revived. But sufficient damage to certain parts of the brain, even if the body continues to function, means the end of the person, and an organism of lesser complexity is left.

Much of the continuity of essential features in the personal discursive individual is a matter of conceptual prehensions, not physical character. This includes both conceptual prehensions inherited from the past and those derived from future possibilities. Elements that sustain *this* kind of derivation of essential features are not only physical but social. Schools teach people how to remember, abstract, and anticipate. The social dimension of the human personality is just as much a matter of essential features as any other dimension. Therefore, the person contains in his organic hierarchy those social factors necessary for his own continuity, the social institutions, personal relationships, cultural heritage, and so forth. The fact that these elements are part of a person is essentially the basis of personal rights. But the fact that the same factors are proper parts of several people constitutes the heart of social problems. Put generally, not only a person's body and isolated physical actions are part of him, but also his social *interactions*. The sense in which social matters are included in or are necessary parts of a person's continuity will be discussed at length in chapter 10.

The continuity of a personal discursive individual is not sameness of character. Rather, precisely because the individual at a present moment derives essential features from the present, and the present involves changing conditions, continuity means an appropriate change of character. The axiological scheme provides a continuity that consists in appropriate changes, not a substratum underlying changes or a fixed form that is merely reiterated. As befits an axiology, the continuity of a personal discursive individual is more like moral continuity than physical endurance.

External Liberties

The distinctions drawn between an organic individual, with the personal discursive individual and the hierarchy defined by it, and its external environment can be used to characterize external liberties generally. *An external liberty is an opportunity in the environment of a person for the maintenance, provision, or exercise of human functions that affect the personal discursive individual.* Although the external opportunities are for things that *affect* the personal discursive individual in the person, they need not be necessary for its continuity through the mutual interchange of essential features; in fact, if factors are necessary in a strict sense then they are proper parts of the person, and only seemingly in the external environment. Most of the conditional features that are to be integrated into the hierarchy of a person's development stem from causal nexuses entering from external sources, that is, sources not necessary for the maintenance of personal continuity. The opportunities to maintain, provide for, or exercise these conditional features of the person are external liberties.

Among the most important kind of external liberties are social ones, in the common sense of "social." A social external liberty is one provided by the shared interaction of many people. Most social external liberties are in fact opportunities for shared interaction. The discussion of dimensions of social freedom in Part 3 deals at length with the internal and external aspects of social freedom, that is, the freedom of interaction.

5

Intentional Action

This chapter and the one to follow concern themselves generally with the problems of free agency, or personal voluntary action. These problems are connected and together are somewhat distinct both from the problems of external liberty discussed previously and from the problems of standards for choice, criticism, deliberation, and so forth to be discussed later.

The problems of free agency can be focused in two ways. The first way, the one undertaken in this chapter, is to ask whether and how a person's will can be effective in the world, given external liberty. The second way, to be undertaken in chapter 6, is to ask whether the will's action is determined by antecedent conditions that do not allow for personal responsibility, or whether it is determined by some mechanism that involves free choice between alternatives.

In experience we distinguish between "events" that happen and "actions" performed by personal agents. Most interesting events have actions in them, and most personal actions have events of nonpersonal elements; but there is a practical distinction between the two.

In experience we also distinguish between voluntary and involuntary actions. Some involuntary actions are really much the same as events, for instance a leg kicking because the knee is struck with a hammer; the fact that the leg can also kick voluntarily leads us to call all kickings actions when in fact the involuntary ones are nonpersonal events. But other involuntary actions are not like events. Of some we say that, although in fact the action was involuntary, the person should have acted voluntarily in the situation, perhaps by performing some alternative action which he could have if only he had prepared himself properly. Discipline gives a person control over situations in which otherwise his action would be involuntary. Of yet other kinds of involuntary actions we say that, although what the person did was involuntary, the reason was that some external force or impediment made him do what he did and prevented him from doing something that would have been voluntary. There are degrees of this external control: it is extreme when an overpoweringly strong man uses your fist to beat your wife against your will; it is less extreme when he uses the threat of beating your wife to force you to rob a bank. It may be said in the last instance that you voluntarily choose to rob the bank as the best alternative of a poor lot. But there is a sense in which you have no choice, since allowing our wife to be beaten is never a live option for you.

At any rate, it is fair to say that all the kinds of involuntary actions, to the extent that they are involuntary actions, are not what Austin Farrer calls "healthy" actions.[1] Either there is too much of the nonpersonal character of events mixed with them, or they are degenerate or diseased cases of properly voluntary actions. It is an experiential truth that a person acts with genuine humanity only when he is acting voluntarily.

The crucial relevant question in the history of philosophy has been, How are voluntary actions distinguished from nonvoluntary actions and events? As Farrer has pointed out, one of the standard strategies for dealing with this question is to distinguish voluntary processes from involuntary ones by distinguishing between kinds of causes.[2] Something like the following argument is made. Events and involuntary actions are caused by antecedent states of affairs determined themselves by antecedent states in a mechanical chain indefinitely antedating the person. In other words, events and involuntary actions are not determined by any peculiarly personal causes. On the other hand, voluntary actions are voluntary precisely because they are caused by the will of persons. An action is voluntary because it is the result of an act of will. So runs the argument.

There is something obviously true about this kind of argument.

1. See Austin Farrer, *The Freedom of the Will*, Gifford Lectures, 1957 (New York: Charles Scribner's Sons, 1958), chap. 6. This chapter is an excellent discussion of many of the points raised in the text.
2. Ibid.

But giving it a proper philosophical interpretation has led to the development of a theory of will as a faculty of person's nature prior to actions that can cause happenings as well as but in a different manner from the way natural causes produce happenings. The distinction between faculties presupposed here is that between the faculty of willing and the faculty of acting as a result of will. The latter is said to be free because it is caused by the former instead of by natural causes.

The difficulties with this distinction between will and action are notorious, and they were pointed out conclusively by Jonathan Edwards more than two centuries ago.[3] Both overt action and willing-to-act are acts. If an overt action is free when and because it is caused by an act of will rather than by a nonpersonal natural cause, what about the act of will itself? Either the act of will is free, or it is a natural event determined by a chain of events stemming from prepersonal states of affairs; in the latter case it would seem to make no sense to call the person responsible, but rather those long past events the make him choose as he does. To distinguish personal from nonpersonal causes is of no help in distinguishing voluntary from involuntary actions and events if the personal causes behave and are determined exactly as nonpersonal ones. So it would seem that the act of will itself must be said to be free, and this is the basis of the term "free will."

But in what sense can the act of will be said to be free? Certainly it is not free in the way actions were said to be: it does not have a personal as opposed to a nonpersonal cause, itself free in some new sense, since this would give rise to an infinite regress. If an action is free because it was freely willed, and the will was free because it in turn was freely willed, and that free willing was free in turn because there was an even prior free act of will, then it would be impossible ever to go from a nonfree to a free process of action. But surely our embryonic protoplasm is not free. We come to be free. Since an infinite regress of this sort (that is, one empirically false as well as logically contradictory) is absurd, an act of will cannot be called free in the same sense in which an action is called free.

The absurdity arising from the claim that an act of will is free

3. Jonathan Edwards, *Freedom of the Will*, ed. Paul Ramsey (New Haven, Conn.: Yale University Press, 1957).

if it is freely caused can be circumvented, perhaps, by altering the view of causation within the soul. It is necessary for an action to have a cause because an uncaused action would be utterly irresponsible. It would be impossible to hold anyone to account or give anyone credit. But perhaps it is not necessary to say every act of will is caused by a prior act of will. Although our actions in the overt sense are ours because we cause them, our mental acts are ours, not because we *cause* them, but because we *are* them (so the suggestion runs). Suppose then that the act of will is spontaneous and is not derived from a prior cause, either free or unfree. Free will in this sense is free because it is uncaused, or at least is *sui generis*.

The difficulty now arises that free will is arbitrary and has no reasons. Surely nature, however nonpersonal, has at least some rational regularity. Absolute whimsy is as far from being a mode of personal existence as mechanical nature. No one really wants to maintain absolute spontaneity for acts of will (although Sartre comes close).

If the only accounts that can be given for how an act of will is free are the disguised mechanistic view of saying that each free act is caused by a prior free act, and the total irrationalistic view that each act of will has no causal connection with antecedently entertained reasons, then the doctrine of free will is in trouble. At this point Edwards thought the wisest course to be the denial of any distinction of kind between overt actions and acts of will. His own view of action was deterministic, and he felt free to deny the freedom of the will, as that position had been argued before him.[4] An act of will for Edwards is an act of choosing, and it can be said to be free only in the sense that it has a real choice open to it. This amounts to limiting freedom to external liberty: a choice is free when nothing will impede it. Choice determines action, and choice itself is determined by prior causes, motives. Why the particular motives operate to determine the exact course of human action must be answered, in Edwards's view, by refer-

4. We must not suppose his determinism to be a naïve one, however. The motive determining the will is always something appreciated by the mind, a moral as opposed to natural cause; he also denied the faculty psychology distinction between will and understanding. See ibid., pp. 141ff and *passim;* also Edwards's *Religious Affections*, ed. John E. Smith (New Haven, Conn.: Yale University Press, 1959), pp. 96–101.

ence to the creator who occasions the whole causal process of nature.

The traditional difficulty with the type of solution Edwards chose is that the responsibility for effects is naturally to be referred down the line of antecedent causes until the relevant factors are temporally prior to any personal elements. Whether this traditional difficulty is well founded is a topic to be discussed in the following chapter.

An action is voluntary when it is personal. But the action extends far beyond the person into the future. Consequently it is necessary and problematic to account for how action arises within a person and extends to far-reaching consequences. It is at the point of the origin of the action within the person that the truth of the freedom-versus-free-will dispute is to be discovered. This chapter deals with the point of origin and its connection with nature, and chapter 6 deals with the question of whether it is a free origin.

Both action and choice require a detailed model of human agency. The focal question for the rest of the chapter is how a personal individual can effect a result external to him. The answer to be given is that he does so by actualizing the antecedent conditions for general laws that then operate to bring about the desired effect. The discussion will deal first with the problem of general laws and then with setting them in motion.

CAUSATION

By a natural law is meant a law of nature that governs behavior in individuals and groups. Natural laws are what Peirce called "real generals." This is to say, they are operative on any existing individuals and groups having certain universal characteristics referred to in the natural laws. To say they exist is to say that they have real effects on individuals and groups, effects that would not exist without the laws. Natural laws are at least partially determinate and hence are a sort of harmonious determination. But the sort of harmony is not that of individuals; nor is it that of the universals that are properties of individuals or groups. The peculiar harmony of natural laws must be understood in its own right; it is not reducible to some other kind of harmony.

The standard philosophical attack on the existential reality of general laws stems from the fact that it is very difficult to find the force or power or bruteness of a general law, especially in theories of experience claiming the only experiential data to be singular images. It is usually thought that only individuals have power or force because it is hard to *imagine* how something general could locate a force anywhere particular.

Furthermore, it seems easy to account for laws on a purely abstractionist basis, to say they are creations of the human mind concocted to handle similarities in observed particulars. The only concrete individual who is continuous from one occurrence of a law to another to yet another, so that the regularity could be marked sufficiently to say it is a general *law* that is operative, is the cognizing human being. Therefore, it is a natural suggestion that the only locus of the law or regularity is in the mind of the knowing subject.

There is a fatal objection to this subjectivizing of natural law, however. The cumulative experience of many kinds, not just scientific, testifies that there are indeed regularities in the observed processes of nature (no one could deny this). How can the regularity be accounted for without saying that there is something in the nature of the things, not just in the mind, that makes them behave in regular fashion? To say there is regularity only in mind is to appeal to constant miracle in nature! The only grounds for saying anything in nature is real stem from what experience forces us to acknowledge. It would require a fantastically complicated and implausible hypothesis about the nature of mind to say it constantly sees regularities in the nature that have no ground in nature itself. Of course, if nature appeared to be more random, then we would say that it appears to have less general law; but nature appears quite well regularized.

The existential reality of a law of nature is a condition of a society of individuals such that the *objective* occurrence of a certain pattern A of universals is subjectively prehended and objectified in a certain pattern B. The proposition expressing the law is, "In the society, if A then B." The extent of the society of which physical laws of nature are conditions seems to include all occasions we can perceive on the micro- and macroscopic level. However, Whitehead warned, significantly, that the general physical characteristics of our epoch may be limited to our epoch, albeit that the epoch is incredibly long. The scientific revolution from Newtonian to Einsteinian mechanics marks the fact that the limited society from which Newton generalized is but an abstract part of the larger society and can be understood in terms of the conditions of the larger society. The extent of the society of which social laws or cultural regularities are conditions seems to be much more limited. Some anthropologists say that every basic culture has its own behavior patterns as conditions, and that such laws are radically relative. Structural anthropologists, following the lead of Lèvi-Strauss, suggest that there are certain conditions applying to all societies of people that merely manifest themselves in different ways in different cultures.[5] The extent of the relevant society for a given condition is entirely an empirical matter.

The *reason* pattern A is followed by pattern B lies in the overall constitution of the relevant society. The society is so constituted that the mutual support its various members give one another is such that B is the best way of objectifying A, as assessed by B's events. Any event in which A is prehended also involves the prehension of all the other past entities. The interrelated constitution of the society is such that the prehension of A plus everything else is best objectified as B. B might be nearly identical with A, in which case the law is one of near reiteration; in this extreme the society is such that in the prehension of A nothing else prehended is of importance for objectification. Most natural laws involve A's being prehended in a way that makes B different from it.

The "subjects" of A and B can be singular or plural. A could be the objectification of the pattern of a single individual momentary existent, or it could be a pattern, various parts of which are the objectifications of several individuals. The same is true of B. Since the objectified patterns are a matter of finished fact, not of subjective process, the individuals exist together in a field, and the pattern may characterize a whole field of individuals. This means that the regularity in laws of nature, the regularity in which A is followed by B, is properly the subject matter of empirical analysis. Coordinate division is the study of the internal constitution and external relationships of individual satisfactions or objectifications,

---

5. See Claude Lèvi-Strauss's *Structural Anthropology*, trans. Claire Jacobson and Brooke Grundfest Schoepf (Garden City, N.Y.: Doubleday, Anchor Books, 1967), chaps. 2, 8, and 11.

and it may determine what regularities there are. Since coordinate division prescinds from the genetic development of individual present existences, it does not ask how or why the regularities are as they are; it is not concerned with why B is the best way to objectify A. Scientific analysis therefore can ignore the philosophical question of whether laws are mere regularities or whether there are some underlying hidden connections.

As a determinate thing, a law of nature is a harmony. It is a harmony of a society such that the occurrence of a certain objectified pattern is itself objectified in a certain pattern. The essence of a natural law, its essential feature or features, is the relative value obtained in the B pattern. The ultimate reason for the B pattern is that it is the best pattern for objectifying the initial objective reality, A, as determined in the B event. It is important to note that the essential feature is a *relative* value. B is the best objectification of A in the relevant society, and as determined by B. The society is a complex conditional feature in the law that allows A to have a regular most valuable objectification. Many patterns are best objectified in different ways in different circumstances, and the response to them may not be relevantly ruled by law. That B determines what is best is not important unless B has free choice, in which case it is very important.

A law of nature is general. It is a general condition of the society that, if A then B. Now the society is composed of individuals, and so is the occurrence of the pattern A, and so would be the occurrence of B. Whence the generality? On one level, it is sufficient to say that the patterns occurring are universal and that the society provides a universal condition because its individual members exemplify universal relations. But the deeper question is how the universals become instantiated in the first place, and how the individuals, the brute facts, can be regulated by mere universals that are not exemplified in brute fact until the regulation has taken place. The question is how something other than a concrete individual can be *normative* for such individuals, imposing regularity.

The answer is that a value is universally normative wherever it is relevant. Given any objective pattern that must be objectified somehow, the best way of objectifying it is what it is no matter how many different subjective processes the objective pattern might be involved in. It makes no sense to say that the best way of objectifying A is B one time and C another, assuming that there are no other relevant factors. The value theory in the axiological cosmology explains why this makes no sense. For a natural law, the society guarantees that there be no other important factors than A and the other objective realities that regularly occur with A; given this social guarantee, the value of B is universally normative for objectifying A. To the extent that the society does not provide the guarantee, or allows occasional lapses where other factors might become important, the law is not absolutely general. This would be the case where the society supports some events of free choice.

The brute forcefulness of a law's normative power, the "long arm of the sheriff," as Peirce called it, lies in existence. In a present moment, an individual prehending A in the relevant society must objectifying it in the best way possible; and if the society does have the condition of the natural law, this way must be B. This is the very nature of present existence: to actualize future potentialities so as to make the best of the prehended past. Whereas the patterns themselves exist only objectively, in past or in future, their normative status brutely governs the process of present existence. The essential features of an individual responding to a prehended pattern according to law must be such as to tolerate the society's provision of factors that make B the best objectification of A. In the case of complex individuals like men, however, the essential features often can make many things besides general social conditions important for behavior and thus allow free choice.

It is often said that laws apply only statistically. This may be accounted for in two basic ways. The first is that the society does not always guarantee the constancy of conditions accompanying A that make B the best objectification. The constancy in society is itself a matter of law, and it is an empirical matter to determine just how much constancy there is. The second is that the prehending individual has its own essential features and may give the socially regular factors a second place to possibilities of its own invention or to prehended entities that are not members of the society. The second reason for the statistical application of law is the more interesting for personal freedom.

Another interpretation of the statistical nature of law's force is that regularities are characteristic of aggregates ,and that laws do not apply to individuals in the aggregate individually. There are two accounts to be given of this. The first is that the aggregate forms a subsociety within the larger law-conditioned society; the relations of members of the subsociety compose a social quality of the whole such that the natural regularity is between some antecedent pattern A and a pattern of the quality of the subsociety. Yet the subsociety is such that there is not a complete determination of the particular contribution of each member to the social quality as a whole; the subsociety only establishes the condition that such and such a proportion of its members do this or that. The production of the B pattern in the quality of the subsociety must be done by members of that society; but there is no determinate relation between the pattern A and the particular members of the subsociety that give the whole subsociety the quality B.

The second account is that, although all members of the aggregate prehend A, not all give it the same importance; B is the pattern resulting from the overall summing up of the ways the members of the aggregate respond. This is like the second account of the first interpretation of statistical law in saying the society does not provide the only objective realities to be taken into account, or the only essential features. If A is for the most part important, then a regular effect might exist that is not a mere summing up of different objectifications; rather there is a limit to how much an individual can ignore, and thereby deviate from, the task of best objectifying A.

The problem of laws of nature was raised because it was claimed that people must use general characteristics of their natural and social environment to effect their intentions. The theory provided now accounts for how causation can be sequential, moving from one present moment to the next, and general, applicable to any occurrence of a certain pattern in the relevant society. The theory of laws of nature has been connected with the model of prehensive occasions. The task now is to elaborate how an individual can set in motion the power of natural law so as to accomplish his intention. That is, how does a person act willfully?

WILL

Will is the intentionally directed ordering in a present moment of the relevant constituent features of a personal discursive individual to produce the pattern that subsequent occasions, according to the general laws of nature, will objectify in the way intended.

Although will includes the whole action *intentionally,* its *actual* constitution is limited to the internal structuring and restructuring of the individual in ways that bring about the effect by the power of the natural laws whose objective conditions they are. Thus will can properly be said to be the beginning of action, not the whole action, and it is limited to the agent's being in the action. This is a happy consequence. Some theories, like Hume's, completely separate will in its intentional identity from overt and public action, with the result that voluntary action is always a miracle. Other theories, like the existentialists', make will and action so perfectly coextensive that action is completely identified with the agent and is not public; the public appearance of the action cannot, on those views, be called personal action but is handed over to the nonpersonal order of physical science. There must be an integral connection between the intentionally private aspects of will and the overt and public deeds expressing it.

Action is a process taking some time. Although will is not coextensive with the whole action, it too may be involved throughout the whole process. A brief self-structuring of the person's constituents can produce effects through laws of nature, but an agent has more control over the effects if he remains in the situation, continually producing more effects to modify his earlier efforts, coping with unexpected obstacles and interventions. This is obviously the case where action involves personal responses with other agents. There is continual adjustment, not only of the intention that develops as possibilities are closed or opened, but also of the means used to accomplish the intention.

Despite the fact that willing is a process interplaying with the process of events in which action takes place, all change comes through present existence, that is, in the succession of present moments. The intentionally directed ordering of the relevant constituent harmonies in the individual must be done on a moment-to-moment basis, and the intentional principles directing the ordering must be brought to bear on that momentary existence. Therefore it is important to be quite clear about the way will works in the moment. The first step is to humanize the cosmological model.

The conditional features ordered in a present existent are prehensions, harmonies of subjective form and objective data, the latter being in turn harmonies of prehensions of previous occasions. What modes of harmonies are relevant for will? There are three especially relevant kinds.

First are those embodying the continuing or inherited character of the person from moment to moment. Some of the obvious modes here are organic discursive ones, for instance hands, feet, muscular habits. Just as important are those structuring the person's identity in subtler ways, exercising their effect on his decisions rather than on his bodily movements—his sense of identity with a family or class or race, his educational background, his funded experience, and the integrated workings of his emotions, rational deliberation, enjoyments, and so forth as they bear upon his exercises of will in a given limited context. Many of these modes are themselves the result of previous exercises of will.

The second class of relevant modes of harmony are those that put the person in touch with the immediate situation in which he has to act. Most obvious are the bodily modes connecting him with other bodies in the existential field. Less obvious but usually just as important are the more cognitive modes of connection allowing for identification of the factors in the situation, prediction of how they will behave, and so forth. The importance of semantic modes cannot be minimized.

The third class are those that anticipate the future in some way. There are modes of harmony whose present being is structured around fulfilling future needs, for instance, cells and organisms whose activity is to digest. Bodily systems with a drawn-out cycle of activity, like that of a person's whole digestive apparatus, are important for their orientation toward future repetition. More important for freedom than bodily future orientations are those modes having to do with personal, social, and cultural ambitions. These are very general modes of harmony, and they function in their effects on more specialized activities, for instance, finishing a job for the day, making up with an alienated friend, doing something excellently for no reason other than the excellence.

Certain modes of harmony are characteristic of human beings and nearly always have a large degree of importance in the exercise of will. Most modes function in any or all three classes or relevance mentioned above. Four modes will be singled out for special comment here.

Bodily modes are nearly always important because all existential connection involves the body directly or indirectly. When action is continuous in a fairly close physical context, the bodily organs usually associated with a human being are important, that is, the hands, feet, the sensitive and expressive organs of the head, and so forth. In personal communication the gestures and movements of the body are themselves relevant in a significatory way. In unusual situations other bodily functions become important. The genetic structure of a couple is important when they have children. With the new devices the army has for detecting ammonia many hundreds of yards away, it is important to enemy soldiers not to perspire.

A plurality of emotions is nearly always important in will. A person who can "will one thing" is not necessarily one who has purged his life of emotions but rather one who has organized his emotions in an order that serves his intentions. This means subordinating some and elevating others in a hierarchy of emotions. Furthermore, it seems good cracker-barrel advice for a person to arrange his life so that all emotions of intrinsic importance get their day of supremacy; this cannot be done completely, of course, but surely the brittle discipline of the person who has always the same emotional priorities ought to be avoided.

Excepting perhaps only those acts of will directed at changing inner habits, the particular involvements of a person are important for his exercise of will. A person is always at some particular place and time of particular importance to somebody, involved in the activities of a whole situation. He always is playing a variety of roles in his various societies, and although he may not be active in them all the time, they may be important. Since most significant human voluntary action involves other people, interpersonal involvements are usually important. Even if the will's intention is to act on an event not due for some time, what the agent does now to shape that future event depends on how he is involved in the particularities of the situation.

No analysis of an operation of will would miss the cognitive elements. As mentioned before, the semantic modes of harmony constitute too great a problem to be investigated profitably with the present categories. But it is possible to note several cognitive functions that must be integrated or ordered by the will as it disposes the agent to effect his intention through the laws of nature.

First and perhaps most important quantitatively is memory. What the agent remembers supplies not only the raw terms for his reasoning, but also the facts and guiding principles forming his assessment of a situation. His character, insofar as it functions explicitly as a cognitive element, comes through memory. This is the conscious element in the inheritance of conceptual prehensions characteristic of a personal discursive individual.

Second, the cognitive grasp of the agent's situation must be taken into account. Physical feels and existential connections are important particular involvements, but the subtlety of cognitive analysis of the situation is required to mediate between preconscious contact with things and the highly reflected terms in which intentions are cast. Intentions point to their ends in terms of the media reason discovers in the various intervening situations.

Third, cognitive anticipations of the future are of utmost importance, for the intention that lies at the basis of will is anticipatory. Not only the goal intended but the means involved in the intention profit from intellectual articulation, and this articulation is predictive.

It is important to note that the constituent features may function in a dual way in the structuring of the agent in voluntary action. On the one hand they are conditional features relating the agent to other things and his own parts to each other. On the other hand they may (or they may not) function as essential features determining the structure of the subjective form of all components prehended. So, for instance, an emotion may not only have its place that must be taken into account, it may also be the ordering feature that determines in part why it and other features have the places they do. More interestingly, the contributions of intellect may function not only as ideas and reasonings to be given a place but as principles for structuring the whole. As will be argued in chapter 7, men have the cognitive power to figure out what is objectively worthwhile in certain limited respects; and to reflect the objective worth of things in their active dealings with those things is the aim of morality as well as a condition of complete freedom.

In summary, we have taken note of certain modes of harmony

relevant to the formation of the will's intention: those dealing with inheritance from the past, those relating to the immediate situation, and those anticipating of the future. The principle here, of course, is the distinction of existence into past, present, and future modes. Of the kinds of relevant harmony, some are nearly always important, of which we noted four: those having to do with body, emotions, involvements, and cognition. Each of these can be important in all three modes of relevance. This was spelled out in terms of cognition, which involves memory of the past, understanding of the present situation, and conscious anticipations of the future.

The next step to clarifying how will works in a present moment is to focus on the question of intentionality.

INTENTIONALITY

To be an agent means to be able to act intentionally. To act intentionally means to act on purpose. And purposive behavior takes place not only in the overt public domain but also in thought. One of the great insights of the pragmatists was that all thought is intentional in the sense of being logically and psychologically related to a purpose. To act on purpose is a highly complex mode of harmony. Like any other mode of harmony, it must be seen for itself to be understood; it cannot be deduced from or completely analyzed into something else.

An intention has an object.[6] The object has a reason for being the intention's object. That is, being an object of an intention results from being a value apparently worth intending here. Therefore the object of an intention is never just some specifiable thing or state of affairs; it is that state of affairs intended under the modality of being worth intending. To intend something is to take it as begin worth intending.

Whether the norm itself is *worthwhile* is, of course, the critical question of all intentional thought. To be an object of an intention, the object only need be *taken* as worth intending. The truth of the judgment later made about whether the object really is worthwhile, or whether its allegedly justifying norm is itself appropriate, is a fragile truth we rarely secure and never secure finally.

---

6. The discussion will be confined to intentional action and will not be focused on intentional thinking; the latter requires only a specification of the argument.

An intentional act always involves an interpretation of its relevant situation. It takes its situation to be such and such and then assesses an appropriate response to some object of intention.

An agent acts for a purpose when the action is taken to have some worth relative to a situation. What is given in the context of action and what is taken in the interpretation structuring the intention (these ought to but need not, sadly, be the same) constitute the raw material for the action to shape correctly. Dewey claimed that men intend consciously only when they interpret a situation as prbolematic, as in need of fixing.[7] His insight into the purposive or intentional character of consciousness was correct (more correct than the Continental philosophers' approach to intentionality that eliminates the normative element for pure eidetic structure). But his vision of what could improve a situation was narrow. Intentional action and thought is aroused not only when something breaks down, but even more importantly and more usually when imagination suggests some improvement to the interpreted state of affairs. And perhaps the most common improvement suggested is that the agent's experience be intensified. In comparative terms we rarely act so overtly as to change the external situation greatly; rather our intentional acts are more often concerned with enriching ourselves, spurred by the boredom of habit.

The norm by which the object of the intention is taken to be warranted is to be derived from the situation intended to be improved. That is, the object is taken as worthwhile because it is thought to improve things. It is not necessary that the norm be consciously specified. Only later judgment can specify the norm, wherein criticizing the norm itself is the functional intention. But the norm relates the object of the intention to the interpretation of the relevant situation by warranting the former as an improvement for the latter.

An intentional act involves not only an object and an interpretation of its situation, but also the relation of the agent to both. An intentional act is the determining of the agent himself and the effects of his self-determination through natural laws to be means toward realizing the intention's object. To intend something is not

7. See his *Essays in Experimental Logic* (1916; reprint ed., Dover Publications, n.d.), chaps. 1 and 2.

only to contemplate an object, nor even to assess it as what ought to be brought about relative to a situation, but is primarily to determine one's own being to bring it about—to be the means toward it. To intend something is to organize one's being to accomplish it. This means that to intend is to function as the directing principle of will ordering the relevant constituent features of the agent to produce the pattern that subsequent occasions must, according to the general laws of nature, objectify in the way intended.

A voluntary act is a harmony including the intention of an object, which is taken as normatively improving a situation (an interpretation of which is included in the act), *and the determing of oneself and the environment through will to accomplish the object.* To intend is the same process as willing, with the emphasis more on the cognitive elements and the determinative results of cognitive thought. A voluntary action begins in intention and ends with an overt and public product; will is the integration of the two.

To will is to do something, to make a change. Therefore the time of an intentional act is the present moment, although we can intend continuously through many moments. This means that the conceived object, the interpretation of the situation, the conceived relation between them, and the knowledge of what to do to bring about the object, must all themselves be delivered up to the moment as objects of the moment's prehensions. The intentional act harmonizing them is in the subjective form. Hopefully, then, the conception of the object is clear and true as a result of previous intentional activity aimed at finding out what to intend here. So also with the other cognitive elements. A continuous voluntary action involves a great shifting and doubling back of intentional activities, clarifying and correcting the objects of the overt intentions.

It is necessary to remember, in specifying the cosmological model of a personal individual to the characteristics of human life, that we have focused on mainly conscious elements of the person's constitution. This is a great abstraction. Most elements in experience are not conscious, and intentionality is a fragile structure of human life riding atop a great wave of other experience. In a moment of present existence, all the factors count in the resolution of the best possible harmony of prehensions, and the value of an intended object may or may not be very important in that ultimate resolution. It is misleading, therefore, to cite a person's conscious intention as the subjective aim determining the subjective form of his satisfaction. The intended object is only one of the essential features involved, and the others might be more important. But we can speak of degrees of the freedom to act intentionally precisely to the extent that there are degrees of importance in the satisfaction of the intended object.

The fact that the intended object is prehended as worthwhile is testimony to its status as an essential feature. In the present moment its function is normative. But a conscious intention is derived from structures prehended from past occasions, and it enters consciousness therefore as a structural possibility; it becomes normative, that is, essential, when the worth of its structure is appreciated. Its genetic history in the occasion, then, is four-phased. It enters as an initial datum aesthetically appreciated. It is analyzed by conceptual prehensions relating it to the future as a possibility. The worth of this possibility is appreciated. And finally it partially determines the objectifications of things in the satisfaction.

Let us focus now on action at a moment. Suppose that all the intentional investigation of possibilities, values, means, and so forth has gone on in prior deliberative activity, and that the results of deliberation figure in the present moment as data prehended. How can that moment function as a decisive point from which follows willful, voluntary action?

All the constituents of the whole individual harmony must have their place in the structural satisfaction of the moment. The subjective harmony resulting from the satisfaction is the objective condition that will have effects through natural law. A person can set the objective conditions from which his intended result may follow by his power of constituting his own objectification of data prehended in the moment.

Supposing that the person has the knowledge in hand, what is required for setting the right conditions? The various bodily, emotional, involvemental, and cognitive factors must be so structured in a harmony that each has a place proper to the fulfillment of the intention and that none has results that frustrate it. Of course, all change within a given moment is restricted by what is possible given the data prehended. An angry person may will in a moment to love his recently offensive enemy but may have subject his emotional life to both distraction and discipline (time-consuming processes) before he can comport himself in a way that has loving results. But he decides in a moment and does what then and there is possible. In each relevant successive moment he makes an advance, maintaining the same object of intention but readjusting his moment-by-moment determination of subjective harmony.

To be sure, we rarely if ever think of constituting our internal selves when willing. Rather, we think of doing some proximate but overt thing—saying something, moving a hand, buying a tool and using it. This fact calls for two points to be made.

First, action usually involves relatively remote intentional objects with a mediated process of accomplishment. We do something now to have a slightly more remote effect. That effect is itself a condition for natural law bringing about a more remote effect, which itself is a condition, and so forth, until the intended objective is reached. We focus conscious attention only on a certain few of these stages of conditions and results, and this is the second point. Conscious attention, and therefore potentially critical cognition, is directed at those critical turns in the process of events where control is needed. We are largely unconscious of the processes that go on with such regularity of habit that critical control makes no difference.

Long before human beings focus conscious attention on such things, they seem to learn how to determine themselves so as to produce results of the sort that can be cognized. The resolution to run a race may have no conscious determination of subjective form other than getting into position at the starting line, but integrated into the subjective harmony with a high position of importance is the increased adrenaline flow. We cannot directly will more adrenaline but our willing to win the race handles the problem of organizing the adrenal constituents. The same general point is illustrated by the football coach, who, knowing nothing of adrenaline, gives his players a hate-the-opponents pep talk. What he does know is that by some devious process (impiously dubbed "spirit") the pep talk results in the extra energy helpful to win.

Voluntary behavior is the process whereby the effects of each of many momentary harmonies add up to a causation of intended results. The chain of events begun in the earlier moments is controlled by qualifying effects intended subsidiarily in the later moments. Of course, the overall intention changes too in the process. The object intended is what it is because it is taken to be normative for the situation at hand, and as the situation at hand changes, so does the objective. The point to be emphasized here is the vast effect an individual can have on a world quite external to him by controlling his own subjective process of harmonization.

Earlier it was noted that an action is voluntary if it is caused by a personal agent in a way stemming from his personality rather than if it is merely a part in a nonpersonal natural process of causation. From the present discussion this may be interpreted in the following way: an action is voluntary if it proceeds from the will of an agent. The will of an agent is intentional and existentially effective in ways described.

There are, of course, practical as well as theoretical problems concerning the freedom to act intentionally, and only the latter have been discussed. It is an educational problem to be sufficiently aware of the effects of one's self to make them conform to one's intentions. There are also moral problems of steadfastness and strength of will, but all these can be understood in the light of the theoretical considerations offered.

6

Free Choice

DETERMINISM AND ALTERNATIVES FOR CHOICE

The problems of free agency, as pointed out at the beginning of the previous chapter, must be focused both in terms of the way a person's will can be effective in the world and in terms of the procedure of choosing what to effect. Chapter 5 explored the former focus and gave a description of intentional action. From the standpoint of intentional action the future is interesting as containing possible effects of personally initiated causal processes. From the standpoint of choosing, the future is interesting as presenting alternatives between which a choice must be made. The first concern of this chapter, then, will be to defend the claim that the future contains alternatives, explaining the general structure of these alternatives relative to a moment of choice.

From the standpoint of intentional action a personal rather than nonpersonal initiation of an action is a matter of moral responsibility because the resolution of prehensions in the critical moment is directed by essential features constitutive of the continuity of a personal life. From the standpoint of choice between alternatives the problem is whether a choice could have been made. The concern here, then, is not with how essential features order conditional ones, but with how essential features themselves are ordered. It would seem that if the ranking of essential features is determined in advance, then although a person might be free to act on the basis of his choice, his choosing is not itself free; although he could have done otherwise if he had chosen otherwise, he could not have chosen otherwise. To say that he could have chosen otherwise is to say that in moments of decision, in contrast to moments that merely resolve prehensions with essential features, there is an explicit adoption of a particular contingent ranking of essential values as the ranking to determine action.

At least this is the hypothesis defended here. Choice is the adoption of a value as one's reason and direction of action. In practical terms, this value then is either the intentional object or the norm approving it for the situation.

There are three main questions to be asked about alleged alternatives between which people have to choose. The first is whether in fact there ever are real alternatives. The second, if the answer to the first is affirmative, is what the nature of alternatives is; this concerns the structure of the future. The third is whether the answers to the first two questions bear in any special way on the nature of freedom and responsibility; in question here is the meaning of the claim that a person acts voluntarily and is responsible for his action only when he could have acted otherwise, and the interpretation of alternatives should give insight into the meaning of "could have acted otherwise."

Why would anyone deny there are real alternatives for choice? Making choices between alternatives seems so much a part of our experience it seems unreasonable to gainsay it. The denial has been made by many philosophers, however, and it is an integral part of the common-sense framework most of us fall into when circumstances or psyche force us into fatalistic moods. The reason for the denial is a belief in some form or other of what can be called the determinist thesis. Its claim is that the present is completely determined both in its own nature and in its dynamic results by past conditions. Since only one future outcome can result from any given present there is never a present time when alternative future results are possible. Since future alternatives are always relative to some present for which they are potential consequences, real future alternatives do not exist.

The experience of choosing between alternatives must therefore be misleading. Men believe there are alternatives only because they do not *know* what in fact has been already determined to result. This position can be made subtle in abstract ways, and it can appeal for confirmation to critical experiences in which we *think* we are making a decisive choice but what happens turns out to be the result of forces that were plainly running things all along; the forces might be nonhuman factors, or they might be psychological propensities.

There is, furthermore, a general trait of experience undergirding the determinist thesis, namely the pervasive indication that what happens does so because of causes. Whether we consider purely physical phenomena or the actions of people, we understand that they follow from states of affairs antecedently given, or from motives antecedently entertained. As Hume pointed out, when we find an event that seems not to follow from its antecedent by any rule, we suspect that there are hidden rules and causes. And in the moral sphere, when a person does something that follows from no motive or cause within him we say that it is an uncharacteristic act—no personal act of his at all—and we attribute it to wholly incidental causes. Even without adopting the extreme Kantian thesis that causation is *logically* necessary for objective experience, causation is so pervasive a part of human experience that the determinist thesis is a natural belief; it is an economical way of simplifying a basic character of experience in a theoretical principle. It must be stressed, however, that the determinist thesis is an abstraction, a simplification, and as such only an hypothesis.

Balancing the experience of pervasive causation, however, is the experience that sometimes people do have the freedom to choose between alternatives. People know they have that experience because they deliberate about what to do. They would not deliberate if they really believed that the issue of events was already determined. Nor would they deliberate without believing they could have a hand in determining what the issue would be. Experience contains too many situations wherein people are faced with difficult choices, and they feel the real bite of deliberation, the pressure of cutting off possibilities. In contrast to experiences of describing, in which people note causes, there are experiences of acting intentionally, and these are often experiences in which the dominant motif is making decisions. Furthermore, *most* experiences are of the intentional action sort rather than the descriptive sort. And most importantly, experiences of decision lie closest to the heart of what really matters in human life.

The defenders of the determinist thesis make the standard argument that deliberation is merely a cause of the choice made, that the deliberation is determined completely by antecedent conditions, and that the choice is also completely determined by the deliberation and other motivations. The basic experience of de-liberating and choosing can be interpreted so as to be consistent with the determinist thesis.

But the rebuttal to this standard move is significant. In many situations of choice, there is a problem of whether to accept the results of deliberation: imagine Masada. How sad but often our intentional action is determined by stupid temptations or rationally irrelevant habits. Human frailty consists so much in the tendency to be moved by one's last feeling rather than one's best. The point is that we *recognize* this state of affairs and sometimes muster sufficient control so as *to choose what motivation we will allow to be determinative*. Sometimes we hold all motivations in abeyance, any one of which is sufficiently strong to determine intention, and deliberately adopt one as the motive that becomes our reason for acting. This is a rare and precious dimension of freedom, and it may be the case that not everyone experiences it; certainly to recognize it requires a peak of self-awareness.

The logical force of this point is that deliberations and other motivations do not always issue directly in a chosen intention, the choice being nothing but the issuing; sometimes there might be a special adoption of certain motivations to be the causes of the intentions, and this adoption is decision. Now although the self-conscious instances of this freedom of adoption are rare, it will be maintained that the phenomenon lies at the heart of all instances of real choice. The abstract description of the phenomenon in terms of adoption can be called the "free adoption thesis," in contrast to the determinist thesis.

The logical state of the problem now is this. There are two basic traits of experience, that of causation and that of making choices between real alternatives. These fit together in common life, but their simplifications on the abstract level of interpretation are mutually contradictory. The determinist thesis contradicts the free-adoption thesis. There must be something wrong with the presentation of the abstract interpretations, then, unless the universe is basically irrational (an hypothesis for which any logical reason would be contradictory). It could be that one is true and the other false, or both could be false; but in either case we would have to explain why they both seem to interpret their respective experiences so well when they are not even related to each other. It could also be that both abstract theses can be fitted into a more general theory so as to be consistent with each other; in this case the universality implied in their isolated expression must be qualified. If such a general theory can be provided, then the prima facie validity of both basic traits of experience can be respected. Since it is the integrity of experience that ought to be protected, and not that of principles, the attempt should be made to find a theory in which *both* traits can be properly respected. The alternative is to hold to one abstract principle, denying the other, and thereby having to explain away the basic experiential trait interpreted by the other.

The aim here is to include both, properly qualified, within the axiological cosmology. The next move, therefore, is to present a cosmological interpretation of real future alternatives. The *universality* of the determinist thesis is something that must be directly denied, however, if the experience of choice is to be admitted, and an argument against it should be given. This will be done in the section entitled "Responsibility," after the nature of alternatives has been interpreted.

POSSIBILITIES AND POTENTIALITIES

The key to the nature of alternatives is to note that they lie in the future and that the future is a unique modality of existence. Much has been written since Bergson to the effect that philosophers too often assume space as a model of reality and reduce time to a spacelike character. It is true that many scientists in their philosophical reflections reduce time to the modality of past time in which every existent looks like a finished fact. Some scientifically minded philosophers, defending determinism, attribute a symmetry or reversibility to investigatable time, a character chiefly appropriate to space. But the reason there seems to be a symmetry to the causal process is that the implicit paradigm time modality is past time, where all relations are finished and therefore completely determinate with respect to one another. The mistake is not first thinking that time is symmetrical, but rather thinking that all the time has only the modality of the past. From this it would follow that time is symmetrical, in a sense like space. The important point to argue here is that not all time is past time and that the future is real and different. A concrete way of making the argument is to appeal to the *experience* of the indeterminateness of the future. This of course would be question begging in the present context; it amounts to an appeal to that very experience we are trying to warrant with the assertion of future indeterminateness. A theoretical interpretation can be given, however, to alternatives as characteristics uniquely appropriate to future existence. This will give the experience second-level plausibility, as it were. Then it will be shown how the theory of experiencing alternatives can also interpret the pervasive causality alternately interpreted by the determinist thesis, thereby neutralizing its venom.

What exists in the future are *possibilities*. This contrasts with present existence, in which what exist are actual entities in the subjective process of actualizing themselves. It also contrasts with past existence, in which what exists is an interrelated system of actualized facts.

Possibilities, according to the axiological cosmology, are universals, relevant to a present state of affairs articulating what actualized states of affairs might result from the present. As universals, possibilities lack the concreteness of both present and past existents. The process of actualizing a possibility adds what is lacking in a possibility to make it concrete.

As relevant to some present existent, possibilities do not include all universals but only some. A distinction is to be drawn between logical possibilities and real possibilities. A logical possibility is any set of universals not self-contradictory as a set. A real possibility is a logical possibility that might be realized in a process of present moments leading from a specified present to the time in which the possibility can be presently actualized. Logical possibilities cannot be possibilities for actualization unless they are also real possibilities. Otherwise they are only possibilities for conception. Only real possibilities exist, since to exist is to have a mode of temporal existence relative to some present existent.

No possibility can be a real possibility unless it exists. That is, to be a real possibility is to have a partially determinate temporal *position* relative to some present time, and indirectly to some past time. To have temporal bearing on a present time, however, is to exist with it as its future.

The test or criterion of existence is to have some existential bearing on some existent. Existential bearing means contributing to an existent a conditional feature that must be taken into account in the existent's determinate nature. The mark of past existence for a present existent is that the past thing is prehended objectively by the present existent and must be objectified in its satisfaction (or be negatively prehended). The mark of past existence for a past existent is that there is a systematic interrelation of cause and effect determining both past existents to be in a causal system. (The idealists' doctrine of internal relations describes how past existents determine each other.) The mark of future existence is that possibilities set limits as to what can be affected by present existents. If possibilities did not exist, then, no matter how a present existent resolved itself, absolutely anything could happen. There would be no limits or determinate relations connecting the present and future. The satisfaction of a present moment would be utterly indeterminate with respect to what might happen next. The presupposition of control over the future is that possibilities are limited and as such determine present existence. If a present existent is to be a cause, intentional or otherwise, it must determine itself this way rather than that because of the limits of the future.

The question now is what structure the limits of real possibilities have. Without any limits, the future is completely indeterminate and absolutely anything can happen. Suppose the limits are so determinate that only one thing can happen. This supposition is a reverse statement of the determinist thesis (the forward statement of which is that the present is completely determinate so that only one result can issue). But then there could be no difference between a possible state of affairs and that state actualized. If the actualization could make a difference, the possibility could be made determinate in a way it had not been determinate as a mere possibility; hence it was not *completely* determinate as a mere possibility. This is the core of the argument to be made in detail against determinism in the next section. The conclusion here is that future possibilities are only *partially* determinate; that is, they include only some of the universals that would characterize an actualization of that possibility.

This means a distinction must be drawn between primary and secondary universals in real possibilities.

Primary universals are those that will characterize the actualization of the possibility no matter in what form it is actualized. From the standpoint of a present, the future possibility is determinate with respect to its primary universals, and nothing the present or intervening presents can do can alter them. Relative to a given present, the primary universals of its real possibilities are determined by its past.

Secondary universals are those characterizing alternate ways in which the possibility might be actualized. From the standpoint of the initial phase of a present moment, the secondary universals of its real future possibility are indeterminate as to which will be actualized. Some might be made determinate for the future by the way the present existent resolves its initial data into a satisfaction. They would thereby be transformed into primary universals. This is the way a present moment controls the future: to act is to transform secondary universals into primary ones. The only real possibility, any of whose secondary universals can be transformed into primary universals by a given present existent, is the possibility to be actualized in the next contiguous moment. From the standpoint of a given present, a remote possibility requires intervening present moments to be completely determined. Even regarding the next contiguous moment, however, a given present can only determine which primary universals it is to have as conditional features or as essential features derivative from the past. The subjective process of actualizing the possibility in its own proper time involves giving those universals an integrated place in a whole harmony; the possibility can become completely determinate only in its own time.

Every possibility has a proper time for its own actualization. Although necessarily future, the proper time of a possibility might be partially indeterminate from the standpoint of a given present whose specific possibility it is. The proper time of a possibility relative to the time of a given present is of utmost importance in describing a possibility. Suppose there is a series of moments, T_1, T_2, T_3 . . . T_x, and suppose that T_N is the proper time of a real possibility later than T_3. The description of the possibility at T_N must include a statement of both what is determinate in the possibility and what remains to be determined, that is, of both primary and secondary universals, identifying which is which. Therefore, since which universals are primary depends on whether the standpoint of the description is T_1, T_2, or whatever, that standpoint must be specific in the description. The description would take something like the form, "At T_1 A, B, and C are primary universals (that is, will happen), and D, E, F, and G are secondary universals (that is, any one might happen); at T_2 A, B, C, and E, are primary universals, F, and G are secondary universals, and D is no longer possible." A description of the possibility from the standpoints of all the earlier times for which it had any primary universals would be a description of how a possibility was made more and more determinate down to its own proper time of actualization. The possibility could not be said to exist for times earlier than those for which it had at least one primary feature, since it must have some limits over and above those of logical possibility in order to exist as a possibility. Without limits it would have no bearing on that earlier time in its present existence. The logic necessary for inferring relations between elements in the coming to determination of a possibility must be a logic of tenses.[1]

It is apparent from the discussion of description of possibilities that a third level of universals must be acknowledged. *Tertiary* universals are those involved in articulating secondary universals; a secondary universal is a harmony of tertiary ones. Some tertiary universals may occur in several of the alternatives, that is, in some secondary universal; other tertiary universals may occur in only one; a universal that occurs in all the secondary universals is a primary universal. In the process of deliberation, the tertiary universals are the "factors" in the situation that deliberation must take account of. The factors can be combined this way or that (that is, so as to exhibit this secondary universal or that one); some alternatives may leave out some factors.

Stated roughly, the primary universals set the general limits for the future within which choice can be made between the secondary universals subject to determination at the moment of choice. The tertiary universals are descriptions of effects in the future of the various things prehended as initial data by the present existent. Interpreting Aristotle's sea-battle example, the possi-

1. For a discussion of the logic of tenses and the cosmological presuppositions of such an undertaking see the articles by Robert S. Brumbaugh cited in footnote 5 of chapter 4.

bility facing the admirals the night before is something like this. The primary universals stipulate that the morrow must reflect some resolution concerning how to carry on the war; the morrow must be strategically significant, as well as have all the climatic conditions and other physical conditions already determined. The secondary universals, at least the most important ones, are, to have a sea-battle and not to have a sea-battle; the possibility includes both as secondary universals. The tertiary universals include all the men, vessels, and equipment that have to be disposed one way or another, for fighting or for not fighting.

In common parlance, the word "possibility" is often used to mean secondary universals. We sometimes speak of alternate possibilities. This is harmless in common parlance, but for purposes of cosmology it is better to restrict the word "possibility" to mean the whole set of universals including the primary, secondary, and tertiary ones. The set as a whole is the real existent in the future that limits the present and can be actualized by transforming some secondary universals into primary ones through the disposition of those tertiary universals subject to the control, by natural law, of the various antecedent presents. The secondary universals cannot be called real possibilities except as together in the whole.

The logical structure of possibilities allows contradictory secondary universals to be compatible, so long as the possibility is future. The law of contradiction does not apply to a statement of the set of secondary universals, although it does to a statement of primary universals. The law of excluded middle does not apply to a statement of what must be true for the primary universals to be actualized, since any secondary universal in the possibility is neither true nor false of that actualization.

Real possibilities, as future existents, are not to be confused with *potentialities,* present existents. In a strictly general cosmological sense, a potentiality is any thing in a present actual occasion that might be objectified or made actual in its satisfaction. This would include both physical and conceptual prehensions. In discussing the moral sphere, however, it is relevant to single out what might be called "action potentialities." These are potentialities not just for reiterating some element of the past but for doing something new with them, an action whose responsibility rests with the present occasion. In the cosmological terms, an action potentiality is a conceptual prehension in a present occasion that might be the subjective form in which the occasion harmonizes its initial data.[2]

Despite the fact that potentialities exist only in a present moment, ceasing to be potentialities either when they are actualized or when they have been excluded, action potentialities are often referred to by the future consequences. In this sense a person has the potentiality now to make his friend happy three days hence by mailing a particular letter now. The relation between an action potentiality and a real possibility is that the universals in the object of the potentiality—the object conceptually prehended—must be the same as (a) the primary universals and (b) one definite secondary universal in the real possibility. That is, the potentiality is the power of a present existent to make a secondary universal primary, determining it to happen. To the extent the causal processes relating a present potentiality to its future consequences are indeterminate, it may be misleading to name a potentiality by its effects.

Another argument that real possibilities exist in the future is that there is a distinction between potentialities and other conceptual prehensions. Some propositions conceptually prehended are possibilities for realization, and other are not. To deny this is to say that everything conceived (not just conceivable) is capable of actualization. Potentialities conform to future possibility, and the other conceptual prehensions do not. Where there are alternative potentialities in the presently existing individual, there must be real future alternatives.

Alternatives for choice, in summary, are the secondary universals in a real possibility that (a) are contradictories of each other, (b) are resolvable by some potentialities (in choosing moments) into a distinction between one universal that becomes primary, and the others that become impossible, and (c) are such that *any* one might be made the primary universal.

Clause *b* is important because the alternatives of interest here are

2. We follow Whitehead in understanding a conceptual prehension to be a prehension (a) whose object is an eternal object (or form) or set of eternal objects and (b) that derives from a physical prehension. A potentiality is a conceptual prehension whose object is the complex universal illustrating a way in which data can be objectified together. The data appear in an object of a potentiality-conceptual-prehension as tertiary universals; the subjective form of a potentiality derives from both the values in the data represented by the tertiary universals and the value of harmonizing that particular way. All objects of conceptual prehensions that are potentialities must be propositions.

for *choice;* that is, the alternatives must be such as to be resolvable in the specified moment of decision. A real possibility contains many secondary universals, most of them insignificant but not all resolvable from the standpoint of a moment of choice (excepting the situation where the choice is immediately contiguous to the proper time of the possibility). The only secondary universals that are alternatives for choice are those that can be resolved in the decisive moment. To resolve an alternative is to make one of the contradictories a primary universal and the others impossible.

Clause *c* is necessary because the choice must have the alternatives. In some situations alternatives might be resolved by human intention where only one of the alternatives can be intended; as we say, there is only one choice open. This is different from having alternatives, any of which can be chosen. Real choice, in contrast to mere intentional resolution, must have alternatives in the act of choosing such that, before the choice is made, any can be chosen. To choose is to select among the alternatives. In effect, an alternative that, from the standpoint of a decisive moment, cannot help but be chosen because the moment is antecedently determined to do so is not really a secondary universal but a primary one. A universal is primary if from the standpoint of a present it is determined to happen by *antecedents* of that present.

The necessity of distinguishing between clauses *b* and *c* stems from the distinction between present and future existence. A present existent is in process only in its own moment, and a future possibility is affected (that is, some of its alternatives are resolved) only by the state of affairs *concluded* by the present. For there to be alternatives for the choice within the subjective processes, in some sense the alternatives in the real possibility must be reflected in alternative potentialities within the subjective process. The importance of this point is reflected in the discussion of responsibility in the remaining paragraphs of this section. Of course the only legitimacy in calling the alternative chosen a secondary **universal** when there is no alternative in the choosing as to how to resolve it, is that the resolving present existent has many other things than choice going on in its subjective process.

RESPONSIBILITY

After this long excursion into cosmology, it is necessary to recall that the discussion of alternatives was necessary to articulate freedom of choice. But freedom of choice is itself important because we say a person must have it to be held *responsible*. Before we proceed to the discussion of choice *within* the subjective process of decision, we should determine what stake responsibility has in the issue.

The word "responsibility" and its cognates are ambiguous, and it will be helpful to specify some of the main meanings.

(a) Responsibility can be used in a straightforward causal sense. "The falling limb was responsible for breaking the plastic flamingo on the lawn."

(b) Responsibility can be used in a sense of moral causation that entails that the agent is praiseworthy or blameworthy. "Butch and Max were responsible for robbing the bank, but Mr. Wilburforce, although he opened the safe for them, is absolved from responsibility because he was forced to help them at gunpoint."

(c) Responsibility can mean an obligation someone has because of his role in some social institution. "The chairman of the board has many responsibilities."

(d) "Responsible" can be used to describe a person who acted with responsibility *b*. Or it can mean a person who habitually fulfills responsibility *c,* his institutionalized obligations.

(e) An "irresponsible" person is one who fails an obligation, institutionalized or not.

The question of free choice has to do primarily with responsibility *b*.

Our moral experience attests that a voluntary action is one for which the agent is to be held responsible (in the *b* sense) for better or worse. This is now to acknowledge something more about voluntary actions than was noted in chapter 5. There we merely spoke of voluntary actions as being the agent's personal ones. Now we are speaking of responsible voluntary actions. Perhaps all voluntary actions are responsible, but whether or not they are, this is a new dimension of the discussion.

What is there in a voluntary act that entails responsibility in this peculiar moral sense? To call someone responsible for his actions usually is to assert that he is the cause of them in a unique way that his conditional antecedents are not. If the line of causation has too much continuity, so that it extends from the deed through the agent's inner recesses back to his parents and environment, we are inclined to say that the agent was a mere machine of remoter causes and is no more responsible, perhaps even less so, than they. Sometimes the law is tempted to excuse a culprit on grounds of expert testimony that he was no more responsible for throwing the rock as he did than the rock was for flying where it was thrown. Sometimes also the law acknowledges that actions done in hot passion are not voluntary because the usual control the agent exercises over his actions is impossible in that situation. Behind both of these excuses is the presupposition that, if the action were indeed voluntary and therefore responsible, it must have been possible for the agent to have done otherwise than he did. If the agent could not have done otherwise, then it is the causes of him that are to be held responsible, not the agent himself, who was only a tool, a mechanical beast.

The requirement that responsibility entails that a person could have done otherwise is complex. If every voluntary action must have an alternative, the alternative must be possibly voluntary. The agent must have been able to choose the alternative rather than the one he did in fact choose.

Some philosophers might argue that the alternative need not be possibly voluntary. Responsibility, they might say, consists in choosing one's action, even if the action one chooses is determined quite apart from the choice. But what meaning could "choice" have here, if not the picking of one out of several possible alternatives? What they mean to say is that one is responsible if he *approves* the action he does; the supposition is that the intention is complex, willing the act on the one hand, given no choice, and liking or not liking it on the other. It is false, however, that one is responsible only when he approves, since people are morally responsible when they choose unwittingly, without being aware of liking or disliking, and one is responsible when having to choose the best of a bad lot.

If all alternatives, the one taken and the ones rejected, are to be possibly voluntary, "could have done otherwise" must mean "could have done otherwise if the agent had chosen to do otherwise." It is not enough that the external situation allow of alternatives. It is also necessary that the agent could have *chosen* otherwise.

Some philosophers have argued that voluntary action requires only an alternative in the overt action. They say an agent is responsible "if he could have done otherwise had he chosen to do so, although he was determined by antecedent causes not so to choose." They argue that the alternative action would have been voluntary had the agent chosen it. The fact that he was determined by antecedent causes to choose what he did choose in no way alters the fact that his action is responsible, because it has a possibly voluntary alternative. He could have done otherwise if he had chosen to.

The difficulty with this position is that, although the set of alternatives is resolved by a predetermined choice, the unchosen alternatives could not have been chosen, and hence were not alternatives *for choice*. In this case they are *impossible* as alternatives for choice, and an impossibility can never be the proper alternative to a voluntary action. The conclusion is that if an action is responsible and voluntary, its alternatives must be such that the agent had the potentiality of choosing one of them.

The argument has brought us to the point of asking how a person has alternatives within the process of choosing. How can there be alternate potentialities? Although the alternatives one chooses between are real future existents of the sort described in the previous section, the process of choosing them must itself allow of alternatives, and this must now be interpreted. We have arrived at this juncture both by considering the nature of future alternatives in the abstract and by considering some of the requirements of responsibility.

The work of interpreting the choosing can be divided into two parts. The first, the task of the next section, is to explain how the process is not determined by antecedents. The second, discussed in a later section, Decision, is to describe what making a choice is.

DETERMINISM AND CONDITIONS OF CHOICE

Paul Weiss has most persuasively made the case that all causation or temporal production implies some kind of indeterminateness in the efficient cause regarding the effect. The efficient cause is an antecedent state setting determinate limits for what the effect or resultant state can be. But the antecedent cannot contain the complete determination of the consequent, since if it did there would be no difference between antecedent and consequent: the consequent in its determinateness would be entirely resident in the antecedent. Time and process would make no difference, and hence different times or moments could not be distinguished by differences in qualities. If time and process are to be significant for the determination of a future state of affairs, then from the standpoint of an antecedent state the future must be partially indeterminate. Weiss claims that the process of causation connecting the cause with the effect is what produces the complete determination of the effect. He allows that the degree of novelty introduced by the process may fall between two extremes. On the one hand it can be as little as "the sheer occurrence, the mere sensuosity or immediacy of the production and the actual effect," or it can be as great as genuinely "novel universals." [3] The basic argument is that the flow of time in a causal process must make a difference, and that therefore a difference must be possible to make in the future effect; unless a difference is possible, a future effect is no different from an actualized one.

The determinist would answer by saying that all characters are completely determinate, past, present, and future. The difference is in the mode of being of the possible versus the actual. The possible is abstract and the actual is concrete. The determinist might go so far as to say that the future is nonexistent, and only the actual exists. In any case there is nothing added to a possibility to make it actual; there is just a change from being possible (or not being at all) to being actual (or coming into being).

Yet what can the difference in mode be if not a determinate one with determinate characteristics? If we know the difference, then there is something we know. To be actual, to be existent, is at least to have a tangible sensuosity, as Weiss puts it.

Even if there is an indiscernible difference in modes, there must be something the remains constant through the change, if the move from possibility to actuality is a modal one. It is impossible to call the change a modal one (or to say there is a change from no mode to some mode) without something constant that changes mode. What could be the constant for determinism?

The determinist can say it is the universals that remain the same from possibility to its actualization. These are completely

3. Paul Weiss, *Modes of Being* (Carbondale, Ill.: Southern Illinois University Press, 1958), p. 44.

determined by prior conditions. All that is meant by the process of actualization is that the universals determined to characterize the future be given concrete instantiation.

But the universals do not remain the same from possibility to actualization. A universal in a possibility is indeterminate precisely with respect to its relations to the heres and nows of its instantiation. This is what is meant by saying that it *might* be here and now but it is not; that it *might* be actualized but as yet is only possible. (The "now" in this discussion is the proper time of the possibility.)

The very meaning of determinism, however, is that the relations of a universal to its concrete instantiation are determined in advance. On the determinist thesis it is improper to speak of a possibility as something that might be actualized; rather, it is something that *must* be actualized when its time comes.

The operative phrase in this stage of the dialectic is "when its time comes." If determinism goes so far as to say that the universals articulating future possibilities are completely determined in their relations to concrete instantiation, then there in effect is no difference at all between past facts and future possibilities. Future possibilities might just as well be called future facts. This is the burden of Laplace's famous remark about complete prediction. If time makes any difference to things other than ordering them serially, it must be in the difference between past and future time, on the one hand, and present time on the other. This shifts the focus of the discussion, however, from (a) possibility versus actuality to (b) future and past facts versus present "presence" or immediate existence (or however one would care to name the "sensuosity" characteristic of present experience). The question now is, what is the difference between a fact's "proper" time, the time when it is present, and its location in past or future time?

The main difference to be noted is that past and future facts are fixed, and that change takes place only in present time. If there are any facts of change, the changing must take place only within the fact's proper time; in its past and future modalities the fact is merely a determinate structure to be compared with other determinate structures systematically related to it.

How can determinism give an interpretation of the present as a time of change, in contrast to past and future as times of structural relation? The answer is, it cannot. If no difference is made to a fact in its passage from future to past, then nothing can happen in the passage. There can be no facts of change, because it is eternally impossible that a thing become different from what it was before. According to the determinist thesis, it is an entirely arbitrary matter which moment is called the present. At no moment can a fact take on a sensuosity that it lacked before or that it will lose when it passes away; for if it did, that moment would make a difference to it. If it makes a difference to it, then before the moment it was indeterminate in a way to be made determinate by that difference.

The determinist might answer that it was antecedently determined that the future fact, when it reached its proper time and became present, would have "presence" or sensuosity or would make the change it is its factual nature to make. But the question is not *when* it was determined that the future fact would become present; rather it is what the *meaning* of presence is. If the presence of the fact, the arrival of its proper time, means any alteration in the fact, then its arrival means it gains determinations it did not have before it became present.

The determinist finally might argue that there is an ambiguity between saying that an antecedent condition determines a consequent one and saying that the consequent one is determinate before it is present. Indeed there is a difference; the former refers to the character of the antecedent to determine and the latter refers to the character of the consequent to be determined. But on the determinist thesis, and only on that thesis, the former entails the latter strictly. One might quibble about the kind of being or nonbeing attributed to the future fact as future, but that makes no difference as to its character. If a future fact comes into existence only when it becomes present, its presence, in contrast to future and past character, is something not determined by its antecedents; for if it were determined by its antecedents, it would always have been present.

The conclusion is that the determinist thesis, if stated with the universality of the claim that an event is totally determined by antecedents, contradicts the thesis that there is real change in present moments. Our very experience of the present, in contrast to the past and future, is sufficient to allow us to reject it. Furthermore, the determinist thesis gains its initial plausibility only by interpreting the experience of causation; since change is incompatible with determinism, the determinist thesis loses its initial plausibility.

It will be helpful to rehearse the argument made here in reverse. The determinist wanted to find an ambiguity in the notion of determination so as to allow him to say a future fact was always determined to enjoy present existence at a certain proper time without saying that the enjoyment of the present existence alters the way it was determined before. The reason he wanted to say that was that determinism needs to show how being present is a different mode of being from being past or future, a mode in which change takes place. It is necessary to talk about change and the enjoyment of present sensuosity because the determinist must give meaning to the notion that there is a difference between the time before a fact in actualized, and the time when the fact's own time comes. Determinism is commited to making sense of "when the fact's own time comes" because it wants to say that the fact is antecedently determined to have such and such a character "when its own time comes." And the reason it wants say that is to interpret its claim that the universals of the future are antecedently determined as to their relations to concrete matters of fact before they enjoy their own concrete instantiation. If determinism did not say that, it would have to admit that the relations to the concrete are added to the future universals to make them actual, and that the future therefore gains determination in becoming actual that it did not have when merely future. But it cannot say any of these things.

The discussion of determinism has been on a general level, abstracted from the problems of freedom. On that same level, it is possible to state the alternate interpretation the axiological cosmology makes of the phenomenon of indeterminism.

Antecedent causes are grasped as conditional features of a present existent by being objects of its prehensions; they necessarily are taken up into the present existent, and this necessity applies to the existent before it becomes present. That is, the real possibility is determined in advance to have such and such objective conditions that it must prehend into the unity of its own satisfaction, positively or negatively. But present existence consists precisely in the process of actualizing a harmony of the prehended objective conditions, and this process involves matters of subjective form that are not all antecedent conditions. The subjective form is a matter of the thing's essential features. Of these essential features, only those derivative from the past are matters of antecedent conditioning in any sense, and even that sense is peculiar. So according to the axiological scheme, no matter how much a future possibility has been made determinate by antecedent choices and happenings, it is always indeterminate until its own proper time with respect to the subjective form it receives in the moment of its actualization. When its own proper time becomes present, the possibility acquires concrete position relative to other actualities and past actual facts by virtue of its own essential subjectivity.

The present moment is the mode of temporal existence in which partially determinate possibilities are transformed into completely determinate past facts. "Past facts" is a redundancy; the present is the bringing about of a fact, and when it has been brought about, its subjective process of coming to be is finished, factum. The axiological cosmology, in contrast to determinism, interprets the the meaning of present existence in this way: it is the process of making a real possibility completely determinate, especially with respect to existential position; once it is completely determinate, it is a past fact. The difference between possibility and actuality is that the latter is completely determinate, and that difference is made by the process of actualization, the process of making determinate. Real possibilities in the remote future are made more and more determinate as their times comes; present existents effect this determination, although real possibilities cannot be made completely determinate; determination of the future as such can be called secondary determination. Primary determination is the actualization of possibilities as potentialities in their own moment of present existence.

It might be argued that the axiological scheme is too essentialistic a theory regarding the difference between actuality and possibility. That is, actuality cannot be simply a complete specification of universals, but must be the instantiation of universals in some concrete present existent.

Axiological cosmology is not an idealism, however. The process of actualization is not merely the determination of additional universals descriptive of a possibility, although new universals may arise because of the contributions of new patterns in subjective form. More importantly, the process of actualization is the giving of position to the objects prehended, which means that the universal possibilities of arranging the initial data prehended are given unique and concrete positions in the particular history of actual facts. The possibilities are instantiated with definite dates and places relative to what else has been actualized. The difference between "elegance," as characterized in the general theory of value, and "contrast," as its specification in cosomolgy, is at the heart of the rejection of idealism.

Elegance is intended as a characterization of the value in anything, not just in cosmological entities. It is a simplification of the value in mathematical systems as well as in persons or buildings. The elegance appropriate to cosmological entities is called "contrast" because "contrast" connotes a greater independence between the harmonized constituents than connoted by "elegance." The reason for the greater independence is that all cosmological harmonies located in the experience of actual entities are harmonies of other, objectified actual entities. Those harmonized actual entities in their moments of subjective process are isolated from each other. It is impossible, of course, for all the factors in an experienced contrast to be independent actual entities, since the experience of the contrast itself involves giving the items subjective form so that they contrast compatibly. But the origin of all conditional features in an entity's experience is physical prehension, and the more of this independence reflected in the final satisfaction, the greater the contrast. In the terminology of the axiological scheme, contrast is the characteristic of value in a harmony whose constituents include physical prehensions.

Contrast must have elements metaphysically simplified as complexity and simplicity; the cosmological versions of these, following Whitehead, can be called width and narrowness.[4]

Width in a contrast consists in the different actual entities directly or indirectly prehended in it. The greater the number of different actual entities, the greater the width. Narrowness in a contrast consists in the function of a few harmonies at the higher levels in the contrast to contain many in the lower levels. A contrast is narrow if the pattern of its highest mode of harmony is very simple, that is, has few constituents, but constituents that themselves include many constituents.

4. See *Process and Reality*, pt. 2, chap. 4.

Degree of contrast is a matter of depth. Depth of contrast is the extent of subjective form that must be added to the initial complexity to achieve a maximization of width and narrowness in the actual contrast. Depth consists in the complexity of the subharmonies that must intervene between the initial data and the contrast so as to achieve the maximization of narrowness and width.

In the actual contrast, width is not merely the number of different actual entities surviving the process of elimination in simplification, but those that survive with their differences; therefore, in the contrast actualized, the degree of width is the degree of difference preserved. Liewise, in the actual contrast, narrowness is not just the paucity of factors directly involved in the higher levels but the function of that paucity in including difference.

Great width in a contrast with little narrowness amounts to a trivial contrast; that is, the togetherness of the different items does little in the way of each enhancing the others in the combination. The opposite of triviality is importance. Great narrowness with little width amounts to emptiness; it is not that the narrow modes of harmony contain nothing, only that what they contain is not distinguished into determinately different things; the contrast is vague on the lower levels. The opposite of empty is relevant; that is, many things on the lower level are relevant to the narrow harmonies on the higher levels.

How, in detail, does the axiological scheme interpret the role of contrast in an occasion? The process of a present moment begins with the initial data of prehension and must arrange these data so as to attain the most valued contrast at the end. To arrange the data is to give them definite places in the satisfaction of the moment. Whereas a particular initial datum might function in a variety of different ways, depending on how the process resolves its relations to the other data, as an objectified datum in the satisfaction it can have only one role.

The positioning is therefore two-sided. In positioning its initial data, the existent gives itself a perspective on the world. Then from the standpoints of subsequent existents, the existent as a past fact has a completely determinate position relative to all the other facts in the world; it is a determinate part of the world for future experiences.

As noted in chapter 2, two analyses of a present existent can be made. A genetic division analyzes the process of moving from initial data to final objectification. A coordinate division analyzes the structure of the objectification relative to that of the objectifications in other actualizations, before and after. Within the moment, the initial data are values whose merits demand recognition; for a genetic division, therefore, the process of actualization is the establishment of definite relationships of relative value, giving to each prehended datum its own unique position of importance in the coherent harmony. For coordinate division, the process is the determination of metric position in the more ordinary sense.

But in both kinds of analyses, it must be recognized that the position is the result of the subjectivity of the process of actualization. For genetic division, the very reason there must be a process from the initial data is that as *initial* data they have no unified position; there is no unified harmony in which each has a place. For coordinate division, there is no attainment of a new temporal or spatial disposition without the construtcion of a new place; if there were no subjective rearrangement of the previous state of things, there would be no difference from the previous state of things. Although coordinate division prescinds from the subjectivity of the process, it does note the change. The error of determinism is to assume, first, that a coordinate division is the only one that can be made, and, second, that everything that happens must have an analyzable reason. The second assumption is proper and gives rise to no difficulty if it is remembered that a genetic division can be made of the process within the moment that accounts for the complete determination of partially indeterminate possibilities. The second assumption plus the denial of the subjective process results in the determinist thesis.

The genetic division of the present existent is the one primarily of interest regarding free agency. In the genetic process there are two kinds of value operative. On the one hand are the values of the objective realities prehended. These are the satisfactions of the previous actual occasions, both of the discursive individual's own past history and of the other things in the past he prehends. Although these prehended satisfactions are structures, ways in which previous entities have attained their own contrasts, they are appreciated in the prehending entity according to their intrinsic worth. The prehending entity then must harmonize them in such a way as to give appropriate place to their intrinsic worths to the degree possible; the fact that not everything is compatible for objectification means that decision will have to be made within the process as to which values will be kept and which eliminated, which will be subordinated and which elevated to a position perhaps higher than their intrinsic worth. The ultimate criterion is not "doing justice to each intrinsic worth by itself" but rather "attaining the greatest contrast of intrinsic worths in the harmony of the prehending entity." This means there must be, on the other hand, the values that rank the objective values prehended (taking "rank" as a neutral generic term for all the sorting processes), values that determine the subjective form in which the objects prehended can be harmonized in the prehending entity. These are the essential features deriving from the past, the present, and the future. The values prehended can be called *objective* values; those functioning essentially can be called *normative* values. The essential features derivative from the past are prehended as objective values; but they were normative values in the objects that are prehended, and they function as normative values in the prehending entity too, although perhaps in a different way.

That there are many essential features, at least three kinds of them, in any actual entity means the process of the moment involves two orderings. There is the ordering of objective data. And there is the ordering of the various essential features to determine which are more important than others, and with regard to what. The former can be called the *process of objectification* and the latter the *process of norm-determination*. Both are aspects of the one process of moving from initial data to objectification. The process of norm-determination must be sufficiently advanced at each stage to determine the parallel move toward objectification. But each stage in the process of norm-determination is dependent on the state of the objectification process at hand for the object of relevance of the norms.[5]

The importance of this distinction is that the essential features

5. This distinction between two orders of determining within the moment parallels Whitehead's distinction between the process of unifying initial data and the process of modifying the subjective aim. The difference between axiological pluralism and the philosophy of organism at this point is that for the latter the whole subjective aim begins as an initial datum subsequently modified by spontaneous factors. For the former the three sorts of essential features function together from the beginning.

derivative from the past, the inherited character of the discursive harmony, could be said to determine the subjective form of the objective conditions, also determined by the past; if this determination is complete, *then there is no freedom of choice.* Put in moral terms, if the conditions of choice *and* the motive operative in choosing are antecedently determined, and if there are no other factors operative in the choosing, then it is impossible that the person choosing could choose otherwise than he does, and there is no free choice.

But on the contrary, if there is a process of determining an order of several kinds of norms for ranking the objective values, and if only one of those kinds of norms derives from the past, then in principle the resolution of the moment cannot be antecedently determined. There are essential features derivative from the present and from the future as well as from the past, and all these must be harmonized into a complex order of values for ranking the prehended objective values. Only the essential features derivative from the past are antecedently determined, and their position relative to the other two kinds of values is a matter of novel resolution within the process of the moment.

It might be objected that we have just pushed the problem back one step further. It will be asked, what determines the process of norm-determination? Might it not be that the essential features derivative from the past dominate that process?

It is categoreally impossible, however, that the essential features derivative from the past alone determine the process of norm-determination. That process includes essential features unique to the moment, and those derivative from the past necessarily are indeterminate with respect to them. Precisely because the norms unique to the moment are utterly spontaneous relative to the past, the norms of habit and character cannot take them into account in directing the process of norm-determination. Therefore, the process of norm-determination includes direction from some other kind of norm, or from a function of all kinds together. The usual *result* of the norm-determination process may be that antecedent essential features are dominant; but in no sense is the determination of the order of norms completely determined by antecedent conditions. In cases of human decision, the essential features *not* derived from the past are nontrivial.

The general discussion of the alternative to determinism can

be made more specific regarding the moral level of human freedom. Neither physical conditions nor antecedent motives can be
said completely to determine a choice. The physical conditions,
as objective data, must be ordered with subjective form by essential features. And since the determination of which essential features will direct that process includes more than those derivative
from the past, it cannot be determined solely by the latter kind.
Speaking now of the values entering into deliberation—those of
which people can be conscious or aware of feeling—let us call
those that enter as *objective* values "incentives"; in deliberation
their intrinsic values provide an incentive for giving them a
place appropriate to their importance in the final satisfaction.
But competing incentives msut be weighed and ranked according
to the satisfaction of the whole. The essential features or normative values derivative from the past can be called "motives"; a
motive is a value in which a person has a personal stake because
it was a norm for him in some sense before. This distinction is
perhaps adding artificially sharp edges to terms that overlap in
common use, but it will be convenient to have terms on the moral
level that reflect distinctions on the cosmological level. The conclusion argued in the last few pages can be stated as the thesis
that neither incentives nor motives can completely determine the
process of valuation constituting the subjective achievement of
satisfaction.

Not all moments in the life of a person are decisive or moments
of choice. Relatively few are, in fact. Most of the time an individual orders himself by characters inherited from the past, maintaining his equilibrium in a changing world and continuing actions
decided upon previously. In these cases, the resolution of the process of norm-determination is to make the essential features inherited from the past the dominant ones. Norms derivative from
the future or spontaneous within the present are then relatively
unimportant. But at times of decision those other norms are indeed important. In any event, whether or not the norms from the
past are important, they are not to be blamed for the resolution of
the process of norm-determination, for alone they are not capable
of it. A motive by itself cannot take into account the novelty of a
moment; the resolution of the process of norm-determination
must.

We must now pay up the promissory note issued regarding scientific description. At any given point someone could claim that the agent is completely determined by antecedent causes, because every element in his makeup is either something prehended, the effect of natural law, or an essential character trait. Why was the boy a criminal? Because he came from a slum background, and the results of that background are to be found in every moment of decision. True. Why did Adam eat the apple? Because he had the ambition common to every man, and that ambition got the better of him. There is no objective element in the character of a person not deriving from antecedent conditions.

Yet, on the other hand, the elements conditioning a person can usually be harmonized in a variety of different ways, and therefore there is something new each moment—namely, the form of their harmony. In a moment an agent can constitute himself in such a way that a new mode of harmony appears not to be found among his conditions. This is his free choice, and it may go on to form his developing character. The slum boy could have disciplined himself to larger society despite his background. Adam could have put his ambition in perspective and refused the apple. There are limits to this, of course; perhaps the elements in the slum boy's background simply cannot be combined in a more socially disciplined way, and perhaps Adam had misunderstood the command not to eat and therefore had no reason to subordinate his ambition. But not always; what freedom of choice people have comes within the limits of compossibility of their conditions.

The deterministic scientist, just because he is looking for conditions that are the effects of previous causes, does not see the novel modes of harmony contributed by the unique essential features. Or if he sees them he reduces them to their components, which of course are the conditions he was looking for. But such a reduction fails to see that the mode of harmony is something with an identity of its own that is lost in its dissolution into components. The new mode of harmony ought to be recognized for its own sake.

The axiological scheme does not pose an irrational roadblock to the scientific investigation of personality development and decision-making. There is no limit to the investigation science ought to make of the conditions involved. In fact, our psychology is gravely lacking in subtlety when it comes to explaining all the things having grades of importance in the harmony of a decision.

Psychologists attend either to the highly reflected conceptual components, conscious or unconscious, or to plainly neurological components, or to expressions of overt behavior. Few psychlogists handle all of these together, and even then the lines of demarcation are crude. Probably many more types of conditions should be taken into account, and someone ought to give a consistent description of their integration possibilities. Until a single language is worked out for describing the components, little can be determined about the compossibilities of components. Yet it is crucial for jurisprudence and other blame-assessing domains of moral thought to be able to distinguish between possible and impossible harmonies; on this discovery hang all particular judgments about whether actions are voluntary or were caused by antecedent conditions beyond the responsible control of the agent.

The mention of responsibility brings us to the last topic of this section. We have talked so far about how a decision might be independent of antecedent causes, the reason being to show how there can be genuine alternatives for choice. But it would seem now that our arguments would make choice adventitious. To choose without a reason is to choose adventitiously, that is, "irresponsibly." Furthermore, people ought to choose for good reasons, reasons about which they have deliberated until they can approve them reflectively. But to choose on the basis of deliberation seems something from which the arguments of this section have disassociated us.

The chief problem for the interpretation of decision, therefore, is to show how the choice can have real alternatives on the one hand and be made for a reason on the other.

DECISION

Of the three kinds of norms involved in the process of norm-determination, those derivative from the past have been sufficiently discussed. As inherited characteristics of the person, or, on the level of deliberative awareness, as motives, they are norms that were either spontaneous or inherited in previous moments of the person's identity.

The norms derivative from the future come from obligations. Those norms are ingredient in the moment as how the individual should relate to what ought to be done, whether or not the obligations are recognized. In a coordinate division they are principles for judging the worth of what the person at the moment does. In a genetic division they are in themselves merely obligations regarding the person's own future. For such norms to be efficacious in determining the process of actualization genetically, there must be a conceptual prehension of them that functions normatively. Any obligation must be conceptually prehended; otherwise there would be no potentiality to choose to meet it, and the obligation would not be a real possibility. But there is no requirement that the conceptual prehension of the obligation be given dominance in the order of norms or that it not be forgotten, or that it even be brought to consciousness. Most of the times when we fail our obligations the trouble is that our attention is turned elsewhere. The obligatoriness in an obligation does not rest in the fact that it is prehended or even that it is consciously seen to be obligatory, but in the fact that it is the best course open.

Spontaneous norms derivative within the moment itself can achieve exclusive dominance over the other norms only as inspiration or divine madness. In this situation, very rare indeed, a person's character is set aside and his obligations are ignored; he can be called truly ecstatic, since the essential features dominant in the moment of experience explicitly cut him off from the continuity with his past and future. Whether or not such ecstasy is a good thing depends on its fruits, a point on which Plato and St. Paul agree. Usually, however, spontaneous norms are not exclusively dominant. When they are *important* in the harmony of norms, the harmony can be called creative. Usually, as individual values the spontaneous norms are not important at all and can be neglected in analysis. Spontaneous norms are spoken of here as individual novel patterns of value for arranging the objective data in the moment. There is another sort of spontaneous norm that characterizes the *overall* pattern of the norm-determination, which will be discussed below.

In every moment the process of norm-determination is resolved, since there is always a harmony of the various norms appropriate for ordering the objective data. But not every moment is one of choice. What is the difference between an ordinary resolution of the process of norm-determination and a decision?

An ordinary resolution is a ranking of norms determined by (a) appropriateness to the objective data at various stages and (b) the maximization of felt combined value. Maximum combined value is the harmony of values achieved in the greatest valued possible contrast in the satisfaction of the moment. The limits to a resolution are set by the compossibility of the norms in various patterns. In Whiteheadian language, there is a categoreal obligation that a resolution of norms be both appropriate and of maximum combined value. Involved in an ordinary resolution are norms from the past, spontaneous norms, and conceptual prehensions (such as exist in the moment) of obligations relative to the agent's future self.

A decision, on the other hand, is a resolution that (a) adopts a norm as dominant in explicit exclusion of some other norms so that (b) a choice is made determining future alternatives with (c) some conscious awareness of the alternatives chosen between and the obligations involved. "Decision" is used here to indicate the peculiar resolution of the process of norm-determination, and "choice" indicates the whole process that includes the resulting resolution of the objective data in turn resolving the future alternatives.

The importance of clause *a* is that not all resolutions are sufficiently focused so that alternative ways of resolving them hang on the adoption of one or another mutually exclusive norms. In a decision there are explicit competing norms recognized as such. In ordinary resolutions the relations between the norms at the initial stages of the process are not so contrasting; rather they are vague feelings too unfocused to be objects of conscious attention and insufficiently self contained to be adoptable, one in exclusion of the others.

The importance of clause *b* is that in a decision the adoption of one norm to the exclusion of others determines the subjective form of the objective satisfaction of the moment in such a way as to transform a secondary universal in a future possibility into a primary one. The decision effects a choosing between alternatives. Consequently, the decision not only involves consciousness of the alternate norms but also of the alternatives in the future possibility and of the connection between them. The connection is that the resolution of the norm-determination process determines the subjective form of the process of objectification so that certain po-

tentialities for intentional action determining the future are eliminated, and one specific one is actualized in the satisfaction. The
degree of consciousness of the connection is not as important as
the consciousness of the way the future alternatives turn on the
present decision regarding what shall be the dominant norm.

The importance of clause c is that the alternatives in the future
from which the decision is made are related to obligation. Each
of the alternatives, if chosen, entails further obligations; these are
the hypothetical imperatives. There is usually a best alternative,
and the obligation is to do the best, a categorical imperative.

The line between ordinary resolutions and decisions is not
sharp. In practical circumstances, however, the important decisions a person faces are those he recognizes as such beforehand and
deliberates about. Deliberation sharpens the contrast between alternative norms and focuses the decision. It articulates the connection between the candidate norms and the results regarding the
future possibilities. A person can have an obligation to make a
deliberate decision if an important future alternative will be resolved willy-nilly by his action; if he lets his intention be formed
by sloughing along with an unaware resolution of his norms, he
fails that obligation.

REASONS

To adopt a norm as dominant in the harmony of essential features is to make it *the reason* for acting. The norm determines the
intentional action resulting from its measure of the objective process. Furthermore, it is the reason the person has for acting that
way. To adopt the norm as dominant is to count it as worthy, in
the moment, of directing action. To decide between norms is to
give oneself a reason, or to adopt a reason, or to make oneself the
one who has the reason, to act this particular way. Whether or
not the reason is objectively valid is a matter for objective, that is,
subsequent, assessment; it is hoped that the person will have anticipated that judgment by prior deliberation and will be able to
weigh, when he decides, the worth of the value he adopts.

To appreciate the worth of something, and to act upon it,
adopting it as the reason one acts as one does, are different things.
Most people have had the experience of knowing the better and
doing the worse. It is naïve psychology, from an experiential

standpoint, to believe that one always pursues the apparent good merely because one would have no reason for doing otherwise. Experience shows that in some crucial instances we choose what to accept as determining reasons, and that we sometimes choose what we know are bad reasons. The very heart of free choice is that a free agent makes himself the person who acts for such and such a reason; he chooses his reason, and he may choose poorly.

This interpretation of free choice differs from that which claims people choose actions and then must accept as their own whatever reason might justify them, good or bad. The difficulty with that position is that it involves plain adventitiousness. The action is chosen without reason, and then after the choice there is an obligation to accept the justification for it, an obligation the person can refuse (in which case he would have chosen in bad faith). Rather, in the genetic process the norm for determining the action is decided upon directly, and the choice of actions results from this.

The theoretical question then is how the decision is made. Is the resolution of the process of norm-determination in a moment of choice determined by norms from the past, future, present, all of these, or none? The answer is, by the norms from the present. Because of the character of present existence, spontaneous norms must function on two levels. First of all, they are on the level with the other norms, presenting values to be realized in the actual satisfaction of the moment. Second, they are the values in fact realized in the determinate harmony of norms. The overall pattern of ranking the norms that in the case of decision involves direct exclusion of some from dominance is a spontaneous product. It cannot be a product of norms from the past, because they cannot be determinate with respect to first-level spontaneous norms. And it cannot be a product of norms from the future, because these are only obligations, and the resolution of the process of norm-determination is a necessity. Finally, it cannot be a product of all or a combination of the first-level norms together, because they do not exist together until harmonized; this is a question-begging candidate. Rather, the integration of the three kinds of norms is unique to the moment; it constitutes the essence of the moment in a primary sense required for distingiushing the present from past and future. Like the pattern of an actual satisfaction, the pattern of the harmony of norms in a moment has conditional and essential features. Its conditional features to be harmonized are the first-level norms. Its essential features are the determinants of the subjective form of their harmony. Those essential features are spontaneous norms.

Because the resolution of the process of norm determination is the heart of free choice, it is apparent that choice is not solely a matter of antecedent conditions, even of deliberation, but of a spontaneous adoption of a reason for acting a particular way.

Then does not this position entail that choice is adventitious? Spontaneity is just another name for adventitiousness.

No, because an adventitious choice is one not made for a reason, one that is made for no reason. Decision, to the contrary, is the supplying of a reason for a choice. A choice determines the objectification of potentialities in a moment so as to bring about one of a set of alternatives in the future, and the choice has the reason decided upon.

The question is whether there is a reason for supplying the reason for choice. Is there a reason for deciding upon this norm rather than that one? If there is not, then it would seem that the selection of the norm is adventitious, and the distinction of levels of norms has just pushed the problem back one step.

In a sense there is a reason, the second-level spontaneous norm. That norm determines the decision; in other words, making the decision one way rather than another is the spontaneous coming to be of the norm unique to the moment. Unlike the first-level norms that exist as initial valued drives to be harmonized, the way a second-level spontaneous norm comes to be in the moment is analogous to the way a satisfaction comes to be. It is a value spontaneously created in the moment. This sense of being a reason, however, is unlikely to satisfy the question asked. The supposition of this question is that the reason must be antecedently entertained and be accepted antecedent to the decision made on its basis.

But this is to beg the issue, namely, that decision is always acting from a reason rather than the adoption of a reason for acting. Of course, there is not a reason for deciding on the norm prior to the decision. Although if there were, then there would not be a free choice; the choice would be determined by the antecedent reason.

Is the second-level spontaneous norm a *good* reason for decision? It is claimed that the resolution of the process of norm-determination is always a maximization of the appropriate values for the subjective form of the process of actualization. Is this still the case with decision?

The answer is yes. The greatest value to be realized in a moment is always limited to the components of the present existent, its prehensions and essential values. From the standpoint of a coordinate division it might be possible to say that the prehensions could have been harmonized in a better way; but that standpoint prescinds from the genetic process, and in that genetic process there were no resources in terms of conceptually prehended essential values that could give rise to the better subjective form. From the standpoint of the genetic process, the decision could not have been better.

But is this not then a commitment to the view that a person always decides for the apparent good? Quite the contrary, the determinant of the decision is not the apparent good or the reason decided upon, no matter how good they are; the determinant is the second-level spontaneous norm. That norm might be such as to elevate an inferior norm to dominance; although that would lead to a bad choice, it would still be a free one. *Given that second-level spontaneous norm,* the best the person can do in one sense is to make a bad decision. This is not a denial of freedom, however, because that second-level spontaneous norm is *not given* except in the making of the decision; it cannot be conceptually prehended within the moment, only subsequently. Therefore, the making of the decision is not antecedently determined. It is the adoption of a reason for action, and the adoption is its own reason.

However, cannot it be said of an adventitious choice that it is its own reason for choosing, in precisely the same sense, acknowledging the same distinction between the reason chosen and the reason for choosing? The difficulty with such adventitiousness is that it is irresponsible; the choice of the reason ought to be governed by what the person is obligated to choose.

On the contrary, an adventitious choice is the choice of an action for no reason, and on the interpretation of the axiological scheme, the choice of the action is made for the reason decided upon; the decision supplies a reason for the action. Obligations are to right choices of actions, and we have accounted for the giving of reasons for these. *Moral judgment is concerned not with the reason for deciding upon the reason for action, but with the quality of the reason decided upon.* The decision is a good one if it decides on the relevant obligation, no matter for what reason the decision is made. That latter reason, in fact, is nothing but the value attained by deciding upon the former reason. A person is morally praiseworthy or blameworthy according to the norms he adopts, not according to the norms for adoption, unless these latter are in some way adoptable. But the norms according to which he adopts do not exist prior to the adoption; they are spontaneously definitive of his being as the decider.

Having dealt with a variety of arguments aimed at showing that the theory of decision begs the question, either falling into adventitiousness or into antecedent determinism, we may now turn to ways in which the different kinds of norms may be integrated in a decision regarding norm-determination.

An obligation can be adopted as the dominant norm or the reason for acting only by objectifying a potentiality for the obligation's fulfillment in the final satisfaction. Or rather, the adoption of such a norm determines the subjective form of the satisfaction to include the potentiality for it as actualized. An obligation can be fulfilled only if there is an objective potential for fulfilling it in the data of the moment; otherwise it is not possible. It is conceivable that an obligation can be adopted as the reason for acting in opposition to all motives and spontaneous urges (excepting the second-level spontaneous norm). In this case the contrast decided between is this obligation versus all motives and spontaneous norms. Kant was of the opinion that unless a person's choice were of this radically exclusive sort it is impossible to tell whether he is acting out of obligation.

The happier state of affairs would be for the adopted obligation to be supported by important motives stemming from the past. Perhaps the decision would involve adopting the obligation and then giving high priority and support to various motives that abet it but would otherwise be subordinate to different motives excluded in the choice. This means altering one's character by enhancing certain parts and downgrading others. The happiest state of affairs would be to have one's most preponderant motives in the situation correspond to obligation; the adoption of the obligation as one's reason would involve no motivational expense. The importance of coordinating motives and obligations in decision is that the continuity of a person's life depends on it. To exclude all motivation is for the person to reject his past. If his past is rotten enough he may be obliged to do it, although it would be remarkable if he could (remarkable in that the second-level spontaneous norm would have to be dancing ecstasy). But for most people the decision to adopt their obligations only calls for a reformation of their past motivations. The Old Testament sense of the happy man, the kind of man Job was before and after his trials, focuses directly on the continuity of past and future that depends on correlating motivations with adopted obligations.

The richest kind of free agency of course is that which integrates first-level spontaneous norms with the others so as to create new possibilities expressing more motivations and realizing greater good in obligation. Spontaneous norms can add new values to which a man can be obligated, enriching his life. Those values might satisfy more of his antecedently determined motivations. Spontaneity is the source of creativity, and this is a new dimension of freedom dealt with in the next chapter.

The reference to the continuity of the person in decision must be commented upon. Because the second-level norm for decision comes to be in the deciding, *a decision is the constituting of the person as a free agent.* Free agency is not a potentiality before the exercise of free decision. There is a faculty of free action, but none of free decision. The person in the moment makes himself a free decider by deciding freely. But this is only for the moment, and a person is a discursive individual with a history and a future. If he decides for his obligations, he includes his future in his free agency.

The important theorem derived from continuity through accepting future obligation is that a person makes himself a free agent in discursive historical character by the decision for obligation. To decide contrary to obligation constitutes a free decision in the moment but is the explicit rejection of the obligations defining future identity. In this sense Kant was right in saying that only the decision to adopt the categorical imperative as the reason for action is a free decision. The transcendental constitution of the self as free depends on a decision selecting obligation as the reason for action; only such a free decision preserves the moral continuity of the whole self.

There is no special obligation for a person to constitute himself a full free agent by making good decisions. The reason for making good decisions is that they are obligatory, simply that. Freedom is not a super goal, for which fulfilling obligations is a hypothetical imperative. A free person is an individual of great intrinsic worth, of great contrast, and there is an obligation to such intrinsic worth.

Transcendental philosophers tend to consider free agency the most important thing for people. Whether it is indeed the most important thing depends on what its alternatives are. Because transcendental philosophers tend to focus so much on free agency, transcendentally interpreted, and to consider concerns for *social* freedom as temptations to inauthenticity, there is reason to suspect that free agency, however necessary it might be, must be understood in a larger social context.

The account of free agency given in the last two chapters may now be summed up. A free agent is one who freely chooses what to do and freely acts upon the intended choice. An action is free in that an agent can determine intended future effects by constituting his present self as an objective condition to be prehended by a series of actual entities and finally objectified as the intended effect; the series is a chain of natural causation initiated by the agent. An action is intentional when it is initiated by the self-constitution of an agent directed to bring about an appreciated result; it is constitution directed by a norm. Free choice involves the resolution of alternative ways in which the future might be actualized. But for these to be alternatives for resolution within the choosing moment, there must be alternate possible choices within the moment; if the choice were determined antecedently, the future would be antecedently determined. A free choice, then, begins with a decision adopting the dominant norm to guide the process of actualization in the moment. The norm for action is freely adopted and is its own reason; or in other words, it is the reason freely adopted for the intentional action. Choosing freely in this way, a person constitutes himself a free agent.

To say a person is a free agent is to say he is morally responsible for his actions, in the sense of definition *b* on p. 148. This means first that the actions must be initiated and controlled by him; otherwise he is not the cause of them, and something else is responsible in the sense of definition *a* on p. 148. Furthermore, for moral responsibility the actions must be personally caused by the agent.

To be held morally responsible for something, the agent must have been able to do otherwise. There must have been real alternatives between which he could choose without being forced by an antecedent cause; if there were such an antecedent cause, then that cause would be responsible, in either the *a* or *b* sense. But then the choice, if only partially determined by the past, must still be the agent's own doing. He must make himself the one who is responsible for the action by adopting the reason for the action as his own. A person is responsible for his actions if it is possible for him freely to choose them, even if he sloughs over the choice and allows himself to be moved by habit or by the last thing he thought of. A person does not necessarily have to exercise choice in order to be responsible for his actions, although he *ought* to exercise choice because he *ought* to fulfill his obligations.

There is an important difference between being responsible for actions and holding oneself responsible. In the latter case the agent's free decision constitutes his continuity with future obligation, making him answer in the future for his present choice. To hold oneself responsible as a free agent requires making the actual decision. The decision need not be in favor of one's obligations, and in fact may adopt a scurvy motive, but to hold oneself responsible the agent must adopt as obligations the hypothetical imperatives attendant upon that decision. Even if an agent chooses adventitiously, which he might in the sense of adopting a spontaneous norm exclusive of obligations and motives, he is responsible because that was a free choice, and he can take responsibility for it by adopting the attendant hypothetical obligations.

Responsibility has been defined in this chapter in terms of the notion of obligation. But the *content* of obligations has not been discussed: an option is *right* for a person if it is *good* relative to him. The next chapter deals with the good.

7

Freedom in Creativity

The Discernment of Values

That a person is a free agent does not as such mean that he chooses and acts well. In fact, part of being a free agent is being faced with the possibility of choosing the worse. But choosing well is not unconnected with free agency since among the norms available for adoption in the crisis of decision are obligations. To the extent that an agent accepts himself as accountable for his actions, he must accept himself as bound by obligations, even if he is seduced to ignore them or is mistaken in identifying them.

The freedom to act well depends on accessibility of the real values of his options the agent. The real values of things about which he acts and of things affected by his actions must somehow be registered, if not in his consciousness at least in his subliminal feelings, if he is to direct his actions so as to act well with respect to them. No one expects the real values to be grasped with perfect clarity or without distortion, but there must be some connection between the real values and the imagined values the agent intends if his actions are to be good in any objective sense. In technical terms, this means normative potentialities in the agent should conform to the values in real future possibilities.

Let us use "deliberation" as a general term for the *processes of discerning* real values relative to action. Deliberation is to be contrasted with the intuition or immediate appreciation of the values of things; it must contain a critical moment to determine whether the values, in some degree at least, are really in the things about which action is directed.

Values by themselves are immediately appreciated. In the grasp of the harmony whose value they are, the normative elements are dominant, since the harmony consists precisely in the normative measure of the things harmonized. This is true whether the harmonies are actual concrete states of affairs, imagined future possibilities, or any other imaginable thing, even a philosophical scheme.

Deliberation is about the *relative* merits of competing values. So the first thing the account of deliberation must do is to develop a doctrine of the discernment of values as relative.

Values by themselves as immediately appreciated or even consciously felt are not discerned as related to the context that might support them. Another task of deliberation, then, is to determine how values in harmonies are related to the actual and really possible world. Most particularly, deliberation must determine how values are related to the potentialities for action in agents who might intend them. That is, the worths of various things must be grasped not only in terms of their relative merits but in terms of their relevance to the factors in the world subject to human control. So the second thing an account of deliberation must do is to develop a doctrine of the relevance of the actual world to the values about which deliberation takes place.

The values immediately felt within present experience, the potentialities for decision and action in fact, are not necessarily those about which men consciously deliberate. Yet they should be. The harmonies with subjective and objective normativeness in an agent are mostly below the level of consciousness, arising as they do from physical and non-negative conceptual prehension. The harmonies about which we deliberate are usually far removed in time, space, and even scale from those in the human nervous system. The great capacity of neural "representation" or "picturing" notwithstanding, it is a problem to correlate remote events about which deliberation takes place with proximate harmonies felt in the deliberative process. This is a parallel problem to the correlation of real possibilities with potentialities. To satisfy the doctrine of the relativity of values there must be some kind of conformation of imagined felt values with intended real future values. To satisfy the doctrine of the relevance of values a causal connection must be grasped between real future harmonies about whose values people deliberate and the proximate potentialities on which their alternative actions hinge.

To satisfy these requirements, then, it is necessary to have a doctrine of the appropriateness of felt values for future values that might be intended.

Although the appropriateness of felt values can be well understood only when we have explored the relativity and relevance of values, in principle the practical demand of appropriateness can be stated now: deliberation ought to be thorough in the respects of relativity and relevance. The more deliberation makes cognizance of the real relative values of things an important and vital part of the agent's makeup, the more the real values as grasped will be presented as potentialities in the moment of decision. And the more deliberation limns out the relevance of the potentialities in the agent to the worthwhile values he might seek, the more his self-constitution will be appropriate to the values he wants to realize. Deliberation is not merely a cognitive enterprise, as if that meant something distinct from practice. Rather the function of deliberative cognition is to make a practical and physical connection between real future values and the present potentialities of the agent. To the extent that deliberation succeeds in making its analyses of values in terms of relativity and relevance *functional* parts of the agent's being, it succeeds in making the agent and the values appropriate to each other.

The phrase "relative values" is systematically ambiguous. It can mean on the one hand the relations values have because of their connection in a harmony. For example, "Good health is necessary for an active mind," "Universal education is a condition for a working democracy," "Great dignity and great self-possession go together," "Either popular support or strong constitutional powers are necessary for leadership in a state." The principles behind this kind of relation are (a) values are determinate harmonies, (b) harmonies are determinate with respect to each other according to the kinds of distinctions between them, and (c) the values of the determinate harmonies are relative to each other insofar as the determinate character of the harmonies constituting the value are determinately conditioned by each other. If harmonies are not determinate with respect to each other in any way affecting their intrinsic values, then their values are not relative in this sense. This sense of relativity can be called "structural relativity."

On the other hand, and more important, "relative values" can mean the relative worth of different harmonies. This can be called "normative relativity" since it involves a comparison of the degrees of elegance in the different normative measures of the harmonies. It is possible, for instance, if A is a constituent of B, that A is far more elegant than B, considering their respective overall normative measures; all the individuals in a mob are more valuable than the mob itself for the reason that the mob harmonizes the people too simplistically. The constituent may be more important than the inclusive harmony because the latter is too complex; people in a chaotic social situation are an example of this. These examples may seem to be misleading because, while we nearly aways regard people individually as more important than any group or situation of people, we are often hard pressed to assess situations where people are harmonized in a profound and richly cultured society that elevates the people to degrees of individual and collective worth beyond what they would have without the culture.

The problem in a deliberative situation is to choose between the wholesale harmonies of all the relevant conclusions alternatively made possible by different courses of action. If we act one way, the net effect will have one degree of elegance; if we act another way, the net effect will have some other degree of elegance. The differences between the wholesale alternatives are made by differences in the constituents. A factor with one degree of elegance in the context of one alternative might have a quite different one in another. A stable personality is more valuable in a basically stable situation, for instance, than it is in one changing at its roots. But the problem for deliberation is to take into account all these alterations of constituents and judge the net effects in the wholesale alternatives.

This kind of judgment is ineluctably aesthetic, distinguishing as it must different degrees of elegance. We noted in chapter 3 that intuition is required to grasp whether a harmony is harmonious. But we also noted that people employ criteria of elegance to judge between greater and lesser elegance in normative measure, even though they cannot separate the criteria from concrete embodiments. The nearest our discussion came to articulating the criteria was to state that greater elegance is greater maximization of simplicity and complexity.

Although discrimination of relative normative value is *ultimately* a matter of this kind of aesthetic judgment, *proximately* it is rarely so. In the first place, there are special problems of incommensurability. In the second place, there is the problem of determining obligation in the face of ambiguity.

The most convenient deliberative situation would be one in which the harmonies structurally related and those normatively related are congruent. This would be a case in which there are a finite number of factors that could be arranged in alternate harmonies so that all the factors would be totally included in each of the alternatives. In this situation, everything would be conceived as completely determinate with respect to everything else in every respect when actualized. Deliberation here would consist in comparing the degrees of elegance of the alternative ways of disposing the same constituents, an idealist's dream. There are three basic reasons the idealist's dream is only that.

First, not all things are determinate with respect to everything else in all respects when actualized. Often the determination is mostly with respect to spatial and temporal location. In a deliberative situation, usually the alternatives on which we can act involve relating the situational factors only in certain respects.

Second, considering structural relativity, the different alternatives involve alternate inclusions of factors. Certain factors are relevant for some alternatives but not for others. Deliberation must choose between alternate harmonies whose constituents are not the same, the structural relativities being incongruent with the normative alternatives. Whereas it is obviously one of the first tasks of deliberation to determine what factors are relevant to take into account in the alternative to be intended, it is equally true that the options open determine, each in its own way, the factors that relevantly can be included in it. One of the hardest moments in decision is the realization that the best harmony requires rejecting something highly prized.

Third, the value of a discursive individual such as a human being is in principle incommensurable with other things because of the individual's *subjective valuation*. His objective values are as commensurable as any objective values, of course; a person's skill as a doctor, for instance, his contributions in carpentry, his influential beauty of soul, all can be related both structurally and normatively to other values in the environment. But what cannot be so related is his own essential, not merely conditional, appreciation of the values in his own experience coming from past and future. The qualities of his past being his own self, and his future being his own possibility, are values not appreciable by others, or commensurable with other values. To be sure, others can know and appreciate the objective reality of his past, can grasp his characteristic essential features as conditions. They can also know what his obligations are and how he stands with regard to justifying his actions in the light of them. The individual himself grasps these kinds of things objectively too. But what the individual does that the others cannot do is to appreciate the normativeness of his past and future essential features as definitive of his own value experience. Others can know that he does this; but they cannot do it for him. The subjective value of a person's own experience, including that of the experience of living, is ineluctably private. Therefore the value of a person's subjective experience cannot be commensurable with other factors that include other people's subjective experience.

Is it possible that a person's subjective experience is commensurable from his own point of view with objective realities in his world *not* including other people or discursive individuals with similar subjective experience? The answer is yes, but the situation is academic. A person's world and the human shape of his own subjective experience results from interaction with other people in society. Therefore it is practically impossible to eliminate other people's experience. Ironically, the only person whose self-experience might be fully commensurable with his world is the idiot incapable of social interaction; it is a question whether his evaluative judgments are problematic in the deliberative sense.

Because things are not determinate regarding each other in all respects, because of the variability of what can be included in alternate resolutions or deliberative situations, and because of the incommunicability of the feeling of one's own experience's values, deliberation is severely limited. The first two sources of limitation require infinite knowledge, which is impossible. So the conclusion must be that in some situations there will be obivously important factors, for instance people, whose values cannot be related sensitively in a satisfactory harmony.[1]

1. See my "Man's Ends," *Review of Metaphysics* 16, no. 1 (September, 1962), pp. 26–44 for a more elaborate discussion of the claim that men face unified possibilities with commensurable values. The claim examined is Paul Weiss's.

The point of all this is that to the extent that real values can indeed be taken into account by agents in directing their actions, *the only way this is possible is through deliberation.* Deliberation does *not* guarantee the real values will be grasped in such a way that the best action always can in principle be determined. But the only way they are grasped critically at all is through deliberation.

What are we to say then about obligation, considering the fact that certainty about the best action is hardly ever possible? An agent's primary obligation is to do the best possible. This is an objective matter. An alternative is a real one if it can be chosen; so long as there is a real potentiality in the agent for choosing it, it is a live option, even if the agent does not know its true worth. Even if the agent is ignorant of true worth, he still is obligated to choose the best alternative; on this level ignorance is no excuse.

In many cases there may very well be a best alternative, but given the finitude of human thought it cannot be determined. Unless the best course is hit upon by chance, moral failure is inevitable. Although choice of the best is possible, it is in principle impossible to choose the best because it is the best, that is, for the sake of its obligatoriness. The most the agent can do is to choose what he thinks is best because, given the limitations of deliberation it is the best he can determine. This is acting with the intention to be dutiful, but with a bottomless gulf between the real values and the apparent ones. In any case, deliberation is the only bridge across that gulf, and when there are incommensurables stemming from the limits of deliberation, the bridge cannot span the gap. Stepping back from the possibilities for action to potentialities for ranking alternatives, there is an obligation to deliberate as best possible.

In summary, concerning the relativity of values, deliberation is nearly always ambiguous in its results, and human action ambiguous in its moral quality. But deliberation is the only means, such as it is, to make intentions appropriate to the real values of things.

It was noted above that deliberation only must determine the *relativity* of values but also *relevance* of things in the actual world for the alternatives being deliberated. In a strict sense, relevance means contributing to a harmony that might resolve the situation. A thing is relevant if its value is somehow constitutive of the overall structure and value of the whole possible resolution. It is irrelevant if it makes no difference to the possible resolution. At the beginning of deliberation the relevant factors are those whose values would be good to maintain and enhance in the resolution and that depend on the issues being deliberated for their maintenance and enhancement. At the end of deliberation the relevant factors are those seen to be maintainable or enchanceable in the most elegant possible resolution of affairs. The values relevant at the beginning but not at the end have suffered the tragedy of not being compatible with the best state of affairs, assuming the correctness of the deliberation.

The form in which deliberation determines relevance is the discernment of a continuum of means–ends, beginning with the actually given relevant data and working through those that must be achieved to bring about the best alternative as the end. Often the relevant factors can be calculated as direct causes of the end. Deliberation is most likely to make mistakes, however, in ignoring necessary environing conditions for traits sought in the end. It is particularly important for deliberation to single out the relevant factors as means that can be controlled by people.[2]

Some thinkers in the Aristotelian tradition have thought that deliberation is only about means, not about ends. Aristotelian theories aside, we do in fact deliberate about ends in experience. The means themselves are things of value. Consequently, they contribute their own value to the end, amplifying the value it would have by itself. The end is a harmony whose constituents are the various means producing and sustaining it. Even if the value of a particular means is bad, perverse, or tragic, if it is genuinely a means the value of the end depends in part on the function of that negative value. It is impossible to consider the value of an end apart from its being a harmony of the values of its means, except by an abstract temporal butchery locating the end in a moment of time distinct from means.

2. Pragmatism traditionally has been associated with this point. Classic texts are William James's "What Pragmatism Means" and "Pragmatism's Conception of Truth" collected in *Pragmatism and Four Essays from The Meaning of Truth* (New York: Meridian, 1955). One of the most cogent discussions relative to deliberation is John Dewey's *Theory of Valuation*, in *International Encyclopedia of Unified Science*, Vol. 2, no. 4 (Chicago: University of Chicago Press, 1939). This is also a classic treatment of the continuity of the means–ends continuum.

The interpenetration of value in the means–ends continuum is even more obvious in the fact that any end is itself a means for further value, even if the further value is not considered in deliberation.

Because things are not determinate with respect to everything else in all respects, a given thing may be a means for an end but also more than a means. This is not to say only that it has a value of its own irrespective of the end with which it is continuous. It is to say that whereas some of its value is relevant to the end, other aspects of its value are not. The end is indeterminate with respect to those other aspects of value; the thing could lose them and, assuming that it does not lose the value relevant to the end, the end would be no different.

Human beings are never only means in this sense because the subjectivity of their own experience is a value incommensurable with any ends they might serve. This is what Kant felt in calling people "ends in themselves." Kant was right in seeing that a part of human life cannot in principle be a means to something else, and he assumed that if there were something in a person ineluctably not a means, it must be an end. But a better way of expressing the point is to say something in human subjectivity cannot be a means because it is incommensurable with other means or with a superior end.

Kant also wanted to indicate that the factors in life making people "ends in themselves" are more important in a way than the respects in which people can be means for something else. This point is reflected in our account by the fact that the incommensurable elements are appreciation of the values in the essential features that define the heart of the continuity of an individual through extended action. A person's heart is the life of his essential features in the series of processes of norm-determination.

Attention should be drawn here to *sets of alternatives* deliberation must cope with. First are the alternate real possibilities. It should be noted that in this chapter we have applied the term "alternative" to the whole harmony being deliberated, including the primary universals that would be present in any alternative as well as the secondary universals distinguishing the alternatives. The second set of alternatives is derived from the alternate conceptual schemes deliberation might use to analyze means–ends continua. Since alternate causal analyses can be given, different configuration of means can be conceived as relevant to a given end. As a result, the determination of ultimate relevance in deliberation is a matter not only of selecting one real alternative but also of selecting a conceptual scheme for analyzing the relation to the real world of the alternative construed as ideal.

This section has dealt with relativity of value and relevance to value. In passing it has commented upon the appropriateness to real values of subjective factors in choice. The overall point concerns appropriateness. To act well is to act with a view to the real values of things. Only deliberation can determine those values, to the extent that they can be determined at all. There is therefore a great value to deliberation.

It is possible in summary to state the factors of complexity and simplicity whose harmony constitutes the value of deliberation. On the one hand, affairs ought to be arranged so as to preserve all the values that have been achieved and that given actual factors make possible. Because everything has a value—and constituents with values—the complexity of deliberation should be infinite. Every potential constituent has a prima facie right to be included in the resultant harmony, with its own value intact if not enhanced. In this sense, everything ought to be relevant. On the other hand, deliberation must narrow down the possibilities to a single state of affairs. That is, it must simplify things, and to do this some things of value must be eliminated; you cannot eat your cake and have it too. The loss in initial complexity ought to be compensated for by a depth of contrast or elegance achieved. The degree of contrast proposed at the end of deliberation reflects the degree of the deliberation's elegance.

The concreteness of human moral life can be illustrated in a comparison with an artist's work. An artist begins with a simple idea suggested by his materials and his past work; contrast comes through the delicate addition of complexity, and at the end of the creative process there is far more than was intended at the beginning. This is true even of "minimal painting," where the additions are mainly significant negatives. In contrast to this, the basic moral task of human life is set originally in complexity. The world is just given, and the moral task is to simplify the given demands to one possibility. The move is from complexity to simplicity. But in the case of art as well as that of the more broadly based human situation of which art is a peculiar variation, the quality of human activity is a matter of maximizing complexity and simplicity in harmony. The more contrast in the harmony, the richer the life.

NORMATIVE INVENTION

The focus on freedom should not be forgotten. What are the essential moments of deliberation that contribute to freedom, that is, have to do with creativity?

Deliberation, not in every instance but in its paradigm form, can be characterized as the "critical art of normative invention." It can be called "critical" because it tests the ideals it suggests. It is an "art" because its practice is itself a normative measure, maximizing the comprehension of complexity in the situational factors with the depth provided by simplicity. It is "normative" because its products are suggested normative measures for harmonizing the deliberative situation elegantly. And it "invents" rather than discovers, because its initial data, its raw materials, are the situational factors and the modes of togetherness they contain.

If a deliberative process begins with fixed goals and attempts only to invent means for their achievement, it is a degenerate form of deliberation. If the goals are inappropriate to the given factors in the situation, then they may exclude important values as irrelevant that ought to be included, and that might be included with different goals. Any goal in a concrete situation probably will exclude some important values—that is the tragedy of the moral life. But the degeneracy in the deliberative process beginning with fixed goals is that it *arbitrarily* eliminates criticism of the goals. Maximum value can be discerned critically only when alternate goals and alternate sets of relevant factors are considered in relation to each other. An authentic, nondegenerate process of deliberation includes criticism of the goals or ends suggested, even if the agent enters the deliberation with an idea as to what his goals ought to be.

In parallel fashion, deliberation beginning with a fixed catalogue of relevant issues is also degenerate. There might in fact be other values worth a chance at relevance. Authentic deliberation requires criticism of both the possible goal and the possible concatenations of relevant factors.

Having distinguished two ways in which deliberation can be degenerate, it is important, in order to single out authentic deliberation, to notice conventional approaches and theories of morals that tend to fix either goals or relevance. Ethical approaches based on a *code of values* are suspect. In the strictest sense a code of values is harmless. The code says that in certain circumstances a certain kind of behavior or intention is valuable, and if the code is a good one that claim is correct. But the code is applicable only where it has critically been determined that those circumstances in fact obtain and that no other behavior or goal would be more valuable. The danger in the code is that it will be applied before such analysis has been made; the very intent of a code is to have a handy rule of thumb for application where there is insufficient time or ability for deliberation. But if the social situation is one of fairly basic flux, then it can almost be guaranteed that the conditions in which the code was developed do not obtain. Moral training in a situation of basic flux should involve not so much allegiance to a preestablished code but rather techniques for psyching out the changes going on. Our present social situation seems to be one of basic flux.

What has been said about code-ethics also applies to *virtue-ethics*. The traits of great value in one social situation may not be the ones needed for another. As Whitehead noted, the only sort of man in contemporary society who would have fitted well into Plato's society is the professional boxer.

In some circumstances the pursuit of relatively *fixed goals* is itself a value perhaps outweighing the values lost by arbitrary exclusion. For instance, a nation strives for consistent policies in both foreign and domestic affairs so that other nations and the institutions of its own society can adjust to them. The need for a consistent policy is greatly lessened, however, if a change in policy can be quickly and perspicuously communicated to those affected by it and if those affected are prepared to shift their own activity in time to take advantage of the new situation. Electronic technology is in fact making the virtue of consistency in long-range planning obsolete. Planning itself is changing from the method of establishing fixed long-range goals to that of establishing *procedures* for *adjusting* short-range goals; the adjustment is desirable as information feedback from present activity opens new possibilities or shows the shortcomings of previous plans. This may mean the end to treaty diplomacy, for instance. The reason the so-called domino theory justifying American military activity in Southeast Asia is not very persuasive, even though it is correct in its analysis of treaty oriented diplomatic behavior, is that people feel the wrong variables are being cited. A deliberative procedure based on fixed goals, in this case certain treaty commitments and economic intentions, is inauthentic, and the flaws become fissures under stress.

On the other side we must beware of the habits of deliberation beginning with a conventional or specialized analysis of the conditions to be resolved. In a changing situation, the factors articulated by conventional wisdom are likely not to have the relevance conventionally assigned to them. Equally dangerous is reliance on a specialist's conceptual scheme transferred to a larger deliberative situation. The presupposition in these cases is that the kind of social variable systematically understood in the special discipline is the relevant kind to consider. This warning is not to say that specialists are incapable of authentic deliberation; it is only to name their prejudicial interpretation of affairs solely in terms of their own specialty as inauthentic deliberation.

Deliberation can now be seen to be the art of inventing appropriate goals or ideals for situations, determining the connection of the ideal with what the agents can do. The ideal should be the best relative to other ideals, if there indeed is a best; it should contain as relevant to it the things genuinely valuable in the situation. And the process of bringing it about should be within the limits of human powers.

Deliberation therefore must contain three basic factors: *analysis, imagination,* and *criticism.* The integration of these three factors is the art of normative invention.

There is nothing obscure about the kind of *analysis* needed for deliberation. The analysis should be empirical and neutral. In contrast to fine art, the moral situation contains given factors to be grasped empirically. The analysis should be neutral with respect to the values desired or the goals initially entertained. In the long run the analysis must show whether the goals are possible; but the goals should not prejudice its view of the empirical situation. This ideal of neutrality is impossible to fulfill completely, of course, since any means of analysis will have been de-

veloped because of some value felt in it. To base the method of
analysis on the goals to be pursued is to suffer, although indirectly,
the inauthenticity of beginning with fixed goals.

The best methods of analysis depend on the situation. But we
should beware of assuming, since the analysis should be empirical,
that empirical sciences are the only disciplines of help. There are
a great many factors, especially those involving human feelings
and aspirations, for which there are no sensitive sciences. An em-
pathetic approach, an analysis of communal responses, of culture,
and so forth, might all be more to the point than an interpretation
of the situation in terms of one of the physical or social sciences.

Imagination is intended here to mean the conception of new
modes of togetherness, modes of harmony. The modes are new in
the sense that they do not derive per se from anything prior in the
experience of the imaginative agent. The things put together in
the mode of harmony are indeed antecedently given in experience; but the modes are new. Without imagination, deliberation
could only fall back on previously tried or discussed solutions.

Imagination can have a feedback effect on analysis. It not only
produces new ways of morally harmonizing the deliberative elements in action, it produces new ways of looking at the facts of
the situation; it provides novel approaches for analysis.

Lacking in imagination, a person is bound to repeat past facts,
and even worse, past thoughts, to the exclusion of any real appreciation of novel possibilities. Because it is the task of the deliberative agent to appreciate the real values in the world, he should
appreciate the real possibilities, some of which are novel.

The concept of imagination is not innocent in philosophical literature and our cosmology should give it formal articulation.
Imagination *in the strict sense* is the spontaneous advent of essential features unique to the moment, harmonizing data given in the
moment. The data given might be conditional or essential features.
The imaginative harmony may be negatively prehended in the
final satisfaction, as is the case with most products of imagination,
or it may find a place there. *In a loose sense,* imagination is the
process of coping explicitly with products of imagination in the
strict sense.

It is tempting to limit imagination to producing conscious conceptual unities, since imagination would seem to involve produc-

ing what we can have an "image" of. But many artists and other creative people are unconscious of the complex work of their imagination until reflection on the novelty in their physical products.

Imagination cannot strictly speaking be called a faculty, since there is no antecedent structure, no potentiality, for producing something spontaneous. At best we can say the universe has a faculty for producing novelty of this sort. We can say "imagination does this" only as a paraphrastic way of talking about spontaneous appearance.

A decision, as characterized in chapter 6, is a work of imagination. A spontaneously imagined harmony is an appreciated value. As a way of harmonizing factors given in the subjective process, its presence is that of a normative measure. Its subjective form includes a feeling of its value, and so there is a rudimentary tendency to accept the imaginative suggestion, actually to order experience with it, and to pursue its ramifications. This rudimentary urge may be cut off by negative prehension, or it may be fed by supporting urges or erotic drives. But from the most subconscious depths there is a peculiar lure to products of imagination that, when it survives to the more or less conscious level, amounts to fascination.

Imagination in the loose sense can be trained. Not that a man can cause spontaneity, but he can develop habits of taking advantage of it. Habits submerging spontaneity in traditional reactions can in part be put aside. This training of the imagination has both negative and positive aspects.

Consider a person, not a professional mathematician, trying to work his way through a mathematical problem. The relevant factors are all such that he carries them in his head. But he just cannot seem to put them together in the right way. All the moves and associations his conventional responses suggest lead down blind alleys. After a while the person knows he has to try something else. So he goes for a walk, hoping that the different physical activity will trigger new associations. Or he forces himself to think about something else. Or he tries to explain the difficulty to a friend whom he knows can grasp only the simplest mathematics. The hope in all these cases, the hope on which we all act when trying to work out of a circle of bad reasoning, is that by inhibiting habits established in the past, an opening will be made for the spontaneous suggestions of imagination to come to the fore. The problem with most problem-solving is that the products of imagination are negatively prehended before they are simplified to the scale where they play a recognizable part in deliberation.

On the positive side, imagination in the loose sense can be taught in terms of habits following out of the leadings of imagination. Primary- and secondary-school training in the fine arts has not been exploited nearly enough as a laboratory for training children in the basic attitudes necessary for the encouragement of the imagination. Facing a moral situation and painting a picture have much in common, for instance. In the former there are always given factors to be coped with, and in the latter there are the lesson limits set by the teacher and the materials. At any point in the process of coping with the problem there is a mixture in both cases of given elements with the agent's own contribution, so that he must be responsible for what he has done. At any point there are enough unknown variables that the agent must follow hunches. The habits built up in art incline one to turn quickly to the suggestions of his imagination. And fortunately, unlike the moral life, the consequences of aesthetic decisions are rarely serious beyond the work itself in the art course.

The suggestions of imagination must be *criticized* in deliberation just as any inherited proposed solution must be. Imagination is in even more obvious need of criticism since its suggestions have not stood any tests of experience. Roughly, the critical phase of deliberation must interpret the imagined suggestion in terms of the facts of the situation and assess whether the harmony it would produce is better or worse than harmonies produced through other modes of togetherness; the assessment is a matter of comparing the elegance in the respective normative measures. Although the process of criticism can have no method, since both at its beginning when it interprets the suggestion in terms of relevant connections and at the end when it assesses the contrast in the harmony suggested there can be no rules, there are still pertinent questions to be answered.

Criticism must determine whether the suggested mode of togetherness genuinely hangs together. Although a mode of togetherness must hang together in some way in order to be imagined, its togetherness may not be of the sort it originally seemed.

Criticism must determine in detail how the imagined suggestion relates to the facts of the situation as determined by empirical analysis. Are the sorts of things harmonized in the imagined product the sorts of things actually to be found?

Criticism must further ask whether the suggestion is a live possibility. Is it really possible to harmonize things in the suggested way? The imagined suggestion may be quite pertinent, but impossible.

Criticism must also ask, looking beyond the imagined mode of harmony, whether there is anything important in the situation that *ought* to be relevant to the solution to the problem but is not in fact given proper place in the suggestion. In the last analysis, in comparing relevant and possible alternatives, it may be that no matter which way the choice is made, something important will have to be sacrificed. But at preliminary stages of deliberation, most of the suggestions of imagination can be weeded out simply because they do not take into account all in the situation they should. The difficulty with most "bright ideas" is unwonted narrowness.

Finally, criticism must determine the various degrees of elegance or contrast. This is a matter of aesthetic judgment, the task of determining, like the statesman, just how much is enough. In this discussion we have oversimplified things to speak only of suggestions for the whole harmony of things to result from action. In reality we deliberate not only about the whole states of affairs but also about a myriad of alternatives within each alternative. However difficult the process of calculating alternatives large and small, in the end the assessment is a matter of aesthetic feeling.

It might be objected that resting deliberation ultimately on *feeling* of worth is to make it ultimately uncritical. To this the following remarks should be made.

First, that ultimate judgment does rest on a matter of feeling, of taste, is just the way things are. Consult experience over a broad range, and it will show that feeling is the ultimate resort of assessment.

Second, this doctrine of feeling is not uncritical. All the various elements of criticism described above are genuine and rational ways of rejecting or accepting alternatives. Criticism can be compared to the work of an art critic. He articulates how the aesthetic object hangs together, what its modes of harmony are, what kinds of things it includes and in what roles, how things differ in importance, and how things are different in the work from what they would be outside it or if some detail were changed. In all this he only articulates what is given to intuition. When he first sees the object, his feel for its value is inchoate because he has not paid attention to the character of its harmony. As he analyzes and lives with it, his judgment becomes all the surer because he comes more nearly to grasp it as it really is. In the same way, the difference between uncritical and critical feeling of value is that the latter is educated. Analysis and imagination show the critic what is the case and what might be. In the end the judgment of relative degrees of contrast or elegance is a matter of educated feeling.

Third, it may be admitted that even educated feeling is ultimately uncritical, though only *in the sense of lacking a determinate criterion beyond its final judgment in terms of which its judgment can be warranted*. But the mere fact of feeling, upon which Hume and others base intuitionist ethics, *is not the ground of the aesthetic judgment*. Rather, the fact of feeling x to be better than y rests on there being more elegance in x than in y; elegance, or contrast on the cosmological level, is the real ground of discerning feeling, in its own way a kind of criterion beyond the harmony appreciated. True, it differs from the kind of criterion rationalistic ethicists would like in not being determinate apart from its expressions in determinate harmonies. But for all that, it is not irrational and can be appealed to in argument even though its recognition is intuitive. We do it all the time, from the mathematician assessing the student's work as correct but inelegant to the businessman rejoicing in the cleverness with which he evades the tax laws.

Although the discussion of deliberation so far has centered on its mechanics, it can be concluded with a mention of three important factors in the content of deliberation. In the first place, although deliberation takes place in and about specific situations, the relevant factors to take into account are not always local. The agent should appropriate his own human nature, history, and aspirations in conscious terms so that they play important roles in deliberation. He should appropriate into consciousness his society's values, its history and culture, its interpretations of the heights and depths of human life. The complexity of all the things prehended, some of which themselves are great simplifications of other realities, must be simplified so that its parts can enter into contrast without flattening out into triviality.

Second, deliberation should orient itself to the possibilities of the technology of the modern world. It is difficult to know which to emphasize first, the humanism depreciated by technologically oriented people, or the technology depreciated by humanists. Fortunately, few people deliberate solely as humanists or as technologists. The virtue of the humanistic orientation in deliberation is that the very process of deliberation goes a long way to ensuring that the attained values from the past will not be lost. The virtue of the technological orientation is that it sees possibilities not dreamed of by the humanist, and it is far more aware of how unseen basic changes have made traditional solutions impotent. The danger of the humanistic orientation is that without the technological outlook it will lose the very values it tries to preserve, not knowing what new techniques are needed to maintain them in a new world. The danger of the technological orientation is that, with the power to do much, it has only trivial values to strive for.

The last point about the content of deliberation is to emphasize the importance of philosophy. In the first chapter it was claimed that philosophy has a great social significance as the discipline distilling what is important in life and articulating the connections at the heart of things. This has great moral purpose. Deliberation must simplify the world about which it reflects in order to appreciate the simple contrasts in the values it wants to realize. Philosophy is the discipline that pays attention to the most general of simplifications. Without philosophy's leaven in society there is no funded articulation of what is most important. Philosophy is western civilization's institution for keeping alive the questions of ultimate and general importance.

CREATIVITY AND PERSONAL FREEDOM

The thesis of this section, and the summary thesis of this book so far, is that *personal freedom is creative activity in the environment of the given world.* A person exercises this freedom continuously throughout his life. Some moments are more creative than others; there are high points and low points, and perhaps points of no creativity. But a person lives well the life of freedom in creativity when even his uncreative moments gain meaning by being related to his creative ones. By activity is meant not only overt agency but also the process of deliberation surrounding and uniting the specific creative acts. And the activity includes the various processes by which prehensions are brought to conscious awareness in experience. Creative activity is prehensive, deliberative, and a matter of agency. Every experience involves all three in various ways, but creative activity requires moments when prehension is in sophisticated contact with the world for the sake of being in direct touch, moments when deliberation sums up trains of assessment for the sake of articulating what is most valuable to do, and moments of direct causal action for the sake of bringing about the best. The life of the inspired musical performer is a good paradigm of personal freedom; the dancer perhaps is best.

The reference to the given environment for creative activity is to indicate that the creative life takes up external liberties as important conditions for its activity. It is necessary in the many ways indicated in previous chapters for a creative person to accept and work with the conditions established in the past for an environment for present and future work. Creativity is not the enemy of tradition but the organ for giving it living value in the present and future, as a musician gives life to a written score. The point is that creativity takes the environment to offer not only opportunities for voluntary action but also the material out of which one's creations are made and the conditions that sustain and make them possible.

Aristotle nicely pointed out that one swallow does not make a summer. One act of free choice, based on deliberation and perhaps even for the best, does not make a life of creativity. Even if the choice is highly creative, introducing a radically new departure in handling a certain kind of problem, making one such choice does not mean the person has freedom in creativity. There are two points being made here. One concerns the difference between free agency and freedom in creativity. The other concerns the difference between one creative act and a life that has freedom in creativity.

An act of free choice initiating voluntary action differs from freedom in creativity in two important respects. First, it concerns the adoption of a reason for acting as one's own; creativity by contrast has to do also with the production of excellent reasons. To be sure, a person cannot in the richest sense be called creative unless he acts upon at least some of his creative suggestions, and the development of creative suggestions itself requires many acts of free choice to follow out imagination, criticize it thoroughly, and so forth. But whereas the creative life includes free agency, free agency is possible without deliberate creativity. Second, an act of free agency is ineluctably individual; its meaning comes from its activity in an individual situation. Freedom in creativity is ineluctably general; it is a life generally shot through with singular creative acts, one whose creative habits and commitments to creativity in the future are essential features determining it at every moment.

An isolated creative act differs from a life having freedom of creativity in that there is no necessity for the act to involve important essential features stemming from the past and future. In a life of creativity each individual act takes up materials that have been created in the past by the individual or by his group to which he is essentially tied. It also involves the commitment to cope creatively in the future with the results of the present creative act. Only such an interplay between creative acts can make up a genuinely creative life. The degree to which a single act is creative and the degree to which a life in general is creative are relative matters. But one inspired performance does not make an inspired musician.

The continuity of creativity from one act to another depends on a feedback from the past and an anticipated feedback in the future. There is a loose sense in which this is true, and a strict sense, the distinction arising from a feedback in terms of conditional elements versus a feedback in terms of essential ones.

In a loose sense we say a person is creative if, like the artist or the moral agent, he works through many stages of a process, at each moment coping with the results of his previous actions in the changing situation. Along with this we call him creative if his creative acts at one time are taken with an eye to producing results he can anticipate coping with creatively in the future. Such a person is creatively prudential, committing himself to a continual responsibility in the situation, creative throughout. We like our statesmen to be creative in this sense. In theoretical terms, such a person is continuously creative with respect to the conditional features arising from the situation affected by his actions. The locus of the measure of this kind of creativity is in the situation itself without much regard for the creative agent.

Most of life, however, is not continuous coping with the same situation. Men move from one situation to the next, and creative people, in the stricter sense of the term, carry their creativity with them. Furthermore, in the strict sense, to call a person creative is to speak of a characteristic of him and his actions, not of a situation on which he has a continuous effect. Therefore, in the strict sense a creative person is one whose essential features are specially creative.

In the strict sense a creative person requires feedback from his essential features in the following way. In a present moment he gives prominent place in the process of norm-determination to those essential features from the past that themselves in their own proper time were creative. That is, the essential features in the past that functioned in analysis, imagination, and criticism are elevated to prominence over those reflecting continuity of character. Because of the importance of imagination in creativity, essential features spontaneously arising in the past moment are accorded unusually high prominence when fed back into a subsequent moment. Creative people are unusually willing to take advantage of chance inspirations; they often prefer the apparently irrelevant thought to the tried and true one. They like apparently random activity and are not bothered by wasted motion or personal inconsistency. A consistently creative person will tend not to be consistent in conforming his present actions to past beliefs, or present beliefs to past action, but will more often elevate into present importance some aspect of past creativity that did not get expressed. Similarly regarding the future, a creative person will anticipate his future obligations to be defined not exclusively by what he does now by way of forming future possibilities, but also by how he might create new possibilities in the future.

The loose sense of creativity depends on the strict sense. The creative life is not based merely on the introduction of novelty; that kind of life would be chaotic and morally adventitious. Rather, the creative life is a harmony of the preservation of achieved values with the introduction of new ones, stressing the latter as the source of simplicity. Instead of taking certain achieved values as the center around which life should be built, the creative person takes the achieved values as the complexity to be simplified and the novel values to be the new forms for simplification. In this respect, the creative person is more likely than the conservative to determine which old values can be preserved and which not according to new forms of organization.

Continuous creativity, in both the loose and strict senses, brings the individual a special freedom from the environment. In the loose sense, the longer the creative person has been creatively involved in his situation, the more his external liberties are of his own making. His opportunities are those he has made himself. Or his situation is one constituted in the main part by the social group to which he belongs and that he himself has helped constitute.

In the strict sense the creative person becomes free from the limits of order exhibited by the physical and social environment. Of course this is only a relative matter, and nearly all our goals for resolving things are suggested by past states of affairs or beliefs; but creative people capitalize on the modicum of novelty. And they develop confidence and faith that they are not bound to repeat the past. This gives a psychological sense of freedom from the environment, and even from aspects of their own pasts, based on real freedom in fact.

Continuous creativity also brings greater internal autonomy or self-determination. This point must be made in contrast to the point that every free choice is an autonomous one. A choice, if it is free, stemming from the free adoption of a reason for acting such and so, is one whose essential features all belong to the person choosing; insofar as the choice is his, he alone is responsible, and essential features from his past, his present, and his future enter it. Not all of his essential features, however, are those he has given himself in any important sense; most derive from unconscious events in his past and from the given structure of things obligating him in the future. Only those deriving spontaneously in each moment, adopted as his reasons for acting in a conscious and responsible way, are those he can be said to give himself, and those are precisely the products of creativity. Through a creative life, more and more of a person's essential features are products of his own imagination given prominence by his own free choice. Continuous creativity means a person is not only the autonomous author of his own choices but is more and more the author of the reasons he has in choosing. A genuinely creative person appears to be idiosyncratic in most of what he does precisely because nearly everything he might adopt as a reason for action, and most of his real potentialities, are of his own making. This explains the paradox that creative people are supposed to be very spontaneous on the one hand and yet have distinctive styles on the other. Not every action is spontaneously creative, but those that are not derive from those that once were, and what is spontaneous is idiosyncratic.

Turning now from the process of creativity to its product, it is important to note that the products of creativity are values. Creativity produces normative measures for harmonizing given data. Of course, there is a structure to the normative measure, and a description of what is created articulates the structure. But the role of creativity in experience is to attain a value of harmonizing something. Subjectively, the work of imagination is a felt value, and if the imaginative suggestion is objectively possible its realization would be a real value.

Freedom in creativity, then, is freedom to do the good. This interprets the thesis expressed in chapter 1 that to be free is to do the good. Neither freedom of external opportunities nor freedom of choice makes necessary reference to the good; but both are contained in freedom of creativity. To do something good is not necessarily to do the best. That any creative product is good stems from the fact that it is a normative measure, and so any act in fact harmonizing things would be an act productive of good. Creative acts are not the only ones productive of good. But creativity is the only dimension of freedom where the freedom consists in acting because of the goodness in the act. Free agency is based, not on choosing the good, but on adopting an alternative as one's own reason for acting. Only creative activity is an exercise of freedom whose freedom consists precisely in the production of value.

Not all acts are equally good, however. Just because every creative effect is a normative measure does not mean all the normative measures have equal elegance. An effect that is less than the best is bad, even though it is the realization of some value. Since very few effects are the absolute best, given the limitations of deliberation, most effects are ambiguous.

Depending on the context, we use two standards of moral praise or blame. On the one hand we assess the distance between the effect produced and the best effect possible. On the other hand we assess the motives behind the action. If a person adopts some reason as his own because he believes it to be the best, even if it is far from it, we do not hold him responsible with the same seriousness that we would have if he adopted something as his reason, believing full well that some alternative were far better. We would hold the person who chose perversely to be morally reprehensible, but we would not trust the person whose sincerest intentions were generally bad judgments.

To say that freedom is freedom to do the good is not in itself to say anything very important. A person is also free to do the bad in the same sense. It would be far more important if we could say a person is free when and only when he does the best, in the sense we have developed for that phrase.

The moral continuity of a person's life from the present into the future consists in the fact that he has obligations. He is obligated to do the best. The effects of his best actions extend far beyond his own person, and so his future self is not defined by the scope of his obligations. But his future self is in part defined in terms of the value it inherits from the moral quality of present action. The future self is the one defined by the fact that its antecedents chose wisely or in ignorance, sincerely or perversely. More particularly, the future self is defined by whether and how its antecedents commit it to live up to their obligations. The choice a person makes in the present is a matter of his present essential features. Those features are inherited by his future self as its own essential features stemming from its past, and the fact that the future self will have to cope with those essential features from its past is an essential feature of the future ingredient in the present.

Because in the future a person will have to cope with the essential moral quality he gives himself now, he now possesses his obligations to act in the external world for the best as essential features. If it were not the case that his future would essentially be defined by his present moral quality, the obligations would merely be conditional features stemming from the fact that his present action has future effects of a certain value. If his future is not essentially defined by his present moral action, then the essential features of his present pass away with the perishing of the present, and nothing is left but objective conditions to be prehended by later moments of experience. But since as a discursive person his future must prehend some of his present essential features as essential features for itself, it is presently an essential matter for him to fulfill his obligations. The reason for the obligatoriness of the obligations is that they are what is best, irrespective of the fact that fulfilling them will make a good moral agent. The continuity of a discursive individual from the present to the future consists in his presently having obligations essentially because of the relation he presently holds with his future. A person has obligations as essential features, not because they are his own future essential features, but because his future essential features will have to cope with the essential features he contributes now by the moral quality of his action.

In less theoretical terms, a person exercises the freedom of creativity most fully when he creates for the best. Creating for the best in the present gives his future the most valuable inheritance, both of its own past and of the world it will have to work on. Furthermore, developing and passing on habits of creativity will better enable the person's future self to create for the best. To do worse than the best is to be creative to a degree less than the best possible. If creativity were defined solely in terms of novelty, greater creativity would not mean greater value but greater difference. But creativity is defined in terms of maximizing the complexity of achieved values with the simplicity derived from novel forms of order. Greater creativity therefore means the production of greater value.

It must be remembered that creativity involves an agent's spontaneously producing a potentiality that did not exist before. Considering the "best alternative" to be one that was possible limited to the initial but not to the spontaneous potentialities, a truly creative act would be *better* than the best.

There are degrees of creativity. The lowest would be that involved in the spontaneous essential features resolving the norm-determination process in free choice. There is no novel order in this case except the determinate ranking of the otherwise given essential features. Degrees above this would involve introducing novel orders that not only make the essential features determinate, but do so in such a way as to achieve greater value. Creativity also involves spontaneous essential features introducing new order into conditional features. Most creativity is of this sort, since it deals with the world conditioning the agent. The upper limits of creativity are known only to the muses who know all possibilities; the only requirement is that the basic factors harmonized be the ones given to the experient. It can be said that everyone has the freedom of creativity to a degree, but the degree can be rather minimal.

Creative activity harmonizes and enhances the dimensions of freedom discussed under external liberty and free agency. In this sense it is the capstone of personal freedom; anyone who lives a fully creative life has personal freedom to the full extent. The unique element of creativity is the process of deliberation, with its analysis, imagination, and criticism. But creativity is a matter of activity: creativity is a characteristic of agents, characterizing their free choices. When deliberation has produced its creative suggestion, it must be chosen and acted upon for the agent actually to be creative. And the action must take advantage of the opportunities provided by the environment. In the lifelong exercise of creativity, nothing of the dimensions of external liberty, intentional action, or free choice is lost.

Moreover, the other dimensions of personal freedom are enhanced. The environment becomes the creative person's own making to a greater or lesser extent. The exercise of free agency becomes not only the self-constitution of the agent in terms of his own reasons for acting but also the enjoyment of choosing between potential reasons the agent himself has created, reasonably in touch with the real values of the world affected by his actions. Without creativity action in the liberties of the external world would involve entering a wholly alien environment. Without creativity free agency would be nothing more than desperate acts to make oneself something, anything. With creativity people can be persons, self-posessed and possessed of their world within the limits of real possibility. There is no gainsaying the irrationality and brute givenness of the world and people's lives. The peculiar quality of human life is the freedom of persons flickering on the surface of the marsh.

It might be said that creativity is the essence of man. We have no evidence of animals other than humans being creative in any significant way, and angels are said to have difficulty doing anything material. Transcendental philosophy would make the imaginative element of creativity the root of man's being and knowledge and the root of the being and knowability of the world. Heidegger, for instance, claims that the common root of both sensibility and understanding for Kant is the transcendental imagination, although Kant thought the root is "to us unknown." [3] Interpreted in a sufficiently abstract way, the doctrine of creativity in imagination developed here rests on the doctrine that any event in time must have essential features spontaneous and unique to itself, whatever other essential features it might have. In this sense spontaneity is the ground of temporality, and imagination is the form of spontaneity peculiar to people as discursive individuals who appropriate their pasts and anticipate their futures in a critical way.

But the essence of man can be spoken of only in the most abstract sense. There is no concrete nature of man, only concrete characters of people. The things general to all people, for instance creativity, are at bottom contingently general. Every person, at any moment of his life, receives an essential inheritance of character from his past, and special essential obligations from his future. But both inherited and anticipated essential features are dependent on the circumstances of the past and future—essential features must be appropriate to the conditional features they harmonize. Furthermore, the inherited and anticipated natures a person has essentially are modified and given a contingent place in present experience by each moment's process of norm-determination. The concrete essential nature of any person is in its way conditional upon the circumstances of time and place in which the person lives. (For all the talk of history, transcendental historicism believes that although it is essential to Man's nature to be in some time or other, the time itself is not essential to the nature of Man.)

More importantly, there is no essential nature passed from one

3. See Heidegger's *Kant and the Problem of Metaphysics*, trans. James S. Churchill (Bloomington, Ind.: Indiana University Press, 1962), pp. 144ff.

individual to another, or from one generation to another. One individual may prehend another objectively, but that is not to make the other's essential features essential features of oneself. The prehension of another's essential features as essential for oneself is definitive of continuity of individual identity. The most that one individual, or one generation, can bequeath to another is the objective conditions, especially the environment, within which individual development can take place. At best, there can be a conscious appropriation of one person's essential character by another; but what is essential to the other is the appropriation, and the first person's essential features become essential to the other only by appropriation, being made relevant to his different conditions.

The seeming exception to this great gulf in the passage of essential features is in love. It would seem that the lover almost literally adopts his beloved's heart's desires as his own, disdaining the requirement that his own essential features must be relevant to his own conditions. But love is far richer than the interpretation of it as a union or merging of individuality. Love is a matter of harmony, and in the world that means contrast. Lovers are inevitably two; this is the richness of love. In love the continuity between beloved and lover is not a given characteristic of the nature of people, but something created by the lover. As any lover will say, love is the most conditional, the most fragile, of harmonies.

Mankind—people gathered under the aegis of the conditional features more or less common to them all—constitutes itself from epoch to epoch. Speculating in an adequately general view, all the characters and distinctions appropriate to cosmology are contingent. They ultimately rest on empirical appeals and in different epochs could be quite different. Perhaps in some other epoch there will be no such thing as freedom as we know it now.

We know now in fact that the nature of people, the harmony of their essential and conditional features, depends on their technology of conditioning each other as people. As conditional features change at the root, essential features must change to be relevant to the harmony of them both. Since technology is in part in the control of people, it now, willy-nilly, determines much of human nature as it exists at any given time. The greatest blindness of our times is not to see the depths at which human nature is being rewrought.

Even progress of the best kind is tragic. Western civilization is passing away. Its roots are already gone and the axe of the Third World is laid to its branches. Even under the best of leaders and the most fortuitous of circumstances the greatness of Western Man will inevitably become a vestige, a relic. Circumstances are rarely for the best, and the ubiquity of human perversity needs no documentation. For all our creativity, we may yet blow ourselves up over a triviality. The only hope of present mankind is in a social concert of creativity. But there is no guarantee, given people's freedoms and apparent perversity, that even this can avert total tragedy.

There is a sense, however, in which Heidegger's concern for the essential nature of mankind, in contrast to its destiny, is well taken. The freedom of creativity can well be called people's authentic being. It is authentic in two senses. To be genuinely creative is being-in-the-truth, as Heidegger would put it with regard to given fact. The whole process of creativity is based on discovering both real facts as they are and real values as they might be. Deception at either the ontic or ontological level makes creativity degenerate. Creativity is people's authentic being also because it is being-for-the-best (a non-Heideggerian notion). Not only is the creative person open to the values to be realized by him, he is essentially inclined toward them.

In this sense, the tragedy of people's conditional fate is sublated under their attainment of conditional and temporal authenticity. As the Stoics showed, there is a sense in which the person who is personally free is exempt from fate. The Stoics of course would have no truck with creativity; but the account of the autonomy stemming from creativity given here accords closely with their own view of rational autonomy in its personal effect.

In the end, however, personal freedom is partial, both in the way we understand it and in its concrete embodiments. We have not yet taken account of people's concrete life—sociality. For all of the public character of social life, it will turn out that the heart of personal freedom, creativity, rests in privacy. And the significance of privacy is its creative contribution to the public.

PART 3

Social Freedom

Preliminary Remarks

Social freedom in the most general sense means free participation in society. But free participation in society has been taken to mean a great many things. It has meant having opportunities and rights: this is the focus of the civil libertarian tradition. It has also meant having real alternatives for social living, where one can choose a way of life with a minimum of dictation from the body politic; this has been the emphasis of the defenders of cultural pluralism. And free participation has called to mind the ability and power to function freely in society, taking advantage of its opportunities; this has been the focus of such diverse approaches as Machiavelli's, Marx's, and Parson's. Most recently, free participation has been interpreted according to the slogan "participatory democracy," meaning the freedom of people to determine their own social environment in various ways.

Perhaps these diverse senses of free participation in society do not make up a general conception at all. Perhaps they are only equivocal uses of the same language, or at best what Wittgenstein called "family resemblances." A similar situation was encountered with respect to senses of personal freedom, however, and it was shown that they could be coordinated according to the cosmological model as various dimensions of personal action culminating in creativity. The same is in fact true of the diverse senses of social freedom. In fact, they can be coordinated so as to parallel and enrich the dimensions of personal freedom.

Parallel to the personal freedom of external liberties is the social freedom of opportunity. Building on the cosmological interpretation of acting in an open environment, the problems to be addressed regarding freedom of opportunity are twofold in nature. On the one hand the opportunities must be prized. Their prizing cannot be merely a matter of idiosyncratic choice but of social importance; that is, our society has decided that certain opportunities are prizeworthy and that it is socially important for individuals to prize them. On the other hand, the important opportunities must be available. Where the importance is great enough, the opportunities are regarded as worth a social guarantee and are called "rights." Exercise of these basic rights has often been regarded as essential to full human life. Chapter 8 will deal with freedom of opportunity.

Parallel to the personal freedom of choice between alternatives is the freedom of social pluralism, the freedom to choose a way to live. The problem is not so much that of choosing—this was dealt with as a personal freedom; the problem is rather that of living in a social structure that tolerates different ways to live, that offers viable alternatives. On one level this is the problem of cultural pluralism. The more basic problem is that of distinguishing the public from the private dimensions of life. What is the function of a common public order that justifiably can set limits to what individuals may do? What are the public functions of different groups, each organized for its own public ends? What is the function of privacy? These are the topics for chapter 9.

Parallel to the personal freedom of intentional action is the freedom of integral social life. Building on the cosmological interpretation of personal natural agency, the problem of integral social life is that of developing a style of experience most attuned to natural creativity in the social environment. But "style of experience" is a cultural artifact, dependent on media of communication. It is a harmonious way of putting together the elements naturally involved in creative social life. To understand it requires understanding the special character of modes of causation peculiar to social interactions. This will be the topic of chapter 10.

Finally, parallel to the personal freedom of creativity is the social freedom of participatory democracy. Participatory democracy is not just an ideal for government, it is an ideal for social behavior. It involves people acting in such a way as to create the social conditions within which they live, taking account of each other's demands, needs, and creative efforts. Its principle is that people ought to contribute to the decisions of social order to the degree that they are affected by the results of those decisions. Participatory democracy is the ideal for free creativity in a social context. Its nature, and the social forms of government and law expressive of it, will be discussed in chapter 11.

"Social freedom" may be taken to refer to socially free individuals or to a free society, one whose structures foster individual freedom. In reference to socially free individuals, freedom of opportunity can be viewed as the culminating dimension of social freedom, for which the other dimensions are antecedent conditions. The free participation in valuable opportunities in one sense is the most individual freedom can be. Being a free agent in history, with historically decisive actions, is indeed the height of individual freedom. But of course the opportunities are only abstract values without the freedom of integral social life, of chosen social form, and of participatory democracy. Participatory democracy can be viewed as the social organization of power such that each individual creates his own opportunities to the greatest degree possible. With reference to socially free individuals, then, the organization of this book can be viewed as an arch. On top of the foundation set by the introductory chapters of Part I, chapter 4 on external liberty and chapter 11 on freedom of political life form the bases of the pillars of personal and social freedom respectively. Each deals primarily with the relation between an individual and the environment. Higher on each pillar are chapter 5 on intentional action and chapter 10 on integral social life, the former dealing with action in the natural environment, the latter with action in the social environment. In the third block in each column are chapter 6 on free choice for personal freedom and chapter 9 on free social form for social freedom, each dealing with the problem of alternatives. The columns reach to form the arch with chapter 7 on creativity and chapter 8 on freedom of opportunity, culminating in historical creativity. One might ask, regarding the metaphor of the arch, what the capstone is; without an odd top piece the columns could not support a centrally placed weight, the notion of freedom as such. The capstone, however, is the cosmology's conception of freedom, spelled out in both personal and social dimensions.

When "social freedom" is taken in reference to a free society, a different conception of the order of the chapters is apparent. The freedom of opportunities is a schematic and somewhat empty approach to defining a free society. To that must be added the further dimension of real alternatives for forms of social life, structures guaranteeing a pluralistic society. But then those alternatives are empty if people do not have integral social styles enabling them to take them up in fully human ways. Even those styles are

8

Freedom of Opportunity

For most people, social freedom is having the opportunity to do what they want. A society is free, in the first instance, if it provides opportunities people desire for action and enjoyment. Two more elements are closely related to this. The society must also guarantee that individuals are not prevented from taking advantage of their opportunities by the unjust intervention of other people or by unjust social strictures. This is the domain of civil rights. Furthermore, a free society must provide the economic and educational resources a person needs to take advantage of his opportunities; the society should provide the power for social freedom. These added two conditions are important for social equality.[1]

Lack of impediment to take advantage of an opportunity has no importance as freedom unless the opportunity is valued in some way. The significance of this for personal freedom was discussed in chapters 4 and 5. There attention was called to the simple act of valuing and to the physical nature of opportunities relative to actors. From the standpoint of social freedom, however, attention must be focused on social values and social opportunities.

SOCIAL VALUES

The most general comprehension of the phrase "social values" takes in all those ideas of value conditioned by the fact that one lives in society, all the values the appreciation of which involves learning and culture. Most human values can be supposed to be social values in this sense. A narrower and more helpful use of the phrase designates those values a society particularly fosters because of its historical experience that those values are worth having. Freedom of opportunity as a social matter involves the op-

1. See John Rawls, *A Theory of Justice* (Cambridge: Harvard University Press, 1971), par. 17.

portunities being prized by people's holding values about them in this narrower sense. An opportunity not prized with such a socially fostered value, but prized by more idiosyncratic values or by direct valuation, can be called a simple external liberty. A social opportunity is one prized with a social value.

"A value," as that phrase is used here does not refer to situations and the values they have. Rather it refers to people's ideas or beliefs about values in situations. Specifically, a value is an idea held by somebody about how a situation might be organized to be valuable. It is the idea of a pattern appropriate for a certain kind of situation, but general with respect to all situations of that kind. It is important to distinguish between the degree of value alleged to be governed by "a value," and the importance that value-idea has for a person's own life, for his commitments and felt obligations. "Values" in the sense meant here are ideals like friendship, security, health, knowledge, a well-ordered society, social freedom in general and social freedoms in particular, for instance freedom of speech, assembly, and so forth. The account of value given in chapter 3 dealt primarily with the intrinsic meaning of value and with its recognition in intuitive judgments of intensity and pattern. Chapter 7 examined some of the elements of the process of deliberation. It is necessary now to deal with values as ideas, particularly as ideas about good opportunities.

Not all social values concern opportunities. In all probability most concern social structures establishing a stable environment, even at the price of removing certain opportunities: security, protection, abundance of food, orderly transmission of power, and so forth.

Questions about the structures of values can be coordinated according to two main axes; doing this will throw light on the special nature of social values. The first is the scale of *comprehensiveness* of the matter to which the value is applied, e.g., a value for individuals, for a social situation, for a culture. Second is an *ordering of dependencies* where the realization of one value depends on the realization of others, but not vice versa; this is an interesting relationship because the more dependent values are usually the ones prized as higher.

Treating comprehensiveness, consider "a value" to be an idea of a pattern harmonizing, actually or possibly, some elements each of which has value itself; this was the conclusion of our previous discussions of value. There is then a scale of increasing and decreasing generality. Any pattern for harmonizing things is of greater, lesser, or equal value to alternate patterns of harmonizing things. The more comprehensive patterns are the more general values, depending on how much they integrate or harmonize. From the standpoint of human judgment, the patterns at the higher levels of generality do not look like those at the bottom. At the higher levels it is possible to specify the antecedent worth of the constituent elements integrated. At the lower levels the values are desires, wants, urges, and so forth, that we usually do not think of as harmonies of less general components. They are usually prized, perhaps uncritically, just for themselves. The account of choice given in part 2 makes clear how even unconscious values are harmonies of values. Social values are much more general, and their components are explicitly prized by some or all of the people they regulate.

A pattern can be called valuable because it is a means for harmonizing things we value independently. In our moral experience we say a certain way of living is good because it allows us to satisfy some wants. A social order is good because it allows us to have the way of living we value. Alternate patterns differ in value as they are better or worse means for integrating values of a lower level.

A crucial distinction must be drawn between who might prize a value-pattern on the one hand and what less general values are integrated by that pattern on the other. For instance, fairly general social values like freedom and justice have to do with harmonizing components in a social order so that the individually prized ways of life of many citizens can be realized. A person might prize justice because it helps him individually. But the worth of the value is to be judged objectively in terms of how well it harmonizes the whole range of comprehended values, including those of other persons.

With some kinds of values, it is not important in practice to distinguish what the pattern does for a particular agent from what it does for all the relevant constituents in its harmony. But we usually label as peculiarly "moral" those values where the objective universality of judgment is important. A person does not have to recognize the worth of a value for it to be objectively valuable as a good harmony of his constituent lower-level values. What we usually mean by a "rational evaluation" is one taking into account the way the value-pattern integrates all its components, not just those immediately relevant to a particular agent.

In light of this brief model, we can now construct a short classification of levels of value-comprehensiveness.

A. *Personal Values:* value-patterns concerned mainly with elements identified as one's own.
  1. *Brute wants and likes:* things a person might want and like without being particularly aware why, for example, physical desires, aesthetic delights.
  2. *Personal values organizing brute wants and likes:* patterns of things in life prized because they allow the combining of lower-level values; they may also have an aesthetic quality themselves. Examples are health, shelter, habits of coping.
  3. *Personal preferences over organizing values (2):* certain value patterns preferred because they (allegedly) organize brute wants and likes better than others, for instance, certain conceptions of health, styles of shelter.
  4. *Life styles organizing preferences:* values having to do with the coherence of some or all of one's typical preferences. A common and basic value-component in nearly all life styles are those patterns accruing and guaranteeing the *power* to attain preferences. The notion of life style will be treated at greater length in chapter 11.
  5. *Preferable life styles:* particular life styles are preferred not merely for their brute aesthetic appeal but because they embody values such as freedom, integrity, honesty, executive effectiveness, and sensitivity.
  6. *Values relating preferable life styles to the exigencies of the environment:* historically or sociologically conditioned values such as "life styles emphasizing flexibility are better in times of profound social transition;" "life styles tending to alienate economic function from self-image are better in times of economic scarcity."
B. *Interpersonal Values:* value-patterns concerned with elements involved in direct, personal interactions.

1. *Economic values* serving brute wants and other components of personal and interpersonal values. For example, fair exchange, being productive of greater capital, pleasure, or the like.

2. *Values for interactions conveying culture* for organizing personal and interpersonal values. Culture includes patterns of meaning for organizing life that are socially inherited. This inheritance takes place in interactions such as those between mother and child, child and its language group, its peers, teachers, and the "cultural" artifacts of its society. Examples are social roles and etiquette.

3. *Values for interactions developing good taste in preferences:* to the extent taste is a matter of convention or whim, these values can be included under rubric B.2. But to some extent taste is the art of eliciting from previously unencountered things the relative values they have. We like interactions teaching taste to be "liberating," "sensitizing," and so forth.

4. *Values for interactions developing "human" qualities making up preferable life styles.* Such interactions should (we usually think) be loving, elicit sympathy and respect for persons, and the like. These are the values of a "good relationship."

5. *Values for interactions that structure the social situation.* The effects of interactions are not only on the people involved but on the situation structuring their interaction. There are values for the institutionalization of relationships, for instance, in families, economic contexts, and the like. Insofar as the alteration of the social situation affects people other than those in direct interaction, a move is made from the private to the public sphere.

C. *Public Values:* value patterns concerned with integrating elements involved as indirect effects of direct personal interactions on people or the sociophysical environment.

1. *Values of the social arrangements distributing qualities, costs, and benefits of private interactions:* these are ad hoc values of the "public" (in other words, the people indirectly affected by the private interactions) existing to control the effects on their lives. For example, values forbidding private agreements to fix prices, values for regulating environmental pollution by private parties.

2. *Values of institutions* supporting such social arrangements as in C.1 with routine, organization of force, and executive personnel; institutions have stability guaranteeing greater effectiveness than the public's mere appreciation of local public values. Governments, symbol systems, and a great many other kinds of institutions give force to the realization of the public's values.

3. *Values of procedures* for employing power in controlling the process of structuring social arrangements. Much of the present social upheaval consists of disagreement over procedural values, for example, participatory democracy versus the role of experts. Chapter 11 will focus on these issues.

D. *Social-Order Values:* value-patterns integrating public values with the social structures enhancing personal and interpersonal values.

1. *Values of social institutions:* whereas some institutions are primarily regulative or sustaining of public values, most social institutions are valuable also because they provide the context for things many people privately or personally want. Educational institutions are obvious examples of this level. Democracy as an institutional way of life for free individuals (not just as a form of majoritarian elective government) is another example. The legal system, and "traditions" as in religion and politics (the mystical tradition, the liberal tradition), are also valuable institutions in this sense.

2. *Values of social balance.* The most comprehensive social-order values are not definite patterns of social arrangements but very formal properties for balancing other social values in a variety of particular patterns. In the West it seems safe to say the main values of social balance have been welfare, security and survival, justice and freedom. *Welfare* in society is a balancing of components to promote the distribution to individuals of the goods and services they should expect by virtue of being members of the society. Resources for *security* and *survival* and the patterns of balancing social components so that under pressure the means to protect oneself will be traded away last. *Justice* in society is a balancing of components so that people receive benefits, burdens, and fair treatment equally, however equality is defined; John Rawls has

clarified this notion brilliantly.[2] *Freedom* in society is a balancing of social components so that citizens have opportunities and resources to exercise personal freedom. The concept of social balance exhibits the more general point that social-order values themselves are a mixture of other values, and each one itself exists usually in some competition with other values. A social pattern must give a finite expression and limited relative importance vis-à-vis other values to each value prized. Normative social thinking in this light is a problem of proper mixing.

E. *Values of Civilization:* ideals interpreting social-order values in terms of transtemporal considerations of what might be achieved by human endeavor. These would be hard to distinguish from social-order values except for the claim each group makes that all societies are to be judged in terms of them, for instance, respect for human dignity, attainment in knowledge, the exercise of creativity. The values of civilization are realized in individuals or in larger social patterns, but they are prized as such because those individual and social qualities form the quality of civilization.

Warning! Ranking values according to comprehensiveness is not the same as ranking them according to importance, intrinsic worth, or relevance for a particular situation. Philosophical idealists have often thought that the most comprehensive value overrides all others.[3] But if it does so, it is for reasons over and above its mere comprehensiveness.

Having suggested a classification of values according to comprehensiveness, we can now take up the relation of values according to order of dependence. It is clear in the classification above that the world is patterned in such a way that some patterns are necessary conditions or environments for others.[4] It is often the case that the values we prize most highly, those that make life most worth living and require the greatest sensitivity, skill, maturity, and wis-

2. Ibid.

3. For a discussion of comprehensive overriding values, see Robert Neville, "Man's Ends," *Review of Metaphysics* 16 (September 1962) : 26–44.

4. This is discussed at some length in Harold F. Moore, Jr., Robert Neville, and William Sullivan, "Contours of Responsibility: A New Model," *Man and World* 5 / 4 (November 1972).

dom to attain, themselves are the most dependent on subtle factors in the environment. We prize love, truth, and beauty. But each requires a massively coordinated environment of lower values; they are luxuries in a world of chaos and violence. Then there are the much lower values, like survival, being able to reproduce, protecting against loss of culture. These are basic environments for the higher values. One of the most common confusions in ethical discussions is between the relative importance of higher and lower values. Or between expendable and fundamental values, to use oppositely loaded words.

The order of values according to dependence is like a pyramid. Are the stones in the base more valuable because they support the top and are most enduring? Or is the top more valuable because it is the achievement of the lower levels, that which gives them significance greater than durability?

We need some terms to distinguish the kinds of relative importance values have when they are related in an order of dependence. It will not do merely to point out the dependence relation, although this should be an essential question to be pursued in moral discussions. It is necessary to label the peculiar priority each pole claims over the other. Let us say that the environmental values are *fundamental values* relative to what depends on them; this means that in a trade-off situation where one side must go, the environmental values will generally be retained. Let us say that the higher values, those more dependent and having more intrinsic intensity, charm, and worth, are *ideal* values. The value of air is fundamental but low grade; the value of diamonds is ideal (and merely ideal for most of us) but high grade.

The relation between fundamental and ideal values might be construed as an instrumental one. As far as the order of dependency goes, the fundamental value is a means to the ideal. But in an instrumental relation, if the ideal end is impossible, the means loses its value. In a situation of values related by an order of dependence, we usually would choose the fundamental value in preference to the ideal one when we cannot have both. The instrumental relation is only part of the story.

It is an abstraction, however, to say that worth of fundamental values is always preferred to that of ideal values when a zero-sum trade-off is required. Most moral problems concretely involve compromise. That is, in pursuit of relatively ideal values, we risk loss of fundamental ones. War is an extreme but illustrative case. Each soldier risks his own life in defense of some ideals for maintenance of his home society. It is not clear that there would be many soldiers if the risk were removed and violent death were guaranteed to each. More prosaically, most of us risk death on the highways for such uninspiring ideal values as seeing films or visiting friends. The risk factor is an important variable in calculations about values.

In a concrete moral context it is no more possible to deduce the greatest value from the dependency relation than it is to deduce it from the level of comprehensiveness. But the argument over which values shall override others must take both kinds of classifications into account.

This discussion so far has explored certain classifications of social values. It must now be made specific with respect to the values involved in freedom of opportunity. In a very general sense, of course, all these values enter into the assessment and valuing of given opportunities, or opportunities not given but desired. This is the sense in which all values are interrelated in deliberation.

A more helpful concept is that of the value-ideas that concern certain opportunities or classes of opportunities, ascribing varying kinds of prizeworthiness to the opportunities. These are the social values the opportunities are believed to have. Of course, the other kinds of social values go into deliberation about the opportunities and may in fact be involved in trade-offs with them. Understanding the other values a person holds is necessary to understanding why he pursues some opportunities and not others, and why he is willing to risk some things in order to have certain opportunities. A value whose object is an opportunity can be called a freedom-value.

Freedom-values are to be distinguished, but not separated, from the values society encourages to be held about freedom of opportunity itself. Certain opportunities are valued, for various reasons; valuing the opportunities is also valued. Freedom-values have as objects the opportunities to be pursued. The higher-order value of freedom itself is not simply another opportunity, but a way of exercising opportunities. That higher value, however, can affect the value of certain opportunities. It will, in fact, be called a third-order freedom-value in the next section. This section has treated it as a value of social balance.

VALUES, RIGHTS, AND FREEDOMS

Let us designate as "first-order freedom-values" all those particular opportunities of which an agent might want to take advantage. For instance, I might want to teach about Kant next Thursday and also to speak out against my mayor on Friday. Each would be a first-order freedom-value. Let us call "generalized first-order freedom-values" *classes* of such values, for instance, the value of opportunities to speak out, or free speech. To use another kind of example, an opportunity to learn about the Romans is a specific first-order freedom-value, as is the opportunity to learn how to fix my plumbing, freedom of education would be a generalized first-order freedom-value. The distinction between "specific" and "general" is of course a relative one.

Specific first-order freedom-values are usually not important for the organized structure of society. They are too ad hoc. But a generalized first-order freedom-value implies value being placed on social structures relating the first-order values as a class. Freedom of speech, for instance, implies valuing a legal structure and judicial system classifying certain first-order values as having special protection because they fall into the class of acts of free speech. Valuing opportunities of various kinds of education as a class implies valuing educational systems organizing the opportunities.

Let us designate as "second-order freedom-values" those social structures and ways of organizing the social environment supportive of generalized first-order freedom-values. These would include institutions, such as the judiciary, civilized traditions, customs of organization, and so forth. In a sense, second-order freedom-values are means to the end of first-order ones. A school system, for instance, is a means to the freedom of education. But in practice access to the second-order value is often the object of primary concern: access to the school system is what freedom of education is mainly about.

First- and second-order freedom-values are opportunities in the social environment in which an agent might participate; the opportunities are systematically structured in the case of second-

order values. But as the catalogues of the previous section should
have made clear, all these freedom-values are involved in competition with a great many kinds of value in life. They may be traded
off ad hoc, or they may be traded off in light of general conceptions
of what it is to be free. In the West, at least, we have generalized
both first- and second-order freedoms to an image of a free person;
this does not refer to personal freedom so much as to the way of
life in which a person is generally free to do what he wants. In
this social sense, a person generally has, or ought to have, freedom
of opportunity guaranteed by the society. There is a shift in emphasis here from generalizing many particular first- and second-
order freedoms to that of organizing them around an image or
sense of what it is to be a socially free person. Whereas the first-
and second-order freedom-values depend contingently on the sociophysical environment, the image of the socially free person gives
an organizing principle for assessing trade-offs in particular freedom-values. Let the main components of this general image of a
socially free person be called "third-order freedom-values." These
are the values defining what it is to participate in society as a free
person, the values of free participation. Our concern in the present
chapter is with these third-order freedom-values. The key to free
participation comes from the cosmological model describing the
relation of a person to his sociophysical environment. First, however, it is necessary to clarify how these values, these ideas about
good patterns for harmonizing situations, relate both to the social
situation to the agent who might enjoy them freely.

When a populace comes to regard certain freedom-values as important enough that public energies and resources be devoted to
guaranteeing them, those values can be called "rights." This is not
the only use of the notion of political rights, but it is an important one.[5] Ungeneralized first-order free-values are rarely called
rights, except insofar as they are derived from their membership
in a class of generalized freedom-values. Most rights that receive
public attention are rights to generalized first-order freedom-
values, such as the right to free speech or to education. These can
be called general first-order rights. When public energies do in

5. With regard to the discussion of "rights" in the sense used here see Brian
Barry, *Political Argument* (New York: Humanities Press, 1965) and Paul Weiss, *Our
Public Life* (Bloomington: Indiana University Press, 1959).

fact provide social structures embodying general first-order rights, for instance judicial protection of free speech or school systems, we can speak of second-order rights to those social structures.

Third-order freedom-values, those definitive of free human participation in the sociophysical environment, have often been called inalienable rights. The reasoning behind that label is that without those rights people would be less than human; this is something more than being deprived of something valuable in the environment. Of course the word "inalienable" is not a description of fact: if those rights could not in fact be denied people, they would not present a worry. Perhaps it is enough to say that those rights *ought not* be taken from people, where the "ought" is much more serious than deprivation of first- and second-order rights because of its connection with definitively human characteristics. But a deeper meaning of the word "inalienable" is that even when a person has been denied exercise of a right, either by removing the opportunity from the environment or by restraining the person, he still possesses the right in a fundamental sense. Because he is human his inalienable rights can only be denied expression; they cannot be taken from him. This reflects the important consideration that to be a human being, to be harmonized in a way definitive of human life, is to make certain claims upon the environment establishing a moral relation between environment and person. In this chapter we shall not make much of the notion of inalienable rights. Rather, we shall speak of certain values as being so important as to be definitive of minimal human existence. To frustrate a person's enjoying those values is to dehumanize him.

A right relative to freedom, then, is a valued opportunity assumed so important that public energies ought to be expended to guarantee it. How does a valued opportunity get to be so prized? The society must recognize that the components harmonized in that value are so important for life that it makes a claim upon the public. The process by which this recognition comes about is an historical one with great ambiguity.

A right is a valued opportunity that ought to be publicly guaranteed. That a person enjoys such a right does not mean he exercises it; this depends on his personal choice. But even if he has the right and chooses it, he still may be unable to exercise it. There are two further requirements. He must also have the talent of pulling himself together so as to act on the opportunity; in other words, he must have personal freedom in the sense discussed in Part 2. And he must have appropriated the resources needed for acting upon the opportunity; having appropriated the resources for exercise is the difference between merely having a right and having a social freedom. The society can guarantee rights, but not social freedom in the complete sense except insofar as it provides resources. To be socially free is to have appropriated the resources for exercising one's rights and also to be able to choose to exercise them.

This is a very complicated situation, with each side in the distinctions contributing to the other sides. One of the main kinds of third-order rights, publicly guaranteed opportunities of participation essential to human nature, is that of profiting from the sociophysical environment. Of course, this means the right of taking up elements in the environment as resources. We shall discuss several of these shortly. But there is a difference between having these resources available and being able to appropriate them to one's own experience and powers. On the other hand, another great class of rights is that of opportunities to act in the environment with the resources and personal choices at one's disposal. How one acts in this way feeds one's abilities to appropriate environmental resources. And so on around.

This brings the discussion to the transition from the valuing of opportunities to participation in the opportunities themselves. As suggested by our cosmological scheme, a person participates in his sociophysical environment in two basic ways: by receiving from it and by giving to it. More abstractly, a person prehends the environment and comports himself so as to be prehended by it in intended ways. A categorial description of this interaction was given in the discussion of intentional action as natural agency in chapter 5.

The structured character of the sociophysical environment adds an extra dimension of order to the more general discussion of receiving through prehension and giving through being prehended. The environment in which there are problems of free participation is ordered so as to be socially meaningful; the elements prehended or responding to one comportment that are not organized in socially meaningful ways are trivial for social freedom. This requires the discussion to be set up according to the following distinctions.

From the standpoint of freedom to prehend the world as a resource for action, two basic notions are important, one general, the other a specification of it. The first notion is that of "massive inheritance." [6] According to our cosmological model, a person at any moment prehends the entire set of past facts, subject to very few limitations. Most of them, of course, are negatively prehended, that is, prehended as being incompatible for inclusion in present experience. For purposes of present experience, however, it is not the individual past entities that are important, but the *patterns* of entities. Patterns, it will be remembered, are ways of having many things together. Therefore, by prehending things in patterns, it is possible to include more things in one's experience, preharmonized, as it were. There is less necessity to prehend negatively. This means two things for experience.

First, by virtue of prehending the past in patterns it is possible to have a stable, ordered environment. This is massive inheritance of stable structures to one's environment. Speaking on the personal level, the brain event involving consciousness, however that might be interpreted, inherits a massively coordinated environment in the form of its body, with neural connections, muscular outlets, and so forth. And beyond the body it inherits the massive system of the natural environment. The order and stability upon which fine human occasions of experience build are derived from massive inheritance of the world in ordered patterns. In fact, without massive inheritance we would have no "world," only a welter of past occasions.

Second, it is by massive inheritance of an ordered environment that the higher levels of value are experienced. Concrete value, of course, is things harmonized in patterns of intense contrast. To inherit the "world," therefore, is to inherit the past as ordered and valuable. By prehending the world as organized into patterns of value, human experience can build upon a base of antecedent achievement. It is only by virtue of the massive inheritance of which complicated human experience is capable that the quality of human experience can have so much greater an intensity of value than that we imagine for electrons.

6. See A. N. Whitehead, *Process and Reality,* 2 chap. 4, and *Adventures Of Ideas* (New York: Macmillan and Co., 1933), chap. 17.

The *problem* of participating in the world as a resource for experience is that some elements of massive inheritance can pass one by. Insofar as certain capacities of massive inheritance are programmed into our biological organisms, they can be taken to happen automatically. But there are certain capacities for massive inheritance that must be learned through experience. Without them patterns ready at hand will be missed and their elements negatively prehended or confused. The line between automatic and learned inheritance is difficult to draw, an extraordinarily complex empirical matter. The problem of free participation, however, has to do with learning to inherit the world in the massive patterns relevant to free human experience.

Social freedom is not concerned with all forms of massive inheritance, only with those endowed with social meaning. Chapter 9 will explore the notion of social meaning as characteristic of traits carried along trains of social causation. Massively inherited trains of social causation constitute *culture,* as philosophically defined. The social meanings involved constitute culture's content; the causal patterns constitute its transmission. Culture is the second concept needed to articulate the problem of participation in the environment as a resource for experience; it is a specific kind of massive inheritance, distinct from other kinds in that appropriating it is a skill to be learned.

Freedoms of opportunity can now be divided into two classes: those of opportunities for receiving experiential resources from the world, and those of opportunities for social action. The former freedom can be reformulated now as that of participating in culture. To be free to participate in culture requires both that the culture is available to be prehended as a massive inheritance and that the person has the ability to appropriate it into his experience in an integral way. In the next section three basic dimensions of the problem of free participation in culture will be explored. In each case it will be pointed out what the peculiar value or importance of the dimension of culture is. From a practical standpoint, then, we shall discuss problems of availability, external problems as it were, and problems of appropriation, internal problems.

After the discussion of freedom of culture in the next section, we shall return to the second class of freedoms of opportunity: freedom to act in organized society. Just as the inherited environment is coordinated in cultural patterns of massive inheritance, so the environment receiving human contributions is structured in political patterns regulating the *power* of effective action.

FREEDOM TO PARTICIPATE IN CULTURE

There is a certain neatness to defining culture philosophically, that is, in terms of an abstract cosmological scheme. If the definition has any practical weight, however, it must be instantiated in the concrete conceptions of culture used by anthropologists and common people. Yet can we obtain a clear and authoritative definition of culture from social science? It appears not.[7] The better wisdom, therefore, is just not to define culture closely. It is better to say everyone knows what culture is, understanding secretly that this is gross mythology. The advantages of this procedure are (1) that everyone does indeed know what culture is in the sense of accepting a range of family resemblances among examples for the purposes of discussion and (2) that everyone can allow, on the basis of the myth, consequent discussions to fix whatever meaning is necessary for the discussion to continue profitably.

We may accept, then, not as a definition but as an opening for discussion, Tylor's famous description of culture as that "complex whole which includes knowledge, belief, art, morals, law, custom, and any other capabilities and habits acquired by man as a member of society." [8]

The point to be emphasized is that these cultural factors are *acquisitions*. What makes knowledge, belief, art, morals, and so forth cultural is that they are acquired social objects.

It would seem that any socially meaningful product of organized society can be prehended as a cultural factor. Most social sciences approach their subject from this standpoint. They ask what cultural factors are operative in a given organized society and treat those factors as determining people in the society the way data determine experiencing individuals. Lévi-Strauss, for

7. This diversity is illustrated, with respect to the study of religious culture, in the excellent discussion of the history of analysis of religion by Annemarie De Waal Malefijt in *Religion and Culture* (New York: Macmillan and Co., 1968), chaps. 3 and 4.

8. Edward Burnett Tylor, *Primitive Culture* (New York: Harper Torchbooks, 1958; 1st ed., 1872), 1 : 1.

instance, believes anthropology to be a science insofar as it can treat its data analogously to the way structural linguistics treats its data, that is, as governed by regularities of relationships between the objective social forms.[9] An approach taking the problem of the subjective appropriation of cultural forms much more into account is the dialectical theory of sociology of knowledge developed by Berger and Luckmann.[10] But even here the dialectical relations are between social forms considered as data; there are social forms having to do with "objective reality" (principally, institutionalization and legitimation) and those having to do with "subjective reality" (procedures for socializing infants, converting people from one social world-view to another, and so on), but there is no relating these forms to actual human interaction as prescribed in chapter 9. Neither structuralism nor the dialectical approach considers social objects in terms of the whole context of social interaction. It is not enough to consider only the socially meaningful products of organized society.

Turning now to the problems of freedom to participate in cultural opportunities, there seems to be three main problematic areas. People would like freedom to have a heritage or history of their own, freedom to appreciate the enriching values of "cultured" life, and freedom to put cultural resources to work in organized society. We shall deal with each in turn.

Freedom to Have a History

Every person and group of persons is conditioned in significant ways by the human-sized affairs of their antecedents. A certain set of human events may *in fact* be the history of the group. But if the effects of the historical events are only in the form of physical, psychological, and sociological results brutely conditioning the affected group, in one sense the group has a history, but in another sense it does not. There is a problem of appropriating the history, of making a human-sized response to the human-sized historical events, of giving the prehended historical events a role in contemporary experience appropriate for human action. When

9. See, e.g., his *Structural Anthropology*, trans. Claire Jacobson and Brooke Grundfest Schoepf (Garden City, N.Y.: Doubleday, Anchor Books, 1967).

10. Peter L. Berger and Thomas Luckmann, *The Social Construction of Reality: A Treatise in the Sociology of Knowledge* (Garden City, N.Y.: Doubleday, 1966).

the history is appropriated this way, it has a new dimension of causality in contemporary experience over and above its brute physical, psychological, and sociological effects.

The first importance of having an historical heritage is that it gives people identities in terms of large-scale human accomplishment. Individuals by themselves might create a great deal, if they are great people. But not everyone can make a significant human accomplishment, and it is possible for ordinary people to appropriate greatness by appropriating a great history.

Even more basic is the sense people have that the particular accomplishments of great individuals rest upon a vast underpinning of human culture; the development of that underpinning culture is a human accomplishment on a scale not even conceivable in terms of individual deeds, except in the language of myth. Now a significant part of a person's identity can be his identification with the historical development of that culture, setting the context for individual virtue. This is not a case of ordinary men attempting to appropriate the genius of great men; it is rather the case of men of any sort of personal accomplishment attaining a dimension of humanity consisting in identifying with the development of human culture.

A person who cannot appropriate a history of this sort must always see himself either as without culture or as dependent on someone else's culture in a way that makes him less than human. For to be human means, among other things, to be part of the race that builds culture. To have a heritage is to be named with the name of the makers of human social life.

There are many histories that can be appropriated, and they need not be "true" histories; myths obviously will suffice, and often without the embarrassment of the facts. Any history will do so long as it can be seen as providing a genuine human culture.

The second reason an historical heritage is important is that it enables a person or a group to have a public face others must take into account in social interaction. If none of the participants in the interactions of an organized society had a heritage, then (prescinding from the first reason for a heritage discussed above) social identification could be centered almost exclusively on the types functional in the social organization as such. That is, all the nonpersonal social identification could be in the form of functional social roles. This would be a culturally shallow but conceivable situation. It is not the usual case, however. In every organized society some of the people, if not the majority, do have articulated heritages. Furthermore, the functions of the social organization are related to the cultural underpinnings of the majority's heritage. American society is based on the cultural heritage of western Europe, a heritage patently exclusive of many minority groups. As long as a person or group has no heritage of its own and must function in an organized society based on an alien heritage, the person or group must think of itself, and be thought of by others, as deficiently human.

It is important to have a heritage for a third reason. If the organized society is to allow and foster a rich degree of social meaning, then the various members and groups must participate in each other's experience. This means that, whereas each group has its own limited heritage distinct from the heritages of others, each ought also, for the sake of social richness, appropriate all the heritages in the name of its membership in the organized society.

This more expanded sense of appropriation does not involve denying or minimizing the uniqueness of one's own heritage. Rather it involves identifying oneself *not only as an individual with a heritage but as a member of a larger social order with many distinct heritages* united in the social interaction of the larger society. Through the mediation of membership in the organized society an individual can appropriate for his own a history that, by its very nature, excludes him from its historical lineage. This appropriation of an identifying history through the mediation of the organized society of which one is a member can be called having a *social heritage*.

The importance of having a social heritage rises as organized society expands to include more and more diverse groups. As the demands for cooperation increase, the pressure for homogenizing social meaning to the lowest level of function will be irresistible unless groups are free to appropriate alien heritages. But if, on the contrary, the social organization itself fosters the appropriation of alien cultures, then diversity can be the strength of the social organization.

There are two basic kinds of obstacles to identifying with a cultural achievement by appropriating an historical heritage: external ones and internal ones. Externally, of course, the problem is that the history is not presented for appropriation. Either because the history of one's group has been lost through dissolution in an alien tradition, or through a return to barbarism, or through one's larger society suppressing the history, people can be too ignorant to appreciate a history that might be appropriated. The internal problems have to do with accepting an alien heritage as the only one possible, complete with the bad faith of knowing it is alien.

The obstacle to appropriating a heritage as one's special public role is that the organized society, as an external matter, does not allow the peculiarities of the minority heritage to play functional roles in the social organization. There is a distinction between the minimum functions of interaction required for social organization, and the cultural enrichment giving the interaction greater social meaning. But the distinction does not mean there is no connection between social organized functions and culture. Quite the contrary. When the cultural traits of a heritage cannot be integrated in an enriching way with the functions of the social organization, they wither under the stresses of the organized interaction. This in fact is one of the chief factors contributing to the decay of historical consciousness.

As an internal matter, the fact the society has no useful roles for a heritage one might otherwise appropriate gives rise to the situation where one does not take the life style of the heritage to be a live option. Of course, one can refuse participation in the organized society, but that is only to make the heritage doubly alien—and it is to abstract the heritage and its culture from concrete society.

The obstacles toward having a *social* heritage, over and above a heritage unique to oneself and different from others in the larger social organization, likewise are both external and internal. The external problem is simple ignorance of world cultures; the alien cultures are not in a form that easily can be assimilated into processes of learning. The internal problem again is more complex. Not only are there alien experiences to assimilate, but there are forms of assimilation unique to those experiences. This point is close to McLuhan's emphasis on the importance of media, namely, that media determine the "ratios" of our senses.[11] Western literate culture, according to McLuhan, gives rise to the habits of integrating experience in linear trains; nonliterate cultures employ what McLuhan calls mosaic patterns. For westerners to appropriate the heritage of the East, therefore, is to require not only new learning but a reconditioning of the basic patterns of integrating experiences.

If having a heritage is important in the contexts mentioned here, and the obstacles are of the general sort described, then the *freedom* to have a history will be disclosed in analysis of the sorts of procedures fit for removing the obstacles. The external obstacle to appropriating a history for purposes of identification is that the history is not presented for consideration. The obvious remedy for this is to promote the study and popular presentation of historical traditions that have been obscured but are indeed appropriate.

The internal obstacle is that people with no appropriated heritage of their own take the alien heritage of the dominant group in their organized society as the only legitimate heritage. They would have difficulty appropriating their own history even if it were presented. It might be said this is entirely a private problem for which the organized society has no responsibility beyond presenting the histories for consideration. But why would people believe an alien heritage to be the only legitimate one? The reason is not likely that they were presented the alien heritage alongside their own and made a free decision to make the alien culture normative for them. More likely, the dominant alien culture was prehended so often and thoroughly in the social interaction that the alienated people did not maintain the options of ordering their experience according to any other standards. Even when their own history was presented, the values according to which they integrated that history with what else they experienced *were those derived from the alien heritage.*

The internal obstacles then require not only the external presentation of a native history, but a reordering of the educational process so as to enable what is presented to be appropriated as one's own standards.

The reordering of social education does not solve the problem

11. See his *Gutenberg Galaxy* (Toronto: University of Toronto Press, 1962).

in its depths, however. Even when one's educational experience makes a variety of histories live options for cultural identification, one option must in fact be freely appropriated if the person is free to have a heritage. As Hegel pointed out, having many options is not itself freedom, since none can be chosen without eliminating the others. Freedom has to do with the way one is chosen. We have used the verb "appropriate" in a general sense in conjunction with coming to terms with one's history. But it must be made more explicit.

To appropriate a history as described here is to elevate its cultural "world" to the status of essential features determining the process of harmonizing experienced data from moment to moment. The heritage would be a set of essential features derived from past prehended data. But its elevation from conditional data to essential features would be an act or series of acts of free decision, as described in chapter 6. It would take an artist to describe the process of this free decision: the appropriation may be gradual or like a conversion, it may be piecemeal or wholesale, superficial or thorough.

After the appropriation of the heritage there probably would be few moments of great decision when the heritage as a set of essential features would be an overwhelming single decisive factor. That is not the only way an *appropriated* heritage functions. Rather the heritage would color every decision in more or less pervasive ways. It would contribute more to the style with which one lives rather than to particular momentous decisions.

To understand having a heritage we have examined the situation where it is lacking and must be appropriated. But what about the people in the dominant groups who have their heritage from birth as it were, whose educational experience from the beginning has made their own history (mythological or real) an essential feature determining the style of their lives? These people may be as brutely conditioned by their heritage as they are by their diet or genes (this is an exaggeration, but unfortunately not often one of much practical significance). Such people are free *to have a heritage* in the sense that the social situation allows it, and in fact insures it up to a point. But they have not *appropriated* the heritage in a sense that can be called free. So we must acknowledge that having a heritage may be free or unfree. Merely having a heritage, freely or not, means self-identifying with a culture of human accomplishment, having a socially recognized historical identity, and perhaps participating in all the cultures of the world. The additional dimension of freedom of appropriation in having a heritage opens a new vista of problems.

Returning now to the function of a heritage in providing a public identifying role as a participant in a unique culture, external obstacles take the form of preventing or excluding the peculiarities of the heritage from functioning in useful ways in the social organization. It is quite possible for an organized society to be monolithic in its own cultural background and still allow other cultures to exist, so long as the idiosyncrasies of the other cultures do not bear importantly on the social organization. Such a society can be called pluralistic only in a weak sense, where the cultural pluralism is not relevant in important ways to the social organizations regulating society-wide interactions. But under these conditions the idiosyncrasies of nondominant cultures atrophy and become mere curiosities, if kept at all. Freedom to have a heritage as a means of public identity, therefore, requires a pluralistic society in a much stronger sense.

Assuming the culture is pluralistic enough for diversity in styles to be a live option, externally speaking, each individual must still appropriate the role stemming from his heritage. This is not merely a matter of appropriating the heritage, as discussed above, although it is at least that. In the nature of the case, the life style stemming from a particular heritage, *considered by itself,* is different from a life style that can be lived in an integrally pluralistic organized society. The style stemming directly from the heritage is a live option only in an organized society culturally monolithic in terms of the heritage. It must be tailored to prosper in a social organization bringing the individuals into interaction with others of a different heritage. A heritage whose life style cannot be adapted to interaction in a pluralistic society is indeed not a live option, and no amount of social reorganization could make it so. Minority religious groups in America, like the Amish, with bizarre customs (from the standpoint of the dominant culture) know that they cannot allow much interaction with other cultures, since interaction tends always to tempt the group's members from the old ways. Certain cultural traditions cannot survive with their essential particularities intact in a pluralistic society. But most traditions can indeed be adapted in life style to some accommodation with the requirements of organized social interaction.

Turning, finally, to the obstacles to having a *social* heritage, again we must address both external and internal obstacles. The former are various forms of ignorance of alien cultures. Freedom will come here through knowledge. It is a particular problem for scholarly disciplines to determine how to study alien cultures, but that problem is being faced in vigorous professional ways. The more difficult problem is to spread scholarly knowledge through the society. The most important current context for the development of the freedom to have a social heritage is that of the confrontation of western European culture with the cultures of the East and of the other non-western peoples.

The internal problem of appropriating an alien heritage through one's place in society is to develop a basic pattern of integrating experience allowing for an appreciation of cultures differing in their very mode of basic experience. In a way this is an impossible task. To the extent the required basic pattern is different from one's native heritage one loses touch with oneself. On the other hand, no heritage is static, and no one form of appropriating one's own heritage can last for long, especially in a pluralistic world.

Since western technology has in fact made one society out of all the world, perhaps that very technology will bring about interactions reconstituting in turn the basic patterns of experience so as to make the world's cultures mutually accessible. McLuhan would argue the basic patterns of experience are determined by the media of communication; this probably is an oversimplification, since there are many kinds of social interaction other than those dominated by organized media. But to the extent McLuhan is correct, technology as the new medium might accomplish the purpose at hand. The problem then would be to make the transition to the new patterns of experiential integrations self-conscious enough to maintain appreciative connections with the cultures of the old patterns. The problem, in other words, would be how each culture could hold on to its own past.

It must be admitted that in some respects a culture simply cannot be inherited in a society with a sufficiently alien form of basic experience. This loss of heritage has happened even within

western culture. It is impossible for most of us to be entertained
and educated by hearing the *Iliad* recited aloud. That kind of appreciation is open only to specialists who can expand their experience in specialized directions. Perhaps in a hundred years, given
the speed of change, no one but specialists would be culturally
educated by a novel. These limits must simply be admitted. But
given these limits, the situation is not as black as it seems to de-
fensive western academics. Often what is appreciable in a cultural
element can be transformed and carried over into a new medium.
After all, we do *read* the *Iliad* with great enjoyment and learning,
and perhaps our novels can be televised with color, taste, and
smell. The excellence of aural poetry is different from that of literate poetry [12] but this does not mean a literate transformation of
an aural poem is necessarily a loss in absolute value; maybe even
the ancient Greeks were a little bored listening.

The discussion of the freedom to have a history can be concluded with the formulation of two rights, two third-order valued
opportunities for social freedom. First, each individual in a good
society has the right of access to a history with which he can identify, along with the resources for appropriating it. This is the *right
of having a history*. Second, each individual, and each group with
a common history, has the right of access to the histories of other
groups that can be appropriated to contribute to a pluralistic society. This is the *right to alien histories*.

Freedom to Appreciate Culture

Appropriating a history or cultural tradition as one's own is
different from simply appreciating cultural elements. It involves
a dimension of self-identification lacking in the latter. Furthermore, it is possible to appreciate a cultural element, or even a
whole tradition, that is alien to one's own heritage. One can appreciate what one would not identify with, in the sense discussed
above. The range of cultural elements we ordinarily appreciate,
or would like to appreciate, is not necessarily congruent with any
one historical tradition. In fact, one advantage of living in a
pluralistic society is the richness of cultural possibilities. The ap-

12. For an excellent discussion of the differences between aural and literate
literature, in relation to their respective cultures, see Eric A. Havelock, *Preface to
Plato* (New York: Grosset & Dunlap Universal Library, 1967; 1st ed., 1963).

propriation of a history does not entail any appreciation of the cultural values in the history, in the usual sense of "appreciating cultural values."

We may recall Tylor's description of culture quoted earlier as that "complex whole which includes knowledge, belief, art, morals, law, custom, and any other capabilities and habits acquired by man as a member of society." When we speak of "appreciating culture," we usually have art in mind, the third of the six examples Tylor mentions. Although there are many theories of the nature of the value of a work of art, most agree that its value is at least intrinsic.

Some philosophers have gone so far as to argue (and we would have to agree in the light of the theory of value above) that anything harmonious has an intrinsic value akin to art. Dewey claims, for instance, that a "consummatory experience" (his phrase for an experience harmonizing many strands entering it) is itself a work of art, and pleads for developing the art of experiencing as such.[13] In short, Dewey expands the notion of art to be the normative form of any cultural or experiential element.

Is every harmony of socially significant things a cultural object to be appreciated for its intrinsic value? No. Even many *general* patterns of organized social interaction are thought to be merely convenient arrangements and not cultural objects. A look over the varieties of distinct cultures, however, reveals that just about any kind of interaction *can* become a cultural object. A harmony of socially meaningful things is a cultural object when its intrinsic value *is appreciated* de facto for its own sake. Beethoven's Great Fugue can be heard as scratches of horse hair on cat gut, or even as background music; but it is not appreciated as a cultural object until its musical value as such is heard. In American culture, background music itself is a cultural object because its calming or screening effects are appreciated, not because its musical value is seen. A person can know by the authority of others that Beethoven's music is of great cultural value without being able to appreciate it, and can desire to learn to appreciate it. In this case we would not say the music becomes cultural when he learns to appreciate its intrinsic musical value; rather we say

13. See his *Experience and Nature* (1929; reprint ed., New York: Dover, 1958), chap. 9; also *Art as Experience* (1934; reprint ed., New York: Capricorn, 1958).

the person becomes cultured, sensitive to identifiable, socially meaningful values.

The freedom to appreciate cultural values refers to the freedom to include in one's experience the cultural objects functioning with due place given to their intrinsic values. The most obvious obstacle to this freedom is that for many people the cultural objects simply are not presented. The tradition of the West has long been that only the aristocrats are fully human in the sense of appreciating the higher elemnts of culture. Everyone suffers, but it is the privilege of the aristocrat to interpret his suffering through the vision of the poets. The law applies to all, but it is the privilege of the aristocrat to understand its real worth, beyond the force of the sheriff's arm. While all men have been accounted fully human in the *theological* sense in the West, cultural privilege has been reserved for the aristocrat.

In America the aristocracy has been expanded to include all those who participate to the full degree in the organized society. The genius of American democracy has been to see access to all humanizing things, culture included, as a problem of interactions in organized society. For that reason the political interest of Americans means something much more than a similar interest would mean for Europeans. Still, American society has many groups not participating fully in the determination of the oragnized society, and they are the ones lacking exposure to culture.

A more internal obstacle is that, in many people, modes of experience are formed that prevent the presented cultural objects from maintaining their cultural character through to the appreciative level of experience. High school students can be taken to concerts but their response may be it's just "long-hair stuff." It is not the case that the music has failed to penetrate to their consciousness; it has penetrated, but they cannot allow it to function as appreciable culture. Their previous experience eliminated the possible role of cultural object in this instance, and they must interpret it as something else. All kinds of cultural objects can be experienced by nonaristocrats; but the nonaristocratic experience has no cultural roles to give the objects.

The obstacles to freedom to appreciate culture can be overcome by altering the modes of social interaction. Reorganizing the avenues of access to cultural objects so as to make them universally available would solve the first kind of difficulty. Reordering the educative processes of social interaction would handle the second, since people can be led to experiences making cultural objects culturally meaningful.

In particular, to give universal access to cultural objects would require reforming the educational system so as to put students in critical touch with the media by which culture is conveyed. The nearly exclusive emphasis in American education on reading and "practical arts" is utter foolishness in the light of this thought. Only literary culture would be opened to students this way. American education has assumed its first task is to give people economic and political power to control the social organization, and to an extent this is a good thing; the availability of cultural objects depends on social organization. But it is an error to think that having the power to avail oneself of cultural opportunities entails the ability to appreciate the culture.

This discussion of the freedom to appreciate culture can be summed up with the formulation of two related rights. First, each person in a good society has the right of access to cultural objects of intrinsic value; second, each person has the right to whatever educational experiences are necessary to allow him to appreciate the intrinsic value of cultural objects. These can be called together the *rights of access and appreciation of culture.*

Freedom to Put Cultural Resources to Work

The discussion of putting cultural resources to work is a transition to the discussion of freedom in organized society. The problem of putting cultural resources to work is largely though not entirely one of social organization. "Cultural resources" here means not only the cultural elements handed down and appreciated, but also the particular heritages people and groups might have or want.

The importance of this freedom lies in the fact that exercising it constitutes general human excellence. Whatever the particular, idiosyncratic virtues a person might have, he is excellent as a human being in the degree and ways he brings his experience of appreciable intrinsic value to bear on his social interactions. Perhaps other things, for instance the virtues extolled by religion, also constitute general human excellence, but cultured behavior is the most obvious form of general excellence, and culture can probably subsume religious *behavior* under itself.[14] If having a culture by both appropriating a history of culture-building and appreciating things of cultural value is definitive of human life, then living in social interaction with culture enriching all action is a prime form of human excellence.

This is an advance beyond what has been said so far. Putting culture to work means not only appreciating the culture, but making it function among the essential features ordering one's actions. One can appropriate a history and be sorry regarding it. But as a matter of culture functioning to constitute human excellence, the heritage must play a cultural, and not just an identifying, role in experience. The *way* in which the heritage is appropriated must be of intrinsic value.

Human life, of course, is a mixture of competing values. General human excellence is only one of the factors to be combined in a *particularly* excellent life. But this acknowledgment of partiality does not mitigate the importance of the freedom to put cultural resources to work.

The special excellence in putting cultural resources to work is that a value transcending the relevant concerns of the immediate situation is given to social interactions. Men seem to feel purely contextual excellence is frustrating, and even if the only excellence they attain is relative to a passing social context, they would like it to have a dimension of intrinsic excellence appreciable outside the context. Culturally informed action is both relative to the context of interaction and transcendent of it.

The external obstacles to putting cultural resources to work have many forms, but most stem from an implicit threat to the organized society posed by the culture in question. In all cases where, relatively speaking, an organized society lacks a particular cultural dimension, the introduction of the cultural dimension would call attention to something of intrinsic value not justified in the de facto interactions of the organized society. The introduction of the cultural dimension ought to enrich the value of the interactions, its defenders would argue, but the possibility remains

14. It is ironic that Tylor, omitting religion from his list of cultural items, is most famous for his cultural studies of religion. In fact, he interpreted religion primarily in terms of *beliefs* giving rise to doctrines and social customs.

that it might alter the interactions so as to make them socially dysfunctional. A hard-working man can be corrupted by books.

Furthermore, an organized society rarely lacks a certain dimension of culture in such a way that the problem *merely* is to introduce the culture. Usually, rather, the society is supportive and expressive of one culture and exclusive of *another* culture in its social interactions. The fear here is that making the alien culture viable in the organized society will threaten the integrity of the dominant culture. Again this is the problem of cultural pluralism.

The internal obstacles to putting cultural resources to work are of two principal sorts. The first is what would be expected, an internalization of the external obstacles. Many people are justly fearful that acting according to their own cultural expression will jeopardize their participation in the organized society. First, the society has likely organized itself against minority cultures, fearful for the integrity of the dominant culture. And second, it might indeed be the case that the new culture *would* undermine the social organization. If a minority culture, for instance, rejects the work ethic within which capitalism is rooted, the American economic system must reject that culture or undergo radical modifications.

The second internal obstacle is more difficult to define. Putting culture to work is an extraordinarily confusing business. Often what appears to be the real substance of culture is only a toothless replica. Real issues are hidden by the cultural symbols, and life is filled with so many things that the struggle for cultural consistency tends inevitably to impoverishment. There is a monumental task of "proper discernment" in living the cultured life in practical society. Of course there are analogous problems in appropriating a heritage or directing one's education to gain true cultural appreciation in the first place. But there is a quantitative difference in complexity amounting to a qualitative difference when it comes to putting cultural resources to work.

The mechanisms for dealing with these obstacles are matters of *social organization*. That is where the "work" takes place. Furthermore, as has been said now in many ways from the beginning of this chapter, the problem is to find a way of organizing society that on the one hand fosters a cultural pluralism and on the other hand fosters the personal integration of all the factors discussed.

This, then, marks a transition in the discussion from problems of the freedom of cultural participation to those of participation in organized society.

Freedom to Participate in Organized Society

The term "organized society" is used in contrast to two other divisions of society: culture (including historical influence) and the myriad of roughly contemporaneous interactions that are not "organized." Precision can be added to this contrast in the following way. A society is "organized" in the respects in which its interactions employ nexuses with general social characters. By "general" is meant not only that the meaning of the nexus is generally recognized, but also that the social meaning of "this" nexus is one recognized as attachable to other nexuses of the same sort. If Jones throws a rock through Smith's window, that is a socially meaningful but not necessarily general interaction. If Jones slaps Smith's face with a glove, however, that is a general interaction in some societies because in all similar actions the slapping is an invitation to a duel; included in the meaning of the interaction is the regular behavior associated with all instances of it. Language organizes society, as does any symbolic activity. Customs and laws organize society in the peculiar sense that sanctions are associated with the regularities involved.

Societies (in the usual sense of that word) differ from one another mainly in having different kinds of organized nexuses. Social scientists, anthropologists, sociologists, psychologists, and the like, usually study a society's organized interactions to the neglect of unique and otherwise unorganized interactions. Only history makes a point of studying unique events, and even here an understanding of such events often involves translating them into some kind of abstract organization (for eaxmple, exhibiting a pattern of the rise and fall of empires).

The treatment of freedom to participate in organized society differs from that of freedom to participate in culture. Both organized society and culture are social phenomena too concrete to be dealt with directly in a philosophical discussion: even the empirical sciences are dubious with respect to the concreteness of their findings. Treating culture, therefore, we adopted the myth that "everyone knows what culture is," and we discussed freedom in terms of various relations that culture has to individuals desirous of freedom. We must now say the same of organized society: "everyone knows what social organization is."

Participation in organized society is not merely or primarily a matter of coping with inherited elements. Rather it is a matter of interaction. Therefore, taking clues from the cosmological model, there should be problems of participating in the *media* of interaction, both as the media carry objects into a person for prehension and as they carry intended effects into action. There should be problems relating to participation in the social construction of *common goals* for organized interaction. And there should be problems of participating in a *style of action* appropriate to social interaction regarding common goals. These shall be dealt with in turn.

Freedom to Participate in Media

Many of the nexuses of interaction in a contemporary society are organized, but they are not all of equal importance for the freedom to participate in the society. Certain general nexuses have systematic bearing on large portions of the whole fabric of interaction, for instance, systems of communication, government, economics. To be able to participate in such systems, therefore, is to be able to participate in large portions of the society. Let us call these important and systematic general nexuses "media"; the word so defined has a domain roughly equivalent to that in McLuhan's use. Free participation in an organized society entails free participation in its media.

In general terms, freedom to participate in a medium means two things. It means first being able to prehend the medium and its content realistically. Anyone can watch television, providing he is not blind; but "uneducated" people cannot grasp its content realistically, being taken in by what appeals to their uncritical sense. Everyone's mode of experience is affected by much television watching, but if McLuhan is right, virtually no one experiences the effects of the medium with critical realism.

Freedom to participate in the medium means, second, that one is able to act freely in employing the medium to effect his intentions. Everyone in America must act with reference to the economic system. But some people do not know how to attain their economic goals; others have unrealistic goals; still others lack the material or spiritual resources necessary to take up an economic role. Some people who do participate in the economic system, even to the point of generally attaining their goals, do so without personal control over their actions: the successful capitalist, alienated from his own humanity, is such a victim. So freedom to participate in the sense of acting with the media as instruments for interaction means the direction of the action must be *personally* free, in the senses characterized in Part 2. The burden of Marx's complaint about capitalism is that men can participate in it in nearly all-consuming degrees, but the participation leads to a bondage of the soul. *Freedom to participate in a medium means not only being able to act with reference to it, but being able to act freely with reference to it, where the free action uses the medium to effect its freely chosen ends.*

The obstacles to experiencing the media and their contents realistically are similar to those preventing participation in culture. Inadequate funded experience in dealing with the media, perhaps stemming from lack of access to the media, is one side. The other side is a matter of positive personality structures prohibiting realistic experience.

Obstacles to free action *employing* the media are more complex. The medium in question may have privately defined social qualifications for participation that exclude some people; racial prejudice in America often takes this overt form. There may be de facto qualifications for participation that also exclude certain people, even though no one intended the de facto qualifications to be exclusive; institutional racism is of this sort (for instance, financial qualifications for attending educational institutions). It could be that participation in a given medium would require certain people to forsake their heritage, something they would be unwilling, or perhaps even unable, to do. Participation in some media requires self-shaming for some people. Most often, the obstacle to free participation in social media is lack of ability. Sometimes the ability is acquired by way of a realistic experience of the medium, and its lack stems from lack of experiential access. But sometimes the ability is a matter of a more sophisticated education that the society does not provide.

Participation in the media of organized society is a two-level affair. The first level is the direct participation in the media for various purposes of interaction that we have been describing. The second level is the formation of the media themselves. Media are formed and altered in the actual course of being put in new connections by interaction. The classical capitalist economic system, in its quite ordinary workings, gave rise to the development of electronic technology, which in turn revolutionized the structure of economics. Therefore, a second-level dimension to the free participation in social media is the freedom to control the formation of the media. The chief obstacle to this dimension of freedom is ignorance of how media are formed. For the most part, westerners have begun to conceive of the structures of society as remedial artifacts just in the last 200 years or so. Only governmental media have been recognized as intrinsically reformable since the beginning of literate thought.

The intent behind the doctrine of equality in modern political philosophy can be interpreted in terms of that dimension of freedom having to do with free activity employing social media as means. The doctrine of social equality need not suppose everyone is of equal excellence; that is palpably untrue. Nor need it demand everyone have equal rewards from social participation; that is practically impossible, and besides, people do not want the same things. Rather, what the doctrine intends is that, because everyone could be capable of free participation in organized society ("could be," since some people are not capable but could have been so given different education and conditions), and because such participation makes people more fully social (that is more human), it would be a great good for all men to be equally free to participate in organized society. The rub, of course, is that equality of freedom is *not* unrelated to condition and station. An uneducated man is not as free to act in a complicated society as an educated one; a poor man requires a greater proportion of his capital to make a given sum than a rich man does. Whereas the Enlightenment thought equality a matter of human nature relative to a few apparently fixed institutions, we know now that the character of equality must be defined in terms of specific matter of free control and that these must be determined empirically. For this reason equality is less useful as an ideological notion now than it seemed before.[15]

15. The best discussion of equality is in Rawls, *Theory of Justice,* chaps. 1, 2, 4 and 5.

The means of overcoming the obstacles to the freedom to participate in social media are primarily educational. Education here refers not only to the processes of attaining abilities. It refers also to the fact that social structures preventing participation in certain media for certain people exist by the sufferance of the whole society and can be changed by re-educating the society. Because something can be done, it is possible to speak of a *right of access to media*.

Freedom of Cooperation

Most social thinkers in the idealistic tradition have thought social interaction is primarily cooperative. Social roles can easily be construed as the different roles necessary to bring about a large-scale unified social conclusion. Even Dewey interpreted interaction by defining interpersonal social meaning in terms of cooperation. There have been various forms of the idealistic thesis, running from conceptions of a monolithic and concrete universal social purpose to a minimal conception of universal order that should be sought by everyone before the pursuit of idiosyncratic goals. But there is a basic sense common to the idealistic approaches; namely, that society is coordinated activity. Then it is thought that since coordination is a unification of many centers of action a good coordination is one unifying the actions into one complex action. Stated more abstractly, this is the principle that diversity is to be unified by subsuming it under some "third" term on a higher level. Recognition of the character of the abstract principle leads to the further inference that the common social goal, being the third term, has a more important and normative status than any of the proximate goals of the individuals' actions taken disjunctively; it is on a higher level. From a logical point of view, this is obviously a bad argument, and no competent idealistic philosopher put it forward in that bald way.

Social activity must indeed be coordinated if socially meaningful items are to be recognized as playing roles in all the actors' experience. The actors' activities must be ordered with respect to one another. But this does not mean they have to be ordered to a common goal. Quite the contrary, a prizefight is an extraordinarily coordinated activity. Nor does coordination mean that socially meaningful items must play the same or similar roles in the diverse experiences of the different interacting persons. The items may play quite diverse roles. The only requirement for meaningful interaction or coordination is that each agent must recognize what the item means for the others in relation to what it means for himself.

So the move from coordination to cooperation, that is, working in a common action ordered by a single complex goal, is not warranted by the requirements of coordination alone. Nor is the elevation of the universal social goal to supreme normative status for society.

Some activity in society, however, is and should be cooperative. Men can accomplish more by working cooperatively than they can alone or by working at cross purposes, and many of the great projects require cooperation and are worthy of it. Men desire a freedom to participate in cooperative activity for common goals. These goals need not be universal through society; nor need they direct activity of long duration. Nonetheless, most significant human activity is cooperative with someone or other.

The most important obstacles to cooperative action and the participation in shared goals come from the fact that men, especially as representatives of a society, expect a *total* sharing of goals. That is, the dominant segment of the organized society expects everyone in the society to share the general goals held by the group and to conform their more proximate goals to what combines fruitfully with those general goals.

What is operational in the tyranny of one group's goals is a conception of a universal purpose that might unite all personal purposes into one common activity, a "third term" goal on a higher level. This universal goal may not be very specific, but it can be determinate enough to eliminate certain competitive types of activity. The "American dream" is almost impossible to state; but it functions in American society in a ruthless way to eliminate kinds of shared activity calling it into question. The dominant goal-group forms a conception of how all its own consistent cooperative activities might be fitted together and then makes that conception an ideal to which all groups and individuals in the organized society ought to conform.

The forms of tyranny are extraordinarily diverse. The dominant goal-group may find ways of preventing the nonconformist actors from participating in the social media necessary for their own purposes. They may bring legal sanctions against organizations with nonconformist goals, arguing a "clear and present danger" case. But basically the tyranny of the dominant goals is unconscious in source and psychological in effect. It builds into the common structure of the society the belief that certain goals—those not given meaning in terms of the overall unifying goal—are unacceptable. Consequently, nonconformist goals are not likely to be thought of, and when they are conceived they are viewed immediately as bad, something out to determine the fabric of society.

Of course, some organized efforts would indeed undermine the fabric of society. But even supposing the fabric of the society ought *not* be undermined, there is still a difference between an organized activity directed by a goal that undermines the *coordination* of society, and one subversive to a conceived super-unity of activity for some one goal. The former indeed is subversive to the society as such. The latter is subversive only to the particular goals of a limited group taken to be universal for the whole.

This is not to overlook the possibility that the goals of one group might be intrinsically better than those of another group, and that the better goals ought to be made obligatory in the society. But it should be noted that if the better goals are made obligatory, and the obligation is enforced with sanctions, then the dissenting group is deprived of the dimension of freedom consisting in the freedom to organize for cooperative activity regarding freely chosen goals. To the degree there is a value to the right of free choice of goals there is a value to the right of cooperative activity toward freely chosen goals, even goals not conforming to unifying ideals of a society.

The remedies for the lack of this dimension of freedom concretely amount to two sorts of things. In the first place, every kind of nonconformist cooperative activity must fight for its own legitimacy. This must be done piecemeal. Each particular nonconformist goal must be shown either not to undermine the organized society, however anomalous it might seem relative to the conceived unifying goal, or to be justified in the changes it does bring about. In the second place the remedy for this lack of freedom must involve the formation of a genuinely pluralistic society. This cannot be done only piecemeal but must be a matter of general social understanding.

Freedom to Participate According to One's Own Style

The notion of style is very difficult to describe philosophically; its concrete description is a matter for art. Abstractly it can be described in this way, consonant with its use in various places above: a person's style is his generally expressed character stemming from his essential features contributing distinctive qualities to all or nearly all his actions. The essential features of style are not the ones usually decisive in important free choices; such essential features may be unique to the particular decisive occasion. Rather, the essential features of style bear upon all actions in some way, giving them a stamp peculiar to the person or to his group. Essential features are those determining the structure of the process of harmonizing the prehensions taken up in an occasion of experience. Some such features are unique to the occasion, but others are operative in a large range of the occasions of a given individual, inherited from moment to moment. Essential features of style are of the latter sort.

Whereas style may give a particular stamp or quality to all actions, it need not determine them decisively, especially when they involve a novel problematic situation. Moreover, the essential features of style need not be especially consistent; a person may have one style for dealing with people in business, another for his family as a whole, and a third for his spouse in private. Style is likely to be more determinative of routine actions than of nonroutine actions. A person's style or styles change as his experience develops. His style may be unique to himself, or it may be characteristic of his group in part; in either case it is something he develops through various forms of social interaction.

A person's style is an important part of his identity despite the fact that his personality is continuously expressed in a multiplicity of situations that otherwise might have nothing of importance in common. Style is not the only factor in identity. A person's identity consists also of what he does on unique occasions; to deny this would be to deny responsibility for past actions. But style is still important in individual or group identity. Although more obviously determinative of actions in stable situations than in unstable ones, style is more important for identity in the unstable ones, since it often is the only clue to continuity of an individual character. So it is important for the sake of identity to be free to participate in society with a peculiar style.

There is a reason it is even more important to have that freedom. What a culture is to an historical group, personal identity is to an individual. The factors of culture most often appreciable and of greatest intrinsic value are the general things. Likewise, an individual's style is his own contribution of intrinsic value to the quality of human life. Just as all individuals need a heritage and culture to be fully human, all need a persoal style or styles. Most individuals by and large appropriate most elements of their styles from other people, from their heritage, or from the exigencies of their organized society. But since style is a matter of essential features, those experienced elements are appropriated in the most complete sense.

Now there is no such thing as a personal style not exhibited in direct social interaction in the organized society. Style *is* a characteristic of such action. So not only must it be possible for a person to work out his style, the social situation must allow him to live it. These two, in fact, are not distinct, since styles are worked out in the living of them.

The obstacles against a personal style for participating in organized society are much the same as those against organizing for cooperative action with reference to strange goals. Just as the dominant segments of society extrapolate their own goals to a super-unifying goal giving them harmonious meaning and then enforce this goal on society, so they take their own sets of styles as normative. They reject styles tending to actions not conformable to their goals. There is no need to rehearse the variations appropriate to stylistic prejudices.

There is a special obstacle in the matter of style, however. Goals are final ends toward which actions can be ordered. But a style of ordering actions, over and above matters of instrumentality regarding goals, has a peculiar normative quality itself. It is fair to speak of styles as ideals for human behavior. Just as we often identify objects in terms of whether they are good examples of their class, so we identify men by whether they are good examples of humanity. This procedure should have only limited use, of course, since the worth of individuals consists as much in the quality of their meeting historically unique exigencies as it does in living up to an ideal type. But human assessment seems unable to do without appeal to types as isolated ideals. And usually in determining the ideal human type, style is one of the most, if not *the* most, important factor.

In organized societies *particular* styles often are elevated as the ideal types. In American society a person or group that does not organize itself first around the economic endeavor, giving life meaning in terms of success in this dimension, is reckoned as lazy, barbaric, and deficiently human. Some styles are better than others, no doubt, just as some goals for cooperative activity are better than others. But, as with goals, the evaluation of ideals is to be settled by the kind of complex normative analysis discussed in Part 2.

The mere fact of some style's being efficacious in a segment of society in itself gives it no normative claim over other segments of society. The case must be decided by harmonizing a great many factors, including differences in organized roles, age, heritage, cultural perspective, and the demands of the unique historical situation. Since historical situations are always partly unique, and the decisive ones importantly so, very few singular actions can be judged by stylistic ideals alone. Only the most general traits of life can be judged in terms of such ideals. Here the ideals, being applicable because they best harmonized the general components of the life in question, must be particular to the various different lives. The ideal style of one heritage is not likely to be appropriate to people of another heritage, just as the ideal style of one generation is not likely appropriate to another.

Again, the remedy for the lack of freedom to participate in organized society with a style appropriate to oneself consists in the creation of a genuinely pluralistic society. That has continually been the conclusion of our considerations of dimensions of social freedom. Social pluralism is not only one among many forms of organization for society: it is the one demanded by social freedom. One can hardly be faulted for suggesting that social pluralism is the most important problem in our age, practically as well as intellectually.

FREEDOM OF HISTORICAL ACTION

The strategy of this discussion has been to divide the freedom of opportunity into two sides: the freedom to participate in culture and the freedom to participate in organized society. Is there any unified sense of participation, however, that brings these sides together? Certainly there is a functional dependence of each side on the other. But is there a patterned value of freedom of opportunity as such?

To exercise full freedom of participation in society is to be an historical actor. As Hegel pointed out, it is difficult to do anything decisive in history.[16] Most people are victims of history; despite their resources and opportunities they are swept up by historical forces they do not understand and cannot control. Even their definitions of happiness are provided by their historical contexts, and whether they are happy depends on chance. They are the objects on which history works its will. Others with more historical consciousness are citizens of their times. Recognizing the values and ideals defining their culture and organized society, they take the defense of those ideals to be among the important defining characteristics of their lives. But they are not creative with respect to those ideals; history gives them serving roles to play. Yet there are others whom Hegel calls history's heroes. They are the ones whose private interests coincide with the interests of the historical forces; they may be great revolutionaries and agents of historical change, but only because they are in the right place at the right time. They are the creative agents of history's forces, not of their own freedom. There are also non-historical heroes, heroes of God or, in Hegel's language, Absolute Spirit. These people attain a closeness to and personal resonance with the foundations of the universe; saints and mystics are the prime examples. But they do this by living in isolation from the historical process. For Hegel, there were no kinds of men capable of free historical action.

A higher ideal of the historical free agent can be discerned, however, even if there are few people of the type. A person makes a free historical action when he comprehends the vectors of historical forces, envisions their alternate outcomes, discerns how those outcomes hinge on the small deeds he might do, and acts with the purity and determination to effect his own choice in the matter. It makes no difference for the ideal how broad the scope of the historical arena is. The arena may involve the moving of

16. See his Introduction to *The Philosophy of History*, published as *Reason in History*, trans. Robert S. Hartman (New York: The Liberal Arts Press, 1953).

nations. Or it may involve decisions in a much humbler scale
of society, one's family or profession. The important factor for
the ideal is that the action take up the historically important
forces and arrange them according to free choice. Most people
are historically determined in all important respects. Most free
choices involve factors of no historical significance. Yet the possibility of a free historical action remains.

Comprehending the vectors of historical forces is an obstacle
almost insuperable in itself. There is no unambiguous understanding of history. Furthermore, the origins of historical forces
in the societies and cultures of the past are not yet perspicuous to
even the best scholars. At the very least, comprehending current
historical forces requires a subtle appropriation of the values and
resources of all the cultures contributing to those forces. The
consequence of this for "western man" is that he ceases to be
capable of historical action to the degree he has not appropriated
the cultures of those with whom he deals. This problem takes on
greater magnitude in the degree that the influence of other
cultures is increasing in the play of world events. The person
of historically free actions is one appropriating the human traditions not just the western ones.

Envisioning the alternate outcomes of historical forces is a
work of great imagination. How easy it is to believe one has
hit upon live options only by suppressing appreciation of certain
overwhelming forces! Nevertheless, there is no reason a priori to
believe all alternatives to the historical process are foreclosed in
advance.

The heart of the cognitive element in historical action is discerning just what one can do that would make a difference. Most
deeds either reinforce antecedent historical forces that would
have carried on anyway, or they oppose them without power. The
former is more likely because the same conditions that support the
moving historical forces support one's own activity. To make a
difference to history requires discerning just what small actions
—what words, what movements, what efforts—tip the balance of
historical forces so as to lead to one's intended outcome. This was
analyzed earlier in the discussion of free choice. The unique
dimension added by history is that the relevant variables to be
ultimately effected and the resources taken in for effecting them,

are often remote from the familiar elements of one's personal life. Although one's decisive movements are of course personal, they are understood in this case not in terms of personal life but in terms of historical causation.

The hardest part of free historical action is attaining the purity and determination to act effectively. "Purity" is a strange word to use in this context. What is meant by it, however, is a motive focused exclusively on the values in the historical lineaments of the action. It is contrasted with motives mixing the values of the action itself with those of the effects of the action on one's personal self and career. The point is expressed in the title of Sören Kierkegaard's book, *Purity of Heart Is to Will One Thing*. The *Bhagavadgita* enjoins: "Act for the sake of the action, not for its fruits." There are many senses of personal self sullying motives, some of them so narcissistic as to distort one's whole view of the world. The demand for purity, however, excludes even those rational assessments of self when they stand in the way of acting for the sake of the historical values in the actions themselves. There is a certain irony in the fact that free historical action requires one to be so at home with oneself, so much in self-control, that one's self can be literally forgotten. The irony is deepened by consideration of the determination required. Action with determination means that one comports oneself continually, through change and stress, so as to effect the desired historical outcome. This entails an extraordinarily sensitive understanding of oneself as a natural and historical cause. But it must not involve a sense of the values of one's own life as having a privileged status among one's motives.

The purity and determination of a free historical agent are rather like the will imagined of God: because He is equally close to all things He creates, none is dearer than any other. God has no sense of self and no narcissistic world. He acts for the world alone. The historical agent must be something like that. The very fact that religious images are best fit for expressing this purity and determination means there can be no *right* to historical free action. No society can guarantee the opportunity, because even recognizing it requires heroism.

Nevertheless, of all the ideals discussed, that of the free actor in history is the highest. His free participation in society serves his

personal freedom in the most complete way. Yet his personal freedom is at the service of the values discerned in and chosen for the
world. Lacking self, he assumes all relevant power and is the most
creative of all.

Freedom of historical action is the highest ideal of freedom in
many senses. It is the concrete expression of the creativity that was
described as itself the culmination of personal freedom. And it
combines both kinds of freedom of opportunity: freedoms of appropriating human values from the environment and the freedoms of acting in organized society. At this stage in our argument,
however, we can only give a relatively empty characterization of
free historical action. In what kind of social organization is the
historical agent most free? The answer we shall give to that question is, A participatory democracy. But why is that form of organization most conducive to historical freedom? Because it is the best
environment for the integral style of social life enhancing any of
the freedoms of opportunity. Why is an integral style important?
In order to give personal unity to decisions whose options are
genuine social alternatives. Why should there be genuine social
alternatives? Because alternatives are required for choice, as was
argued in Part 2. And social choices require social alternatives.
Freedom of opportunity is one dimension of social freedom. Freedom of genuine social choice is an addition to it, enriching all
the opportunities, and essential to free historical action. The organized structure of genuine social opportunities is a pluralistic
society.

9

Freedom of Social Pluralism

One of the most important freedoms of opportunity is to live according to the social forms of one's choice. The notion of "social form" is difficult to define, and it probably would be a mistake to define it too explicitly. It includes an individual's life style, and perhaps the style of his group. It might include participation in certain institutions peculiar to an ethnic group, or idiosyncratic practices of education. There are many areas of life both large and small that center around ways of doing things that may be peculiar to a person or group. These are prized if they give some special meaning to people's lives. They are valued as freedom-values insofar as some people want them to be available as options.

It is not enough for an analysis of freedom to note that diverse social forms are valued as opportunities. A society is not free unless it sustains a social order tolerant of the plurality of valued forms. The "social order" in this case means an organization of the society to safeguard the pluralism. A free society should conceive the protection of social pluralism as a special principle of its order, as an important component of its ideal self-understanding, and perhaps even as an element in its government and law. Without this special attention, two unfortunate conditions would obtain. First, no social form would have the time for slow development to rich and intense value because the range of tolerance would be contingent upon the social mix of feelings about what is immediately nonthreatening. No unusual traditions would have the time to develop because almost surely they would be threatening at some time to someone who had the power to undermine them. Second, the social forms of minorities would be suppressed, not only because they are perceived as threatening but also because of the more general chauvinism whereby each dominant group usually thinks its own way of getting along is really the only good way. Therefore, a pluralistic society must undertake special measures to protect its pluralism through the perils of passing fancy.

The first special measure that can be taken, although perhaps not sufficient by itself, has to do with the way a society perceives itself. In most respects, the idea a society has of itself, indeed its mythical ideal, sets limits for what it is possible to do in the society. A society that perceived itself as pluralistic, as guaranteeing that dimension of social freedom, at least could be called to task by its prophets when it acted intolerantly. The aim of this chapter is to examine what is involved in the very conception of a society as pluralistic.

There is something of a paradox here, however. A person or group believes in the value of its own chosen social form. How can he also prize the social form of people different from himself without being merely eclectic? Somewhere, each person distinguishes between his private values for life and his public values for pluralistic social order.

Pluralism becomes a problem when diverse people privately want freedoms incompatible with the form of public order at hand. There would be no problem if what the diverse groups did in private conflicted in no important way with public order. But private idiosyncrasy cannot be limited to the private domain, especially when the values privately held must be exercised in the full range of social interaction in order properly to be appropriated. Much of what men claim a right to do in private has public effects, or so it seems. This suggests that the distinction between the public and the private domains of social life lies at the heart of the problem of pluralism.[1] The distinction between the public and the private, like the meaning of culture, is something everyone believes he understands, a belief patently false. But it is wise to note at the beginning some of the things everyone believes to characterize the distinction.[2] Everyone recognizes a dif-

1. John Dewey also held to the importance of the distinction between the public and the private and urged it to be substituted in political theory for the distinction between the individual and the collective society. See his *The Public and Its Problems* (Denver: Swallow Press, 1927), pp. 13ff.

2. It is hardly less than ironic to footnote something claimed to be believed by everybody. Interesting general discussions of the distinction between public and

ference between a person's private responsibilities and his public ones. Parallel to this is a distinction between a person's private life and his public life. We also distinguish between people who are "in private life" and those who are "in public life." The latter are defined by the society in terms of some official role, and the former, although possibly just as influential, have no obligation to an official *role,* however much they have public responsibilities due to their influence. Further, we recognize a difference between institutions in the public sector and those in the private sector.

Everyone also recognizes that the distinction between private and public affairs of life is a shifting one, depending on circumstance. In time of war, for instance, many affairs usually thought private become public. The problem of how this line shifts relative to changing conditions lies at the heart of the distinction between public and private.

Even more complicated is the common recognition that there are relative degrees of privacy and publicity; the governor of a state may enter into public lobbying with other governors to get federal funds for the state; but he would resent the other governors telling him how to run his state, his private affair. On another level, his life as officer of the state is a public one, distinct from his private life with his family. Even in his family there is a household "public" he must respect and from which he seeks seclusion in his "private study."

Parallel to the relative degrees of privacy and publicity for individuals is a scale for groups: so long as a subculture in a larger society fulfills its responsibilities to the group as a whole, its way of life *in respects not seriously affecting the whole* is its private matter. This was the argument of the cultural pluralists early in the century regarding the integrity of Jewish culture, and it has been widely accepted in principle.

The cash meaning for the distinction between private and public is generally recognized to lie in the supposed right of men to

private, however, are to be found in the following contemporary writings, among many others: Brian Barry, *Political Argument* (New York: Humanities Press, 1965), chap. 11; Charles Fried, *The Anatomy of Values: Problems of Personal and Social Choice* (Cambridge: Harvard University Press, 1970), chap. 9; and Paul Weiss, *Our Public Life* (Bloomington: Indiana University Press, 1959).

do what they want in legitimately private affairs, whereas in public affairs they must give moral regard to "the public good." This does not mean only public affairs are subject to moral considerations. Quite the contrary, it might be the case that private affairs are strictly governed by norms. Some segments of our society think private affairs are nonmoral, others take them to be moral matters. But it is generally agreed that it is not public responsibility to determine how one behaves in private; this is the bite of the distinction. Our laws, for instance, are coming to recognize a private domain of actions over which they should exercise no jurisdiction, however reprehensible some actions might be.

Some people, of course, argue that certain matters usually thought to be private are in fact public responsibilities. For instance, they might argue that sexual matters ought to be regulated by public laws because the moral fabric of the public is undermined by sexual corruption. This only amounts, however, to denying these matters are in fact private. Regardless of how the lines are to be drawn between public and private affairs, it is commonly recognized that what should be understood by the distinction is that it is not the responsibility of the public to regulate private affairs. In fact, our society has come to regard privacy in certain matters as a right to freedom from interference by other persons or by the public. Freedom as the "right to privacy" will be explored in a later section of this chapter.

Another, perhaps not so prominent dimension of the distinction is the belief that public affairs should be dealt with reasonably and with due measure. Public affairs are thought to be subject to public check, continually open to examination according to public standards. Private affairs, on the other hand, while they may be moral matters, are the arena of creativity, imagination, and idiosyncracy. John Stuart Mill believed so strongly that creativity depends on privacy that he desired to limit the domain of public respectability as much as possible.[3]

3. See his *On Liberty*, ed. Currin V. Shields (New York: Liberal Arts Press, 1956), chap. 3, esp. pp. 81–82: "Precisely because the tyranny of opinion is such as to make eccentricity a reproach, it is desirable, in order to break through that tyranny, that people should be eccentric. Eccentricity has always abounded when and where strength of character has abounded; and the amount of eccentricity in a society has generally been proportional to the amount of genius, mental vigor, and moral courage it contained."

A final point commonly recognized is that public aspects of society should be consistent with one another, whereas the private aspects need not be. Of course, it is impossible for all the elements of public action to be consistent on every level; but this is taken as the ideal. Regarding private matters, it is often cited as a great virtue of western society that unmeasurable diversity is possible. Private affairs need not be made consistent with one another because they do not conflict; to the extent they do conflict they take on a semblance of publicity. But the more diversity that is possible in private matters, the richer the society is supposed to be.

There are some special features about common notions of privacy that require further mention. They have never been universally believed, but they have been fairly influential in forming the common-sense notion of privacy. They are instances of the general belief that the move into privacy is a withdrawal from participation in organized society. This belief may reflect the etymology of the word, which stems from *privatum,* the Latin term for being deprived of an office, or bereaved.

Private life has sometimes been prized as a context for withdrawing from full participation in organized society to an enjoyment of the pleasures of culture. This amounts to an attempt to alienate oneself from the social freedoms discussed in the previous chapter under the heading of organized society and to adopt only those, or nearly only those, discussed under culture. The attempt is bound to fail, however, in a significant sense over and above the practical difficulties of avoiding organized society. Culture cannot be enjoyed unless it bears upon activity in organized society. Some people are willing to pay this price, of course, enjoying the pleasures of culture only in attenuated ways. But carried far enough, exclusive concentration on culture leads to eccentricity with no redeeming features, a dehumanizing state of affairs. This sense of private life, therefore, is dangerous because, although it is defined in reference to public life, it is defined in exclusion of it. The lesson, therefore, is that a good understanding of private life is likely to require some sort of interaction that includes the public side.

Private life has also been thought of as a context for withdrawing from organized society and its values to the exercise of whim.

This is an extreme case of what John Stuart Mill had in mind when he justified the social usefulness of eccentricity, an extreme case because it is not apparently socially useful. For a balanced personality, one balanced by a full participation in the important affairs of human life, whim might mean *play*, the importance of which cannot be overestimated. Of course, whim is an essential part of creativity when involved with other aspects of freedom. But when whim becomes the dominant character of private life, a person's life is disastrously bifurcated into publicly defined roles and private chaos. This perhaps has been the intent, or at least the result, of modern liberal political theory, which has emphasized justice and equality for public definitions of people and the irrelevance of norms for more unique personal characteristics. But it is indeed a disaster, from two points of view. From the view of the society, people's private lives have no meaning or enriching function. Because many people privately are *not* whimsical, but greedy and calculating, a public order defined with indifference to the quality of private life presents a special problem of corruption, a sad lesson still unlearned by liberalism. From the view of the individual, his public roles and private whims have no bearing upon each other. Whim alone is an impoverished personal freedom, allowing no self-possession; definition by public roles allows no autonomy unless creatively related to choice. The attempt to define privacy in terms of whim undermines a sense of integrity or personal unity unless other crucial features are added.

Another meaning often given to private life is that of being a context for withdrawing to one's family or small coterie of friends, in contrast to participating in the larger and more impersonal society. There is nothing necessarily exclusive about this, since a person can be in the impersonal world at some times and in his private world at others. This sense of private life is fostered by views such as those of Harvey Cox in *The Secular City* that distinguish between personal relationships, I-thou, and impersonal but still important and social relationships, I–you.[4] Private life is thought to be the domain where I–thou relationships predominate (for instance, within the limits of family or friendship

4. *The Secular City: Secularization and Urbanization in Theological Perspective* (New York: Macmillan Co., 1965), chap. 2.

cliques) and are protected against impersonal social encroach-ments by socially recognized structures. In contrast to the two previously mentioned interpretations of private life, this one has all the personal richness one might desire.

This interpretation stands in a peculiar sort of jeopardy, how-ever. Insofar as the private personal relationships are not mere happenstance but stem from some social organization, such as the family structure, they are subject to the controls determining such organization. These controls often lie in the hands of the outside impersonal society. Personal family relationships, for instance, are organized in large part according to the meanings of family roles; those roles are now changing radically and always will as long as the society at large is characterized by social mobility. And the causes of those changes often are remote from the concrete characters of the personal relationships in the family. A striking example of this change concerns education, in its full sense of becoming human, not just in terms of reading, writing, and arith-metic, which were nearly always public matters. One of the ear-liest ideals of American society was that the education of its chil-dren was a family's private affair. But it was also early recognized that an uneducated citizenry is a public liability, hence the public interest in education. As things have developed it has become much more efficient for the public to take over education in more and more respects. But this has meant that education, which was a matter of predominantly personal relationships when it was centered mostly within the family, has become a more imper-sonal matter. The lesson here is that the relation between private life and public life cannot be maintained with integrity if its structure is a function of the interactions of the whole society, as most social structures are.

Private life, finally, has often been taken to mean the context from which a person can criticize his organized society. "Criticism" here means not the reforming criticism that stems from a critical interaction with the basic forms of organized society, but rather a radical or revolutionary criticism that takes up a stance against the whole. The separation cannot be complete, but it can involve a private style of life explicitly rejecting the fundamental organi-zational principles of the society, and perhaps formulating a whole-sale alternative. Due to the difficulty of living at odds with most of one's society, the private life of radical criticism is likely to be unhappy. But it is not to be depreciated. Such a private life has an intimate public side, namely its public critical witness as viewed by the rest of society; this is a perfect consistency of private and public life. Withdrawal from organized society to private radical criticism does have a simple disadvantage, however. It is most likely to become ineffectual, and there is nothing more dehumanizing than unrelenting lack of success. What may originally have been a vision of a better society so often turns to sheer negativity. The only way the life of radical criticism can be successful is if the organized society prizes and gives place to such criticism. A life of criticism that arises by rejecting the basic organizational principles cannot be lived without an active participation in the restructuring of society; private criticism must be lived in a life of intense public involvement.[5] This is another lesson.

We can summarize the hidden values that have appeared from this consideration of privacy as withdrawal from organized society: (1) private life should be defined in terms of a life of interaction with a public side, (2) private life as well as public life must contribute something to personal identity; an individual should not be defined indifferently by publicity or privacy, (3) the valuable distinction between private life and public life does not rest legitimately on some de facto social structure; rather, it is likely to rest on a difference in ways of relating to social structures, (4) private life cannot mean a critical rejection of the organization of a society unless it is coupled with a critical public involvement in changing the organized society.

Our discussion of the pluralistic society began with a consideration of the distinction commonly drawn between the public and the private. After reviewing several of the usual ways of drawing that distinction, discussing them in the special contexts within which they are drawn, we examined several beliefs about the meaning of private life. Although none of these concepts of the public and the private is adequate to our systematic interest, each expresses something felt to be true in human experience, even with its limitations. Therefore, one of the important tests of ad-

5. For a splendid discussion of radical criticism in the commune movement see Rosabeth Moss Kanter's *Commitment and Community: Communes and Utopias in Sociological Perspective* (Cambridge: Harvard University Press, 1972).

equacy of a proper philosophical distinction is whether it can render these common notions plausibly. We now turn to two candidate philosophical formulations.

DEWEY'S PUBLIC AND MCLUHAN'S MEDIA

Social pluralism depends on most of the above characterizations of the distinction obtaining in certain proper ways. The great defender of social pluralism, of course, was John Dewey, and we shall begin with a consideration of his procedure for drawing the distinction between the public and the private. He formulated the problem in quasi-evolutionary terms, that is, as how a society that recognizes only private interpersonal transactions might come to recognize a public domain. He calls this the formation of "The Public," and we shall quote at length from his summary of the argument.

> Conjoint, combined, associated action is a universal trait of the behavior of things. Such action has results. Some of the results of human collective action are perceived, that is, they are noted in such ways that they are taken account of. Then there arise purposes, plans, measures and means, to secure consequences which are liked and eliminate those which are found obnoxious. Thus perception generates a common interest; that is, those affected by the consequences are perforce concerned in conduct of all those who along with themselves share in bringing about the results. Sometimes the consequences are confined to those who directly share in the transaction which produces them. In other cases they extend far beyond those immediately engaged in producing them. Thus two kinds of interests and of measures of regulation of acts in view of consequences are generated. In the first, interest and control are limited to those directly engaged; in the second, they extend to those who do not directly share in the performance of acts. If, then, the interest constituted by their being affected by the actions in question is to have any practical influence, control over the actions which produce them must occur by some indirect means.
>
> So far the statements, it is submitted, set forth matters of actual and ascertainable fact. Now follows the hypothesis.

Those indirectly and seriously affected for good or for evil form a group distinctive enough to require recognition and a name. The name selected is The Public. This public is organized and made effective by means of representatives who as guardians of customs, as legislators, as executives, judges, etc., care for its especial interests by methods intended to regulate the conjoint actions of individuals and groups. Then and in so far, association adds to itself political organization, and something which may be government comes into being: the public is a political state.[6]

The nub of Dewey's argument is the distinction between direct and indirect consequences of social interactions. The distinction as he makes it out seems clear enough, even if certain consequences are hard to classify. But of equal importance with that distinction is Dewey's insistence that the indirect consequences must be perceived for there to be a public. A public is not generated by having consequences affect it; it generates itself because of consequences that do or are believed to affect it. There is no "right" of public organization before there is actual organization.

But is not the root meaning of "public right" the legitimacy or authority of the public to control certain kinds of consequences? Not for Dewey. A government, perhaps, has such legitimacy, but not a public as described here. The reason industries should heed the demands of antipollution organizations is that the demands are justified, not that they are authoritative. In the end, the question whether the public or the private agents will control the indirect consequences comes down, in Dewey's view, to which has more power. In fact, he complains more loudly about the evil violence performed by government and organized publics than he does about the violence of private agents too powerful to be controlled.[7]

The second major factor in Dewey's analysis is that publics are all relative to the active forces producing the indirect consequences. It is important to note there is a variety of publics. As problems are local, with no serious consequences extending be-

6. *The Public and Its Problems*, pp. 34–35.
7. See, e.g., his *Liberalism and Social Action* (1935; reprint ed., New York: Capricorn, 1963), pp. 62–67.

yond a definite group, so publics are local. A given individual may belong to several overlapping publics. And as the transactions producing the consequences are often temporary, so publics may be temporary. Dewey was perhaps insensitive to the tendencies of organizations to perpetuate themselves beyond their relevance to actual problems. What would happen if an organized public exercised control over private parties long after the parties ceased to affect the members of the public? Dewey would have to say the organized public had become a private party with indirect consequences, directly intended, perhaps, for the previously private parties who now ought to constitute themselves as a public to control the other organization.

How does a whole society organize itself as a public, according to Dewey's analysis? He does not dwell on this problem, although the answer can be deduced from what he does say. Some actions do indeed affect everyone in the larger society; of course, not everyone is affected to the same degree, but the effects may be universally serious nevertheless. A public may be as universal in a society as perceived effects. Furthermore (and this is the more important factor), the various small publics recognize this by organizing among themselves so they can tap a larger reservoir of power when it comes to dealing with their own relevant problems. Dewey himself emphasizes that larger publics are formed by the "recognition of extensive and enduring indirect consequences"; but it is not contrary to his analysis to emphasize the concern for power.[8]

In an important respect, then, Dewey stands Hobbes on his head. Whereas Hobbes feared unauthorized power, Dewey takes it to be at the heart of society as it actually works, and a good thing. There is no reason, thinks Dewey, to believe that power concentrated in the hands of a public official will be any less evil or violent than in the hands of a private individual, unless each man in the public actively participates in the determination of the official will. Dewey has confidence that a participatory democracy

8. For a careful empirical analysis of the formation of a public according to Dewey's categories, see Raymond J. Bucher, O.F.M., "The Current Academic Crisis: Toward a Solution According to John Dewey's Notion of the Public" (Ph.D. diss., Fordham University, 1970). Bucher analyzed the role of the Ocean Hill-Brownsville school dispute in the formation of a self-conscious public community organization.

will be more or less just. Unlike Hobbes, for whom individuals seemed isolated centers of life, Dewey takes proper human experience to be participation in the experience of all members of the society. Therefore, in a properly experiential society a minority's feelings and sufferings will not be left out but will be made part of the experience of all. By virtue of an ideal of experiential participation, the ideal of democracy is to leave each man with his powers, to alienate him as little as possible.[9]

Dewey's distinction between the public and the private is imbedded in his larger view of society. Nonetheless, there is something peculiarly unhelpful about the categories he employs to make it out, namely those of direct and indirect consequences. In the first place, they are rough categories. Most social interactions between specific individuals bleed off into the larger society not only in consequences but also in participation. Since the line between direct and indirect participation in the interaction is so indistinct, categories other than those Dewey offers will have to be brought out to deal with most individual cases. Such supplementation of general categories is always necessary in dealing with cases, but in this instance the supplementation would have to be so great as to suggest the categories themselves do not do the work they should.

In the second place, the model of the evolutionary development of a public is misleading. The perception of indirect consequences by an unorganized group whom they affect is one thing. But what about the situation where the public is organized and already takes an active part in most social transactions? Even more than in Dewey's time, the American government is a partner now to nearly every industry, having a large say in investment possibilities, prices, advertising and so on. And the government's presence as an active participant in social interactions is not limited to the economic sphere. For all practical purposes, then, the public as represented by the government is directly, not indirectly, involved in the transactions. We are, in fact, witnessing the formation of a new public in America composed of social *radicals,* people who reject enough of the organized interaction between established society and established public organization *to feel themselves affected only indirectly,* and therefore demand a greater voice for

9. See his *Democracy and Education* (New York: Macmillan Co., 1916), esp. chap. 7.

reformation. This testifies to the basic validity of Dewey's position, but also to the unwieldiness of his categories, since there is an obvious sense in which the government must be considered an arm of the public. The evolutionary model is misleading in a developed society.

In the third place, and most important for our present purposes, the categories of direct and indirect consequences do not tie in to the problem of social pluralism. It might be said social groups can be as diverse as they please so long as that diversity has no serious indirect consequences on the rest of society, but that concerning indirect consequences they must conform to the established dictates of the relevant publics. The difficulty with this, however, is that social pluralism will not resolve the problems of social freedom raised in chapter 8 without allowing diversity to express itself in a *full-blooded* way throughout the whole range of social interactions. A gaggle of ghettos is not a free pluralistic society. Of course, an idiosyncratic group or individual must take account of public opposition to his culture, goals, and style, and this taking account might have the form of opposing his power to that of the public. But Dewey's categories at this point have not advanced our appreciation of the fact that social pluralism is a problem.

It will be argued in the remaining sections of this chapter that Dewey's basic vision regarding the public is correct. But a radical revolution in society is necessary before his notions become *descriptive*. In other words, his view is more nearly appropriate for today, which is in the midst of such a revolution, than it was for his own day. But a different philosophical analysis from his will be required to see what the revolution consists in and how his categories do in fact apply.

The difference between the private sphere and the public is marked, on the public side, by how much the public can demand (legitimately or de facto) from individuals. What the public can demand varies with conditions. More affairs are private in time of peace than in time of war. In time of economic stress the government takes more control over money than in time of economic stability.

What is the implicit principle governing the de facto or de jure settling of the scope of public demands?

Suppose we say that the public has implicit demand over the

whole range of socially constituted general media of social interaction.[10] The society, the most general public, can control the general media of interaction for its own good because the media
(1) exist by the resources of the organized society as a whole and
(2) are the underpinnings of that society. So in whatever circumstances u the public good is served by extending control into an
area within these media previously left to private control, the
public can in fact and de jure extend its control. The justification
for this public extension is that citizens, even in their private roles,
enjoy the media because the media are sustained by the society as
a whole, not because the citizens created them. On the other hand,
in those areas of organized or unorganized interaction, *not* constituents of the general social media, a person has private freedom
to do what he wants. This can be called the "media" thesis, reflecting McLuhan's suggestions about the importance of media.

The media thesis has the advantage of giving a rationale for the
sliding boundaries of public and private life. The areas of life not
constitutive of general media are inviolately private. But regarding the general media, the public always has implicit control and
can exercise actual control according to the changing demands of
the public good. Now the distinction between the private and the
public is not morally important except insofar as there is a conflict between an individual's good and the public's good. The
media thesis resolves this conflict by making the public good the
sole criterion regarding the limits of control on the only area of
possible conflict, the media.

The media thesis has the further advantage of avoiding the intuitive appeals to "rights" that have characterized classical modern
social theory.[11] For instance, there is no need to say there is a
"right" to property, even a right to possess one's own body as
property. "Property" is a notion depending on a socially legiti-
mized form of transferring title. Such a form of transfer would
be an obvious example of a general medium. So those aspects of
life consisting in possession of property are in fact public affairs

10. A more technical discussion will be given in the next chapter of concepts
such as social interaction and social meaning being carried over media.

11. For a thorough and profound discussion of the difficulties of "rights" theories
in modern society, see Leo Strauss, *Natural Right and History* (Chicago: University
of Chicago Press, 1953). See also Paul Weiss's defense of such a theory in *Our Public
Life,* chap. 2.

regarding their "propertiness," that is, their title transferability. Possession of money and transferable goods is possible only where there is public definition of rights of transfer, and so for the public good such possession can be regulated publicly. In those cases where it makes sense to speak of transferable possession of one's own body, for instance as an economic unit of labor, or when one's executors might sell or donate one's dead body for medical purposes, it is conceivable that the public good might demand regulation of title. The public good usually, however, is thought to profit by as little actual public regulation as possible.

Yet another advantage of the media thesis is that the determination of what in fact is a general medium is an empirical task. Economic and judicial systems are obviously media. So are languages and other media of communication, although they are difficult to control even if the public wanted to. But what happens in wartime? It seems then that the medium of the society's survival includes nearly all the aspects of life for its citizens. Those Americans who remember World War II recall how otherwise private backyards became Victory gardens, how used tin cans had to be stamped flat and saved for the "war effort," and how job selection was a matter of picking your vital industry. Some people have even argued that the medium of military defense includes the thoughts and attitudes of citizens, justifying an extensive use of propaganda and censorship. Whether the public good in fact demands the inclusion of people's thoughts as parts of the war effort, or whether a war effort that must include regulation of thought is in fact in the public good, is an empirical matter. In empirical fact the regulations of the public may do well or ill; but if it is shown that the possession of backyards, rubbish, jobs, and thoughts is dependent on the society's successful waging of the war, then those things may be claimed as constituents of the general medium of social self-defense. The trouble in practice with most arguments justifying public control based on forms of the "clear and present danger" doctrine is that they move too quickly from showing the dependence of a particular version of the factor in question on the preservation of the society to a dependence of its existence in any good form. It might well be argued that even if the society capitulated to the enemy, people could still think and work, and maybe even have rubbish and backyards.

The difficulty with the media thesis is that it conceives the location of the boundary between public and private to be too much a matter of the initiative of the public, where the boundary in question is the place on the various media where the actual regulation of the public ends. The shifting of the distinction between public and private, according to the media thesis, is a shift on territory that is implicitly all public, and where the determination of the boundary, therefore, is up to the public. Yet the empirical evidence indicates that the determination of the boundary is a matter of others factors. Sometimes the public attempts to set limits unacceptable to people in what they successfully assert as their private roles. Governments, the official representatives of most general publics, are well aware that they must operate within the limits of acceptability. Of course, what a government can and cannot do is in part a matter of plain force; but the government's force is limited in the long run by what is acceptable. As Dewey would point out, the limit of any public is the potentiality of counter-publics being formed. The factors determining overall acceptability in this case are the ones truly determining the boundary between public and private. Helpful as the media thesis is, it must be rejected in favor of a theory locating the determination of the boundary between public and private not in the will of the public alone, but in the factors that determine also what is acceptable throughout the society at large regarding the boundaries.

It must be remembered throughout this discussion what the logical structure of the argument is. We are not trying to deduce a definition of the distinction between public and private. Rather we have elucidated various unintegrated things people universally or in special situations believe to be true about the distinction, and we are hunting a general theory to make sense of them. Therefore, it is legitimate for us to use notions of the public and the private spheres, derived from common lore, when in fact we have not given a formal characterization of them. The theory we will propose will in fact have to be tested against what people commonly think. In the same way, the ambiguities in the discussion at this point about whether a public is "legitimately constituted," or whether a de facto boundary between public and private matters is where it ought to be, are harmless. It might be argued, concerning the criticism made of the media thesis, that the public *should not* be the prime determinant of shifts in the boundary; this may be true, but its proof would require an elaborate theory about public and private obligation on a delicate point not yet established. Only if we know in fact what the determinants of the boundary are would we be able to say that the public has limits it should not overstep.

THE ENVIRONMENT–CREATIVITY THESIS

The hypothesis to be considered next and defended can be called the "environment–creativity" thesis, namely, that the distinction between public and private rests on a distinction between social environment and creativity within that environment. The distinction is made in terms of concern. The public has to do with concerns for maintaining a sociophysical environment in which creativity can take place. The particular kind of environment an organized society requires is relative to the kinds of creativity prized in the society. Privacy has to do with concerns for creating valuable things that enhance the environment. Not only are works of art products of creativity in this sense, products that can take their place as part of the social environment, but the same is true of the little acts of kindness and love in a family that elevate the personal relationships above the environmental family structure. All the various ways in which men are creative depend on a social environment in which that creativity can take place; concern with the environment is a public matter, concern with the creative activities as such is private, according to our hypothesis. Most actions of life, even most concerns, are neither public nor private.

Before examining the distinction in detail the equivocations of language concerning privacy and publicity (detailed on pp. 257–62) may be interpreted in terms of the thesis. A person's "private life" consists in those aspects of his experience that are creative, particularly or generally, whereas his "public life" consists of those aspects that involve maintenance of the social environment; most of his activities have aspects of both. "To be in public life" is to have a recognized social role whose function it is to maintain the social environment; to "be in private life" is not to have such a role, but instead to have a role that might be creative. "Private life" is primarily a negative term; the president of General Motors is in private life because it is not the defining responsibility of his role as president to preserve the environment, even though he does so indirectly by paying taxes; as a private citizen he might form an antipollution committee and would then be assuming a public role. The "public sector" would be those organized aspects of society, especially institutions, concerned with maintenance of the environment. The "private sector" would be the institutions desiring to use the environment for creative purposes. Business-men, those defining the private sector, would claim they are cre-ating new products, jobs, and money, thereby enhancing the en-vironment that supports them, whereas radical critics would say the private sector is just part of the establishment maintaining a dynamic but balanced environment of an economic sort, thereby *improperly* being called "private." The distinction between pub-lic affairs and private affairs is "relative" in the sense that a broad environment may be maintained for a creative task that itself is the maintenance of an environment for another creative task. A governor's grant of federal funds maintains an environment in which he can cope creatively with the problems of the state, which in turn is maintenance of an environment for the mayor's creative work, and so forth; the governor's job is an environment supporting his creation of a family life, which in turn is the con-text for his creative thoughts about statecraft. The boundary be-tween affairs to be controlled by the public and those to be con-trolled by private individuals shifts according to whether the af-fairs are taken as necessary for the environment or as instrumental to creative endeavors. The phrase "the public" refers to the col-lections of people considered abstractly as identified with their participations in the social organizations concerned with maintain-ing the social environment. Defining the public in terms of or-ganizations with concerns allows recognition of the fact that peo-ple *not* affected by relevant consequences, either directly or in-directly, can join an organized public to remedy a situation just because they feel dispassionately that it ought to be remedied, a fact Dewey's account must miss. A person's "privacy" refers to those organized elements of his life that reserve resources and energies for creative activities that arise from the demands of en-vironmental preservation.

If the environment–creativity thesis is to sustain critical examination, it must be given a theoretical formulation. This shall be done in terms of the categoreal scheme already developed.

In chapter 4 we discussed in detail the distinction between what is internal and what is external to a person. What is internal are his essential and conditional features, and what is relevantly external are the other things involved in nexuses leading to his conditional features. (What is external and not relevant is irrelevant.) The environment, therefore, would seem to be a matter of external things, and we shall find that it is, with one qualification.

As Whitehead pointed out so elegantly, the endurance of a living organism requires an environment that is somewhat stable.[12] The various nexuses or organic causal processes and individual enduring organs in a body must maintain a regular pattern of interaction, massively inherited, if the organism as a whole is to endure. But the enduring components of the organism themselves are in many respects termini of causal nexuses entering from the outside. The relevantly external things must tolerate the organism and sustain it. But since the organism requires fairly constant components for its overall organic pattern of interaction to be reiterated, the external things must also be fairly constant to tolerate and sustain the organism. All the relevant external things are *in* the organism's environment; but when there is a problem of *maintaining* an environment, what usually is referred to are the things that must be relatively stable in the environment for the organism to survive. To speak, then, of an organism's environment is to speak of those relevant external things that must continue in a constant character for the organism to have its characteristic features. Elements in an organism's environment change; for instance, a species of animal the organism eats dies out. But the environment still tolerates and sustains the organism if the organism can adapt to the change; that is, if the oragnism can find something else to eat.

The human environment, of course, is social as well as physical. It includes all the elements of culture that can be handed down by tradition or appropriated as matters of heritage, as well as all the socially meaningful elements involved in social interaction. It also includes the forms of interaction making the interaction possible

12. *Process and Reality*, pt. 2, chap. 3. See also the discussion of "massive inheritance" in chapter 8.

under the more general environmental conditions. The social environment must tolerate and sustain the human organisms as social beings.

The distinction between the public and the private does not rest on the distinction between environments and organisms, but rather on the distinction between environments and creativity. Creativity must now be explained in this context.

Creativity is a matter of what individuals do in their subjective moments with the prehended data given. Every moment, in a strict sense, is creative for any occasion of experience whatsoever. But in the present context let "creativity" refer to a subjective process wherein a novel outcome is adopted as the determining essential feature of the process. That is, the novel outcome, with its novel value, is made its own justification and the guiding principle of the process. In this sense we say the process is creative and the outcome is something created.

A creative process of this sort contrasts with a process that, although producing a novel outcome as all subjective processes must, has as the essential features determining its subjective form either factors inherited from the past or adventitious novelties of the moment itself. Human activity that is public, by contrast, is determined by the motive, the essential feature, of maintaining the environment. However inventive the means of this activity might be, the dominant essential features are those of environment maintenance derived from the past. Now there might have been a free choice to make environment maintenance one's goal; this is a free choice of putting oneself into public service. But the activity of pursuing that goal, though free in other senses, is determined by the goal inherited from that previous decision.

Human creativity is activity that produces valuable novelties for their own sakes. These novelties then can become part of the environment, as cultural objects do; or they can be used to maintain the environment, as technological inventions do; or they can be destructive of the environment, and this is where the clash between public interest and private creativity begins.

Creativity requires an environment in a general and in a special sense. In a general sense, the organism doing the creating must be maintained, and consequently both the environment of the organism and the organic body itself as environment for the creative activity must be maintained. This is the qualification mentioned to the thesis that the environment is everything relevantly external to the conditional features of the organism: the conditional features of the body and social constitution of the creative agent must also be included in the environment. The physical health of individuals and their social education are environmental factors for a person's creativity.

In the specific sense, the creativity requires an environment to supply its activity and to receive its products. Every society has certain kinds of creativity it prizes, and it tries to provide an environment that fosters those kinds. It provides the kind of education needed, the kinds of tools, the kinds of appreciative attitudes, and often the sanctions necessary to spur people to creative action. These are specialized environmental factors for the kinds of creativity at hand.

The concern of the public is to maintain environmental factors of both the general and special kinds. It might be argued the function of the public is to maintain an environment for the sake of the sheer endurance of the individuals in it, not for the sake of their creativity. If turtles have public lives, they might indeed organize for sheer endurance. But as noted in previous chapters, items of intrinsic value are things the appreciation of which is constitutive of human life. To be human is to be a culture-maker and appreciator. So the endurance of *human* individuals' lives means the tolerance and sustenance of creativity. The appreciation of this is probably more primordial than the development of a social structural distinction between the public and the private. If all creativity were impossible and the only option were a bare maintenance of biological human life, it is doubtful human society could long sustain a workable public.

The objection raised against the media thesis is that it does not recognize that the ultimate powers for settling the boundary between public affairs and private affairs lie in the patterns of acceptance characteristic of the society at large. The environment–creativity thesis does not have that difficulty. What the public is organized to control is what is generally recognized as pertaining to jeopardized environment. There of course may be disagreements about this. The government may say it should control one thing and the majority of the people may say another. This is a disagreement about either what elements of the environment are in jeopardy or about what to do about it. In the long run what the government can do depends on what the people accept—the people constitute the environment for the government. Or different factions within a society can disagree about the boundary; this is a disagreement about jeopardized environment and what is to be done about it; in effect two different boundaries will be operative in the society. Part of the problem of social pluralism consists in the fact that what is environmental for one group's kind of creativity is not environmental for the others'; in fact it might be destructive of the others' environments.

It would seem from what has been said that the concern of the public would always be to maintain the environmental status quo. But obviously there have been reforming public movements, and in America it is accepted gospel that the function of government is to improve things.

Our hypothesis is not committed to saying the public must defend the status quo. All our hypothesis requires is that the environment articulated as the ideal in the public concern be relative to certain prized kinds of creativity. If the ideal is perfectly realized in fact, those kinds of creativity will in fact be fostered and appreciated. But if, as is more likely, the ideal is only imperfectly realized, the prized kinds of creativity will be possible only in imperfect form. Conversely, to the degree the prized kinds of creativity are not possible and appreciated, to that degree the public concern will be for an ideal that is contrary to fact. The difference between reform movements and revolutionary movements is that the former seek environments for kinds of prized creativity in part already enjoyed and the latter seek environments for prized kinds of creativity quite distant from the facts.

The environment–creativity thesis can interpret Marx's conception of the aim of history. The aim is an environment wherein people can be perfectly free, that is, not free in terms of abstract principle but concretely free.[13] At this point the state would wither away as a government of people, and all that would remain

13. See, e.g., Marx's review of Bruno Bauer's *The Jewish Question,* in *The Writings of the Young Marx on Philosophy and Society,* ed. and trans. Loyd D. Easton and Kurt H. Guddat (Garden City, N.Y.: Doubleday, Anchor Books, 1967), pp. 216–41.

of an official sort would be a regulation of things. Marx's conception of the state, of course, is the organized power of a class of people for coercing some other class. In the perfect environment there would be no need for coercion of people. In terms of our thesis, Marx's view would be the enjoining of the withering away of the public insofar as the environment with which it is concerned is the social one. There still would be a need, presumably, to control the physical environment, and a public would be concerned with this. But there would be no need to control the social environment. The result would be a state of universal privacy, excepting concern for the physical environment; the privacy, of course, would be the context of creativity, Marx's characterization of concrete human freedom.[14]

The means to freedom, Marx thought, involved the dictatorship of the proletariat, where the proletariat controls the state so as to coerce the capital-owning classes to conform to the kind of environment that tolerates and sustains perfect freedom, an environment with no private property. He thought that when this environment had been attained the proletarian dictatorship would have undermined itself and would wither away. History has shown, it seems, that Marx misidentified the "contradiction" in the proletarian dictatorship. When the ideal environment, relative to an ideal of freedom so far from actual realization anywhere, is as abstractly conceived as the Marxist ideal must be, the concern of the public becomes fastened on the revolutionary movement as the goal itself. Instead of the future ideal, the structure of the revolution itself becomes the environment about which the public is concerned. And since a revolution is not itself the kind of thing that can be stabilized, the concern becomes the maintenance of the *form* of the revolution, that is, the ideology and the bureaucracy. So long as the revolutionary spirit remains alive there must be repeated revolutions against the public created by the revolution; the revolutionary bureaucracy must be purged again and again. This has happened in the Soviet Union and, more recently, in China.[15]

14. See the selections from Marx in Part 1 of the collection edited by Max Eastman: *Capital, The Communist Manifesto, and Other Writings* (New York: Modern Library, 1932).

15. See Robert C. Tucker, *The Marxian Revolutionary Idea* (New York: W. W. Norton, 1969).

Repeated rejuvenations of the proletarian dictatorship cannot escape the basic contradiction involved. Of course actual progress might be made in terms of particular economic and social programs; but this concerns the content of public action and not its dialectical form. Progress has never been speedy enough in Marxist countries for rejuvenation of the public to be unnecessary, where it can just be allowed to wither. Consequently, the true contradictory of the proletarian dictatorship asserts itself, namely, liberalism. Liberalism in this context means the freedom of people, proletarian and others, from the dictatorship of the proletarian public. The proletarian dictatorship assumes all privacy into the public concern for establishing the environment for perfect freedom. Liberalism reasserts the rights of privacy over against the public dictatorship, and it does this short of accomplishing the original goal of the revolution of the environment for perfect freedom. This is what has been happening in Eastern European countries.

The reemergence of liberalism in Marxist societies amounts to a denial of the basic concept that Marx in his early writings called man's "species being." [16] Species being is to be understood in contrast to what he called the egoistic conception of man. The egoistic person seeks his individual interest, and freedom for him means freedom from hindrances to that egoistic pursuit. Egoistic people's participation in political society is only abstract, their concrete lives being led in a civil society only abstractly regulated by political forms. But an egoistic person must fully appropriate his political life if he is to guarantee his egoistic civil freedoms. And yet he cannot do that without giving up his egoism and taking up political freedom as a concrete mode of life. But this transforms the political sphere from an abstract regulator of a society of egoistic individuals to a mode of life for individuals whose freedom is the freedom of the whole society or species. Man's species being finds concrete freedom in the freedom of the whole species. Concretely a person is not an egoistic individual (which he must be thought to be for capitalism to be the appropriate economic form) but a species being. This justifies the abrogation of individual liberties in the dictatorship of the proletariat;

16. See *The Writings of the Young Marx*, p. 237. The term derives from Feuerbach.

individual liberties limiting the public are a remnant of egoism. This is why "orthodox" Marxists say Marxist liberalism is a backsliding into egoism.

The historical development of Marxist countries, however, into the "bad infinite" of repeated revolutions against the bureaucracy, or the dialectical transcendence into social liberalism, suggests there is something wrong with the analysis of human life in terms of egoism and species being. Although this is not the place to trace the point in detail, the suggestion can be made that the difficulty lies in the implicit understanding of the distinction between the public and the private. Conceiving private life as the egoistic claim to a sphere of control limiting an abstract political government, Marx could say that a person's true freedom consists in an abrogation of private control in favor of species control. But if privacy consists rather in creative activity, and if the function of the public is to tolerate and sustain this, then the assumption of man into a species being destroys not only the egoistic version of privacy but the creativist also. It frustrates creativity as such because creativity requires an environmental tolerance for the establishment of new values. A person's species life in the revolutionary movement must accept the essential revolutionary goals, however, and there is no room for creativity, at least of the social sort. This means the revolution has undermined itself at the outset: an environment for perfect creativity cannot be sought through a social form that itself becomes an environment denying creativity. Creativity must become the enemy of the revolution. The paradox that the revolution aims at an environment allowing perfect social privacy and yet assumes a form excluding social privacy is in fact a contradiction undermining the revolution itself.

There is much room for doubt about the value of dialectical analyses in terms of contradictions of historical developments. The very approach assumes a dubious unifying quality to historical periods. It would be better to consider the Marxist theory a theory about society and contrast it with alternatives, such as the one being developed here. Since the Marxist would prefer the historical to the theoretical arena for adjudication, however, the effort we have just made is appropriate. But in theoretical terms we may suggest that the Marxist theory is in difficulty because it fails to see the importance of the basic human distinction between crea-

tive and noncreative activity as it has been spelled out here for
social theory, that is, for the distinction between the public and
the private.

In this section we have presented an hypothesis about the formulation of the distinction between the public and the private.
The hypothesis is that the distinction rests on the more basic cosmological distinction between human environments and human
creativity. That is, when people classify various things as public
or private, they have in the back of their minds the recognition of
the crucial difference between concerns for the environment and
concerns for creativity. The distinction, according to our hypothesis, is made in practice by the appeal to something like the cosmological theory's distinction between environment and creativity. The cosmological distinction provides largely prereflective criteria for making the social distinction between the public and the
private.

An almost inevitable confusion should be avoided here. It is one
thing to say the cosmological distinction between environments
and creativity provides the criterion for the social distinction between the public and the private. It is quite another to ask what
the criterion would be for ascertaining whether that whole assertion is true. Obviously the criterion for the latter would be an
empirical sampling of the ways the distinction between the public
and private commonly is made, to see whether those ways are
would one would expect on the belief that the environment–
creativity distinction is the operative principle. This has in fact
been the strategy of this chapter: the first section put together a
common-sense sample, the second section a sample of philosophical attempts to make the distinction.

The status of our hypothesis now is a descriptive one. The
claim is that the environment–creativity distinction is the one people in fact use, or grope for, with more or less insight and consistency. Should they do so, however? To put the question another
way, is a division of public and private affairs de jure when it
accurately reflects the difference between concerns for the environment and those for creativity?

A Kantian might argue transcendentally that the very possibility of making a normative distinction between public and private affairs, with sufficient de jure status for establishing authority and so forth, presupposes that the environment–creativity distinction itself be normative. But the de jure status of the ordinary uses of the public–private distinction is not itself well established.

The dialectic of the argument must be more subtle than that. It must tease out, as was attempted in the first two sections of this chapter, the values we commonly and unsystematically see in the public–private distinction. Showing this distinction to be most intelligibly interpreted according to the basic cosmological distinction, it must proceed to tease out the more simplified and basic values we feel in the relation between the environment and creativity, when that relation is spelled out. The authority of the cosmological concepts then returns to justify the practical social distinctions drawn—not just in this theory but in social practice—on the basis of them. In a sense the value of the dimensions of experience simplified in the cosmological concepts has support from all the reasons for believing the cosmological theory. So the arguments about the value of creativity presented in Part 2 lend their weight to our present claim that privacy is prized because of its connection with creativity. The argument should also work the other way, however. That is, we ought to be able to see new elements of value in the social environment and in creativity because of their connection with the way we distinguish the public and the private.

In all this, the justification for normative claims is never more than an appeal to what values we in fact feel when the distinctions are presented. As chapter 3 made clear, the judgment of what things are valuable, and to what degree, is empirical, even though the *nature* of value is a formal matter.

The next two sections have as their tasks the eliciting of stronger senses of the value of the environment–creativity thesis. The next will show how it undergirds the very strong value commonly put on the "right to privacy," a sense of privacy barely mentioned in the first section. The following will show how the distinction between the public and the private relates to social pluralism, expressing the cosmological conditions of environment and creativity.

THE RIGHT TO PRIVACY

There is a sense of privacy much stronger than any of those discussed so far, except for its own mention in the first section: the sense of a private sphere protected by public mechanisms from encroachment by other people or by the public itself. Certain kinds of privacy are taken to be so important that the public voluntarily limits its own power of interference even in times of stress, and it commits its energies to the protection of that privacy from unwanted encroachments of other parties. This sense of privacy is stronger than those involved in the previous distinctions according to which the public does not or should not exert control or deliberate influence. It is so strong that the public itself guarantees it.[17]

It was remarked in chapter 8 that an opportunity prized so much by society that social resources were committed to its guarantee is a right. The crucial notion there was the public commitment of resources to guarantee the opportunity. Privacy is not an opportunity, except in roundabout ways. But certain kinds of privacy are protected by structures of social order, in situations where the value of that social guarantee is felt by the society to be warranted. In the case of privacy as a right, the "society" is the relevant public. A right to privacy is guaranteed because some public values it.

The public guarantee of the right to privacy, however, is a double-edged sword. If the public guarantees the right, it also can abridge it. The public guarantees in fact often take the form of establishing the right with the provision that it may be abridged by due process. The Third Amendment to the United States Constitution says, "No soldier shall, in time of peace, be quartered in any house without the consent of the owner, nor in time of war but in a manner to be prescribed by law." The Fourth Amendment says,

17. Charles Fried attempts in *The Anatomy of Values* to account for the value socially conveyed upon privacy with the notion that privacy provides the context in which love, trust, friendship, respect, and self-respect make sense. He is surely right in his claim that privacy is necessary for those other ends or values; and from this privacy takes on a certain necessary instrumental value. But the value of privacy is more than this. We would say that a person's privacy ought to be respected even if he is unlovely, untrustworthy, and so forth. Even failing those basic human ends, his privacy deserves respect; not to respect it in some sense is to treat him as something less than human.

> The right of the people to be secure in their persons, houses, papers, and effects, against unreasonable searches and seizures, shall not be violated, and no Warrants shall issue, but upon probable cause, supported by Oath or affirmation, and particularly describing the place to be searched, and the persons or things to be seized.

Similarly, laws protecting private property are usually complemented by clauses specifying procedures for public exercise of its own right of eminent domain. The right of privacy, created by public interest, is subject to qualification by public interest. The very strength of the public valuing of privacy is all the more significant in light of the fact the public guarantees the privacy by specifying the conditions under which it might be abridged.

The notion of "right to privacy" is vague in its domain. What kinds of privacy or private affairs are involved? The constitutional amendments themselves list one's home, effects, papers, and persons. The law also recognizes certain relationships to be private in the sense that spouses need not testify against each other in a court of law; also there is a protection of confidentiality in the case of priests and physicians, and respecting certain kinds of personal records. Perhaps most interesting because it is only now gaining careful legal formulation is the right of patients to refuse medical treatment.

What is the common thread here? Two things stand out. First, each one of the examples involves a personal object over which the state might have a clear and pressing interest to exert control. The need to confiscate private property in time of war serves the real need for security. The need to search and seize suspected criminal quarters and persons serves the need for justice. The need for information about persons serves not only the need for justice but also various interests in discovering qualified personnel. And of course individual ill health is a social as well as personal burden.

Second, from the strict viewpoint of social needs, the private object protected is not particularly valuable. Its protection cannot be justified by any simple utilitarian argument to the effect that keeping the soldiers out of one's house contributes to the social good more than quartering them. In fact, insistence upon the right of privacy often seems either perverse or indicative of guilt. To be sure, much of the original impetus behind legislation insuring privacy, such as that in the Bill of Rights, came from experience with abuses of public power: privacy was invaded when no question of social good was involved. But the laws are sufficiently strict that social goods of a fairly high degree are limited by the right to privacy, and the privacy by itself seems of little importance to the social good. Privacy is not an obvious means to social good.

These two points suggest the following thesis, that in the right to privacy we find a recognition of a special value to those aspects of human life not defined by social roles. Sociologists define "social roles" in terms of systems of social interaction. The notion of social roles is more useful philosophically when generalized. Let us suppose the "system" to include not only systems of human interaction but any system wherein items and plays are meaningful in some sense or relate to human values. And let us suppose the roles to include not only universal variables in a system that could be played by anyone in the same position, but also the unique relationships a person might make out in his sociophysical environment. The systems of a person's social roles then would comprise all those systems that might be referred to in order to explain his character, behavior, possessions, and so forth. His social roles would include all those features of his life that are "objective" by virtue of being implicated in patterns of interaction including items outside his person.

What is left, however, undefined by the set of a person's social roles thus expansively characterized? It would seem only his whims, his choices that are not predictable according to the confluence of his social roles. "Whim" perhaps bespeaks the trivial end of the spectrum of choices. Some choices, of course, pick up the threads of complex systematic interactions and weave them into patterns whose value, adopted as the agent's own, bears important social consequences. The only aspect of such a process of historical choosing not covered by the various social roles is the act of choosing itself, the act of adopting one of the potential motives as the determining reason of one's action. The act of choosing that is not forced by the antecedent pressures from the agent's roles and that is considered before the choosing has become a factual choice with systematic consequences—the subjective process of choosing— is privacy in its inmost meaning. And most such choices are not about important things with great consequences but (unfortunately) are generally random, trivial, and impotent. Choosing by itself is rarely objectively valuable; mostly it is whim.

The right to refuse treatment for medical care illustrates the extent to which we prize that innermost privacy. A person's health can be viewed as a kind of social system. Both physical and mental health have to do with the ways in which he systematically interacts, or can interact, with various factors in the environment. The health roles can be in good shape or bad shape, and the values of those systematic harmonies are publicly observable and recognizable. It is better to be in good health than in bad, whether or not the person recognizes this. Nevertheless our society is coming to believe that the values directing a person's health care should be those chosen by him. The right to refuse treatment allows a person in effect to define what is important for him regarding his health; the balance of factors in health is itself a matter of valuation. The same right allows a person to put other values ahead of health. There are two levels of this allowance. First, although good health is better than bad, other things, for instance family loyalty or heroic action, might be better than good health and justifying of bad health. The right allows this choice to the person. Second, the right allows a person to refuse treatment for no reason whatsoever, or because of stupid reasons, or simply because of perversity. One of the great difficulties in the current attempt to define the right to refuse treatment carefully stems from the legal concept of mental incompetency. Perhaps there are many mental conditions in which a person is systematically prevented from thinking freely about his condition by the illness; in these cases the person is declared to be incompetent, and the right to refuse treatment is alienated from him. But it is a perverse abuse of the concept of mental incompetency to take unreasonable (according to society's reason) refusal of treatment as itself evidence of mental incompetency. If this were allowed, unreasonable refusal in principle would be impossible. Our policies regarding the right to refuse treatment must provide mechanisms for avoiding this subtle abuse.[18] A person is not exhaustively defined by his social roles, including that of health; his definitive value also resides in part in his free choice.

But why do we so greatly value this inner privacy, this whim?

18. In this connection see Nicholas N. Kittrie, *The Right to Be Different: Deviance and Enforced Therapy* (Baltimore: The Johns Hopkins Press, 1971).

Certainly not only because of the value of its products, the choices chosen. If that were so we would simply prize only good choices and not respect the bad ones; there would be no right to refuse treatment, only a right to persuade the doctor to change his estimation of the person's desires.

The value must lie in the act of creating value as such. Let us call this the "subjective value of choosing," in contrast to the "objective" values of the components entering into the choice and of the fixed choice itself. The point is, the subjective value of choosing is worth prizing even when the objective values produced are not.[19] In fact, it is worth prizing even when the objective values are far worse than alternatives that could have been chosen or imposed from without.

What is the subjective value of choosing? Part of that value might lie in a chooser's being the creator of the objective values chosen. Not only does he determine his character by the objective values of his choices, he also determines himself to be the chooser of them. But this is only to return to our previous thesis that whim per se has value, and we would like some progress in finding out what that value might consist in. That progress might in principle be impossible, however. Usually what we mean in asking what a value consists in is a request for the components that the value pattern harmonizes; grasping the components together allows us perhaps to feel the value's intensity. But in the case of the act of choosing, prescinding from the objective components entering and the objective outcome there are no components in the relevant sense.

This forces us to suggest a new distinction for the cosmological scheme. Suppose we say that the relation of a thing to its objective values is that of "enjoying." The values a thing has includes those in its own patterns, in the effects attributable to it, and so forth. These all have to do with the "being" the thing attains and causes. In distinction let us say that the relation of a thing—an agent for all practical purposes—to its subjective values is that of "creating." There are therefore two fundamental orientations to values, each of which is involved in prizing objects. One is the value the thing enjoys or has. The other is its value as creating. The former is a harmony and is measurable in the senses discussed in chapter 3.

19. This is the point not registered in Professor Fried's account; see note 17.

The latter is a process whose prizeworthiness does not derive from the value of the harmonies it produces but rather from its status as the creator of values.[20]

This special value of creating is subtle and cannot be substantiated by appeals to particular experiences. Our mode of approach to it is not to appreciate, purify, and assess, as we do with objective values. Rather our response is more like the religious one of awe and silent respect. Creativity is one of the fundamental mysteries of the universe, a factor so basic as not to be expressible in any one of the things created. The creating we respect in a person is not to be measured by the objective values he creates. In fact, it is strangly alien even to the person's personality. He has the value not because of who he is (a matter of his objective character) but because he is a person. *Any* person deserves that same respect, and the individual cannot take credit for being respected as a human being. In trying to express the value we feel should be respected in people universally we quickly slide off into quasi-religious expressions such as "infinite dignity." It is because the person has creativity in him that he has the dignity, and creativity is indeed infinite. Of course it is not infinite in him: he chooses only this and that. But his creativity is respected because it is a portion of the creativity of the universe, the essence of process. Most religions call this creativity by divine names: Tao, Siva, Spirit. But the creativity is particularly obvious in human choices of the sort described, because there the creative choice is somewhat free from antecedent conditions. Those cultures with finer perceptions of the divine force find the same creativity in animals, plants, and even geological structures. It is enough for us that a human being's choosing is a locus of special value distinct from the values of his choices.

There is a crucial problem here, however. Whatever our religious perceptions, social structures acknowledging values of various sorts must always treat those values in the form of trade-offs. The protection of any value is at a price, and the society must provide mechanisms for saying that in certain circumstances the price is too high. Regarding privacy there are always procedures for

20. For a more elaborate discussion of this subject see my "The Limits of Freedom and Technologies of Behavior Control," in *The Human Context* 4, no. 3 (1972): 433–46.

abrogating it when deemed necessary, for instance through search warrants, eminent domain, or declarations of incompetency. But infinite dignity cannot be measured and traded off. Only objective values can be weighed. Therefore, in respecting the right to privacy, the social forces cannot be dealing primarily with that inmost privacy itself, the subjective creating. What then?

Society does not directly prize a person's inmost privacy. Rather it prizes the person himself. And a person is not a bifurcated value animal with objective and subjective values. A person is an integral harmony of the two. The very nature of subjective choosing is to make choices harmonizing one's objectively attained values with one's subjective value of creativity. "Integrity" is a good basic word for this harmony of objective and subjective values. It results from subjective choice but is objective in its form and social function. As a harmony it is somewhat peculiar. Its components are not other value-patterns combined, but rather such value-patterns combined with the value of creating. In explicating integrity, therefore, we would be forced in individual cases to remark not only on the objective values a person attains but also on such notions as that he is a person, a creator. The particular character of one person's integrity might show in his style of life, or in the lineaments of certain decisions and actions. But in drawing it out, we would always have to add to our description of the pattern of integrity, "and he also is a subjective human being, not a mere object." Because in fact we do this in discussing a person's definition as a social being, with rights, it is reasonably safe to say our account is on the mark.

We have come in the West to prize personal integrity and protect it with social resources. Because of this social valuing of integrity, we respect people's privacy. We ask their consent in medical treatment. We would like criminals to understand why they are punished. And we set limits to the powers of the organized public to control people according to their merely objective sides. The recognition of the value of social pluralism arises from a prior recognition of the value of individual integrity, a social pluralism with as many social forms or integrities as there are persons.

The aim of this section has been to show why privacy seems valuable enough for society to limit itself out of respect. The reason underlying this interest is to add weight to our distinction of the public and the private on the basis of the cosmological distinction between environments and creativity. The inmost sense of privacy did in fact turn out to be creativity. It seems, however, that social respect for privacy, structured according to a respect for integrity, does too much for social pluralism. Indeed we seem to have an account of the society as a public and the individuals as private, when what we want is an account of society's tolerating a plurality of social forms.

Social Pluralism

Pluralism becomes a problem when people privately want social forms incompatible with the form of public order at hand. But this is only the beginning of the problem. People's private desires for social forms of their own choice become public.

A social form might be desired privately by a person as the way he wants to live his creative personal life, as the social form of his integrity. But this includes making certain demands on the public environment, for instance those of freedoms of opportunity for having a heritage, culture, and so forth. Now, in general, the public is supposed to provide those environmental supports for the creativity prized by the person as part of his chosen social form. But the public itself is a group of people organized, as Dewey pointed out, to protect itself against the indirect effects of various private transactions. The people in the public either include those demanding certain resources for their social forms, or they do not. Either way, however, all those people wanting certain resources constitute themselves a special subpublic relative to the larger public, a public organized with the special interests of eliciting from the environment resources for their own prized kinds of creativity. A society is likely then to have a great many subpublics, each concerned with arranging the environment to support their desired way of life. In any situation of scarce resources, as most social situations are, there is conflict and competition between these publics.

What is the most desirable way of harmonizing these diverse social-form oriented publics? We shall pursue a typology of answers. The typology in itself elucidates the structure of the issues.

First, the competition may simply be that of a free market. Each public uses force, guile, and bargining to arrange the environment for its own interests. This is the anarchy Hobbes feared. It is difficult to know which is worse, unending fighting or victory establishing a hierarchy of powers. As to perpetual war, Hobbes's statement of the price cannot be surpassed:

> In such condition, there is no place for Industry; because the fruit thereof is uncertain; and consequently no Culture of the Earth, no Navigation, nor use of the commodities that may be imported by Sea; no commodious Building; no Instruments of moving, and removing such things as require much force; no Knowledge of the face of the Earth; no account of Time; no Arts; no Letters; no Society; and which is worst of all, continuall feare, and danger of violent death; And the life of man, solitary, poore, nasty, brutish, and short.[21]

As to victory and the establishment of a peck order of publics, the consequence is the diminution and eventual elimination of all but the most powerful.

Second, the competing parties may recognize the advisability of ground rules for the struggle, enforced by a central government. Is the chief of state from outside the society? What guarantee would there be that he would respect the justice of competing claims of the various publics? Should he come from within the society, representing one of the competing publics? This would lead again to a hierarchy of publics regarding their power to make demands on the environment. The best that could be accomplished with either of these arrangements is the establishment of a feudal society where those publics are tolerated that interact in a productive way with the others. But not only does this generally remove the freedom of choice individuals would have for their desired social form, it would also limit the kinds of social forms that would be available. Of course, some limitation on diversity of social forms is necessary, but it should be arrived at through pursuit of the most efficient use of resources, not through a social government whose very form dictates the social options.

Third, the competing parties, following Locke and the liberal tradition, might conclude that the best central government is a representative republican democracy. This would include a con-

21. *Leviathan*, pt. 1, chap. 13.

stitutional protection of each important minority subpublic, as well as a forum for distributing resources that compromises power demands with *tu quoque* appeals for respect. The difficulty with this conception of the liberal democracy is that in practice it recognizes only one public social form, that of the governmental process itself. People's public lives are defined by voting rights and their protections and powers under the law. But the social forms having to do with their concrete ways of life are pushed back into the private domain, unacknowledged by the government. Two unfortunate results follow. People lose their sense of concrete social life and identify with their abstract democratic public roles. This was the gist of Marx's criticism of man as an egoistic being. On the other hand, the competition between the publics over social form goes on unnoticed and unregulated. Every person is equal before the law and has civil rights of franchise, but only those in the strong and favored publics are able to take advantage of these opportunities. Those in the other publics are suppressed, kept ignorant and impotent. Abstract civil equality is the very thing that prevents the liberal government from seeing the real nature of the competition and from acting to preserve social pluralism.

Fourth, Marx's own suggestion is that the harmony of the diverse publics comes from the form of the economic competition itself. Whatever the governmental form might be, that is insignificant compared with the real forces of social unity, those of the struggle itself. The situation is not anarchic because each public in the struggle feels, if not consciously perceives, its own self-definition to be its opposition to the others. Of course, according to Marx one public will dominate and exploit the rest, so that the social pluralism is at best that of feudal society. But there is another disadvantage to this conception of social unity: the whole of each person's life is exhausted in the public struggle. There is no privacy, no integrity. The very reason for social pluralism in the first place—free choice of social forms—dies away.

The Marxist interpretation has opposite faults from the liberal one. The Marxist conception of social unity has no room for significant privacy, socially acknowledged and protected. The liberal conception has so much privacy there is no public recognition of the public demands of the pluralism of social forms. A proper

10

Freedom of Integral Social Life

Suppose that one's society offered all the opportunities for free appropriation and action that might reasonably be desired. Suppose also that it tolerated and supported all the important social forms one might choose as desirable ways of life. There would be yet another dimension of social freedom missing. In the complex relation between the structure of society relative to individual free action and the structure of the free individual relative to social environment, our story has reached a new pass. How does the individual integrate his personal character with the social opportunities and options of form of life?

The problem of integrating one's social life into a whole is a new dimension of freedom. Although such integration obviously rests on concepts developed with respect to personal freedom—continuity through past, present, and future; responsibility; dealing with environments already influenced by one's choices—integrity of social life is not merely personal unity. Personal unity is cheap enough if one restricts himself to a protected environment, puts aside claims of history and social change for attention, and worries only about his integrity. There is, in fact, a sort of occasion in which we employ the language of "personal integrity" to say something polite about the person who is socially alienated, native to another era, irrelevant in concerns, and impotent in projects. Of course personal integrity does have a value of its own expressed in the discussion of creativity. But there is a sense in which it is insufficient and empty without an integral social dimension.

Integral social life means that a person's integrity includes an harmonious involvement with various factors in his social environment. The discussion of personal freedom in Part 2 was vague with respect to the characteristics of the environment within which a person works out his freedom. But the last two chapters have shown that even the personal dimensions of freedom make demands on the social order, demands for opportunities and demands for real options for choice. There should, then, be special characteristics of individual unity reflecting the social character of the required environment. Of course not everyone attains an integral social life. People can have personal creativity while maintaining a vagueness with respect to society and still live in a society of opportunity and pluralism without integrating these. As it requires action to obtain opportunities and to establish a pluralistic society of live options, so it requires action to achieve an inclusive, relevant integrity.

The concept of "integrity" was appealed to in the last chapter to refer to the basic harmony of one's private choice with its public expression. This is perhaps the most fundamental element of integrity. But it also refers, as an extension of that fundamental usage, to all functions of harmonizing the diverse objective and subjective elements of life into a whole of personal identity. Insofar as one's identity is a single unified thing, it must come from integrity of efforts at harmony, not from solidity of unchanging substance, for a person is no solid substance.

Social integrity might be thought to derive from an integrated social form. In planning for our children, for instance, we try to think them into coherent life situations with a happy blend of spouse, career, and place. Because such plans do not have to deal with real contingencies, their contemplation is a fond luxury. But hardly anyone enjoys a single integrated social form. Social forms are so dependent on external circumstances that they change inconstantly through life. Furthermore, most people participate in a great many social forms, most of which are not coordinated with one another except by the personal efforts of the individual. Therefore, the external form cannot be counted on to contribute to integral social life. In fact, social forms that are too integrated seem themselves to be bondages, obstacles to free choice.

Integral social life must be a characteristic of the experience of the individual, including both his subjective choices and their objective conditions and consequences. It might indeed be the case that social conditions demand such diverse and inharmonious responses that a person's life simply cannot be integrated except by devotion to abstract principles such as justice. That person would enjoy the happiness of the virtuous, but not the happiness coming from concrete social living. Where the latter is possible, however, it cannot consist in an imposition of fixed personal character on changing events. The very meaning of the social dimension to integrity is that the social conditions are an integral part of the response, not something upon which personal character is imposed. Rather the concrete integrity must take the form of a style of life, expressed in every diverse action and response, but not so determinative of the personal contribution as to distort true perception and authentic action.

To discuss "styles of experience" in any but the most popular and superficial way requires a rigorous analysis of the social dimension of an individual's context. We have referred in previous chapters to various social elements, assuming that their philosophical significance either could be taken for granted or questioned later. Now is the time to raise the basic questions about the social aspect of experience. We must supplement the cosmology of individual freedom delivered in Part 2 with a cosmology of its social dimensions.

In its vague common-sense meaning, a person's social nature has to do with his relations with other human beings. Therefore, in the language of the cosmology, people's social characteristics are located in their conditional features that relate somehow to other people. A conditional feature, it will be remembered, is one a person has in virtue of his connection with something relatively external to him. The conditional feature is a relative terminus of a causal nexus whose beginnings are external. Let us propose, then, that social conditions in the common sense are *conditional social nexuses* in the technical cosmological sense.

Social conditions are always relative to individuals. The challenge of getting to outer space is a social condition for people in technological countries; but it is hardly a social condition for remote tribes of Indians in the Amazon valley, or at best only an indirect condition. Exactly *how* a given state of affairs socially conditions different groups of people is a relative matter; sociologists have made class distinctions on the basis of these differences in modes of social relations to the same conditions.[1] Because social conditions are relative to individuals, it is important to characterize them as *conditional* nexuses, in the sense of that technical term developed above. A conditional nexus is one terminating in the conditional feature of some individual. This singles out as important the fact that a social condition is connected as a nexus with some individual to whom it gives conditional features.

An individual has a conditional feature in virtue of its connection with something external. That connection might be *necessary*. For instance, whereas the exact spatial location of a human being is conditional upon what is around him, it seems necessary for him to have some place or other. Likewise, it seems necessary that people as we know them have certain sorts of social conditions, for instance those that teach at least rudimentary languages and distinctions necessary for survival. Other social conditions seem much more *contingent* upon history. For instance, three hundred years ago the state of life in China was largely if not entirely a neglible social condition for most Americans; now it is an important and influential condition.

It might be argued that certain kinds of social conditions must be present for life to be human. This is true only if large presumptions are made as to what constitutes human life. Certain presumptions are safe enough, for instance, that to be human means to be conditioned by a language. Yet if McLuhan is right about language, dangerous equivocations lurk in what that statement means. Western technological people would be inclined to say that a good diet, properly modish dress, "adequate" housing, and an education up to a certain rather high level are all necessary conditions for genuine human life; they would cite the dehumanizing effect of deprivation in these areas. Yet we know of exemplary human beings who live in conditions of continual hunger, poverty, exposure, and ignorance. What is truly human by way of social conditions seems to have more to do with varying constellations of conditions rather than with any universal constants; what con-

---

1. E.g., in his classic study, *Elmtown's Youth: The Impact of Social Classes on Adolescents* (New York: John Wiley & Sons, 1949), August Hollingshead distinguishes social classes in part by relations to different conditions (different classes tend to attend different churches) and in part by relations to the same conditions (all classes attend the same high school but relate to it differently).

stants there are have more to do with *discovering norms for coping with conditions* than with the conditions themselves.

Returning to the cosmological characterization, a social condition should be called a nexus because (1) it must be causally efficacious in individuals to condition them and (2) the characters of the objects "named" as the conditions must be carried through the causal process. What Mao Tse-tung does in China conditions the American people, but as a social condition what he does must be united with the causal routes connecting China with America. The social condition is the whole nexus, and its identifying character is the one passed along with the occasions in one form or another.

What is it that makes some conditional nexuses social? A conditional nexus is social if it significantly carries through its occasions a trait that is peculiarly human. This might mean that something human is conveyed directly, as in personal relations. Or it might mean that the structure of the nexus itself is significantly determined by human life.

The focus of the question has now shifted to identifying conditional social nexuses by their connections with individuals and by their carrying a "peculiarly human trait." But we are not in a position to characterize the connections of conditional social nexuses in any but the most categoreal way, quite in abstraction from the concrete realities of social life. And how can we discover what makes a trait peculiarly human? Surely not by a further elaboration of the categoreal dialectic. It is tempting to say that something is peculiarly human if it is involved essentially with the free agency described in earlier chapters. Such agency is indeed the factors distinguishing human beings from less complex individuals. But this is inadequate for two reasons. First, there may be other elements of freedom deriving from human sociality that are precisely the relevant factors for defining the peculiarly human quality of social relations. Second, it is likely that there are many elements both of sociality and of the unique qualities of human life that are not directly involved in freedom; freedom is not everything, although it may be involved in everything.

Consequently, before it is possible to tackle the problems of the connection of social nexuses with individuals or problems of the nature of the peculiarly human, we must elaborate more of the connections between empirical data and our abstract categories. We shall re-approach the issues of society and individuals, and the nature of the peculiarly human after we have inquired into the shape and limits of society. The limits are set, of course, by the extent of social connections, part of our main problem.

A society is bounded only by limits of the set of social nexuses that condition any of its members. People are in the same society if they are related by social nexuses; the relations may be direct or they may be mediated by intervening social nexuses. A person fails to be in a society with some other person only if there are no social nexuses carrying a human trait from him to the other. Although it is practically inconceivable that two people be related by only one social nexus (usually social nexuses relate one person as a member of a group to another person as a member of some other group, and such intergroup relations are very complex), even if there is only one nexus, the people still are members of the same society. Many points must be made to explicate this thesis.

First, the strategy is to give a characterization of the broadest and most neutral mode of human interaction. The term "society" is admittedly an arbitrary choice. It is not meant here in the sense of "high society" versus "working-class society," but as the most neutral term for human association.

That people are socially related in this sense does not necessarily mean that they have a common culture, belong to the same organized groups, or share a common spirit. They need not appropriate in a human way the same history (although, since they are causally related, they must have some common history, namely, the conditions sustaining the connecting social nexus). And they need not be comtemporaries.

Second, with reference to the cosmological categories developed, it is profitable to note that a society is a harmony of people. Even where all the causal action is one-directional, where it is misleading to speak of interaction, the causal relation fits people together into some kind of structure, tentatively at least. The profit in making this reference to cosmological categories is that, since any harmony has a value and intrinsic norms for its own organization, there is a value to and norms for societies as such. John Dewey long argued that causal analyses of social situations are the source of sound knowledge of what is genuinely good or bad. His usual argument for the point was that causal analyses revealed possible constellations of affairs and that the relative worths of these alternatives made their intrinsic appeal to our imaginations.[2] The intrinsic appeal of a state of affairs, according to Dewey, consists in its overall unifying quality, something akin to the notion of harmony developed above.[3]

To call social relations harmonies is to speak on a more general level than that of the dispute between "order" versus "conflict" theories of social change.[4] Since conflict is an obvious case of causation, conflicting things must be said to be in a harmony.[5] The paradoxical sound of the language derives from the social forces being harmonious enough to fight, but not harmonious enough to cooperate on certain more complex levels of harmony. The commitment of the present characterization of society is only to the former level of harmony. In point of fact, the analysis to be given below is closer to "conflict" than to "order" theories on most issues. But again, since even conflict is a kind of harmony, there are norms for good as opposed to bad conflict.

Third, moving from categoreal to practical connections, if the limits of a society are set by the extent of interconnecting social nexuses, our world today is in most parts one society. Perhaps a few remote tribes neither touch nor are touched by the rest of the world. And of course, as in any harmony, some features and connections are not very important. But increasingly it has become the

2. See, e.g., his *Theory of Valuation* in *International Encyclopedia of Unified Science*, vol. 2, no. 4 (Chicago: University of Chicago Press, 1939), esp. sec. 7 and 8. See also his *Human Nature and Conduct: An Introduction to Social Psychology* (New York: Modern Library, 1930), pts. 3 and 4.

3. Regarding unity and quality see his *Experience and Nature* (1929; reprint ed., New York: Dover, 1958), chaps. 8–10; *Art As Experience* (1934; reprint ed., New York: Capricorn, 1958), chaps. 6 and 7; and "Qualitative Thought" and "Peirce's Theory of Quality," in *John Dewey: On Experience, Nature, and Freedom*, ed. Richard J. Bernstein (New York: Liberal Arts Press, 1960).

4. This distinction is discussed with subtlety by Dahrendorf in *Class and Class Conflict in Industrial Society* (Stanford: Stanford University Press, 1959), pp. 157ff. Dahrendorf finally distinguishes two meta-theories in sociology, the *integration theory of society* that "conceives of social structure in terms of a functionally integrated system held in equilibrium by certain patterned and recurrent processes," and the coercion theory of society that "views social structure as a form of organization held together by force and constraint and reaching continuously beyond itself in the sense of producing within itself the forces that maintain it in an unending process of change."

5. Dahrendorf himself makes this point in ibid., p. 164.

case that nearly all peoples, customs, traditions, and aspirations are affected by worldwide mutual interaction of one sort or another. Industrial disturbance of the world's natural ecology alone makes this point.

Recognition that one world means one society (in the sense defined here, not in the sense of one culture or one political organization) is not new. But even recognizing the point, many western thinkers understand the world society with a peculiar and unnecessary bias. Geoffrey Barraclough is probably correct in claiming that in this century no single historical "theme will prove to be of greater importance than the revolt against the west." [6] But it is a mistaken bias that reads the development of the nonwestern countries solely or even primarily in terms of Western variables. As Barraclough says,

> [T]he current tendency to treat westernization as the key to the revival of Asia and Africa leaves out some relevant facts. The more we know of Asian and African societies before the advent of the Europeans, the clearer it has become that they were neither stagnant nor static, and it would be a mistake to assume that, but for European pressures, they would have remained anchored in the past.[7]

Barraclough goes on to cite the determination of Asians and Africans to maintain, reshape, or create their own personality, distinct from the West and based on their own prewestern backgrounds.[8]

What this means for an understanding of our society, therefore, is that our western scholars must appropriate the histories indigenous to nonwestern countries, just as we must appropriate western history, if we are to understand even our own portion of society. Needless to say this calls for a major and painful revamping of our educational system, one that will leave nothing the same, not even the western values of scholarship.

It is clear by this stage in the exposition that our theory of society is based upon notions of causality—special kinds of social causality. This approach contrasts with that of the social contract tradition for which the root notions have to do instead with a

6. *An Introduction to Contemporary History* (Baltimore: Penguin, 1967), p. 154.
7. Ibid., pp. 149–50.
8. Ibid., p. 197.

special kind of intentionality underlying cooperation; social causation is that which takes on human meaning in terms of the social contract.

An intuitive reason for our approach is that social causation is presupposed in the development of common language, conflicting interests, and other features of human life to be understood as prior to the making of a contract. Of course, a contract theorist might argue that the "state of nature" contains genuinely human forms and that the move to "civil society" only involves taking on a certain kind of government. But this takes much of the force from the contract position. Not only is the contract not essential for society, it is not essential for those modes of organization and authority required for social interaction. At most, then, the contract gives expression to the justification of a certain kind of ideal for society. This seems to be the extent of John Rawls's appeal to the "original position" of the contractors: it is a heuristic device for conceiving fair judgment unbiased by personal advantage.[9] The result of this modification of the contract tradition is that the contract is no longer definitive of civil society; it is simply a way, among others, of seeing certain values to be ideal or normative. Our own approach easily includes a Rawlsian defense of justice defined his way as one kind of important social value. The more basic substratum on which social values are layed, however, is that of social causation as such.

Our argument is now at the point of having defined the social nature of human life in terms of nexuses of social conditions. Nexuses of social conditions in turn have been defined as carrying traits that are peculiarly human. Because what is "peculiarly human" is so closely related to human sociality, this seems a circular definition. The task of the next section is to explicate how nexuses of social causation can bear peculiarly human traits. This is to define the "sociality" in social causation.

SOCIAL MEANING

According to John Dewey, society is both the cause and effect of language or signs.[10] Social activity is a particular sort of inter-

9. See John Rawls, *A Theory of Justice* (Cambridge: Harvard University Press, 1972), chap. 3.
10. *Experience and Nature*, p. 173.

action between people, particular in that the interaction itself is meaningful. Signs are not prior to society, nor society to signs: society is the set of interactions that are meanings or signs. Therefore, to understand the meaning of meanings or signs is to understand what makes some interactions, and the relations through which they take place, social.[11]

Dewey analyzes a situation of meaningful interaction as follows:

> *A* requests *B* to bring him something, to which *A* points, say a flower. There is an original mechanism by which *B* may react to *A*'s movement in pointing. But natively such a reaction is to the movement, not to the *pointing,* not to the object pointed out. But *B* learns that the movement *is* a pointing; he responds to it not in itself but as an index of something else. His response is transferred from *A*'s direct movement to the *object* to which *A* points. Thus he does not merely execute the natural acts of looking or grasping which the movement might instigate on its own account. The motion of *A* attracts his gaze to the thing pointed to; then, instead of just transferring his response from *A*'s movement to the native reaction he might make to the thing as stimulus, he responds in a way which is a function of *A*'s *relationship,* actual and potential, to the thing. The characteristic thing about *B*'s understanding of *A*'s movement and sounds is that he responds to the thing from the standpoint of *A*. He perceives the thing as it may function in *A*'s experience, instead of just ego-centrically. Similarly, *A* in making the request conceives the thing not only in its direct relationship to himself, but as a thing capable of being grasped and handled by *B*. He sees the thing as it may function in *B*'s experience. Such is the essence and import of communication, signs and meaning. Something is literally made common in at least two different centres of behavior. To understand is to anticipate together, it is to make a cross-reference which, when acted upon, brings about a partaking in a common, inclusive, undertaking. . . . Neither the sounds uttered by *A*, his gesture of pointing, nor the sight of the thing pointed to, is the occasion and stimulus of *B*'s act; the stimulus is *B*'s

11. See ibid., p. 175.

anticipatory share in the consummation of a transaction in which both participate. The heart of language is not "expression" of something antecedent, much less expression of antecedent thought. It is communication; the establishment of cooperation in an activity in which there are partners, and in which the activity of each is modified and regulated by partnership. To fail to understand is to fail to come into agreement in action; to misunderstand is to set up action at cross purposes.[12]

At the outset attention should be called to the ease with which Dewey moves from watching the movement of pointing to the recognition of the movement *as* a pointing and the transferral of focus to the object pointed at. There is, of course, a colossal difference between the three, and the transition from the first to the last is at the heart of socialization. But for Dewey's purposes and ours the difficulty is not relevant. He is trying to explain the logical structure of social interaction, not its genesis. With regard to the question of genesis, for our purposes it is enough to say that the particular happenings rearranging things so as to bring about uniquely social patterns need not themselves be social. What those original causal factors are is an empirical matter not bearing directly on the problem of what sociality itself is.

There are three positive points to be singled out in Dewey's account before moving to assess it. What Dewey calls the "essence and import of communication, signs and meaning" is that a meaningful object or a sign is interpreted by each person in terms of how it functions *in the experience of the other* as well as in his own experience. In other words, the object is social if to grasp it is to grasp it in terms of someone else's experience. Let us call this the doctrine of *the diverse experiential location of objective meaning*.

But what if only one person in the social relationship adopts the other's experiential standpoint? Is the relationship social? Surely many situations are like this, especially when adults deal with young children who are just learning that objects are social. To handle this Dewey emphasizes that the experience of interpreting might be what he calls "potential." *B* interprets the object

12. Ibid., p. 178–79.

in terms of how *A might* but does not in fact relate to it. But is the situation really social if one of the parties *never* performs a reciprocal interpretation? Would this not be like a situation in which a human being deals with a brute animal: the man looks at objects from the beast's point of view, but the beast is always egocentric, to use Dewey's term.

It is one thing when *A* does not adopt *B*'s standpoint although *B* adopts *A*'s. It is another thing when *B* adopts *A*'s standpoint in the sense of looking at objects as they potentially function in *A*'s experience, and those objects in fact never do function that way in *A*'s experience. An adult can interpret how a dish functions in a child's experience without the child's interpreting the dish in the adult's experience; but this is different from the dish never functioning in the child's experience as the adult interprets. This is not a simple ambiguity, however, not just a confusion of words. Meaning, and hence sociality, applies primarily to *conjoint behavior* with respect to objects, and only secondarily to the objects themselves.[13] This can be called the doctrine of *the social primacy of interactive behavior*. The structure of this point is similar to Aristotle's illustration of a certain kind of analogy: an animal is healthy in the primary sense, and its food and urine are healthy in different and secondary senses to be understood in relation to the primary sense. Dewey points out that behavior of a certain sort is meaningful in the primary sense, and objects are meaningful in derivative senses to be understood only with reference to the situation of communicative behavior. Likewise, we say sociality refers to behavior in the primary sense, and to objects in a secondary sense.

Regarding the ambiguity, the following can be said. When one person does not ever adopt the other's experiential standpoint with respect to objects, the situation is not a social one because there is no conjoint activity. There is no social behavior, and the person who adopts the unreciprocating being's standpoint is only entertaining himself, as often is the case with people who keep

13. "Meaning is not indeed a psychic existence; it is primarily a property of behavior, and secondarily a property of objects. But the behavior of which it is a quality is a distinctive behavior; cooperative, in that response to another's act involves contemporaneous response to a thing as entering into the other's behavior, and thus upon both sides" (ibid., p. 179).

pets.[14] On the other hand, cooperative behavior in a larger context regarding other objects might be related meaningfully to the function falsely imputed to the object. Here the persons to whom the experience is imputed might *learn* to give the object that function, and he would learn it because of conjoint behavior regarding related objects; this is how children learn. Or it might be the intention of the imputer to *prevent* the other from interpreting the object in that function, and he might direct the conjoint behavior to hide the possible function. Or the imputing person might simply be mistaken with regard to the other's experience, falsely interpreting their conjoint behavior as indicative of that function in the other person when it is not there. In all these cases the object can be regarded as socially meaningful in the secondary and derivative sense because it is related to meaningful behavior. But for the object to be actually meaningful for the person in whose experience it is imputed to have the meaningful function, that person must actually engage in meaningful behavior. Otherwise, the meaning is only potential for him.

Meaningful behavior is intentional for Dewey.[15] Objects are viewed both as consummatory, as the flower would be when A enjoys it, and instrumental, as the flower is the means to A's enjoying it because it can be carried to him by B. Dewey stresses the instrumental character of the flower's portability. In the situation *all* the behavior, A's pointing and speaking, B's interpreting and fetching, etc., is directed by reference to the goal of satisfying A with the flower. This includes A's behavior of interpreting how B will respond to the request and how the flower functions in his experience, and B's interpreting of the flower's function for A. Not all behavior is for the sake of the goal, since B could have refused the request; but it is meaningful because of its positive or negative instrumental character with reference to

14. Some people claim pets do, in a rudimentary way, adopt their master's experiential standpoint; but this would only support the general point.

15. "Primarily meaning is intent and intent is not personal in a private and exclusive sense. A proposes the consummatory possession of the flower through the medium or means of B's action; B proposes to cooperate—or act adversely—in the fulfillment of A's proposal. Secondarily, meaning is the acquisition of significance by things in their status in making possible and fulfilling shared cooperation" (ibid., p. 180).

the goal. Reference to the goal need not be verbal or even conscious.[16] But reference to the goal is necessary in some sense for the behavior to be communicative. This can be called the doctrine of the *common intentionality of social behavior.*

Dewey's answer to what makes something social is that it functions meaningfully in the experience of those acting conjointly, an answer summarized with the principles we have called "the diverse experiential location of objective meaning," "the social primacy of interactive behavior," and "the common intentionality of social behavior." We shall now assess the adequacy of Dewey's suggestion for purposes of our own analysis.

The principle of "diverse experiential location of objective meaning" deals with meanings insofar as they are related to human intentions. There is an important distinction, however, between the content of an assertion and its form, the structure that gives it social significance in the first place. In defining sociality, the form may be more important than the content intended. Therefore we may generalize Dewey's doctrine to include the social significance of a meaning's form as well as its intentional content. An object is social if it is conveyed in a conditional nexus such that (1) the subjective form of its prehension must connect it with the prehension of a possible mode of its being prehended by some other human subject, and (2) the subjective form of the prehension in the second subject must connect the object with the possible mode of its prehension exhibited in the first subject. On Dewey's level, this is to say that the experience of each subject includes an interpretation of how the object functions in the experience of the other. But the generality of the new formulation allows many aspects in the experience in which the object may function, some of which are implicit and some explicit. It does not emphasize meaning as explicit functioning in intentional behavior.

The new formulation can be called the doctrine of the *diverse experiential location of social significance.* It has brought us a long way toward filling in the blanks of the statement made early in the chapter that a social conditional nexus is one exhibiting

16. Dewey would say consciousness arises only when the behavior is problematic in some sense. See the Introduction to his *Essays in Experimental Logic* (Chicago: University of Chicago Press, 1916).

in its own structure a trait that is peculiarly human. The problem was to determine what a peculiarly human trait would be without begging the question. Now we can say, at least provisionally, that a trait is peculiarly human if its prehension involves the recognition of its functioning in several subjects of experience. This is defining "peculiarly human" in terms of sociality, a point to which we are indebted to Dewey, and of course this is circular: we had appealed to the peculiarly human to define what makes a conditional nexus social. But the circularity is informative, not vicious, since we have specified what sociality is the second time around in terms of the doctrine of the diverse experiential location of social significance.

Dewey's doctrines of the social primacy of interactive behavior and of the intentionality of social behavior elaborate and specify the relation between the subjective forms of the prehensions of an object in several subjects. They may be taken as completing the point begun in the doctrine of diverse experiential location; the latter doctrine needs the two others to be specific.

The critical question now is whether the sociality of something consists in its functioning in an interaction between two or more subjects, prehended as described above. Or are there objects that are social by nature apart from such interaction? The best argument *against* the social primacy of interactive behavior is McLuhan's claim that media, and by extrapolation other social objects, determine how we experience and interact, not the other way around. If the nature of people's social interaction is determined by the social media they use, then it is hard to see how the media themselves can be constituted as social entities by the interaction.

Arguing against McLuhan's reasoning, we may say that objective media are not only *given*, but are *taken up* in prehension with a subjective form that is novel, perhaps adventitious in part, perhaps the free and deliberate contribution of the subject. The objection raised here, then, against the social primacy of interactive behavior is likely to be met only by a consideration of how objects are taken up in experience. Or, to put the point in our more recent language, how is it possible for two subjects to prehend a common object, including in the subjective form of each person the subjective form of the other's prehension?

Consider the hardest case, the prehension of a social object by two contemporaries. Because they are contemporaries, neither can prehend the subjective form of the other directly in that same present, since the object of a prehension must always be finished or past. Consequently, each subject must construct, in the process of harmonizing his data in the present, what the subjective form of the other subject *might* be. The construction, of course, may be incorrect, but then the sociality of the object depnds only on the inclusion of a possible subjective form of its prehension in another subject. What are the conditions for the process of this construction? The obvious answer is twofold. First, that the two subjects be mutually engaged in some conjoint behavior, wherein each subject has prehended various responses of the other in varying contexts to the object. The conjoint behavior must involve the object, since the character of the object determines that it cannot be prehended except as social. The imaginative construction of the possible mode of prehension in the other subject is not a matter of subjective legerdemain—it is a conformity to truth about the object. Second, since part of what the first subject constructs in the mode of the second subject's prehension is the second subject's construction of the mode of the first subject's prehensions (and so on to triviality), only interaction in conjoint activity can give the data for the depth of reflection required. All this is not merely to say that interaction is necessary as a means of access to the subjective life of other people. It is to say the meaning of the object as social is constituted by the fact that it functions in the experience of several subjects mutually reflected in all, and that this mutual reflection is made possible by interaction.

The case of the prehension of a social object by noncontemporaries is less difficult. An historian, for instance, grasps the social significance of a writing in a dead language by constructing what it must have meant to contemporaries who spoke it. If the writing is in the historian's language, there is a direct interaction in the form of the ancient writer's imagining how a reader will respond to his text and adapting it accordingly, and the historian's constructing the writer's intent. In the case of prehistoric objects about which there is doubt regarding their social quality, the point at issue is precisely whether the prehistoric people interacted socially with regard to the object.

Having shown interaction necessary for the mutual reflection of the object's prehension in several subjects, we must ask what interaction is, in terms of our model. The answer is, continuous behavior by several subjects, each of whom employs his construction of the subjective form of the others' activity as essential features for determining the subjective form of his own activity.[17] There cannot be interaction without social objects in terms of which to interact, but the objects are social in virtue of the diverse location and mutual reflection of their functionings in experience. This is the answer to the objection against the social primacy of interactive behavior.

At this stage in our study, the social primacy of interactive behavior means a causal nexus can be conditional in a person in a social way only if it conveys or conforms to a trait, the prehension of which in the conditioned person involves including a possible subjective form of its prehension by another subject, and so forth as described in the doctrine of the diverse experiential location of social significance. There can be conditional social nexuses only where there is the possibility, and some actual occurrence, of social interaction.

Regarding the doctrine of the common intentionality of social interaction, the question to be raised is whether the goal in terms of which the interactive behavior is directed must really be common. It would seem the definitive kind of social interaction today is not cooperation, as Dewey expresses it, but conflict.[18] Social

17. If an interpreter's construction of the subjective form of another's activity were used only as a conditional feature, his experience would not be essentially social, as in fact it is. That the construction is used as essential does not mean it is essential to use the construction; that is, an interpreter can ignore his construction of his neighbor's experience, negatively prehending it. But if he positively prehends it, the construction is essential to his own activity.

18. It is an empirical question whether social conflict can be as deep as suggested in this paragraph. The next chapter will offer ways of understanding it philosophically if indeed it is that deep, and examples will be given. From a methodological point of view it has been argued by some sociologists, conflict theorists, that the presumption of pervasive and deep conflict leads to fruitful empirical research, and this is testimony to the reality of the conflict; see, e.g., the two chapters of Georg Simmel's *Soziologie* translated by Kurt H. Wolff and Reinhard Bendix as *Conflict* and *The Web of Group-Affiliations* (New York: Free Press, 1955). Given the magnitude of the problem of conflict in present society, it seems best to devise a social theory that allows conflict to be basic even if the conflict turns out not to be as deep as supposed.

objects seem to be uninteresting when their roles are defined by cooperative behavior; like warranted beliefs in Dewey's epistemology, they are unnoticed until fought over.

It would seem incumbent upon us, in this day of wholesale conflict between cultures, to articulate a meaning to sociality that does not ignore the conflict or relegate it to a degenerate form of authentic cooperation. The kind of solution to social problems that appealed to the idealists and to Dewey, the advocation of resolution of conflict by moving to higher ground, cannot maintain itself when the conflict is about fundamental issues. When the conflict is fundamental there is no higher ground to go to, and possible agreement is limited to the proximate and relatively trivial. It is a revolutionary age when the fundamental issues are the open and important ones.

To what kind of commonality of goals is Dewey committed? It might be thought that the participants in the interaction must share the same goal in order to interact. Certainly Dewey's example about the flower would suggest this, as well as his advocacy of cooperative action. But as we noted, interaction takes place even when one of the parties rejects the expectations and desires of the other.

Is it the case then that the meaning of an object as social depends on being related to some goal in the experiencer's view, even when the goal, and hence use of the object, might be rejected? Not necessarily. The meaning of a social object stems from the fact that each of its experiencers interprets in the light of a possible way that it could function in the experience of the others. This function need not as such be instrumental to a goal. For Dewey it could be simple enjoyment. The goal for Dewey enters the logical structure of meaning as the directive of the interaction needed for men to participate enough to share social meanings. As long as sufficient interaction is possible, men can disagree completely about the worth of social objects and can mutually reject as stupid, untrue, or malicious the roles they see the objects play in their neighbors' experience. All that is necessary is enough interaction to identify the various roles in the various individuals. This kind of conflict-bearing interaction seems possible.[19]

19. It is unclear whether Dewey would accept this. He was enough of an idealist not to dwell on empirical facts of radical conflict but to move immediately to the

How is such conflict-bearing interaction possible? It is necessary for the subjects to be involved in a common field of activity,
that is, one where the causal effects brought about or influenced
by some subjects condition some others, directly or indirectly.
Where the individuals are not contemporaries and the causal
action seems to be one way, as in the example of the historian and
the ancient writer, the interaction depends heavily on imagination; but the interaction is social so long as the causal chain conveys a character, in this case the writing, in terms of which each
subject interprets a role in the experience of the other. What is
common is not the goal directing action, but the field of action
with common objects. The objects have natures limiting what
can be done to them, with them, and around them, and these
limits force themselves on the people in the field. The roles given
the objects may differ radically, depending on the perceptiveness
of the experiencer and on his particular goals; the objects may
have social meaning if they are interpreted in the experience of
each person in terms of how they function in terms of other
persons. But the interaction with respect to social objects does
not demand a common purpose among the social subjects, only a
common field.

To be sure, not every social interaction is as good as it could
be, and many things worth doing require cooperative, not merely
conjoint, effort. But the need for cooperation characteristic of the
industrial mentality may be much less in a world characterized
by centers of pattern organization.

Dewey would be quick to point out that cooperative social
interaction enriches itself in consummatory social objects by its
very cooperation. But there are two points militating against the
claim. First, it is by no means empirically clear that cooperation
enriches experience more than conflict. Supposing the conflict-
bearing interaction does not blow itself apart, it maintains in a
tense harmony values that otherwise could not be together. This
leads to greater complexity, one of the chief components of richness or value. Cooperation can lead to dull uniformity, the opposite but equal danger to blowing up.

Second, cooperation on a large scale consists in making certain

---

goal of resolution; he would not take kindly to the suggestion that radical conflict
is more desirable than cooperation.

areas of experience the focus of controlled change and in assuming that the great bulk of experience is settled and noncontroversial. The great bulk of settled experience is the foundation of common interpretation and values underlying cooperation. Dewey emphasized the importance of what he called the "funded experience" of the race and pointed out that only the surface of experience comes into question. Our own time is different, however, since the conflicts are at the foundation. We may agree in the short run on superficial points for short-run cooperation; but for the present our civilization cannot be based upon long-run cooperation. What was a great mass of funded experience for Dewey, today for many people is a scaffolding of beliefs that obfuscate and mislead.

For our own position, the doctrine of the common intentionality of social interaction must be rejected. Social interaction involves intentionality on the part of the participants and a common field of affairs, but it does not necessarily involve a common intent. In substitution, we may hold to a doctrine of "individual intentions in a common field."

Let us sum up our argument at this point by giving an answer to the basic question of this chapter so far. In what does the social nature of human life consist? What makes people social beings? What constitutes the connections of sociality as such? These are all variants of the original question.

The complicated strategy has been to look to the cosmological scheme for a suggestion about sociality and then to put flesh on the abstract bones. The cosmological suggestion was that the social nature of human life consists in the contribution to life of the conditional social nexuses that bind people. Asking what makes a nexus social, we examined first what the limits would be of a society defined by the interconnection of conditional social nexuses.

We then said that what makes a conditional nexus social is that it conveys or is structured by a trait, called here a social object, the experience of which necessitates including a view of how the object functions in other people's experience. Along the way we have found it a defining characteristic of human nature as such to be able to have social experience, to experience objects in terms of the way they are experienced by others. This theory of social experience and the interaction constituting it has been outlined in terms of the doctrines of the diverse experiential location of social significance, the social primacy of interactive behavior, and individual intentionality in a common field.

In connection with the theory of society, it is possible now to define a concept crucial for the political considerations to come, power. "Political power" is the control of the nexuses of social causation, that is, those conveying social meanings around the social order. Those social nexuses not only determine the resources people have for acting, they determine their possibilities. Control of the nexuses can be of many forms; it is as rich a notion as that of political power in general. The human traits can be manipulated, as can the ahuman elements conveyed, the form and style of the medium of transmission, and the mode of appropriation or conditioning.

SOCIAL CHANGE, REVOLUTION, AND NEW SENSIBILITIES

Since the social environment is constituted by the interactions of the society itself, including the various creative activities going on, its most striking feature is nearly continuous change. But since the creative activity is what is most likely to introduce drastically novel factors, and since the creativity depends on its environment, the change is likely to be localized in proximate affairs and environments, leaving the more remote environmental factors relatively untouched. Changes in the most basic environmental factors would undermine the processes of creativity and the media communicating their novel results to the foundations of society. That is, radically creative action, especially that aimed at changing society, tends to undermine itself, setting proximate limits to its own effectiveness by destroying the very environmental factors usually counted on to carry over intended effects.

Where creative action tends not to undermine the basic environment, there still is no guarantee that the environment is stable. The various interactions themselves, creative or not, feed back into the environmental conditions, and the whole society changes, the environment more slowly than the focal points. It was in recognition of this that Plato advised in the *Statesman* and *Republic* that a good constitution in society (by which he meant a happy blend of basic environmental factors) is best served by a conservative government whose chief aim is to maintain that environment. The original development of such a constitution he thought to be almost incomprehensively difficult, depending on a preeminently powerful statesman of creative vision who could blend the given environmental factors well. Such a man was above constitutional constraints. But Plato recognized that in the long run even the best environmental blend must get out of phase. Short of another true statesman who would rule the society as his private preserve, things could only go downhill, the constitution quickly becoming evil and inappropriate to conditions. When environmental factors break down, that would sustain and tolerate the values of the society, the distinction between the public and the private breaks down. This is as characteristic of the rapine avarice of the corrupt forms of government as it is of the dictatorship by the statesman who is responsible only to himself and to the ideal.

It is important to distinguish between the *causes* and *roots* of a massive social revolution. Causes are factors that are to be traced to the old order, insofar as they are social and not physical (for instance, climatic). Causes of massive revolution are elements of the old order, themselves to be understood in terms of the old forms of interaction, but having effects that cannot be tolerated in the old order, forcing its change.

Most commentators trace the present revolution of the West to industrial technology. They acknowledge that the rise of industrial technology is a development quite at home in western history but that in turn it undermines the basic forms of interaction of that history. McLuhan, for instance, attributes the revolution to the development of electronic technology from mechanical technology. Marcuse attributes it to the effect of technology on the psyche.[20] Drucker believes the revolution stems from the patterns of economic organization associated with mass production.[21] And so forth.

The *roots* of the revolution are the basic environmental factors altered by the causes and in turn giving rise to the various mani-

20. See his *One-Dimensional Man* (Boston: Beacon, 1964); *Eros and Civilization* (Boston: Beacon, 1955; New York: Vintage, 1962); and *Reason and Revolution* (1941; reprint ed., Boston: Beacon, 1960).

21. *The New Society: The Anatomy of Industrial Order* (New York: Harper & Bros., 1950).

festations. For Marcuse the roots are new psychological patterns and pressures; for Drucker the roots are social organization and its control of the sense of human life; for McLuhan the roots are a new "ratio of the senses." The causes of the revolution are factors that might happen anywhere in the society, but the roots are located in the foundational environment. The truth of this point is not trivialized by the recognition that we often do not realize a particular factor is part of the foundational environment until it brings forth the revolution.

The *manifestations* of a revolution are the changes in the society resulting from the alteration of the root environment. In America the commonly recognized manifestations include the disenchantment of youth with the American dream, with their parents' values, and with their parents' claims to authority; these are summed up as the "generation gap." There is a more general disenchantment, not confined to youth although perhaps primarily expressed by them, with the old conceptions of national interest, of the importance of alliances, of citizenship, and of the violence permissible for political ends.

One of the manifestations to be expected of any massive social revolution is a boundary change between the public and the private. That alteration is a function of contingent conditions, but a crucial distinction must be drawn at this point. It is one thing for the boundary to shift when the basic environment of the society remains stable, as, for instance, during a war that does not change the basic environment. It is quite another thing for the boundary to change when the basic environmental factors themselves change. In a society undergoing a basic revolution, and not just a superficial adaptation of social forms to new conditions, the alteration in the environment means the society loses its sense of the concerns of the public. The confusion this brings about only compounds the difficulties of the revolution, since the society no longer shares an understanding of the public mechanism for adjudicating the revolutionary changes. The revolution in the West is characterized by extreme confusion over the environmental factors toward which various publics might organize their concern. There consequently is a feeling of helplessness—there is nothing public to be done.

It is hard to conceive, then, a more pluralistic situation. Relative to each kind of manifestation of revolution—and there are many more than those few singled out above—there is a confrontation of those allied with the old order and those with the new. This situation cannot be called an *organized* pluralistic society. The pluralism results from breakdowns and conflicts of organizations. But if a new organizational principle could be found that would justly order the revolution as such, that order would be the foundation of a genuine organized pluralistic society.

What does "continuing revolution" mean? To Marxists it would mean that the revolution continues to alter social conditions step by step until the goal of concrete human freedom is attained. But a revolution based on an alteration in the basic environment is a different matter. The revolutionary manifestations stem from a change that has already taken place to a significant degree in the basic environment. So it is to be expected that after the manifestations all fall into line with the new environment a new period of relative stability will ensue. So much may be true. But what is usually meant by a period of stability is that affairs take place within a stable frame of public order, that is, of institutions maintaining the environment. Theoretically, there are many kinds of order; the distinction between stable orders and dynamically changing ones is basic. Western society has been ordered by an ideal of stable order, that derived from law.[22] But as we shall see in the next chapter, the disintegration of stable order is one of the chief manifestations of the present revolution. Rather, the new order seems to be dynamic in some sense. And this is the sense in which the revolution can be called continuing. The "new order" must include patterns of interaction that cope with continually changing patterns of interaction. So long as the socially important patterns are in continual change, society will always be pluralistic, divided between groups of the old and the new.

To speak of the "present social revolution" perhaps presumes too much. Even supposing that the philosophical lineaments of

22. For further discussion of factors in the social environment undermining the authority of statutory law as the primary vehicle of justice in the West, see Robert Neville, "Justice and the Future of Statutory Law," *The American Journal of Jurisprudence* 17 (1972) : 92–110.

social revolution are as has been described here, is it true that western society exhibits them now? In one sense that simply cannot be answered: only history will show what the ultimately important variables are in our present situation. But in another sense, the revolutionary character of the present situation seems undeniable. The reactionary moves of law and order, and of economic tightening, are moves on the level of manifestations; the roots of society are in transition, and this is interpretable in many ways discussed below.

New sensibilities of social order are emerging from the present social revolution, sensibilities setting the limits of the public and private domains and providing the tolerance, such as it is, for social pluralism. At a profound level, the revolution seems to be warfare between the emerging and the declining sensibilities. Warring sensibilities are the most pervasive manifestation of the alteration of the basic social environment. Strife over what is and is not acceptable is expressed in nearly all manifestations of revolutionary conflict.

What alteration in the environment gives rise to the new sensibilities? And what, more directly, are the characters of the new sensibilities? These questions lie at the heart of the social order for social pluralism and the dimensions of freedom it fosters.

The question of the basic environmental variable can be raised by contrasting two suggestions about the problem. One is that the root variable is the fundamental pattern of social organization itself, a thesis pressed by Peter Drucker in *The New Society*. The other is that the root variable is the basic pattern of style of human experience, a thesis maintained by McLuhan in the form of the claim that revolution stems from a change in the "ratio of the senses." We have discussed McLuhan's thesis above and now will sketch Drucker's. According to Drucker,

> [The] true revolutionary principle is the idea of mass-production. . . . The mass-production principle is not a mechanical principle. If it were, it could never have been applied beyond manufacturing and independently of assembly line, conveyor belt and interchangeable parts. It is a *social* principle—a principle of *human* organization. What was new in Ford's plant was not the organization of mechanical forces,

but the organization of human beings performing a common task. And this explains the shattering impact of the new principle on traditional cultures, on the relationship between man and society, and on the family.[23]

The *cause* of the revolution may have been the success of the mechanical operation of mass-production, but the *root* is the new social organization mass-production entails. In the new social organization the worker is divorced from the product made and from the means of production; he has a limited job in the total context of the enterprise. But it is the enterprise as a whole that produces, not the worker. Social status, self-conception, and family organization are no longer based on producing a product with a particular character, but rather on how one integrates into the social system of the overall economic enterprise. According to Drucker, the enterprise, for instance making Ford automobiles, is a local and relatively complete community with a variety of interlocking roles calling for a variety of skills. The great anxiety of this type of social organization is fear of being cut off from the productive enterprise, since this means to be cut off from the whole community and all social values.

It is in a sense unfair to criticize Drucker's particular thesis as expressed in *The New Society* since the book was written in the late 1940s and reissued in 1962. The radical depth and breadth of the revolution have only become apparent since that time. The revolution is most obvious in the fadism of student enthusiasm— now spent in civil rights, now in antiwar activities, every three years in a new cause—showing that the real revolution lies underneath these issues. But Drucker's thesis can be examined as a *type* of analysis, namely, that of social organization as such. The emergence of a new social organization, with its resultant conflicts, exhibits a severe dislocation of previously held values. But it must be asked how and why the emergent social organization is basically acceptable. There are many novel and competing organizations brought about by industrialization; why should one in particular, the enterprise, win out?

An analysis of the organization as such cannot answer this question. The root of the revolution must lie in the organization's ac-

23. Ibid., pp. 1, 4–5.

ceptability. Economics has not always been the determining factor of social organization; according to Drucker, the "primacy of economic performance" is unique to industrial society.[24] Why is that accepted now? It might be argued that acceptability is something determined by social organization, not the other way around. But that would not allow a change of social organizations to be explained in revolutionary terms. The enterprise organization, if that indeed be our social organization (ironically, it seems to be the prime target of the new revolutionaries) is accepted because of our new sensibilities, not vice versa. Of course, it affects the sensibilities, but not at the most basic level.

The question why some particular social organization is acceptable can be answered by showing it to fit a particular basic style of experience. McLuhan's thesis is that the ratio of the senses, or basic style of experience, is determined by quite ordinary factors, such as the character of the media of communication, but that it itself is the root of the way men respond in all situations of social interaction, including those of organizing and reorganizing society.

The argument McLuhan needs can best be made by reference to scholarly studies of different cultures from our own, since the important factors for analyzing our own society are the very things in question. The basic study here is Eric Havelock's essay on the development of Greek and western society, *Preface to Plato*.[25] Havelock's problem is why Plato would attack the poets and poetry in the extreme way he did in the *Republic*. He suggests that Plato was attacking a conception of poetry having a particular function in nonliterate society and that Plato's literate society called for a type of thinking antithetical to poetic thinking. From an analysis of Plato's description of poetry as *mimesis* Havelock argues his intent was to do away with a whole style of experience stemming from oral poetry. In a nonliterate society the social laws and mores must be conveyed in oral form, and the great problem is to *remember information*. Memory is aided by casting the information into verse formulae and metrical structures. The poetry is not memorized as mere ideas and words; the memory is in the muscles. Recalling oral poetry is a matter of acting it out, of filling

24. Ibid., pp. 50–51.
25. *Preface to Plato* (New York: Grosset & Dunlap Universal Library, 1967; 1st edition, 1963).

oneself with its emotions; this personal and emotional identification takes place in the reciter of the verse, and also in the audience. Havelock cites massive evidence to show how the Homeric epics were cultural encyclopedias, unifying a Greek culture dispersed in colonies; how successful leaders were those able to formulate thoughts in memorable verse; and how the appropriation of verbal communication implied extreme identification with both the content and form. Social behavior in preliterate society is the sort based on imitation of examples of behavior that can be grasped in narrative form. "Critical distance" from verbal content is impossible.

The literate society of Plato, the society in which there were not only writers but also a large audience of readers, was fundamentally different; or, rather, Plato wanted to bring out the difference. The writing of words allows them to take many forms other than poetic; it allows them to convey abstract ideas and moral principles divorced from narrative events. It allows the development of abstract logic and theory. And the virtue of abstract thinking is critical distance from any verbal form. Havelock elaborates in detail how the fundamental patterns of experience of western literate society were emerging in Plato's writing, and how Plato saw profoundly what issues were separating the sensibilities of the nonliterate style of experience from the emerging intellectual style.

What interests us about this analysis is not the causes cited but the conception of basic experiential style and how it determines a whole pattern of society, including social organization. As long as western people were unconscious of the difference between the styles of experience characteristic of nonliterate and literate societies they were unaware of the contingency of such styles. And as long as their cultural communication was primarily literature, with only literate cultures as objects of study, they had no reason to suspect nonliterate culture's basic style of experience to be any different from their own. The only access to nonliterate cultures was through archeology, art history, linguistics, and in the case of contemporary nonliterate tribes oral questioning and observation. But having identified experiential form with that communicable in literary form, alternatives were not recognized. The fact that scholars now are studying nonliterate societies from nonliterate points of view is testimony that our own society is gaining perspective on the basic style of literate experience.

The perspective gained by studies like Havelock's has been exploited by McLuhan in his varied analyses of the development of literate society and of the current revolution away from that basic experiential style.[26] The notion of "ratio of the senses" perhaps represents human experience as more passive than it is. But McLuhan's main points can be carried over into a theory of basic experiential style interpreted by the cosmological view we have been developing. We have spoken of experiential style as the general pattern or set of patterns characteristic of the way an individual integrates his prehended experiential data into his unique action. There are many elements of style, some more basic than others. If McLuhan is correct that style is a function of communications media, then the styles of different literate language groups would differ in respect to the differences in language, but not in respect to the characteristics of literacy. Western European society, although involving many national cultures, has been literate for a long time. The question now is what style of *most basic* experience is emerging through the current revolutionary changes. The ultimate question is whether the new style tolerates and sustains the desirable social pluralism discussed earlier.

A Pluralistic Style of Integral Social Life

The aim of this section is to describe a pluralistic style of experience appropriate for an integral social life. It should be clear from the discussion just how the features of this style conduce to integrity in a pluralistic social situation. The source for the description is really twofold. On the one hand we will look to the categoreal scheme developed so far for clues to the fundamental structures of experience. On the other we will look to actual historical changes away from the literate style of experience, some of which have been highlighted by McLuhan, others of which are pointed out by the cosmology. Now this second source has an ambiguous status. It would be tempting to say it is an emerging style bound to supplant the literate style as electronic technology becomes more abundant. A conclusion from this would be that a pluralistic style is just about inevitable. This kind of confidence

26. See, e.g., *Understanding Media* (New York: McGraw-Hill, 1964).

seems unwarranted, however. Our claim will be instead that a pluralistic style can be discerned among the new possibilities and ought to be brought to fruition. For this to happen, however, other root factors in the environment should be made to harmonize with it and reinforce it. These include various freedoms of opportunity, choice among social forms, and particularly a social order of participatory democracy. Whereas the literate style laid the foundations for pluralism with its support of universalistic thinking, only the pluralistic style provides for an integral social life in a pluralistic situation.

The discussion is arranged around three themes relative to the categoreal model: the new sensibilities regarding (1) perception, (2) the person as the center of action, and (3) the character of *social* action as interaction. The first is the theme on which McLuhan has dwelt. The second is the primary locus of the new style of basic experience; it is in terms of the particularities of this point that the others receive their interest in the present discussion. The third deals with the pattern of social organization and moves from the basic environmental variables of the revolution, to the manifestations of interest, to the problems of social pluralism.

In an occasion of experience a distinction is to be drawn between (1) the initial data of prehension, (2) the phase of working the perception into a unity, and (3) the resolution of the occasion in some action. According to the interpretation of experience given in Parts 1 and 2, the stage of perception is an advance upon the initial data of prehension in that the latter have been harmonized to the point where they can be objects of consciousness. Although perceptions need not be objects of consciousness they have the relatively sophisticated form of something that *can* be. At the stage of perception, however, the task still lies ahead of integrating the perceptions with all the other elements of experience, including the essential features, so as to produce an actual state that initiates a causal event external to the occasion. Again this is a relative difference, the final action perhaps not being much different from perceiving. But for most occasions there is a relevant distinction between the initial prehensive data—the elements at the perceptive level—and the creative outcome of the moment.

The theme to be developed here concerns the form of the perceptive moment. The pluralistic style of experience, far more than the literate style, appreciates perceptions in patterns of *contemporary* relations rather than of *linear* relations. The literate style of perception was more receptive to patterns of linear relations; that is, things were perceived as being in logical and temporal sequences, and the clues to their perception were based on the places they might occupy in serial orders. In contrast to this the pluralistic style relies less on serial forms and is more apt for naïve and relative immediate identification with isolated perceptive elements.

Whereas the literate style introduced a critical element into perception by receiving only sequentially orderable perceptive data, the pluralistic style throws itself into things less critically. For the pluralistic style, criticism comes later. Its pattern of perception, therefore, resembles what McLuhan calls a mosaic. The logical, causal, or other higher level ordering patterns are derived in a later stage of experience than the perceptive. Of course it would be an exaggeration to say the sequential form of perception is dropped completely.

In the technical language of our categoreal scheme, the pluralistic style de-emphasizes the perception of occasions in terms of *patterned* nexuses and emphasizes a tolerance of all sorts of irregular nexuses. The simplification in terms of patterned nexuses comes after the initial perceptive stages.

The first consequence of the pluralistic style is that many things of intrinsic importance can be recognized in the perceptive phase that otherwise would be neglected because they do not play a role in a recognized patterned nexus. In the literate style of perception the prehended data not playing roles in recognized patterned nexuses tend to get negatively prehended or radically transmuted or reverted before reaching the stage of perception.[27] Of course, the literate style's insistence that perception emphasize patterned nexuses will have the effect of leading men to discover more patterned nexuses; but the pluralistic style enriches experience more

27. These technical terms for what can happen to a prehension in the passage from the initial to the final stage of an occasion come from Whitehead. Anyone interested in the qualifications lurking in this sentence may refer to Part 3 of *Process and Reality*.

radically at the perceptive level. As a consequence, more things of interest and intrinsic importance can function as potential objects of consciousness.

The second consequence of the pluralistic style is that discernment of pattern on the perceptive level is more an empirical matter than it was with the literate style. By "discernment of pattern on the perceptive level" we mean the perception of pattern in what is *given* rather than the conception of pattern to be *imposed* within the experience. Since all experience is creative in the sense of giving rise to novel patterns, every occasion does in fact impose new patterns, altering the old ones given in perception. But since moral experience involves the critical imposition of pattern, the analysis of what is *given* in the moral problem is of great importance. And much of that analysis is accurate perception of patterns. According to the literate style, only perceptive elements conformable to serial ordering tend to be perceived. According to the pluralistic style, patterns relating perceptual data are to be perceived.

A pattern, considered in itself, however, is just a way in which a variety of things can be consistently together. If data do arrive at the stage of perception, then they are together as perceptive data and there is a pattern of their relation to be perceived. But to the extent things are not serially related, their de facto relation as unconnected on any higher level is also something to be perceived.

Just as the pluralistic style of experience is able to bring to the perceptive level more things of intrinsic importance not in linear sequences, so it is able to neglect things lacking importance that do happen to be serially connected with important things. When young people complain about the "irrelevance" of what their elders want them to pay attention to, what they mean is not irrelevance but unimportance. A thing is relevant to something if it is in a patterned nexus with it. But it may be of no intrinsic value or importance. The only reason to pay attention to it would then stem from the concern for the patterned nexus, which the young people tend not to have.

The literate style of experience has tended to exaggerate the importance of patterned nexuses for valuable things because such nexuses are built in as conditions to perception. Furthermore, it has tended to transmute the importance of the valuable member of the nexus to the whole nexus; this would be justified only if the value does depend on the nexus. And having transmuted the value of the member to the whole, the literate style of experience tends to neglect the negative values of the other members, if such there be. This point was brought out by radicals' criticism of the American war in Indochina. In the first place they distrusted the arguments from long-range prudence that would justify the war, suspecting on the basis of how they perceive things that the long, serial, causal relations hypothesized are not to be trusted. In the second place, they did not perceive the horrors of the war to be in a serial nexus as necessary means to the good end of international stability. Rather they put those things side by side, prescinding from hypothesized but unperceived causal relations, and judged the horrors to be far worse than any perceivable good wrought.[28]

The fact that the pluralistic style of perception makes the problem of pattern or order an empirical one does not mean it neglects the questions of perceptive truth, of getting the right relation between perceptive elements. The same pragmatic tests can be applied to suggested relations according to the pluralistic style that could be applied according to the literate style. The new style does entail, however, that linear *reasoning* is less important than sensitivity for discovery of what is there to be given. Complex empirical problems like those in science involve an elaborate prolongation of the perceptive stage, including all sorts of rational deduction as instrumental for the perception. In fact, the scientific procedure can be called perceptive only by analogy—it surely takes more than one occasion of experience. But the point still stands that for the pluralistic style, a person who reasons about perception without sinking himself into the maelstrom is not to be trusted, since he is likely to sneak the serial orders back in as a priori to the perceptive level.

The third consequence of the pluralistic style is that experience through time is like a dynamic kaleidoscope of perceptions. The perceptive phases of each occasion succeed one another like a succession of mosaics, aptly described as kaleidoscopic. This contrasts

28. For a fine development of this point, see Stuart Hampshire, "Russell, Radicalism, and Reason," *The New York Review of Books* (8 October, 1970) : 3–8.

with the literate style, in which important perceptive experience would tend to be limited to sporadic occasions and would receive a dominance in consciousness only when the serial trains of thought would lead to it (excepting surprises). Though only relative, this contrast is an important one. A person with pluralistic style is at home in a constantly changing environment, guided by little of the antecedent preparedness of familiar trains of thought. This point is borne out in art and music, both popular and sophisticated, and it helps understand the contemporary style of social and political opposition. In such an environment people of the old literate style feel ill at ease, unable to concentrate, and overburdened by what they take to be an excess of sensory stimuli.

The pluralistic style of perception, expectant as it is of instability and novelty, leads to a distrust of the stability of personal character that assumes a stable environment within which one can manipulate factors. Perceptive people, for the pluralistic style, are those fundamentally responsive to changes. The literate style stable personality seems, to the pluralistic style, to result from an unfortunate disengagement from the world. As to planning, the pluralistic style fosters planning as much as does the literate, but only with the expectation of continuous reinterpretation of the conditions and aims; a planned activity, the successful completion of which could have been imagined at the beginning, is expected to be an amazing coincidence.

This leads to a discussion of the character of a moment of experience as a whole, the second main theme. The pluralistic style of experience is a new style of integrating prehensive data from beginning to end. It integrates *perception, thought,* and *action* in a new way.

The literate style tended to order perception, thought, and action so that discursive thought is the dominant character of experience (the importance of consciousness in some philosophical traditions attests to this); perception's primary role is to provide premises for discursive thought, and overt action is something withheld until blessed by critical thought. The whole style was oriented to give manifestation to the development of human criticism.

According to the categoreal model of human experience developed in Parts 1 and 2, reception of data, mental ordering of it, and the constitution of the self as agent by initiating external

causal events are parts of every occasion of experience, each needing the others. In particular occasions of experience, they are not
of equal importance, however; some occasions are dominantly perceptive, some dominantly critical, some dominantly active. According to Havelock, preliterate Greek experience tended as a
general style to leave the second phase undeveloped. Perception
established an immediate contact with the social environment uncritically passed on in the action. This is mimicry, *mimesis*. According to McLuhan (Havelock is more cautious in criticizing
literate culture), literate cultures tend to exaggerate the second
phase, truncating perception and making men as agents strangers
in their environment. Relatively speaking, then, the pluralistic
style balances out the phases. Although every "experience" has a
peculiar bias, each is supposed to have a perceptive sensitivity, a
discursive creation, and an overt action. In the pluralistic style
the person is conceived not as a rational animal but as a sensitive
and creative center of action.

Part of the pluralistic sensibility, then, is an appreciation of
sensitivity, even sensuality. Not to demand perceptive items be in
rational sequences at the perceptive level allows the development
of both these. To be receptive anywhere to perceptual data requires developing sensitivities other than those taught in the
learning of speech. Whereas the emphasis on sensitivity, and the
training of sensitivity as such, seems like uneducated inarticulate-
ness to literate-style people, it is likely to be far richer in perceptive content. The danger, of course, is that the development of
pluralistic sensitivities will take place in a form that cannot be
handled creatively or turned to action. Without a correlative development of forms of working up the perceptive content, the
pluralistic-style perception leads to impotent passivity.

Beyond developing sensitivities, the pluralistic catholicity of
perception encourages sensuality, a special sensitivity to the physical and bodily components of perception. All perception involves
a causal nexus connecting the "object" perceived with the perceiver, and the medium of the nexus, especially the perceiver's
body, has a character in terms of which the mediation of the object's features is accomplished. In the literate experience the character of the medium is made inconsequential, and the focus is on
the sequential career of the "objects" perceived. In common sense

the media are transmuted in terms of the characters of the perceptive organs (for example, visual objects have optical sensations
ascribed to them), and in science even the character of the perceiver's body is eliminated, except for spatial and temporal positioning. In the pluralistic style, care is taken to appreciate and
savor the particular characters of the perceptive medium as well as
the objects perceived. The importance of the object as an enduring and external thing is likely to flicker in experience. It is not
that the pluralistic style loses any objectivity; it is only that it ties
objectivity closer to what is perceived, and how, rather than to any
a priori categoreal structure.

Most importantly, the pluralistic style gives a new sense of the
form of self-identity. To be a self is to be an active agent who, in
every moment of experience, organizes all the conditions given
him, including his mosaic of perceptions, into a determinate identity for himself with external consequences. That is, the agent is
the *center*, receiving given conditions and resolving them into an
action. As a continuing individual a person's identity must take
the form of characterizing his intentional and imaginative integration of his given conditions, including his own past states. This
contrasts with the literate sense of identity that was, in effect,
bifocal: from the outside, a person's identity is his career, described as an ordered sequence; from the inside the identity is a
self-contained world of discursive thought.

The pluralistic sense of self includes a new sense of the locus
of personal freedom. Where the literate style emphasized freedom
only when important action was necessary, the pluralistic style
sees its need in every experience, even when action is not important. The literate style also tends to believe the exercise of freedom ought to be postponed until it could be exercised with mature judgment. The pluralistic style sees this as a perversion of
experience and demands social opportunities to exercise freedom
while yet in the formal process of social education.

The pluralistic sense of self also involves a new sense of authority and responsibility. Since every experience is viewed in
terms of what the individual himself does with what conditions
him, his every action is his own responsibility. The limits of authority can only be to give advice. To accept authority as authority instead of mere expertise is to treat a conditioning feature as

an essential one without acknowledging that elevation to be a free act for which one is responsible oneself. Viewed as advice which one has the responsibility of accepting or rejecting, the demands of authority are often seen to have clay feet.

Finally, the pluralistic sense of self gives rise to a heightened sense of the importance of creativity, in the broad sense. If one's identity is in terms of what he does with his conditioning factors throughout his life, then the value of his identity depends on his capacity to create things of value. According to the literate style, one's career is the important thing, and that career might be routine and deadly, so long as it plays a valuable role in the social organization. The pluralistic style thinks much less of careers in terms of their value in the social organization, and much more of life as a continuing locus of creativity. Where the literate style took unbridled imagination to be a threat to patterned behavior, the pluralistic style takes it to be a sign of both success and opportunity. Where the literate style, considering the interior of identity, placed great value on reflection about the given conditions, the pluralistic style places emphasis on the reintegration of them to greater values, reflection playing a more instrumental role. Where the literate style took good action to be that which contributed to the valued order of society, the pluralistic style appreciates creativity as "doing your own thing." Each agent is the center of his own creative action, and that action constitutes his identity. There is a new appreciation for privacy.

The pluralistic person is at home in a radically changing environment. He suffers little loss of identity when his external career is dislocated or when conditions give him things to think about. The literate-style person needs stability for both senses of identity. The value of the pluralistic identity consists in the ability to cope with great creativity.

The new sense of the person as a center of action finally gives rise to a sense of nonisolation. The pluralistic style of experience has little sense for a continuing "inner life," at least on the level of daily affairs. Whereas for the literate style a person's individuality consisted mainly in the history of his thoughts, and his privacy in his inner consciousness, for the pluralistic style a persons' identity consists in his creativity in an environing medium. The environment includes the elements perceived and the effects of his creative action, however far off they might be. The inner life of reflection involved in the critical phases of creative activity flickers on and off relative to his perceiving and his overt acting. Identifying with the process of his creating, a pluralistic style person sees himself as a center operating in an environment. The environment is no more separable than his essential features governing his creative process.

The third main theme of the pluralistic style of experience is that, for it, social action means *interaction* with other centers of creative living. It is from this point that the principles of a participatory social order will come. The very language of interaction Dewey introduced anticipates the social life characteristic of the pluralistic style of experience. Perhaps no one had ever meant to deny that social action is a matter of interacting with other centers of creative experience. Certainly Kant's conception of the kingdom of ends reflects the view that moral action ought to treat people as centers of experience not reducible or instrumental to anything else. But Kant's view exhibits the old style of literate experience in that proper social interaction for him means treating people *indifferently* as ends; the only differentiation comes as a matter of nonmoral considerations about one's own inclinations. As we shall see, the pluralistic style finds little justice in the conception of law's treating everyone alike.

The first point to emphasize, then, is the derivation of the social character of the environment, for the new style of experience, from interaction with other people considered as creative centers of experience. Other people are taken neither to be isolated individuals with a purely self-contained integrity, nor to be players of social roles, but rather to be creative centers operating in a medium or environment shared with oneself. The character of a *proper* social medium, therefore, must be one amenable to being shared by the society of creative centers of experience.

The second point about the social sense of the pluralistic style of experience is that it entails a higher degree of involvement in social affairs than the literate style. In fact, for the latter a certain amount of detachment was considered a good thing, a necessary vehicle for criticism. At times, although never wholeheartedly, the literate style has fostered social roles that seem extremely detached, the "academic" being the stock example. The pluralistic style, to the contrary, sees detachment as a sign of fear and impotence, parasitic to boot on the perceived and addressed world from which it attempts separation. Proper criticism for the pluralistic style is the judgment formed by active participation in affairs, both perceptively and directively. Although only a shift in emphasis, this is an important one.

The third point directs what the first two have said to the problems of a social organization expressive of the pluralistic style of experience. The point can be put simply. The organizational structures of society must be such that the ways in which they determine human life must be respectful of the character of human life as styled pluralistically. Considered as formulas for the regulation of social effects, the structures cannot be well formed unless their "use and mention" of people defines the people as creative centers of experience. Social structures forcing people to function as indifferent tokens can be tolerated only when a trade-off in other values is justified. New structures fostering the particularity of specially located centers acting in a particularly located medium will have to be developed.

The problem of this chapter has been to articulate the dimension of social freedom consisting in an integral social life. All the social opportunities in the world, and all the options of forms of life, do not make a person socially free unless he can appropriate them to his own integrity as a person. Personal freedom considered alone is vague regarding the social nature of human life. The human being is a social animal, and the very meaning of his personal freedom requires this to be recognized. The strategy of the chapter has been to explore (1) the peculiarity of social life and (2) the contours of an experiential style reflective of social freedom. In the first connection the basic concept developed was that of interaction. In the second the basic notion was that of a stylistic integration of perception, thought, and action. These points are intrinsically incomplete, however, without a further discussion of the social order in which the exercise of *power* exhibits social freedom.

A further comment is appropriate here regarding an aspect of the argument that has surely not escaped the reader's attention. Throughout the discussion there has been a dialectic between actual states of affairs described and ideals relevant for them.

Whereas in chapters 8 and 9 the ideals were taken to be values actually prized as ideal by our culture, in this chapter the ideal of a pluralistic life style has been put forward as one people ought to recognize but perhaps do not. That is, now the discussion has entered into advocacy for disputed ideals, and in the next chapter this advocacy shall be undertaken even more directly. The formal plot of the argument is something like this: we actually prize certain social ideals (chapters 8 and 9); the conditions for attaining these ideals require a pluralistic society whose social (chapter 10) and political (chapter 11) structures become higher level ideals. The somewhat hortatory flavor of the preceding few pages and of those to come reflects the shift from rationalizing accepted ideals to advocating new ones. But the quality of the argument must shift in a logical sense now too. We have not only to make sense of the proposed ideals, rationalizing their principles and tracing some of their more important implications, but also to assay just how far their adoption would in fact tend toward the attainment and consolidation of our actually prized values.

The normative argument in justification of the social ideals of a pluralistic life style and participatory democracy is made especially difficult by the fact that those ideals in principle cannot contain within themselves certain other values they limit. For instance, there is no way by which an ideal of social organization can encompass the idiosyncratic values of privacy. It can reflect our social prizing of those values and attempt to keep a place for privacy, but it cannot, as Hegel mistakenly thought, fulfill those values in itself. There is no way by which a social ideal, such as participatory democracy with a pluralistic lifestyle, avoids the tragic paradox that a person can legitimately choose to reject public life, thereby depriving himself of the power to sustain even his private life.

On another level, the social ideals affect but do not encompass the religious dimension of freedom. The pluralistic ideal of social style applies to the affairs of cosmological causation; religious freedom makes sense only in light of the problem of coming to terms with the ontological foundation of the cosmological process itself. The inner life revealed in the ontological quest is quite different from the inner life of private continuity through time.[29]

29. For a more complete discussion of these distinctions see my *God the Creator*, Part 3, and *Spiritual Liberation* (New York: Seabury, 1975).

The person whose life style is pluralistic might *also* participate in the yoga of identification with the ground of all being; but that is a different matter, not regulated by ideals of social life.

The discussion to come, then, must be sensitive both to the limits of the ideals proposed and to the need to justify them as worthwhile in light of previously accepted values.

11

Freedom of Political Life

The discussion of free social style must remain vague and abstract until it is joined to a theory of how to organize the social environment so as to make it concrete. This brings us to the question of how to deploy the powers of individuals to bend the social environment toward freedom in all its dimensions. If politics is the arena of the deployment of human powers to structure society, our topic is political freedom.

Politics is not identical with government, although government is perhaps its most obvious institutionalization. If the Marxists are right, the most important political struggles concern economic ownership of the means of production. Recent discussions have shown that there are important political structures in the mores of sexual role distinctions. "Politics" in this chapter should be taken to include all the habits and structures involved in deploying human power to alter the social environment or to maintain the status quo.

Our task is to find a general ideal for political life, one that resonates with and enhances the various personal and social dimensions of freedom discussed previously. We need to articulate an ideal for free political order in which free people can participate and that in turn reinforces social styles, the values of privacy, diverse cultures, and prized opportunities. Because the organization of power has a special place in receiving the accomplished abilities of free people, and in fostering the conditions for those abilities, it is yet another dimension of freedom—the freedom of political life.

In our search for an ideal, it is necessary to say something more about the function of political ideals. Political ideals, like many other kinds, relate to processes, not static states of affairs. A utopia is not a political ideal, but rather the description of a society embodying certain political and cultural ideals in certain ways. A utopia can even be as "developmental" as H. G. Wells desired: "The Modern Utopia must be not static but kinetic, must shape not as a permanent state but as a hopeful stage, leading to a long ascent of stages." [1] But it would not be a political ideal, only an ideal political state. A political ideal is abstract and general; it is embodied in different situations in different ways, with different institutions to accomplish the same ends. The ideal of justice, for example, can be instanced in many alternate forms. Furthermore, it can be instanced more or less well: certain institutional changes in a situation may be called for by the ideal, such that when they are accomplished, even more changes are called for. But the political ideal itself should be understood somewhat in its abstract character precisely so that its alternate embodiments can be compared for the relevance to the present situation.

Plato's ideal of justice in the *Republic,* for instance, calls for a harmony of all needed kinds of people in the polis, each performing his own unique role relative to the others. This ideal is abstract with reference to which classes a state in fact needs; Plato illustrated it in the *Republic* with appetitive, spirited, and rational classes, and in the *Statesman* with the gentle, brave, and mixed classes. Our ideal for political order should be equally abstract. And it should be conceived to apply to *processes,* not to structures. The ideal is valuable because of the *changes* called forth in its pursuit, not for some end product. Plato surely was right that ideals could never be actual states of affairs but rather are ingredient in actuality by virtue of directing processes. Our question, then, is what ideal best would direct our political activity so as to channel our powers to foster and enhance all the dimensions of freedom met with so far, as well as other social values constituent of political activity.

Because of the engagement in the social environment characteristic of a free style of social interaction, it seems irresistible to call the political ideal "participatory democracy." That title connotes creativity in the social sphere parallel to the personal creativity

1. *A Modern Utopia* (Lincoln: University of Nebraska Press, 1967; 1st ed., 1905), p. 5.

capping the dimensions of personal freedom. Yet "participatory democracy" has become a slogan in recent years for every alienated person who wants the social order to listen to him. Of course, if a person does not have a voice in the decisions affecting him, participatory democracy is not functional; but there are usually more pertinent reasons why it is not functional than the fact that some other political ideal is operative. At any rate, the recent appeals to partcipatory democracy have not been strong in articulating the ideal theoretically, with an assessment of its implications and the principles needed to make sense of it. This chapter intends to do just that, spelling out the ideal and the subsidiary principles it requires in order to be a worthy ideal.

Robert A. Dahl, in his elegant political treatise, *After the Revolution,* poses certain criteria for a democratic ideal and lodges certain criticisms against the ideal of participatory democracy.[2] His remarks provide a convenient foil for our discussion.

The ideal of participatory democracy, in the form to be defended here, can best be expressed in the form of a basic principle that should be exhibited in any actual social order that would profit from being so arranged. The basic principle can be stated as follows: *The general organization of social interaction ought to guarantee that individuals participate in determining the organizational elements of the society in the respect and in direct proportion to the degree those elements affect them.*

Now Dahl takes this principle—phrased somewhat more simply but essentially the same—to identify participatory democracy with what he calls primary democracy, the condition in which each person votes his own opinion on each issue, the town meeting. The other forms of democracy he singles out are committee democracy, referendum democracy, representative democracy, and democracy of delegated authority. Dahl's main thesis is that there is no one form of democracy best for all occasions; and in fact each has various appropriate uses.

It is a very basic mistake, however, to believe that the ideal of participatory democracy directly concerns governmental structures or, as he calls them, structures of authority. Rather it is an ideal for the general form of social interaction. It is not an ideal for in-

2. Robert A. Dahl, *After the Revolution: Authority in a Good Society* (New Haven: Yale University Press, 1970).

dividual behavior or for government, as the notion of democracy has usually been interpreted. Participatory democracy of course bears on individual behavior and on methods of government, but as such it need not be conceived as an ideal for either.

If participatory democracy were an ideal for individual behavior, it would be self-contradictory: individuals might choose to ignore their prescribed participation and the right to do so is guaranteed in the individual liberty democracy is supposed to foster. Also, individuals could choose to establish a tyranny, destroying the democratic organization, and they could do so in exercise of their democratic freedom.

If participatory democracy were an ideal for government, instead of for organized society taken inclusively, the government legitimately might extend itself to totalitarian proportions, determining most of the important social organizations of the state. Dahl points out the liability of Rousseau's *Social Contract* in this regard. But by this extension the distance between the individual contributions to the democratic government and the governmental determination of social organization would be so great that individual participation would be almost completely diffused. A person's participation would bear on affairs relating to himself no more than to anyone else affected by the state's organization ("state" meaning here an organized society with a political government).

The principle of participatory democracy, construed as an ideal for the general form of social interaction, does make normative claims on individual behavior and the structure of government, to wit, whenever they affect the general form of social interaction. But not all individuals' actions are important for the organization of society, and not all the structural problems of government are important in defining the overall society as a participatory democracy.

But what can it mean to talk about the general form of social interaction if it does not mean government? It means the processes of setting the conditions under which political decisions are made, not necessarily the making of those decisions themselves. It is in the setting of the conditions for the decisions that the ideal prescribes participation of those possibly affected. Although this point will be analyzed in greater detail below, it is useful to make it here in order to deal with Dahl's criticisms of participatory democracy.

Dahl's first criticism, leveled against Rousseau as its best spokesman, is that participatory democracy will inevitably lead to factionalism and powerful leaders whose presence would skew the balance of participation, disenfranchising some citiezns. This complaint, however, depends on equating the government with the participatory context. If the context setting the conditions for decision-making is not the government, but rather the "people" who legitimate certain forms of government, they may very well prize factionalism and leadership. Political parties, for instance, may be politically economic ways to allow individual citizens to express power in decisions affecting them that they would not be able to express without factional organizations. The political ideal, here, would be to make sure the right factions are formed so as to bring the genuinely affected parties into contact. As will be shown below, the expectation of adherents of participatory democracy would be that conflict would be fostered and organized. As Dahl points out, primary democracy—one man one vote—may be a very inefficient form of participation. The government established by a participatory democracy, contrary to Dahl's expectation, would very likely call for all forms of "democratic authority," and some nondemocratic ones as well.

Dahls' second criticism is that the notion of participatory democracy does not tell us who the "people" participating are. Who should count as citizens? The notion of "citizen" is one defined in relation to government and state. Yet the principle of participatory democracy claims that the relevant "people" are those affected, or possibly affected, by the decision. These may or may not be identical with a state's citizens; but insofar as the criteria of citizenship affect persons who are not citizens, the principle of participatory democracy suggests those others should be included in the process of defining citizenship. Participatory democracy needs a principle of relevance, establishing both who is potentially affected by decisions and in what degree; this will be dealt with in detail below. Contrary to Dahl's complaint that proponents of participatory democracy have been short on giving criteria for "the people," John Dewey's theory of the Public, discussed in chapter 9, deals extensively with the problem. It is unfortunate that Dahl took Rousseau instead of Dewey to be the best advocate of participatory democracy.

Dahl's third criticism is that while a participatory democracy must be small in size, there are some problems, for example pollution, that cannot be handled in small units. This again presupposes that a participatory democracy is such by virtue of its government. A participatory democracy need be small only if the people must get together to talk in one room about setting the conditions for decision-making. But there is no reason to believe that setting those conditions is so much a matter of talk; it is rather a matter of conflicts focused in relevant ways. In principle there need be no limit in size to the population conflicting in a participatory democracy, although of course there are size limits to its effective government. This point should not be taken to minimize the problem of finding ways to focus conflict relevantly on a broad scale; but surely the formation of large-scale interest factions is one good way, and it does not presuppose all the people with the same interest need congregate in the same stadium.

In a sense the principle of participatory democracy is much wider in scope than would be an ideal for individual behavior or for governmental structure. It applies to any kind of social organization. A family, a business enterprise, a church, and a school should all be participatory democracies in their own ways. And so should all the unnamed kinds of relations included in organized society; relations between races, between social classes, between generations, between geographical areas, and between any divergent sorts of life. To the extent that these relations are organized, even informally, they ought to conform, where relevant, to the principle of participatory democracy. But of course this does not mean all decisions must be made on the basis of one man one vote.

Dahl makes the point that there are many organized activities in society for which participatory democracy would be silly, including some of those mentioned in the previous paragraph. True enough, if participatory democracy is a form of government. But there is a deeper point at issue. Participatory democracy is an ideal (as alleged here) because it fosters the other dimension of freedom. Lurking behind its attractiveness is the sense that attending to its pursuit in setting of conditions for decision-making will make people freer in all the other senses, as well as reinforce the habits of participation itself. It is very important, therefore, that the ideal of participatory democracy be universally applied to all contexts of social interaction deploying power. This is a practical point, because it may significantly tip the balance in matters of consultation, truth-telling, and the like. Dahl makes the point that for Rousseau, the participatory democrat, "the only legitimate source of authority is primary democracy" (p. 81). If one shifts the meaning of primary democracy from governmental forms to the broader context suggested for participatory democracy, that statement comes down to the claim that basic authority to affect decisions rests in those potentially affected by them. There is a fundamental truth to this. People exercise their basic authority in setting conditions for the decisions potentially affecting them. All other authority, for instance that in the decisions themselves, is lent or delegated authority, depending for its legitimacy on the basic authority disposing it. This belief, underlying the value seen in participatory democracy, gathers much of its strength from the previously analyzed kinds of freedom having to do with creativity and historical agency.

An objection will surely be forthcoming from defenders of Dahl's criticisms, namely, that the account here distorts the popular meaning of participatory democracy. When the students behind the barracades in the 1960s shouted for participatory democracy, they had in mind no such subtle and elusive distinction as that between decision-making and setting the conditions for decision-making. But is that true? When students demanded a voice in faculty tenure decisions, for example, did they demand that the committee be composed of faculty representatives plus the entire student body? No, they usually suggested some representative procedure, rarely if ever more than parity with faculty representation. Indeed, they had just such a distinction between marshaling the forces of those affected by the decision and focusing those forces in an economical way for decision-making.

With these preliminary considerations setting the stage for what must be explored in detail, our discussion must now turn to making the principle of participatory democracy precise.

The notion of participation is the most important concept to clarify, and the most difficult. It is most difficult because, except in an abstract sense, the nature of relevant participation depends on the kind of social organization in which participation is taking place. Sometimes the obvious kind of participation is exactly the wrong thing. In cases calling for expertise, the direct participation of a layman may result simply in his losing all power to direct the flow of events, no matter how much he is affected by them. A more effective participation would be for him to hire an expert who could give him the control. Yet the transference of the management control to experts in itself leads to loss of participation. The experts gradually take over the task of setting goals and defining what the affected layman's participation ought to be, and the layman becomes the tool of the expert who strictly speaking has no participatory interest. This kind of problem can be resolved only in a direct analysis of a particular case.

On the more abstract level, however, we can say what is important in participation by reference to our categoreal scheme. To participate in the formation of a social organization is to form it by interacting with it and its other formative elements. This means participation requires all dimensions of interaction. To participate requires then both perception and causal access.

Perception is essential so individuals can take conscious and deliberate possession of the factors involved in their social organization, including the factors relevant to controlling or changing it. According to our cosmology, all individuals prehend everything completed for them to prehend; but the structure of their experience necessitates the negative prehension of most of what is prehended. The data of prehension must present themselves in a certain way to be taken up in perceptive form. There are obvious ways in which social organization might prevent the perception of relevant kinds of data. It might condition people to filter the data out. And it might just keep things a secret: the fact that everyone prehends the election structure of an act of political chicanery does not mean they perceive it as chicanery. Humanly significant events like chicanery should be made public in the same terms in which the direct agents in the interaction conceive them for delibrative purposes. One of the things the principle of participatory democracy means for the distinction between the public and the private is that matters pertaining to the environment, that is, to the sociophysical organization, should be "made public" and not be kept secret or private. This has been known since the beginnings of democracy in America, and has been emphasized again and again by Dewey, however reluctantly and partially it has been accepted in practice.

Causal access to the crucial factors on which the social organization turns is also essential to participation in organized social formation. Nondemocratic societies can be defined as structured so that causal access to the crucial factors is limited to a certain class of empowered individuals without regard for who is affected by the organization in question. The limitation itself is a matter of social organization. In a participatory democracy certain elements of social organization ought to ensure that perception and causal access go principally to those affected. If practical, it should also organize ways of preventing participation in the determination of the organizations by people *not* affected.

The principle of participatory democracy is *not* a rule for making decisions, as mentioned above. It is a rule for *setting the conditions under which decisions or determinations are made.* This is an extremely important logical point. How decisions are made is something relative to the case or kind of case at hand. It might be decided that the way to make decisions is to give every affected party one vote, or to give affected parties weighted votes in accordance with how they are affected. This would seem to make the rule for making decisions equivalent in practice with the participatory conditions for the decisions. But it is by no means clear that this is the best decision-making procedure, or the one that in fact is the best measure of the proper participation. In a business enterprise, for instance, management is a highly specialized affair, and a worker not skilled in management would participate in the enterprise best, determining the results of the organization to turn out best as he would like them to affect him, by doing nonmanagement work and turning the management over to experts. His degree of participation would be registered by the degree to which his experience in the results of the enterprise is well accounted. Voting procedures, appeals to experts, waiting for consensuses, and the like, are all methods for making decisions appropriate in different circumstances for participatory democracies.

There are two important reasons for interpreting participation as a matter of the conditions for decision rather than as a means of making decisions. The first concerns power and conflict. The second concerns wisdom and executive excellence.

POWER, CONFLICT, AND SOCIAL CHANGE

The dynamic rule of social change is that social ordering is the result of a conflict of powers, the result taking the shape of the vector of all the forces, qualified by the nonsocial elements in the situation. When the forces are diametrically opposed, the greater wins; but usually a compromise is attained with each party getting a share of the pie in rough approximation to the relative power he brings to the conflict. This principle of social change is meant to be an empirical generalization about how things work, and as such it might be empirically wrong. Stated as vaguely as it is here, however, it seems quite plausible. It would run into trouble only when specifications as to the nature of social power are made.

The principle of participatory democracy is an ideal for the general form of social interaction insofar as it determines the organizations in society. The rule of social change is a description of the basic dynamics of social change. It is important to understand the logical connection between these two principles.

Participatory democracy is suggested as an ideal for the general organization of the conflict generating social change. The conflict can be organized in many other ways than according to that ideal, although it is doubtful it could be significantly *un*organized. Anarchy is possible only as a limiting ideal, and not a good ideal at that; an unorganized state of affairs is most liable to being controlled by a sudden and not necessarily very powerful coalition of organized forces—that is, anarchy tends to breed irrational organization.

The reason participatory democracy is claimed to be an ideal is that it is claimed to organize the process of social organization with the greatest value. This, of course, must be substantiated, and its substantiation comes in large part by way of showing participatory democracy to be the general form of organization expressive of the other dimensions of freedom.

The trouble with many ideals of general social organization is that they ignore the fact that conflict lies at the heart of the determination of social order. Social contract theories, for example, might acknowledge conflict as basic outside the social order but intend the establishment of their prescribed order as a replacement of conflict activity with contractual activity; or if not a replacement at least a circumscription. But the empirical truth of the matter seems to be that even in contractual or cooperative activity the *basic* determination of social organizations is a matter of the conflict of forces; and where the social ideal attempts to stabilize things by law of contract or ideal of cooperation, the stable structures quickly become means whereby the group with the most power tyrannizes and deprives the lesser groups of power. An ideal for a situation described by the conflict principle as a basic dynamic ought to acknowledge and enhance the way social change takes place.

In this regard, the principle of participatory democracy says social conflict ought to be organized so *the people affected by the outcome of the conflict contribute their own power to the conflict by participation in it.* Injustice in this regard arises when a particular conflict issues results for those not freely exerting their power in the conflict.

An important prudential argument for participatory democracy, therefore, is that it can be a constant social ordering principle, where its alternatives cannot. A general social form other than participatory democracy would alienate some affected powers from the process of determination, and these powers in the long run will turn and undermine the process. This is in fact what happens in revolutions: powers denied access to the arenas of determination of social organizations affecting them finally gather themselves to force their way in. The principle of participatory democracy would put all of the relevant powers there to begin with.

It is necessary, regarding decision-making, for participatory democracy to have a *principle of relevance.* When is a person or group affected by the outcome of a decision, and how is this measured in relative degrees? The principle of relevance then must have two main clauses:

> 1. *A person is a relevant participant in setting the conditions for a decision when its outcome affects his creativity, either directly or indirectly through the environment.*
> 2. *The degree of a person's relevance is measured first in*

a ratio to the number of other people affected in the same way, and second, according to the relative intensity of value the affect has in the person's experience.

The first clause means that a person is relevant to set the conditions of decision-making if the decision can modify the conditions of his creativity. Some of these conditions are general ones of environmental structure, perhaps even the object of some public's concern. Other conditions are unique to the person's own situation. If a decision has two possible outcomes, one of which affects a person and the other does not, the person is relevant to the decision-making process because the decision deals with both possibilities.

The second clause marks the inevitable compromise between the claims of those who are affected alike and the claims of those to whom the affect is more important than it is to others. It is clear from the discussions in previous chapters that the same factor can play different roles in the experiences of different people. In fact, free choice is the ability to give the same factor any of several roles. The fact the clause marks two incommensurable conditions means that the best compromise must always be a matter of harmony, with all the aesthetic balancing involved in this, as described in chapter 3. What the best blend is of the two conditions must be decided by social experience in each kind of situation. No rule can be given except as a description of an aesthetic sense of what is most important.

The principle of relevance lends itself to abuse. A person for whom an affect is not very important may exaggerate his feeling of its importance just in order to get recognition. The decision about his right to participate—a meta-decision-making process—is just and moral to the extent that it accurately measures his true concern. Of course, the criteria of the just and moral are different from the reasons for predicting how such a decision-making process might come out. The principle of relevance is an ideal concerning who has the ideal right to participate, however, and not a description of who gets to participate. It is possible (and usually the case) that those who in fact participate are not identical as a class with those who are relevant to participation, according to the ideal of participatory democracy.

This highlights the distinction between degrees of relevance to participate and degrees of power one brings to the procedure for setting the conditions of decision-making. A person with only minimal relevance might wield extraordinary influence. It is necessary, therefore, in describing the ideal of participatory democracy, to articulate a principle parallel to the principle of relevance, namely, a *principle of power. A participatory democracy ought to render each person the power to influence the conditions under which decisions are made in a proportion commensurate with his relevance.*

This principle obviously has negative and positive aspects. The social order ought to prevent people from using too much power when their relevance to the decision does not warrant it. And the social order ought to take special steps to see that individuals do have the power when their relevance warrants. Again, there is a distinction between who does have the power and who ought to. These principles articulate the ideal; they do not describe the facts. Nevertheless, according to the rule of the dynamics of social change, it is the actual power people have and can garner that needs regulation. The principles therefore are ideals for the appropriate facts.

Discussion of the principles of relevance and power calls attention to the important truth that the most significant decisions in a society are those interpreting how those principles are to be applied (or misapplied or suppressed). That is, the important decisions are those setting the conditions for important decision. In these decision-making processes of the highest generality, everyone has a relevant interest. This is why a participatory social order is called a democracy: a democracy is not merely a form of government but an order for arriving at end altering a government.

WISDOM, AUTHORITY, AND EXPERTISE

Any decision-making procedure should be understood both according to both how it works and how it ought to work in order to make good decisions. Not only is it an advantage for an ideal of general social organization to be compatible with, in fact be based on and expressive of, a conflict model of social change, it would be an advantage for it to make sense of the claim that good decision-making is wise decision-making, and that good determination of affairs is excellent executive virtue. When democracy is interpreted as a rule for making decisions and executing policy in terms of voting and so forth, a "good" decision, that is, a legitimate one, is merely the result of the vector of forces, the count of votes. But there is no logical connection between the result of a conflict of forces and the wisdom and excellence of a decision or determination of the process. Although a population of well educated and informed people might more often than not act in its own best interest, these conditions are almost never met. And since some people in any society are better educated and informed than others, the very fact allows them to become tyrants. The distinction between a good outcome and an outcome merely the result of forces has been recognized as long as the specialization of management has been appreciated. It is usually thought democracy necessarily is opposed to the distinction. But that belief is false in the case of the principle of participatory democracy.

In a participatory democracy the participating parties might hand over the actual decision-making to experts, in particular cases; or the parties might insist they be well educated and informed themselves to enter the process of determination. These things can be done without jeopardizing the principle of participatory democracy, since that principle governs the *conditions* for determining social organization, not the actual determination. Whether the rule by experts is consistent with the principle, or whether it tends to undermine it, depends on whether the experience of the affected parties is taken into account. It probably is a wise maxim that the affected parties not separate themselves too much from the process of decision itself; but there is nothing from the standpoint of participatory democracy to say they cannot.

Whether the decisions regarding social organizations are made well or poorly is a matter of justice on a more particular scale than justice regarding general social organization. That is, it would have to be determined whether the decisions make the affected people happy, whether they lead to richer lives, more free and creative, more secure against dissolution, more full of vitality and contrast, and so on. Simply because a society is a participatory democracy does not mean it will be well organized on all levels; it is a problem for a participatory democracy to make particular decisions well. And democracies do not have a monopoly on good decision-making; a benevolent dictator has all sorts of advantages when it comes to ruling, as does a well-trained aristocracy. Dictators and aristocracies tend to neglect both the experience and the powers of the people they rule, however, and the free exercise of power seems important for happiness. Even when a dictator makes all the right decisions, his people are likely to want to rule themselves just because that is part of what it is to be mature people, people self-possessed of their powers. At any rate, the principle of participatory democracy does not say a democratic decision is a good one. It says only that it is good that decisions be made democratically, and that making good democratic decisions means going beyond the principle of democracy to whatever sort of excellence is appropriate to the occasion.

Distinguishing the conflict principle of social change from the principle of participatory democracy as an ideal, and those in turn from the problems of coming to particular good decisions, forces a distinction between levels of generality in social organization. The principle of participatory democracy is an ideal for the way which social organizations should be determined and changed. But as an ideal it is a matter of organization itself. Now if it were limited to government, governmental organization could be conceived as the general form of organization within which all other kinds of organization could be controlled. But that would lend itself to a democratic totalitarianism: there is no reason to believe that even perfectly wise and benevolent government control should be applied to everything. The principle is rather like a theme to be applied to all instances of social organization. There might be organizations in a society aimed at instilling the theme of participatory democracy in all conflict situations, for instance schools, news media, and so forth. But the organization of conflict in terms of participatory democracy is not a separate and higher organization from the organizations that the principle determines. It is an ideal for any organized activity of determining social organization.

Finally, regarding participation the issue of representation should be addressed more directly. Given the construction we put on the principle of participatory democracy, there is no reason why a party affected by a determination of a social organization might not participate through a representative. We have already noted how an expert might be lent a participating individual's power. And living in a representative state we cannot help but be aware of the efficiency of execution coming from simplifying the participation of many people into that of one representative. The grounds for the transfer of authorship of participation from oneself to a representative have been thoroughly explored by the social contract theorists.[3] The point to be noted, however, and underlined again and again, is that *how* particular decisions are to be made *well* under participatory conditions is a matter to be determined over and above the setting of the participatory conditions. In each particular situation the participatory interaction determines the procedure for deciding each issue, and the procedure determined might be representative, an appeal to experts, a matter of direct vote, or whatever. If the particular procedure chosen does not accurately reflect the individual's participatory interests, his participation in setting the procedures will work against it.

Two practical morals can be drawn from this. First, it would be unwise to let direct participation in the decision procedure ever get very far from the affected agents. Since the procedures instituted in particular instances tend to organize themselves in a self-perpetuating way, it is dangerous to allow the use of experts and representatives to move the decisive determinations from local contexts. When the choice of procedures is a matter of local control versus distant expertise, the value of the latter ought to be carefully hedged about with lines of quick appeal back to the affected community.

Second, it should be borne in mind and reflected in the articulation of decision procedures that they are expressions of a participatory democracy more basic than themselves. To the extent that they fail to be expressions of the more basic participatory democracy, they are unfaithful to the basic theme of social organization, and the wrath of neglected power should be expected to strike them down. This means in effect all definite procedures for decision-making are proximate, contingent, and temporary. They fail to be genuine democratic institutions, under the principle of

3. For an excellent discussion of representation in a participatory democracy, see Aldo Tassi, "American Political Philosophy: 1763–1776" (Ph.D. diss., Fordham University, 1970).

participatory democracy, when they fail to be accurate embodiments of the proper participation of the people affected. This point has radical consequences for the belief in constitutional government and rule by law. Under a participatory democracy the social order must be constantly changing to be faithful to the affected participants. This is the kind of social order that seems to be formally necessary for the new style of experience.

The fact that society is the arena of conflict calls for the general principle of participatory democracy to be specified in two further principles, the *principle of authority* and the *principle of publicity*.

The principle of authority is: *a person's authority to exert his relevant power resides inalienably in himself and can only be delegated to another by his explicit will.*

This means first of all that a person is responsible for making his own decisions and for wielding his own power. In a participatory democracy it is immoral, according to this ideal, to evade that responsibility or shirk the duties of power. Of course, in many situations people are unaccustomed to exercising responsibility and unprepared for it. The traditions of paternalism militate against the sense of responsibility suitable for a participatory democracy.[4] When people are timorous or feel powerless, they surely should be helped. But in the main, the institutions and social arrangements of participatory democracy, respecting the principle of authority, ought to reinforce the taking up of responsibility and preparation for dutiful exercise of power.

Two qualifications of this principle must be mentioned. The first is that of the person incompetent to exercise his own authority. Incompetence is a most dangerous concept. It is tempting to conclude that because a person is not prepared to exercise some dimension of freedom fully, he therefore is not competent to make free decisions on his own authority. This temptation seduces us into such immoral acts as commiting merely odd or socially deviant people to mental institutions, depriving students of reasonable options because their elders know what is "better" for them, and generally exercising exploitative power in the name of greater wisdom. Nevertheless, there are situations where people are incompe-

4. See Gerald Dworkin, "Paternalism," in *The Monist* 56, no. 1 (January 1972): 64–84.

tent to exercise the authority that ought to be exercised in that situation. Small children and seriously ill mental patients, for instance, are in no position to exercise their authority with any discrimination about certain matters that might be at hand. As medicine has shown, proxy authority is often indispensable in saving lives and in returning patients to a position from which they can exercise authority in matters of their own health.

We ought to say then that society in these clearly defined cases ought to prevent a person's authority from being exercised and have decisions made on the authority of proxies that derives from the judicial public. The cases would be those in which the person has no possibility of judging reasonably about the case and where the publicly authorized decision would contribute if possible to the person's eventual assumption of his own authority. The last clause would justify proxy authority for children in most cases. In the case of retarded people and others in whom responsibility even at a minimal level cannot be expected, the justification of doing things to and about them assumes that they never have personal authority and that they are permanently in the authority of others. This does not mean that they should be treated as less than human just because they cannot participate in decision-making: exercise of authority is not the minimal criterion of being human.

In no case should a proxy authority be construed to exercise a person's authority except on the explicit and authoritative consent of the person (in which case it might better be called "delegated" than "proxy" authority). Except for explicitly delegated authority, proxy authority derives from the society, not from some special relation the proxy bears to the person, such as kinship. Society may decide kinfolk are the best proxies, but that is a separate matter. The reason it is preferable to say that proxy authority derives from the public consists in a two-step interpretation of the grounds for authority. First, under these conditions the person has not authoritatively given his authority to another, and hence the proxy's authority cannot derive from the person that would have it in the first instance. Second, all authority derives ultimately from what the society values and, in its organized public form, is willing to sanction. Our society values authority resting in the person affected by the action; this is for good reason. But society also values authority being placed elsewhere under certain circumstances, namely those in which the person has no possibility of reasonable judgment. The determination of what reasonable judgment consists in ultimately belongs to the public. Nevertheless, a particular person can contest society's interpretation of the notion of reasonable judgment while still claiming to be more faithful than society to its own ideal of "authority resting in reasonable judgment." The force of the general claim that authority derives from society is that a person should not be held responsible for decisions made by his proxy; he should have legal standing to sue the society's formal agencies (not perhaps his individual proxy) for damages in the case of bad decisions.

The second qualification to the principle of authority is that society has the obligation to suspend an individual's authority in its own protection. Although there are doubtless many examples of this sort, criminology and mental-illness cases probably furnish the outstanding examples. Protection of course refers to prospective situations; there is no protection against what has already happened. Therefore an unhappy compromise must always be worked out between society's interest (as a participatory democracy) in maintaining personal authority and its contrary interest in self-protection.

This second qualification is paradoxical. It seems primarily to be giving special authority to the state to suspend individual authority. Its effect, however, is to prevent a tempting abuse of the first qualification, namely that of saying a person has no authority because he is unreasonable, when in fact he only has bad or evil reasons. What this second qualifications suggests is that such a person not be deprived of authority, or declared to be a non-authoritative human, but rather that his personal authority ought to be prevented from being exercised under certain conditions. In practical language, a person should be locked up only because he is dangerous, not because he is a nonauthoritative human being. A criminal acting out of political motives might be dangerous to society and worthy of incarceration, but he should not therefore be subject to "therapies" that would change his motives on the ground they are not authoritative. Suspended authority is still authoritative, and the person still enjoys that element of dignity. The suspension only should mean that the person's freedom to implement his decisions is circumscribed. The principle of participatory democracy entails responsibility for evil acts, and therefore authority for those acts should not be denied, only circumscribed, except in cases where the person cannot act reasonably. "Reasonably" means only that the person makes a fairly accurate judgment about what to do on the basis of his values and motives, be they good or bad. In cases where others are not endangered, the person should be free to choose his own values and motives, according to the ideal of personal freedom.

A final meaning of the principle of authority is that no authority rests in expertise alone. An expert is authoritative only in cases where he is personally relevant, according to the principle of relevance. Experts are often given authority by groups or individuals to make decisions. The principle of participatory democracy would suggest that this giving is only a matter of *delegation*. The authority remains the individual's, even when he has the expert make the decision for him. When things go wrong, therefore, he should blame no one but himself. Of course, he should be able to sue the alleged expert for false representation, if that in fact is the case. But generally it is the individual's responsibility to delegate his authority only to those for whom he will take responsibility. There are many areas in our current society in which people have avoided responsibility by delegating power to experts in areas where their expertise is simply not relevant. Medicine and the priesthood are areas in which authority is often delegated to an extent unwise regarding the real expertise.

A special problem must be raised at this point. "As ideals, the principles of relevance, power, and authority are fine," a critic might say. "But they all suppose that each participant in the society, exercising his relevant power with authority, has an understanding of what is going on. But this is patently false now, and probably always will be. People *hide* their actions so that counter actions cannot be taken. And if the actions are not hidden, those to be affected might choose to ignore knowledge about them until too late. Even if people wanted the knowledge, it may be impossible to communicate. Or if it is communicated it may be impossible to assimilate and bring to bear intelligently on the issues except for the most sophisticated person. In all, participatory democracy demands too much of people. It demands that they be participatory heroes."

So it does. But that is not a bad thing for an ideal. The criticism would be relevant if there were in fact nothing that could be done about the difficulties. But there is, and it is expressed in the *principle of publicity: People ought to have access to any information about matters over which they are among the relevant authorities. A participatory democracy should also, through its institutions, facilitate the accumulation, communication, and personal assimilation of this information in any ways possible.* This principle suggests that participatory democracy should first admit a *right* and then to implement a worthy program.

The right is that of *access to information about oneself and one's situation.* This means, practically, that a person ought to be able to see his medical records, to be told his doctor's real opinions about his physical and mental conditions, to see personality, aptitude, and achievement records, and to see any files a business or agency might keep on him. On a larger scale it means a citizenry ought to have access to the deliberations, records, and commitments of its government. There are limits to this right, as to any other. For instance, a person's access to information might compromise another person's confidentiality and privacy; how to balance these rights is a social decision to be made respecting diverse kinds of cases. But it seems illegitimate for a person to have information withheld from him simply because knowing it would do him harm. If it might do him harm, that is his problem, with which society might help him; in a participatory democracy that is part of being a responsible participator. Clearly, a participatory democracy ought to reward and reinforce people's learning how to handle dangerous information, rather than having some "expert" decide what they should know about themselves. Only where knowing the information would render the person *less* capable of exercising relevant authority, as might be the case in certain severe kinds of mental illness, would withholding information be legitimate. Even then the burden of proof ought to be on the withholder of information.

The program, of course, is that a participatory democracy ought to devote its resources to enabling people to handle information well. Where before we said people have a right to participate in educational media, now we suggest the society has an obligation to provide educational media. Not only should facts be communicated, but also methods of handling them and perspectives on the relativity of facts and methods. Perhaps more important, however, is the obligation to educate people in the emotional attitudes and personal strengths needed to face information squarely. This means a variety of things from character development to spiritual perfection, including learning to live for dying. It does not mean, however, that the social order best discharges its obligation in this regard by public institutions. Public schools are not a priori solutions to the public right of people to have an education; the public right is only to the *resources* necessary for education. Much less will spiritual enlightenment come from the Government Printing Office. But a participatory democracy has an obligation to educate through the best means apparent, including mass media. In all this, the discharge of the democracy's obligation to education must be compromised with each individual's right to privacy. In light of the effects of education on creativity, perhaps there should be a right to refuse education.

The fay supposition of sufficient education is only the first-line objection made by the critics of participatory democracy. The more profound criticism, because the more practical, is that the democratic ideal would entail such constant alteration of the basic structure of society that individuals would be unable first to find out where the crucial decision points are and, second, to hold any one "publicly delegated" decision-maker responsible.

In practical terms, it is not enough for a person to be aware of the decisions being made in society relevant to his life. He must also know where those decisions are made and how his own limited powers might be brought to bear on them. But in a constantly changing society as described for a participatory democracy in continual revolution, the nodes of power too shift. What is likely to result, according to this criticism, is the development of a supermanagerial class expert in sniffing out the changing power structures. Authority will be delegated to these people because only they will have the power to alter decisions. But the authority will be incapable of recall because the managerial class has a monopoly on access to decision structures.

This is a powerful criticism, of course; but it is an old one and the mechanism for its resolution has already been developed. The resolution can be formulated simply, if somewhat pretentiously, as the *principle of rule by law: Any issue, for which there is a relevant public of people affected, ought to be decided according to public mechanisms determined in advance and to which the relevant public has the right of access.* This is only to say that the people ought to contribute to the setting of conditions under which decisions relevant to them are made. The principle points out, however, that they have to know what these are in advance of the decisions. And it entails, most importantly, that the structure of setting the conditions for decision-making should not alter faster than the society can reprogram the educational institutions. In practice this means that the most general structures of social order for setting conditions for decision-making, for instance those of the governmental constitution, should change slowly. Other structures of setting conditions for decision can change faster, relative to how easily those conditions can be assimilated educationally. A simple way of putting the point is to say that the relevant exercise of authoritative power in a participatory democracy requires publicized, not secret, politics.

It is sometimes said classical modern social theory construes the freedom of individuals as more important to social organization than the virtue of individuals. Or at least that it is not an organizational or public problem for it to make individuals virtuous, only free. The principle of participatory democracy agrees with this emphasis in the following way. The claim that participatory democracy is the ideal for setting conditions for determination of social organization, plus the claim that those specific procedures must be subordinate to the interests of participatory democracy, amount to saying the basic theme for all social organization is more important than, and normative for, the particular determinations made. Participatory democracy itself is the social form for freedom on the basic level, and the problem of wise decisions that might make men virtuous is secondary. Our theory puts more weight on freedom in this sense. But in the context of our interpretation of personal freedom, the dichotomy between freedom and virtue is a false one. In the full sense, freedom means choosing and acting for the best, in personal and social matters. Virtue prescinding from freedom can at best be a matter of determining prehended conditions by habit. But unless the habits are freely appropriated through criticism, this is a less than human virtue.

The argument could be made on the basis of the theory of value that right action, not freely appropriated, is not as good in the main as free action that sometimes makes mistakes. And even apart from such a lofty kind of argument, virtuous habits are almost impossible in a very fluid situation; what is virtuous in one context is pernicious in the next, and the man of hardened habit is greatly to be feared. So, a social organization *conditioning* men to right action is a genuine impossibilty as a general matter.

INSTITUTIONS AND GOVERNMENT

The principle of participatory democracy says nothing directly about specific institutions of the society. If it did, it would be subject to the kinds of criticisms Dahl raises. In this it contrasts with *ideologies* interpreting social change in terms of specific changes in institutions; for instance, the socialization of industry, the abolishment of private property, or the defense of private property, the limitation of government, or the establishment of one-man-one-vote.

Institutions are one sort of social organization. The term "organization" has been used in this and other chapters in the sense of a structure of interaction where activities are ordered in relation to an end. Thus, not only organizations in the usual sense, with stated objectives, officers, and so forth, are to be counted, but any kind of intentional social ordering where the structure of the interaction, not just the individual actions, is related to an end. We have already singled out general social media as organizations. Institutions as well can be singled out; an institution is the general structure of a general medium. For instance, the institution of capitalism is the general structure of an economic medium, as democratic elections are of a political medium, or as groups of parish churches are of a religious medium.

The contrast of the principle of participatory democracy with ideologies whose ideals are institutions of some sort is important. The principle of participatory democracy allows all institutions to be structured according to the pragmatic needs of particular situations. In some cases a socialistic economy might ensure the greatest relevant and proportional participation; but when it gets bogged down in bureaucracy it can be a far cry from an expression of participatory democracy. In other situations a system of free enterprise might ensure greatest participation. But most likely, in any complex situation a great variety of institutions, not at all compatible with one another on a theoretical level, might be appropriate.[5]

The upshot of this fact is that a social revolution in favor of participatory democracy would have no great programs, where programs are defined in instituitional terms. It would instead have a lot of proximate and contingent suggestions, where the motive behind the demands is to make a particular organization more susceptible to participation by those affected by it. In institutional terms the demands of participatory democrats might seem contradictory—they might seem Marxist here, Keynesian there, liberal here, conservative there. The revolution is not about institutions, but about the method of controlling social organizations, and there the contradictory institutional demands might be quite consistent.

The participation of people in the American government is interpreted in terms of electing representatives who themselves determine policies by vote.[6] The mere fact of interpreting democracy in terms of election compromises the effectiveness of the principles of relevance and power. The president is elected not just by those affected by what he might do, and their votes are not weighed according to the degree of affection. Members of the House and Senate are elected according to geographical distribution, not according to the relevance or degree of affection. To be sure, the pressures of getting elected serve to make representatives sensitive to the need and interests of their constituency, but only at a far remove from the direct participation of the constituency. This is compatible with participatory democracy only to the extent that by the time the effects reach from the government to the people, those affected could have participated in the determination of those effects as much as if they had participated from the beginning. Of course, this is very difficult, and it is therefore safe to say a government as big as the American one is too big; too

5. Dahl calls this situation a polyarchy.

6. See James M. Buchanan and Gordon Tullock, *The Calculus of Consent: Logical Foundations of Constitutional Democracy* (Ann Arbor: University of Michigan Press, 1962).

many determinations of social organization are made on the national level where the effects are local.

A principle is called for, then, that would determine the level on which determination of organizations ought to be made. The principle in operation at present is roughly this: affairs pertaining to local communities ought to be handled on the local level, even if there are analogous affairs in parallel localities. Affairs whose effects are inclusive of several localities ought to be solved in a representative body higher than the localities but representing them. So matters of foreign wars, highways and interstate communications, and welfare programs involving migrations of people from one locale to another are taken to be matters properly decided on a national level. But this principle of determining the level of decision, even if it could be well inculcated, which it is not, would be inappropirate. There are affairs that have effects on local levels and that could be administered on those levels and yet depend on affairs in other levels. For instance, it seems a good thing for local communities in a large city to control their own schools; but poor communities must run their own systems with money from wealthier communities. How can there be interdependence with regard to money but independence with regard to educational policy? At this time it is difficult to say what a proper principle would be for establishing the scope of governmental relevance for various issues, but certain factors the principle would have to cope with can be pointed out.

First, the structuring of the levels of government would have to be flexible. The age when fixed assemblies can decide whatever happens to come their way is about to pass. We are learning too much about the appropriateness to specific problems of the structure of decision-making bodies to tolerate for long one kind of institution for deciding all kinds of issues. We have rediscovered the old truth that issues are decided in many areas other than official ones. The intentional scope of the ideal of participatory democracy would have to be broadened to make them explicit.

Second, relations among different levels, and among different localities on the same level of government, must be worked out in terms of the causal lines of interaction of the issues to be decided. The plain force of affairs in practice marks the relations between these decision-making centers turn on causal lines of interaction.

But today the interactions involved in the issues are too confused with the interactions involved in the bureaucratic relations between centers of government.[7] In fact, the causal lines of the issues are often forgotten in the face of the difficulties of procedural interaction. No structured government can be purely diaphanous, letting the issues shine through without distortion. But if governmental centers were related to each other in ad hoc ways, relative to specific and passing issues, the tendency to monolithic distortion of the real relations of the various localities affected by the issues would be minimized. Only a faithfulness to the causal lines of interaction among different affected groups will allow relevance and due proportion to be given to the participation of the various affected groups in organizing the interaction justly. This point must be qualified, however, with the recognition, that it would conduce to tyranny if the requirements of publicity and rule by law are not met.

Third, the model of appealing to a central and higher authority in the case of conflict will have to be severely limited and the direction of the appeal reversed. Appeal should be made not to an authority above the conflict but to the various individuals affected by it. Western civilization has acculturated itself to appeal to the higher authority during the rise of literacy with the help of two environmental factors that are dissolving today. The authority, having centralized power, was better able to *enforce* a resolution on conflicting parties. And the authority could claim detachment by mediating his relation to the affected parties by laws. Today people are withdrawing their power from central authorities and employing it in their own involvement in social organization. And detachment is no longer a pure authoritative visage; sometimes involvement is more authoritative.

Institutions have yet to be modeled that would redirect arbitration down to the affected people rather than up to a higher authority. But it is clear they are needed and in fact are coming into focus. The increasing frequency of strikes by public employees in the United States is forcing the issue. The parties to the conflict simply are not satisfied with the determinations made by higher arbitration panels, and wildcat strikes are uncontrol-

Responsibility: A New Model," *Man and World* 5 / 4 (November 1972).
    7. See Harold F. Moore, Jr., Robert Neville, and William Sullivan, "Contours of

lable. The laws against strikes by public employees are ineffectual; there *can be no effectual statutory law* in these matters, because law itself is no longer regarded as more authoritative than certain kinds of demands made by those affected. Positive law can be effective only when it is massively accepted, and people are coming to accept less authority for law as such. What is authoritative is a settlement worked out by those directly affected, and we have few institutions for effecting such settlements.[8]

Although it might seem that the advocates of participatory democracy are only complaining about a kind of government too large and too unresponsive, on reflection the complaint is radical and might shake society to the core. The shift of appeal in conflict from higher authority down to those directly affected would be as major a change in social organization as the shift from the authority of the Achaean warlords to that of Justinian's laws. This is not to say a hierarchical government would cease to exist or perform vital functions. But it would become much less important in society, lose much authority, and give way to new procedures for adjudicating conflict, procedures of participatory democracy.

The image of the ideal free society that emerges from the principle of participatory democracy is of a group of people interacting in such a way that each is the creative center of his own experience. Each person's experience is unique, and the pattern of the society as a whole continually shifts, both as to individual activities and general structures. Although each person acts uniquely, the interactions are such that on the one hand his creative inventions enrich the harmony of the whole and on the other his public activities foster the kinds of creativity in which he engages. Each person provides for his external liberties by his participation in the public sphere. His involvement in the social context with an integral style is an expression of his intentions. His interactions in the pluralistic society call for choices between alternatives. In

8. The United Federation of Teachers' strikes in protest of actions of the experimental school district in Ocean Hill-Brownsville is a classic case of an issue allowing no appeal to higher authority; each side was able to destroy the settlements unacceptable to it again and again. A splendid study of this situation in the school system focusing on the formation of a public and the concept of participatory democracy is Raymond Bucher, "The Current Academic Crisis: Toward a Solution According to John Dewey's Notion of the Public" (Ph.D. diss., Fordham University, 1970).

the environment fostering creativity he is under constant induce-
ment to choose critically and to invent new and better standards
of action. He participates in his culture in ways unique to his relation to the social environment, with his own way of appropriating
his heritage, enjoying cultural achievements, and putting these resources to work in his social interactions. His participation in the
ordering of society's effects upon himself grants him access to public media and enables him to pursue his own goals, in short, to
have his own style of life. This is a society for free people.

The Limits of Freedom

But alas, that very fact may be the most serious objection to the
ideal. It is an ideal for a society of free people. Freedom has been
the theme throughout for our cosmology, for the conception of
the various dimensions of personal life, and for more satisfying
social structures. As a multifaceted thematic ideal, freedom is very
basic to the aspirations of all people. But does it have alternatives?
And would those alternative themes, if developed through cosmology, the conception of personal life and of society, give rise to
different basic ideal structures? And if so, how are they ranked?

That is a much more difficult question than any other dealt
with in this book. And of course since this book began as a reflection on freedom, no one should trust its conclusion to be a
fair judge in its own case. Only after one had made as thorough
a study of potentially competing ideals could one approach the
problem fairly. The methodology, parallel to that of this book,
would then be to give a cosmological interpretation of life according to each ideal, comparing them with respect to greatest intensity of value and assessing potential integrations and rankings.
That is a task for another time.

These caveats having been expressed, a brief attempt to deal
with the objection must be made. Three candidate alternative
ideals can be considered as case studies: security, satisfaction, and
justice.

If "security" were the topic of the book, with "survival" at one
extreme and "development" at the other, the cosmology would
have emphasized the reinforcements and threats to an individual
from his environment and would have interpreted process in
terms of adaptive evolution. The discussion of the dimensions of

personal life would have focused on the powers people have, materially and intellectually, to affect their environments. The discussion of social life would have focused on the problems of cultivating the various environments so as to secure to people their continued and enhanced existence. None of these things need contradict what has been said about personal and social life in the context of freedom. But when the crunch comes, and one must choose between alternate imperatives—to maintain security at the cost of freedom or to attain freedom at the cost of security —which is the better option?

The answer to this would depend on distinguishing the various dimensions of each. But most of us would say something like this. "Promote the security of the social group and environment first in those respects that are preconditions for freedom. Do not promote participatory democracy in the service of freedom before developing reasonable resources in the society to provide the requisite education (remembering that the social organization has a power of its own to call forth certain resources). On the other hand, once steps have been taken to make reasonable provision for the security of the group and environment, it is preferable to put personal freedom in various dimensions before personal security. After all the qualifications coming from social responsibility have been acknowledged, there is something demeaned about the person who puts his personal security ahead of the exercise of freedom. This was the lesson of Dostoyevsky's Grand Inquisitor."

Respecting the developed western nations, then, the ideals of freedom are more deserving of attention precisely because, by and large, the requirements of security have already been provided for. Except for particular circumstances, the problems of security have been solved, and the resources are available to address those of freedom. For relatively undeveloped nations, freedom may not be the theme through which to reflect on personal and social life; but again, since undeveloped nations are demanding freedom, perhaps the level of security needed to be attained before freedom becomes a predominating ideal is not as high as we had thought in the West!

Consider the ideal of "satisfaction." What is meant by satisfaction is not the subjective sense of "having enough," but rather the more abstract sense of "attaining things humanly valued."

Developing this ideal thematically would treat the attainment of culture and virtue, of artistic accomplishment, personal development, and pleasure in all its guises. It would treat security as a minimal base of satisfaction, and justice as a principal norm for distributing it. Threats to the ideal of satisfaction would include personal suffering, social poverty, and the decay of the finer attainments of civilization. In a cosmological discussion, "satisfaction" would mean anything attained by a concrescent occasion, or more particularly, any form figuring significantly in the many occasions composing a society. This is not only compatible with but entailed by the cosmology of freedom. A discussion of personal satisfactions would deal with the kinds of things Aristotle thought constitutive of happiness—eudaemonia. The social dimension of satisfactions would include all the various environing conditions necessary for personal satisfactions, especially those pertaining to culture and organization that in themselves enrich personal satisfaction. Again there would be nothing to contradict, only to supplement, the discussion of freedom.

But when the choice is forced between an imperative for important satisfaction and one for an important dimension of freedom, what is the better option? The very question appears to stack the deck in favor of satisfaction. What is the value of a free act, or of a free style of living, if not its product? The value of the act derives from the value it produces; or so it would seem on a utilitarian calculus. But the extreme high value western society has placed on freedom would itself be unexplainable on a utilitarian calculus of the satisfactions produced by free acts. At least it does not seem intuitively plausible that people with a high degree of creativity receive more satisfaction overall than people with low creativity, unless a peculiar kind of satisfaction in creativity itself, apart from the created products, is counted. On the social side the point has often been made that nondemocratic forms of organization better provide human satisfactions than do democracies, unless the special satisfactions of a free society itself are taken into account.

Whether or not freedom is prized *more* than satisfaction, there seems to be a special kind of value felt in freedom through its many dimensions, different from the kind of value felt in the satisfactions of actual accomplishment. This can be seen on the abstract cosmological level. The value of satisfaction is that of the objective order of achieved and enjoyed facts. The value found in freedom is a peculiar way the subjective order of concrescence enjoys value. But all the language for "having value," for example, "enjoying" it or "attaining satisfaction," refers to the objective order's mode of being valuable. Immanuel Kant attempted to work out a language for the value felt for subjective freedom or "practical reason." But somehow the value he found there, the value that would have to underlie and make reasonable our high prizing of freedom, was too closely connected with being "right." And the peculiar value of freedom must be distinguished with all the values of free activity's products.[9]

However we might account philosophically for the nature of the difference between the value of satisfaction and that of freedom, there remains the problem of weighing them when they offer conflicting imperatives. There appears to be no formula for ranking them. Still, it would seem that the realistic pursuit of some dimension of freedom at the cost of some satisfaction is preferable to the sacrifice of basic freedoms for satisfaction. To be sure, the development of certain freedoms, for instance those involving education, requires certain satisfactions as prerequisites. And the attainment of certain satisfactions, for instance human respect, requires accession to certain freedoms. But the person who accepts poverty of satisfaction in the name of freedom is a hero. The person who accepts personal and social bondage for great satisfaction is despised; even if the person never had a real chance to become free, and traded off illusory ambitions of freedom for the substance of comfort, he is pitied. This suggests that the ideal of ever-deepening freedom is at the heart of being human, whereas the ideal of ever-enriched satisfactions is a matter of making the best of circumstances. From this some confidence may be drawn that whatever values of freedom have been revealed are at least not thoroughly misleading, however they might be compromised by those of satisfactions in particular circumstances. Whether to be free is close to the option of whether to be human in the best sense. Whether to attain satisfactions is a contingent matter of making the best of circumstances.

9. This is discussed at greater length in my "Limits of Freedom and Technologies of Behavior Control," *The Human Context* 4, no. 3 (autumn 1972): 433–36.

The ideal of "justice" has been thoroughly developed by John Rawls; if his account is short on the kind of cosmological interpretation so important for the present book, it is long on a detailed examination of its implication for social order. A comparison of the various dimensions of justice with those of freedom is too large a task for these concluding pages. In general, however, distributive justice is both a norm for freedom at a certain level and a necessary stage in the development of the higher dimensions of social freedom. That is, in order for social freedom to take the form of freedom of opportunity, the opportunities must be open to any individuals who might qualify for them. If they were open only to those who, by ad hoc historical developments, chanced to be in the right place at the right time, the opportunities would not be guaranteed by the humanly meaningful structure of the social organization. There is an element of universality in the notion of "meaningful structure of social organization" that makes sense of social opportunities by addressing them to people in what Rawls calls the "original position." The social opportunities are social precisely because they are addressed to and guaranteed for individuals in their capacities as "contractors" to the social organization. The value of freedom of opportunity presupposes the ideal of a just distribution of opportunity. That we value privacy illustrates all the more the prior value of just distribution of respect.

The relations of freedom to security, satisfaction, and justice are ordered in various ways. In the evolution of human society, freedom in its various dimensions builds on a minimal base of security. Freedom as the value in subjective process is strictly coordinate with satisfaction, the value in objective fact; whereas freedom is the ideal of being a good person in the sense of subjective development, satisfaction measures the person's worth here in fact. Justice is a necessary component of the ideal of social freedom and enters on as basic a level as the freedom of opportunity.

To develop any of these other values would enrich and complement the discussion of personal life and social order centered around freedom. The cosmology guarantees that, in principle at least, those other values would not contradict the claims made by the theme of freedom about the nature of things. Or the cosmology *would* show that, if it could be used to interpret security, satisfaction, and justice as it has been to interpret freedom.

Where particular circumstances present conflicting imperatives —and there is no reason to doubt the likelihood of those conflicts simply because there is a unified cosmology—people must attempt to compromise and balance the conflicts in the most harmonious way. Those values, like many others, are not easily made commensurable. And as the discussion of value theory above has shown, harmonizing incommensurables is the heart of normative judgment.

What this very abstract point means is that failure shall attend our activity not only because we fail certain ideals but more poignantly because we fail one ideal in the service of another. The ambiguity of the moral life is essential to the human condition.[10] Coping with *this* fact requires the perspective, not of another cosmological ideal, competing with freedom, security, satisfaction, and justice, but that of an ideal interpreting the meaning of human existence itself. The cultural embodiment of that perspective is religion.

More important for the study of freedom than its conflicts with other values is a potential conflict between its own dimensions. Despite the fact that a certain degree of attainment in any one dimension is a precondition for attainment in the others, there is always a potential conflict between maximizing one dimension at expense to others. These potential conflicts cannot be avoided, mediated, or transformed to more intense experience without wisdom, yet another ideal whose pursuit is essential to rich life. The greatest potential conflict between dimensions of freedom arises from the gulf between personal and social freedoms. Integrity of personal life requires the freedom to act in such a way as to undermine both one's power in the public arena and also the social structures making personal life possible, however unwise that might be. Responsible public life and political structures have the power, indeed sometimes the obligation, to prevent the ex-

10. The essential conflict of ideals is discussed in my "Man's Ends," *Review of Metaphysics* 16 (September 1962) : 26–44. The religious significance of this is developed in *God the Creator* (Chicago: University of Chicago Press, 1968), esp. chaps. 10 and 11.

pression of personal freedom. Each side depends in part on the other, personal freedoms needing opportunities and resources from the free social environment, social freedoms needing personal integrity as their reason for being. Nevertheless, when choices are forced between the demands of personal freedom and those of social freedom, as they often are, conflict cannot be avoided. In many cases of conflict, wisdom can show a way of compromise, sustaining both sides. But in principle a person can follow the call of his personal freedom to self-destruction in the social environment. And because of its respect for privacy, a free society must tolerate that. When this conflict occurs, too often the rebel hero who begins by marching to a different drummer ends in paranoid perceptions, ridiculous reflections, and unfocused, impotent actions, pathetic in his loss of self-possession. Freedom's liability to pathos, however, results from the fact that the tools needed for its attainment also serve to destroy it. Understanding this about the pathetic victim of freedom, his condition is also the human tragedy and therefore noble.

John Rawls ends his *Theory of Justice* with a discussion of how a grasp of the "original position" from which the principles of justice are approved enables rational people to unite all perspectives *sub specie aeternitatis*. He concludes, "purity of heart, if one could attain it, would be to see clearly and to act with grace and self-command from this point of view." [11] But can we take to heart the tragedy ineluctable to freedom, and perhaps also to justice, from the point of view *sub specie aeternitatis?* Of course we can, for the empathy drawn out by the perception of tragedy dissolves our finite perspectives into triviality and puts us "eternally" in the position of the other. This kind of eternal perspective, however, is not the achievement of rational abstraction from perspectival differences as Rawls's Kantianism would suggest. It is rather an achievement of perfected participation.

This concords with a paradoxical character of freedom in all its dimensions. On the one hand freedom appears as disengagement from bondage—from external chains, from an impotent will, from prior determination of choice, and from routine values—from impoverished opportunities, from social totalitarianism, from alien social forms, and from political bondage. On the other hand free-

11. *A Theory of Justice*, p. 587.

dom is a move in each dimension to a deeper engagement: to the occupation of an environment, to the alteration of that environment, to choices that define oneself, to the creativity of one's self and world together, to historical action, to one's own idiosyncratic culture, to one's integral social style, and to full participation in political life. Although these are two sides of the same coin, if freedom is perceived only in terms of disengagement, it will always be felt to conflict with satisfaction and to be abstract and self-destructive. To perceive freedom in terms of the new engagements, however, requires an investment of personal life and social resources sometimes alien to the spirit of disengagement. Yet engagement is the more inclusive view of freedom, adding human significance to disengagement and making wisdom and justice integral components of the free life. Such a free life, incoporating wisdom and justice, is worth more than can be reckoned.

Bibliographical Essay

In the essay that follows I have attempted to mention for each chapter the classic sources forming the general culture of the problem, as well as those recent writings in whose ambiance the text is contoured. Publication information is given only for the first mention of each title; thereafter the reader is referred to the page in the bibliography on which the full citation appears.

CHAPTER 1

The demand for freedom can be documented in countless ways. Two of the most interesting are the Charter of the United Nations and Geoffrey Barraclough, *An Introduction to Contemporary History* (Baltimore: Penguin Books, 1967). On the role of intellectuals in the social process, see Plato's *Republic* and *Gorgias,* Dewey's *Reconstruction in Philosophy* (1920; reprint ed., Boston: Beacon Press, 1957) and *The Quest for Certainty: A Study of the Relation of Knowledge and Action* (New York: Minton, Balch & Co., 1929), and my "The Social Importance of Philosophy," *Abraxas* 1 (fall 1970) and *The Cosmology of Social Thinking* (forthcoming). Alfred North Whitehead is one of the critical foils throughout this book; regarding the role of intellect see his *The Function of Reason* (1929; reprint ed., Boston: Beacon Press, 1958) and *Modes of Thought* (1938; reprint ed., New York: Capricorn Books, 1958). For surveys of the notion of freedom see Mortimer J. Adler's monumental *The Idea of Freedom,* 2 vols. (Garden City, N.Y.: Doubleday, 1958–61) and Gajo Petrović's "What Is Freedom," in his collection of essays *Marx in the Mid-Twentieth Century* (Garden City, N.Y.: Doubleday, Anchor Books, 1967). Basic sources shaping the history of philosophy about freedom include Thomas Hobbes's *Leviathan* (New York: E. P. Dutton, 1950); Benedict Spinoza's *Ethics* in *The Chief Works of Benedict Spinoza,* trans. R. H. M. Elwes, vol. 2 (New York: Dover, 1951); Immanuel Kant's *Critique of Practical Reason* (1956) and *Foundations of the Metaphysics of Morals* (1959), both trans. Lewis White Beck and published by Bobbs Merrill; Georg Hegel's *Philosophy of Right,* trans. T. M. Knox (Oxford: Clarendon Press, 1942); Karl Marx's *Writings of the Young Marx on Philosophy and Society,* trans. and ed. by Loyd Easton and Kurt Guddat (Garden City, N.Y.: Doubleday, Anchor Books, 1967); Jean-Paul Sartre's *Being and Nothingness,* trans. Hazel E. Barnes (New York: Philosophical

Library, 1956); and Paul Weiss's *Man's Freedom* (New Haven: Yale University Press, 1950). Gerard Radnitzsky's *Contemporary Schools of Metascience,* vol. 2 (New York: Humanities Press, 1970) contains an interesting discussion of freedom in the continental tradition from Kant through the Frankfurt School. Concerning the general problem of philosophical abstractions and experience see Richard J. Bernstein's *Praxis and Action* (Philadelphia: University of Pennsylvania Press, 1971); Robert Brumbaugh's "A Preface to Cosmography," "Cosmography," and "Cosmography: The Problem of Modern Systems," all in *Review of Metaphysics,* 7 (1953) : 53–63, 25 (1971) : 337–41, and 26 (1973) : 511–21 respectively; Martin Heidegger's *An Introduction to Metaphysics,* trans. Ralph Manheim (New Haven, Conn.: Yale University Press, 1959); Edmund Husserl's *Ideas,* trans. Boyce Gibson (1931; reprint ed., New York: Collier, 1962) and *Cartesian Meditations,* trans. Dorian Cairns (The Hague: Nijhoff, 1960); William James's *Some Problems of Philosophy* (New York: Longmans, Green, 1911); M. Merleau-Ponty's *Phenomenology of Perception,* trans. Colin Smith (New York: Humanities Press, 1962); Wilfrid Sellars's, *Science, Perception and Reality* (New York: Humanities Press, 1963); Peter Strawson's *Individuals* (Garden City, N.Y.: Doubleday, Anchor Books, 1963); Paul Weiss's *Modes of Being* (Carbondale, Ill.: Southern Illinois University Press, 1958); and Ludwig Wittgenstein's *Tractatus Logico-Philosophicus* (London: Routledge and Kegan Paul, 1922). My own argument profits most from John E. Smith's *Reason and God* (New Haven: Yale University Press, 1961) and *Experience and God* (New York: Oxford University Press, 1968), and from chapter 1 of Whitehead's *Process and Reality* (New York: Macmillan Co., 1929).

CHAPTER 2

The basic texts for this chapter are Whitehead's main systematic writings: *Science and the Modern World* (New York: Macmillan Co., 1925), *Process and Reality* (New York: Macmillan Co., 1929), and *Adventures of Ideas* (Cambridge: Cambridge University Press, 1933); the best secondary introduction to Whitehead is Victor Lowe's *Understanding Whitehead* (Baltimore: Johns Hopkins Press, 1962); the best systematic commentary is William Christian's *An Interpretation of Whitehead's Metaphysics* (New Haven: Yale University Press, 1959). The most important background for twentieth-century options in metaphysics and cosmology is the move from Hegel's *The Phenomenology of Mind,* trans. J. B. Baillie, 2nd. ed. (London: Allen & Unwin, 1931), *The Science of Logic,* trans. Johnson and Struthers, 2 vols. (New York: Macmillan Co., 1929), and *The Logic of Hegel,* trans. William Wallace (Oxford: Oxford University Press, 1892), to the systematic writings of Charles Peirce in *The Collected Papers of Charles Sanders Peirce,* ed. Charles Hartshorne and Paul Weiss (vols. 1–6) and Arthur Burks (vols. 7–8), (Cambridge: Harvard University Press, 1931–58), esp. vols. 1, 5, and 6. Whereas Charles Hartshorne's *Creative Synthesis and Philosophic Method* (LaSalle: Open Court, 1970) continues the Whiteheadian tradition in a brilliant way, I believe that tradition's most significant contemporary alternatives are represented by Martin Heidegger's *Being and Time,* trans. John Macquarrie and Edward Robinson (London: SCM Press, 1962); Bernard Lonergan's *Insight: A Study of Human Understanding* (New York: Philosophical Library, 1957); Sellars's *Science, Perception and Reality* (see p. 372) Weiss's *Modes of Being* (see p. 372); and Wittgenstein's *Philosophical Investigations,* trans. G. E. M. Anscombe (New York: Macmillan Co., 1953). My own alternative views to Whitehead's are expressed in *God the Creator* (Chicago: University of Chicago Press, 1968) and in a series of articles: "Neoclassical Metaphysics and Christianity," *International Philosophical Quarterly* 9 (December 1965) : 605–24; "Whitehead on the One and the Many," *Southern Journal of Philosophy* 7 (winter 1969–70) : 387–93; "Genetic Succession, Time and Becoming," *Process Studies* 1, no. 3 (fall 1971) : 194–98; "Response to Ford's 'Neville on the One and the Many'," *Southern Journal of Philosophy* 10, no. 1 (spring 1972); "The Impossibility of Whitehead's God for Theology," *Proceedings of the American Catholic Philosophical Association* (1970); and "Experience and Philosophy," *Process Studies* 2 (fall 1972).

CHAPTER 3

My basic line of thinking follows Plato's in the *Republic, Parmenides, Philebus,* and *Statesman.* The best interpretation of Plato's own view is Robert S. Brumbaugh's in *Plato on the One* (New Haven, Conn.: Yale University Press, 1961). A somewhat different but equally interesting interpretation is Edward G. Ballard's *Socratic Ignorance* (The Hague: Nijhoff, 1965). My account also draws heavily on Leibniz's in the *Monadology* and *Discourse on Metaphysics,* both in *Discourse on Metaphysics et al.,* trans. George Montgomery (LaSalle: Open Court, 1902). J. N. Findlay's *Axiological Ethics* (London: Macmillan & Co., 1970) provides a good historical survey. Contemporary alternatives and contributors to the view defended are: Brand Blanshard's *Reason and Goodness* (New York: Macmillan Co., 1961), John Dewey's *Theory of Valuation* (Chicago: University of Chicago Press, 1939) and *Logic: The Theory of Inquiry* (New York: Henry Holt, 1938), Robert S. Hartman's *The Structure of Value* (Carbondale, Ill.: Southern Illinois University Press, 1967), Ralph Barton Perry's *General Theory of Value* (New York: Macmillan Co., 1926), and Charles

Stevenson's *Ethics and Language* (New Haven, Conn.: Yale University Press, 1944).

CHAPTER 4

Hobbes's *Leviathan* is the foil here. Leo Strauss's *Natural Right and History* (Chicago: University of Chicago Press, 1953) presents an interesting interpretation of Hobbes's significance. For the cosmological topics see Aristotle's *Physics* and *Metaphysics* on act and potency; Paul Weiss's *Nature and Man* (New York: Henry Holt, 1947) on the distinction between what is external and what is internal; Henri Bergson's *Creative Evolution* (New York: Henry Holt, 1911) on the spatializing of time; Immanuel Kant's *Dissertation of 1770* in *The Philosophy of Kant,* ed. C. J. Friedrich (New York: Modern Library, 1950) and the *Critique of Pure Reason,* trans. Norman Kemp Smith (London: Macmillan & Co., 1929) on the nature of existence; and Adolf Grunbaum's *Philosophical Problems of Space and Time* (New York: Knopf, 1963) and Bas C. van Fraassen's *An Introduction to the Philosophy of Space and Time* (New York: Random House, 1970) on space and time. Donald Sherburne's *A Whiteheadian Aesthetic* (New Haven, Conn.: Yale University Press, 1961) has a fine analysis of the notion of pattern.

CHAPTER 5

Historical references for the view that freedom is voluntary action are Spinoza's *Ethics* (see p. 371), and Jonthan Edwards's *Freedom of the Will,* ed. Paul Ramsey (New Haven, Conn.: Yale University Press, 1957). See also David Hume's essay "Of Liberty and Necessity" in *An Inquiry Concerning Human Understanding,* ed. Charles W. Hendel (New York: Liberal Arts Press, 1955). For contemporary treatments see Austin Farrer's *Freedom of the Will* (New York: Scribners', 1958) and Stuart Hampshire's *Freedom of Mind* (Princeton, N.J.: Princeton University Press, 1971). On "action theory" see Hampshire's *Thought and Action* (New York: Viking Press, 1959), Bernstein's *Praxis and Action* (see p. 372), and "The Contours of Responsibility: A New Model" by Harold Moore, Robert Neville, and William Sullivan, in *Man and World* 6, no. 4 (November 1972). On laws of nature, see volume 1 of Charles Peirce's *Collected Papers* (see p. 373).

CHAPTER 6

The literature of the freedom and determinism controversy is enormous. Indispensable items are Aristotle's *Physics,* bk. 2, and *Metaphysics,* bk. 9; also Charles Peirce's *Doctrine of Necessity Examined* in

Collected Papers, vol. 6. See also Sartre's *Being and Nothingness* (see p. 371) and Jonathan Edwards's *Freedom of the Will* (see p. 374). Paul Weiss's best treatments of chance and causation are in *Modes of Being* (see p. 372) and *Man's Freedom* (see p. 372). The contemporary discussion is still formed in the main by Kant's position; see *The Critique of Pure Reason* (see p. 374), *The Critique of Practical Reason* (see p. 371), and the *Foundations of the Metaphysics of Morals* (see p. 371).

CHAPTER 7

On deliberation see Plato's *Statesman,* Aristotle's *Nichomachean Ethics,* and Dewey's *Human Nature and Conduct* (New York: Henry Holt, 1922). For interpretations of types of ethical approaches, see Dewey's *Theory of the Moral Life* (New York: Holt, Rinehart & Winston, 1960) and Stephen Toulmin's *Reason in Ethics* (Cambridge: Cambridge University Press, 1950). On imagination and intuition, see Kant's *Critique of Pure Reason* (see p. 374); Heidegger's *Kant and the Problem of Metaphysics,* trans. James S. Churchill (Bloomington: Indiana University Press, 1962); Dewey's *Art As Experience* (New York: Capricorn Books, 1958); John Cage's *A Year from Monday* (Middletown, Conn.: Wesleyan University Press, 1967); Ralph Waldo Emerson's *Essays: First Series* in *The Complete Essays and Other Writings of Ralph Waldo Emerson* (New York: Random House, 1940); Charles Peirce's discussion of "musement" in "A Neglected Argument for the Reality of God," *Collected Papers,* vol. 6 (see p. 373); and my "Intuition," *International Philosophical Quarterly* 7 (December 1967) : 556–90, and "Man's Ends," *Review of Metaphysics* 16 (September 1962) : 26–44. Concerning "authenticity," see Heidegger's *Being and Time* (see p. 373) and Alexander von Schoenborn's "Authenticity and Inauthenticity: A Groundbreaking in Philosophical Anthropology through the Work of Martin Heidegger" (Ph.D. diss., Tulane University, 1971).

CHAPTER 8

On the notion of social values and rights see Charles Fried's *The Anatomy of Values* (Cambridge: Harvard University Press, 1970), Blanshard's *Reason and the Good* (see p. 373), and Paul Weiss's *Our Public Life* (Bloomington: Indiana University Press, 1959). For a case study of social values, see the Institute of Society, Ethics and the Life Sciences, *Ethics, Population and the American Tradition* (a report to the President's Commission on Population Growth and the American Future, September 1971, forthcoming from the U.S. Government Printing Office). Leo Strauss's *Natural Right and History* (see p. 374) is a fine analysis of the history of the concept of natural right; a thorough and penetrating analysis of Strauss's own view is given in Victor Gourevitch's "Philosophy and Politics," *Review of Metaphysics* 22, no. 1 (September 1968) and 22, no. 2 (December 1968). The freedoms of participation have usually been studied in terms of their absence—alienation. In addition to works of Marx and Sartre cited earlier, see for instance Leszek Kolakowski's *The Alienation of Reason,* trans. Norbert Guterman (Garden City, N.Y.: Doubleday, Anchor Books, 1969) and *Toward a Marxist Humanism,* trans. Jane Peel (New York: Grove Press, 1968). Concerning freedom of historical action, see Hegel's *Reason in History,* trans. Robert S. Hartman (New York: Liberal Arts Press, 1953), *The Bhagavad-gita,* trans. S. Radhakrishnan (London: Allen & Unwin, 1948), and Freud's essay "On Narcissism: An Introduction," in *A General Selection from the Works of Sigmund Freud,* ed. John Rickman (Garden City, N.Y.: Doubleday, Anchor Books, 1957).

CHAPTER 9

On the distinction between the public and the private see John Dewey's *The Public and Its Problems* (Denver: Alan Swallow, 1927); John Stuart Mill, *On Liberty,* ed. Currin V. Shields (New York: Liberal Arts Press, 1956); Hegel's *Philosophy of Right* (see p. 371); John Locke's *Second Treatise on Government* in *Two Treatises of Government,* ed. Thomas I. Cook (New York: Hafner, 1956); and Jean Jacques Rousseau's *The Social Contract,* trans. Charles Frankel (New York: Hafner, 1947). On the notion of media, see any of Marshall McLuhan's books, for instance *Understanding Media* (New York: McGraw-Hill, Signet Books, 1964). Regarding pluralism, see Harvey Cox's *Secular City* (New York: Macmillan Co., 1965), Dewey's *Freedom and Culture* (New York: Capricorn Books, 1963), and Nicholas N. Kittrie's *The Right to Be Different: Deviance and Enforced Therapy* (Baltimore: Johns Hopkins Press, 1971). Concerning the points about Marxism, see Milovan Djilas's *The Unperfect Society: Beyond the New Class,* trans. Dorian Cooke (New York: Harcourt, Brace & World, 1969) and Adam Schaff's *Marxism and the Human Individual,* ed. Robert S. Cohen, trans. Olgierd Wojtasiewicz (New York: McGraw-Hill, 1970). Regarding information and privacy, see Alan Westin and Michael Baker's *Data Banks in a Free Society* (Chicago: Quadrangle Books, 1972).

CHAPTER 10

Classic background books on the theory of society include Plato's *Republic;* Aristotle's *Politics* and *Nichomachean Ethics;* Hume's essays in *Of the Standard of Taste and Other Essays,* ed. John Levy (New York: Bobbs Merrill, 1965); Hegel's *Phenomenology* (see p. 372); Jeremy Bentham's *The Principles of Morals and Legislation* (New York: Hafner, 1948); *Marx and Engles: Basic Writings on Politics and Philosophy,* ed. Lewis S. Feuer (Garden City, N.Y.: Doubleday, Anchor Books, 1959); and Josiah Royce's *Problem of Christianity,* introduction by John E. Smith (Chicago: University of Chicago Press, 1968) and *The Philosophy of Loyalty* (New York: Macmillan Co., 1908). See also John E. Smith's *Royce's Social Infinite* (New York: Liberal Arts Press, 1950). The basic foil for this chapter is Dewey's *Experience and Nature* (New York: Dover, 1958). See also his *Philosophy and Civilization* (New York: Capricorn Books, 1963) and *Essays in Experimental Logic* (Chicago: University of Chicago Press, 1916). On related topics see Whitehead's *Mode of Thought* (see p. 371) and my "Creativity and Fatigue in Public Life," in *Toothing Stones: Rethinking the Political,* ed. Robert E. Meagher (Chicago: Swallow Press, 1972). A book bound to affect philosophical theories of society is John Rawls's *A Theory of Justice* (Cambridge: Harvard University Press, 1971). Behind the discussion of revolution lie the previously cited works of Marx, as well as Herbert Marcuse's *Reason and Revolution* (Boston: Beacon, 1960) and Peter Drucker's *The New Society* (New York: Harper & Row, 1949). Eric A. Havelock's *Preface to Plato* is basic to the interpretation of differences between styles of experience.

CHAPTER 11

Books on democracy are legion. A good representative collection would be Spinoza's *Theologico-Political Treatise* in *The Chief Works of Benedict Spinoza,* vol. 1 (see p. 371); *The Federalist Papers* in any edition, for instance Henry Steele Commager's (New York: Appleton-Century Crofts, 1949); Aldo Tassi's "American Political Philosophy: 1763–1776 (Ph.D. diss., Fordham University, 1970); J. Buchanan and Gordon Tulloch's *The Calculus of Consent: Logical Foundations of Constitutional Democracy* (Ann Arbor: University of Michigan Press, 1962); and "Port Huron Statement of the Students for a Democratic Society," in *Philosophy for a New Generation,* ed. A. K. Bierman and James A. Gould (New York: Macmillan Co., 1970). Concerning social conflict see Georg Simmel's *Conflict* and *the Web of Group-Affiliations,* trans. Reinhard Bendix (New York: Free Press, 1955) and Rolf Dahrendorf's *Class and Class Conflict in Industrial Society* (Stanford: Stanford University Press, 1959). Concerning social authority see Walter Lippman's *The Public Philosophy* (New York: Mentor Books, 1955) and John Dewey's *Liberalism and Social Action* (New York: Capricorn Books, 1963). For various approaches to proxy consent in medicine see

Index